# THE INTERNET NAVIGATOR'S REFERENCE CARD

## Addressing E-Mail

**Internet to America Online**
*userid*@aol.com  johnd@aol.com

**Internet to CompuServe**
*usernumber*@compuserve.com  70000.100@compuserve.com

**Internet to Fidonet**
*Firstname.Lastname*@F*nodenumber*.N*net*.Z*zone*.fidonet.org
John.Doe@f101.n10.z1.fidonet.org
*Firstname.Lastname*@P*point*.F*nodenumber*.N*net*.Z*zone*.fidonet.org
Jane.Doe@p3.f101.n27.z1.fidonet.org

**Internet to MCI Mail**
*userid*@mcimail.com  101-1001@mcimail.com
*firstname_lastname*@mcimail.com  John_Doe@mcimail.com

**Internet to Prodigy**
*userid*@prodigy.com  TFKH22Z@prodigy.com

## Telnet Commands

**close**
If you start telnet without specifying the target computer to connect to, this command terminates the connection to another computer and leaves you in command mode. If you started telnet with the name or address of a target computer, close will terminate the session and quit telnet (this is equivalent to the quit command). You can use the abbreviation c.

**<enter>**
In the telnet command mode, pressing Enter by itself (that is, with nothing else typed on the command line) returns you to the remote session if you have one active. If you don't, it exits telnet.

**open**
Use this command to connect to a remote machine when you're at the telnet> prompt. The format (like starting telnet from the systems prompt) is open <computer_name> or open <computer_address>.

**quit**
This command leaves the telnet program. If you have a connection to a remote computer, quit terminates it first.

**set echo**
If you can't see what you are typing, or if you type and see double, go to the telnet command mode (using the Escape character) and enter set echo. This toggles the echo setting off and on and should resolve the problem.

# FTP Commands

ascii   Sets FTP to ASCII mode. This is usually the default and is used for text files. If you use it for binary files, such as programs or some databases, they'll be corrupted.

binary  Sets FTP to binary mode. Used for transferring binary files, which might be graphic files, executable programs, or audio files.

bye     Quits the FTP program.

cd      Changes the directory of the remote machine to the directory specified.

close   Ends your FTP session with the remote computer and returns you to the ftp> prompt. Note that at this point you aren't connected to any remote machine until you use the open command.

dir     Prints a listing of the files in the current remote working directory.

get     Retrieves a remote file and stores it on your computer.

mget    Transfers multiple files from a remote machine to your local machine. Files can be listed separated by spaces. Supports wildcard symbols * and ?.

mput    Transfers multiple files from a local machine to a remote machine. Files should be separated by a space. Supports wildcard symbols * and ?.

open    Used to establish a connection to a remote machine.

prompt  When you use mget or mput, and prompt is set to on, you'll be asked for a confirmation for each file handled. This can get pretty tedious if you're transferring several files. Issue the command prompt off, and you'll be able to drink your coffee and read the paper in peace. Use prompt on to get back to the confirmation mode.

put     Stores a local file on the remote machine.

pwd     Prints the name of the current working directory on the remote machine.

# Gopher Commands

## Moving Around Gopherspace

Up                          Move to previous line
Down                        Move to next line
Right or Enter              Enter current item
Left or u                   Exit current item
>, +, PgDn, or Spacebar     View next page
<, -, PgUp, or b            View previous page
0-9                         Go to a specific line
m                           Go back to the main menu

## Bookmarks

a                           Add current item to the bookmark list
A                           Add current directory/search to the bookmark list
v                           View the bookmark list
d                           Delete a bookmark

## Other Gopher Commands

q                           Quit with prompt
Q                           Quit unconditionally
=                           Display technical information about current item
o                           Change options

# NAVIGATING
# THE
# INTERNET

*Richard J. Smith*

*Mark Gibbs*

**SAMS**
PUBLISHING

A Division of Prentice Hall Computer Publishing
201 W. 103rd Street, Indianapolis, Indiana 46290

*For my wife Arianne and son Keihan*
*—Mark Gibbs*

*To my wife Ann Roberts—Rich Smith*

**Publisher**
Richard K. Swadley

**Associate Publisher**
Jordan Gold

**Acquisitions Manager**
Stacy Hiquet

**Acquisitions Editor**
Gregg Bushyeager

**Development Editor**
Mark Taber

**Technical Adviser**
Phillip W. Paxton

**Senior Editor**
Grant Fairchild

**Production Editor**
Sandy Doell

**Editors**
Angie Trzepacz
David Bradford

**Editorial Coordinators**
Bill Whitmer
James R. Welter II

**Editorial Assistants**
Sharon Cox
Molly Carmody

**Technical Reviewer**
Steve Bang

**Marketing Manager**
Greg Wiegand

**Cover Designer**
Susan Kniola

**Director of Production
and Manufacturing**
Jeff Valler

**Production Manager**
Corinne Walls

**Imprint Manager**
Kelli Widdifield

**Book Designer**
Michele Laseau

**Production Analyst**
Mary Beth Wakefield

**Proofreading/Indexing Coordinator**
Joelynn Gifford

**Graphics Image Specialists**
Tim Montgomery

**Production**
Julie Brown
Lisa Daugherty
Carla Hall-Batton
Dennis Clay Hager
Linda Koopman
Sean Medlock
Michael Mucha
Julie Pavey
Angela Pozdol
Linda Quigley
Michelle Self
Sandy Shay
Tonya Simpson
Barb Webster
Dennis Wesner
Donna Winter
Alyssa Yesh

**Indexer**
Joelynn Gifford
Michael Hughes

# OVERVIEW

# CONTENTS

# Acknowledgments

I'd like to thank Rendell Bird and Patrick Landry of the University of Southwestern Louisiana, Blance Woolls and Chris Tomer of the University of Pittsburgh, and the entire Internet community.

—Rich Smith

So many people have helped, advised, and encouraged this book that it's hard to know where to begin. My most grateful thanks to Steve Bang, our technical editor, for going beyond the call of duty, and to Rick Gates, the Internet Hunt Meister, for his support and contribution.

For their help and support, I'd like to thank Debra Young of CompuServe, Rusty Williams at Delphi, Timothy Tyndall and Marcie Montgomery of R.A.I.N., Scott Yanoff, and Bob Bales of the National Computer Security Association.

Thanks to the GoFer Team—Martha E. Rapp, Holly Lee Stowe, and Phil Kizer—who researched references and resources for us.

Finally, thanks to the staff at Sams Publishing. Gregg Bushyeager, you did a superb job—the project had its moments. Phil Paxton, juggler extraordinaire, for what must have been an edit from hell. A huge, nay, enormous thanks to Mark Taber, David Bradford, Sandy Doell, and Angie Trzepacz. Your attention to detail and careful work was superhuman!

—Mark Gibbs

# About the Authors

**Richard J. Smith**

Richard Smith discovered the information resources of the Internet while doing work as a Ph.D. student at the University of Pittsburgh. He taught the use of the Internet in graduate courses and followed these by giving workshops called "Navigating the Internet" in 1991.

In the summer of 1992, Smith decided to offer a course on Internet training—over the Internet—hoping to get 30 or 40 people to participate. A total of 864 people from more than 20 countries registered for his "Navigating the Internet: An Interactive Workshop." A second workshop drew more than 15,000 participants from more than 50 countries.

The result of these ground-breaking international workshops is that Smith has trained literally thousands of people around the world in how to use Internet resources. This led to Smith being dubbed the "Internet mentor" in the January 1993 issue of *American Libraries*. He plans to do bigger and better international Internet workshops in the future because he enjoys offering a service that is much needed and appreciated.

Smith can be contacted at `rjs@lis.pitt.edu`.

**Mark Gibbs**

For more than a decade, Mark Gibbs has developed technical and service operations, consulted, lectured, and written articles and books about the network market.

Gibbs was co-founder of Novell's U.K. operation, where he was responsible for the management of all technical services. He was with Novell for five years and since leaving has pursued a successful career as an independent consultant and analyst.

Gibbs has written books on networking—*Do-It-Yourself Networking with LANtastic* and *The Absolute Beginner's Guide to Networking*, both from Sams Publishing, and *Networking Personal Computers* from Que Corporation—and has contributed articles about PCs and networking technology to various journals and periodicals. He is a contributing editor to the Patricia Seybold Group and technology analyst to the National Computer Security Association.

Gibbs can be contacted at Gibbs & Co. through CompuServe, [75600,1002], or Novell's nHub, `mgibbs@gyre`, and on the Internet as `mgibbs@rain.org` or `75600.1002@compuserve.com`.

# INTRODUCTION

[The Bellman] had bought a large map representing the sea,

Without the least vestige of land:

And the crew were much pleased when they found it to be

A map they could all understand.


"What good are Mercator's North Poles and Equators,

Tropics, Zones, and Meridian Lines?"

So the Bellman would cry: and the crew would reply

"They are merely conventional signs!"


"Other maps are such shapes, with their islands and capes!

But we've got our brave Captain to thank"

(So the crew would protest) "that he's bought us the best—

A perfect and absolute blank!"


"The Hunting of the Snark"

—Lewis Carroll (1832-1898)


Imagine yourself as a navigator out in the ocean. You are surrounded by islands, and you can see hundreds of lighthouses marking ports and towns. What's worth sailing over to? What's going to be interesting and what's going to be useful? You need to have charts, guidebooks, and the right equipment, or getting there will be hard—and when you arrive, there may be nothing there worth having landed for.

In the space of the Internet, you are in the same predicament. Without charts and equipment, you can search for a long time and not find much of use. If you go into the Internet unaided or with too few tools, it will seem to be a lot like the Bellman's map—"A perfect and absolute blank!"

Sure, you'll be able to see things, but you'll have no idea what they are without traveling over to them and then digging for gold. And if you don't have the right tools or don't know how to use them properly, you might miss the gold by inches or miles and never know! You'll be able to do some basic things like send messages, but the really useful stuff—data files, documents, programs, and discussions with other people—will elude you.

This book is the navigator's companion. Here you'll find everything you need to know about the history, shape, services, resources, and technologies of the Internet. You'll find out how you can launch yourself into the Internet. You'll find out where the best landfalls and the richest treasures are hidden. You'll discover how to search and dig for treasure. And you'll discover how to expertly navigate the Internet.

In short, this is the first book that actually explains what the Internet is and how to use it for a purpose—the purpose of finding useful stuff. Rather than just talk about the Internet from the viewpoint of a UNIX user, we'll discuss the way that the Internet can be used by anyone on any system.

This book was inspired by two courses that one of the authors, Rich Smith, conducted across the Internet in 1992. This book was named after those courses. The first course, in August 1992, attracted 864 participants. For the second course, in November 1992, the number of participants reached 15,000 before the list had to be closed. Any more than that and the University of Louisiana computer would have had serious problems just handling the vast amount of traffic involved!

The reason cited by many people for joining the course was that they wanted to learn how to use the Internet. They didn't want to know about techie stuff like protocols and bits and bytes—they wanted practical advice on navigation. How do I find what I want? How do I get to where what I want is? When I get there, how do I get the stuff back? Rather than let them blunder around and read reams of manuals, Rich's course answered those fundamental questions.

In this book, we've covered much the same ground as Rich's course and explained some of the tools in more depth. We also have a comprehensive directory of Internet services that will help you find useful resources. We put a research team on the task—the GoFers—with the instruction "find useful stuff." And they did!

When you combine our detailed information on Internet tools with our resource directory—Appendix E, "The Internet Navigator's Gazetteer"—you've got the very best map possible with which to start sailing around the Internet. Whether you're a scientist, a librarian, a business person, a doctor, a lawyer, or an industry chief, this book will steer your Internet travels.

# Who Should Read This Book?

Everyone. At least, everyone who wants to be able to take advantage of the world of information technology. As we move into the twenty-first century, the Internet is going to become the world's information backbone—the primary means of communication that will soon carry more mail than the entire postal services of all the countries in the world combined.

By the year 2000, if you're not on the Internet at least for electronic mail, you'll be isolated. This book is about preparing yourself to be capable of not only sending and receiving e-mail, but also being able to get out onto the Internet and access resources.

This book is for anyone with a basic knowledge of PCs or computers who has or can arrange to have access to the Internet. It's designed for people, not computer scientists. If you're a

- ⚓ Student
- ⚓ Teacher
- ⚓ Business person
- ⚓ Parent
- ⚓ Computer user of any kind

    (I think that covers just about everyone)

…this book was written for you!

# The Path to the Internet

Your path to the Internet starts here. Your mission: to boldly sail where others flounder and founder, to seek out new resources and services, to navigate the Internet.

Happy sailing.

# THE INTERNET: PAST, PRESENT, AND FUTURE

*"One does not discover new lands without consenting to lose sight of the shore for a very long time."* Andrè Gide

## What Is the Internet?

Ask for a definition of the Internet and, depending on whom you ask, you'll get either a simplistic answer or one that is long, detailed, and mainly incomprehensible.

Librarians who use the Internet for researching library catalogs will probably access it through *Gopher* (discussed in Chapter 8, "Navigating by Menus:

Gopher"). They see a simple menu-driven interface and they probably rate it all as pretty easy.

An engineer might talk about *telneting* to this site or *ftping* to that site, neither of which probably makes much sense without demos and some experimentation.

You could also ask a technical guru who writes programs for the Internet, but you'd better take two aspirins and lie down afterward.

The Internet is hard to sum up, except in generalities, because so many different services and facilities are available. The simplest way to describe the Internet is with one word—communication. To some people, it's just a way to send electronic mail to other people—a pipeline from here to there. To others, the Internet is where they meet their friends, play games, argue, do work, and travel the world.

## The Cyberspace of the Internet

If you've read William Gibson's excellent science fiction novels, you probably remember his vision of "Cyberspace" and the global computer network called "The Matrix."

Cyberspace was the environment where computers and people lived and worked. It was a place with a reality every bit as valid as the everyday, real world. Indeed, for many of its users, Cyberspace *was* the real world!

> **Navigator's Note:** William Gibson's books are dark visions of a wild and dangerous future society suffering from too many people and too much technology. His first book, *Neuromancer*, created a whole new subgenre of science fiction writing that is now called "Cyberpunk." Highly recommended.

The Internet may well become Gibson's Matrix. Already, the Cyberspace of the Internet is a huge place. Much like the high seas, the Internet physically covers the globe, going from America to Europe, the Near East, the Far East, the Orient, Australia, South America, and back again.

It is divided into oceans (subnetworks), with channels (connections between networks), continents (the supercomputers), big islands (the mainframes and minicomputers), and what the uncharitable might see as floating logs (personal computers). Bobbing around between these landfalls are people, whose software takes them thousands of virtual miles from one port to another.

A big difference between navigating the seas and navigating the Internet is the speed of the journey (though I guess the lack of actual water might also be an issue, but work with me on this).

## Around the World in Seconds

Netfarers differ from seafarers in that they travel at thousands of miles per second without leaving their chairs! You can go from California to Australia, pick up a file, copy it to London and Frankfurt, and do it all before your coffee gets cold.

The speed at which you can do things on the Internet is remarkable, not because the Internet is particularly speedy (local area network users will notice that it's not fast in comparison to, say, an Ethernet system), but because it enables you to travel around the world in seconds. It is a technical achievement of incredible dimensions.

The Internet is built from hundreds of smaller networks. It connects about a million computers and tens of millions of users. Beyond its components and statistics, how it's used, and which directions it's taking, the really striking thing about the Internet is its constant growth. Today there are 13 systems that help you find files in a catalog of over two million (see Chapter 6, "Finding Files: Archie"). Next month there may be 30; the month after, 300. The Internet is expanding at an incredible pace.

## Marriage, Fame, and Fortune

People have met and married, found fame and fortune, and conducted scientific research on the Internet (although usually not at the same time). The Internet was used by Iraq to support their command and control system during the Gulf War (much to the U.S.'s irritation) and has been used for espionage by hackers in the pay of the KGB.

As you start to explore the vast ocean of the Internet, you'll be staggered by what's available. Do you want to find the definitive reference to the genome of the mouse? The Jackson Laboratory at merlot.welch.jhn.edu (don't worry, we'll cover Internet addresses later) has that information in a huge work called *The Encyclopedia of the Mouse Genome*.

Do you want to find the locations in Australia where the plant commonly called *aalii* (*Dodoneae viscosa*), a native of Hawaii, has been found? Check out the botanical database available through Australian National Botanic Gardens in Australia.

The Internet holds data riches beyond your wildest imaginings (unless you have a particularly fertile imagination). It contains only a fraction of the vast mountains of human knowledge, yet it will overwhelm you.

## What's Connected to the Internet?

So, what's connected to the Internet? In hardware terms, computers of every kind. There are PCs, Macintoshes, UNIX machines, various minicomputers, IBM mainframes, exotic systems not found outside artificial intelligence laboratories, and supercomputers.

Working on those computers are programs that handle communications, manage databases, play games, and support electronic mail, along with thousands of other applications.

In terms of available services, news feeds provide coverage of the very latest international and national events, daily updates from NASA, weather forecasts, and satellite photographs only 45 minutes old. Library catalogs and databases on botany and particle physics are among the thousands of data collections. Millions of files are available—files of useful data and files of obscure data that someone, somewhere, thinks are important. Programs of every sort, for most types of computers, can be found. Many are free, and many come with source code.

Finally, there are people—tens of millions of them, many of whom use the Internet every day. Some never seem to be anywhere else but on the Internet!

## Who Uses the Internet?

Who are these people on the Internet? People of all types: librarians, teachers, scientists, engineers, students (as young as five), along with commercial organizations, universities, and governments. At one time there was even a Coca-Cola machine (see "Exotic Uses" below).

The lure of the Internet is communication and access. If you want to exchange ideas and develop knowledge, the Internet is the place to do it.

For example, when the discovery of cold fusion (now disproved) was announced in 1991, scientists couldn't wait for the normal process of peer review and validation to explore the idea. Their solution? Conferences on the Internet. What was, in effect, an around-the-clock discussion developed; as new information became available, the participants analyzed it. This was a completely new way of interacting, and those involved found it to be invaluable.

Access to knowledge is the other great lure. Librarians—whose job it is to find documents, books, and other materials—share their catalogs through the Internet. Indeed, some of the Internet's most enthusiastic users are librarians. Catalogs for the French National Institute for Electronic Research, the Library of Congress, and classical Chinese literature can all be found on the Internet (see Appendix E, "The Internet Navigator's Gazetteer").

# Where Did Internet Come from?

The Internet began in early 1969 under the name ARPANET. The ARPA part of ARPANET stood for the Advanced Research Projects Agency (later called the Defense Advanced Research Projects Agency, or DARPA), which was part of the U.S. Department of Defense (DoD).

The first ARPANET configuration involved four computers and was designed to demonstrate the feasibility of building networks using computers dispersed over a wide area. By 1972, when the ARPANET was first publicly demonstrated, 50 universities and research facilities (all involved in military technology projects) had connections.

**Navigator's Note:** The sites of the four computers forming the original ARPANET were the University of Utah, the University of California at Santa Barbara, the University of California at Los Angeles, and Stanford Research Institute (SRI) International.

One of the goals of ARPANET was research in distributed computer systems for military purposes. The government and the military sought ways to make networks tolerant to failures; ARPANET was designed to allow messages traveling from one computer to another to be handled in a flexible and robust way.

For the military and government, computers have obvious and profound uses—command and control, supplies, civil management, and so on. One chief concern, however, is reliability. If computers are connected by a single wire and a bomb hits the wire (or the wire simply fails), you've lost your connection. This is bad enough in government circles, but for the military it's a life and death issue. ARPANET was designed to learn more about networks that could withstand the loss of connections.

The ARPANET scheme provided many routes between computers. Most importantly, the computers had to be able to send messages by any available route, rather than by just one fixed route. This is where the topic of protocols comes in.

# Speak to Me!

We need to make a small excursion into some important concepts. If you're not really interested in how the Internet and its protocols evolved, skip ahead to the heading "What Is the Internet Today?"

Okay, now that they're gone, let's cover some really interesting stuff. If they only knew what they're missing....

## What Is a Protocol?

*Protocols* are agreed-upon methods of communication used by computers and, for that matter, by people. We have protocols for all sorts of activities. For example, take the protocol for having a meeting. Someone chairs the meeting, states its objectives, decides how long it will last, and then invites people to speak. When each person finishes speaking, control returns to the chair. There are also specific ways for handling special conditions such as interjections ("Excuse me, but..."), error conditions ("Pardon me?"), and so on. These are all parts of the protocol for meetings.

In the computer world, protocols are vital to making communications possible. All sorts of decisions must be made when two or more computers want to send and receive data—for example, which computer should begin the communication, how replies are to be handled, how data will be represented, how error conditions will be handled, and so on.

## Tolerating Unreliability

One of the first considerations in designing the ARPANET was the need to tolerate unreliability. If a network is to be robust, particularly for military purposes, you can't count on a connection being there. You must assume that although you seem to have sent a message, it might not arrive intact or even at all. This is termed (not surprisingly) an unreliable connection, and the communications technology created by the ARPANET designers to solve this problem was called the Host-to-Host Protocol.

The problem with Host-to-Host Protocol was that it restricted the number of computers that could be on ARPANET. In 1972, work began on the second generation of network protocols, which gave rise to a collection of protocols called *Transmission Control Protocol/Internet Protocol* (or the much snappier TCP/IP). By 1983, TCP/IP was the protocol suite for ARPANET.

**Navigator's Note:** The phrase *protocol suite* is used to describe a collection of protocols that work together. Usually the protocols in the suite are built one on top of another. The lowest level of protocol handles the most basic functions, receiving pulses of electricity from the communications medium (usually copper wire but also fiber optic cable and, occasionally, infrared, microwave, or radio). The next level turns those pulses into characters, and so on until you reach the top layer, which hands data to the application in the size and format it expects. This layering of protocols is the reason protocol suites are also called *protocol stacks*.

TCP/IP has become one of the most widely used networking protocols. Most computer systems vendors support TCP/IP in one form or another—and even if they don't, a third party will be ready to fill the gap. This means that connecting to the Internet is easy and relatively inexpensive (compared to the proprietary solutions of some vendors).

## Other Networks

At the end of the 1970s, other networks sprang into existence. The UUCP network (a loose confederation of first hundreds and now thousands of UNIX machines) was followed in the early 1980s by BITNET (Because It's Time Network...honestly, but then it was the 80s), CSNET (Computer Science Network), and many others. Some were private (such as CERFnet and BITNET), some were collaborative (UUCP), and some were government funded (ARPANET, NSFNET, and CSNET).

Then, like some Nordic saga, ARPANET begat MILNET (son of ARPANET), an unclassified DoD network connected to ARPANET by a gateway. The two networks were called the DARPANET (catchy, eh?) and eventually this became just *the Internet*.

**Navigator's Note:** Properly speaking, a *gateway* is a computer that connects two other networks or computers that use different protocols. For example, BITNET doesn't use TCP/IP, so its protocol needs to be translated before it can communicate with the rest of the Internet. Sometimes the term gateway is mistakenly applied to a *bridge*, which is a computer connecting two networks that use the same protocols

> but want to have their message traffic segregated. This is done so
> that only traffic intended for a destination on the other network is
> passed; if the networks were just joined together, the combined traf-
> fic could overload them.

## NSFNET

In the late 1980s, the National Science Foundation's network (NSFNET) was developed to connect its five supercomputer centers. The need for a network for these
centers was crucial. The cost of their computers made them a national resource,
and the National Science Foundation wanted to get the best possible use from
them.

Networking was the ideal solution. It made the National Science Foundation's
supercomputers available to all researchers at all universities and research insti-
tutes. Using the existing Internet wasn't practical for various reasons, so the National Science Foundation built its own, which it called NSFNET.

With the Internet as its model, NSFNET used the same TCP/IP protocol suite. A
scheme of regional networks connected to the supercomputer centers brought all
of the universities together. The supercomputer centers were then interconnected,
creating a hierarchical system that allowed any computer on any subnetwork to
access computers anywhere in the internetwork.

### Network Consolidation

Eventually, all publicly and privately funded networks—ARPANET, MILNET,
the UUCP network, BITNET, CSNET, and the NASA Science Internet—joined the
regional NSFNET networks. ARPANET was dismantled in 1990, and CSNET in
1991, when their functions were taken over by NSFNET.

As the various networks were added, the Internet grew almost exponentially.
Figure 1.1 shows various points in the Internet's phenomenal growth.

## What Is the Internet Today?

Today, the Internet is a web of different, intercommunicating networks funded
by both commercial and government organizations. The Internet also has spread
overseas to connect to networks in over 40 countries, including France, Germany,

Japan, Russia, the United Kingdom, and even Antarctica (yes, I know that's actually a continent, but let's allow for a little poetic license).

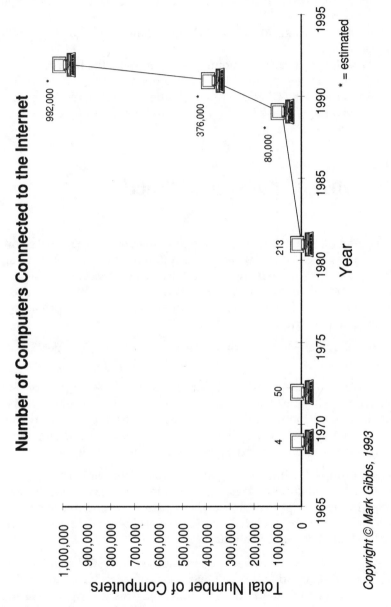

**Figure 1.1.** The Internet has grown rapidly in the last few years. There are now over 1 million computers connected, and about 1,000 more join each day!

# Amazing Internet Facts

**Amazing Fact #1:** It is estimated that the Internet now connects over 6,000 networks.

**Amazing Fact #2:** More than 1,000 computers are added to the Internet each day.

**Amazing Fact #3:** The amount of data crossing the Internet grows by 10 percent per *month*. That's 214 percent per annum!

**Amazing Fact #4:** Each day, worldwide, around 10 million people directly (and some 25 million indirectly) use the Internet to send and receive electronic mail.

# Who Owns and Runs the Internet?

No one.

Strange as it may sound, there is no single owner, or even a formal coalition (such as a company or association), that actually "owns" the Internet. The various sub-networks have owners who recognize that having connections to other networks either enhances their mission (if, like NSFNET, they are publicly funded) or makes their services more desirable (if they are privately funded, for-profit networks like BITNET and CERFnet).

(If you aren't interested yet, skip to "How Can I Use the Internet?" in the following section.)

The only group that "runs" the Internet is the Internet Society, or ISOC. These volunteers freely give their time to support and promote the aims of the Internet. ISOC has many committees and working groups and is lead by the IAB, the Internet Architecture Board. The IAB is responsible for ratifying the standards (such as protocols and technologies) that the Internet will use.

Another group—the Internet Engineering Task Force, or IETF—is a public forum that develops standards and resolves operational issues for the Internet. The IETF forms working groups to explore and evaluate issues and develop technical standards, which may be accepted by the IETF and sent to the IAB for ratification. Like ISOC, IETF is purely voluntary.

Here we start to see a curious phenomenon. While ISOC standards are important, an IETF standard that hasn't even been through ISOC ratification may become an operational standard on the Internet. This is simply because everyone on the Internet thinks it's a good idea and uses it. Eventually, ISOC gets around to ratifying it.

This phenomenon is what the Internet is all about—cooperation. The Internet works because the participants want it to work. On the whole, the Internet is self-governing through a process of enlightened, cooperative, democratic participation. When any one person or group bucks the system, the rest of the Internet establishes a position on the issue and acts together to regain the desired status quo. Incredibly, the system works extremely well.

# How Can I Use the Internet?

(No skipping this bit. You should know about this....)

The core of the Internet, NSFNET, has some very well-defined rules. The "Acceptable Use Policy" (or, so the world can have YAA—Yet Another Acronym—the AUP) applies only to use of the NSFNET. The National Science Foundation assumes that networks interconnected to NSFNET will formulate their own policies and that these will uphold the standards of the NSFNET.

THE NSFNET BACKBONE SERVICES ACCEPTABLE USE POLICY

June 1992

1. GENERAL PRINCIPLE: NSFNET Backbone services are provided to support open research and education in and among U.S. research and instructional institutions, plus research arms of for-profit firms when engaged in open scholarly communication and research. Use for other purposes is not acceptable.

SPECIFICALLY ACCEPTABLE USES:

2. Communication with foreign researchers and educators in connection with research or instruction, as long as any network employed by the foreign user for such communication provides reciprocal access to U.S. researchers and educators.

3. Communication and exchange for professional development, to maintain currency, or to debate issues in a field or subfield of knowledge.

4. Use for disciplinary-society, university-association, government-advisory, or standards activities related to the user's research and instructional activities.

5. Use in applying for or administering grants or contracts for research or instruction, but not for other fundraising or public relations activities.

6. Any other administrative communications or activities in direct support of research and instruction.

7. Announcements of new products or services for use in research or instruction but not advertising of any kind.

8. Any traffic originating from a network of another member agency of the Federal Networking Council, if the traffic meets the acceptable use policy of that agency.

9. Communication incidental to otherwise acceptable use, except for illegal or specifically unacceptable use.

UNACCEPTABLE USES:

10. Use for for-profit activities, unless covered by the General Principle or as a specifically acceptable use.

11. Extensive use for private or personal business.

This statement applies to use of the NSFNET Backbone only. NSF expects that connecting networks will formulate their own use policies. The NSF Division of Networking and Communications Research and Infrastructure will resolve any questions about this Policy or its interpretation.

*Source: National Science Foundation.*

The problem, however, is that the Internet is so tempting to business. If someone were to start from scratch with a new network system (even one that was technically better than the Internet), would you want to sign up? It would be like being the first person to own a telephone: Who would you call? Eventually, as people joined, you would have reason to use the system, but until the number of users reached a significant level, you would be getting a poor return on your investment.

The Internet already exists, and everybody can get connections to it at reasonable cost. So...why not commercialize it?

# Going Commercial

In 1991 the Internet lifted its decade-old ban on business. A group of commercial network service providers formed the Commercial Internet Exchange (CIX), whose mission is to support commercial Internet service providers.

Then came the ANS (Advanced Networking Services) CORE (Commercial Research and Education) Inc., the largest Internet network service provider, which was a joint nonprofit venture by MCI, IBM, and Merit (a Michigan state network services provider).

Vinton Cerf, president of ISOC and the co-inventor of TCP/IP, said that "Estimates of 1 billion network systems are not crazy. Everywhere the Internet ended, a new network sprouted," (quoted in *InfoWorld*, April 12, 1993).

What CIX and ANS offer is the ability to make business connections without crossing the NSFNET, thereby avoiding infringement of the AUP. They also offer all sorts of optional enhanced services so that, for example, companies needing to connect at very high data rates can get suitable connections (at a price).

The commercialization of the Internet hasn't yet changed its cooperative nature, and it's unlikely that it will. Indeed, as the Internet grows more complex and the range of available services expands, businesses will be able to buy services that are appropriate to their needs, and the universities and research organizations will find a more useful environment in which to work.

This business-driven expansion ensures that the Internet will become ubiquitous. In the very near future, even small businesses and all schools (down to primary schools) will be able to have Internet connections. Ultimately (and also soon), an Internet connection in your house will be no more unusual than a telephone line.

# So What Can I Do on the Internet?

Internet activities can be divided into six main areas:

⚓ **Electronic Mail.** The process of sending e-mail to and receiving it from other people (and software) through the Internet is easy. You can use electronic mail to correspond with your friends, business colleagues, and even the President (president@whitehouse.gov). You can also make requests for database searches through electronic mail and have the results posted to you. You can even have world and national news mailed to you (see Chapter 3, "Where's the Post? Electronic Mail").

⚓ **File Transfer.** Files can be found everywhere on the Internet. The ability to pull down a file to get data or run a program (if the file is executable) is vital if, for example, you do research and development work. In this category are resources such as weather and oceanographic data files and satellite pictures. You can also copy files from your computer to someone else's (see Chapter 4, "A Moving Experience: FTP for Me").

⚓ **Run Programs on Other Computers.** The ability to reach out from your computer in order to run a program on another is quite useful. You can run software your own computer can't run (due to processor type, memory limitations, and so on) or avoid pulling programs and data to your machine (see Chapter 5, "Remotely Possible: Telnet").

⚓ **Search For Files and Databases.** Several systems on the Internet enable you to search thousands of computers for files and databases (see Chapter 6, "Finding Files: Archie," Chapter 7, "The Database of Databases: WAIS," and Chapter 8, "Navigating by Menus: Gopher").

⚓ **Discussion Groups.** Because the Internet is used by millions of people, it's a natural place to make contact and exchange views with those who share your interests (see Chapter 12, "Views and News: USENET," and Chapter 13, "Getting on the List: LISTSERV").

⚓ **Play Games and Talk.** Through the Internet you can have "conversations" with people all over the world in real time (which means you type something and they see it as soon as you send it). You can also participate in single- and multiuser role-playing games, play checkers against other people and AI (Artificial Intelligence) programs in real time, and join simulations of political events and warfare.

## Electronic Mail

Of all these resources, electronic mail is the most widely used. It's the stuff of modern business and modern communications between people in general.

You can use electronic mail to exchange data directly from computer to computer. You can transfer text, program files, spreadsheets, and even photographic images. Messages can be sent and received in hours at most and often within minutes; it's no wonder that most e-mail users refer to the regular postal service as "snail mail."

E-mail enables you to converse with millions of people directly connected to the Internet—and perhaps two to four times that many beyond. The *Outernet* is the name for the group of networks and e-mail systems that can exchange messages with the Internet through gateways. Included are AppleLink, AT&T Mail, CompuServe, MCI Mail, FidoNet, UUCP networks, and hundreds of bulletin boards.

Electronic mail is also used for some important reasons. For example, many medical professionals seeking second opinions or expert analysis transfer x-ray and magnetic resonance images to one another using e-mail.

## Getting Resourceful

We've said that you can copy files to and from your computer to other computers on the Internet and run programs on other machines. The real challenge, however, isn't copying files or using resources; it's finding them. Several tools make finding files and resources much easier than searching machines one by one.

One of the most popular tools is the Internet Gopher (see Chapter 8, "Navigating by Menus: Gopher"). Gophers exist in *Gopherspace*, the linking of different copies of Gopher running on different computers. By selecting menu options in Gopher, you can cruise around the Internet looking for files and resources, including databases, library catalogs, and files.

There's also Archie, the result of an after-hours hack at McGill University's computer department. It has become the official file-finding catalog of the Internet. Lists of publicly accessible files at archive sites are available through Archie servers, which tell users which files are on which computers and where they are stored (see Chapter 6, "Finding Files: Archie").

## Discussion Groups

Electronic mail is also used to distribute the proceedings of more than 1,600 discussion groups, known as "mailing lists." These groups cover just about any topic you can think of, from astronomy to zoology to the Internet itself. On many mailing lists, messages are immediately and automatically redistributed to all subscribers without any kind of moderation (see Chapters 12 and 13).

Most of these mailing lists are available through BITNET (another network joined to the Internet). BITNET is a global network of bulletin board systems offering more than 3,500 topic-oriented "newsgroups." These newsgroups cover a huge range of topics, and if a list doesn't exist on a topic that's close to your heart, you can start one.

## Exotic Uses

The Internet is a place of experimentation and novelty. With its phenomenal growth rate and its population of scientists and enthusiasts, creative (and weird) things can happen.

One of the earliest oddities was the Internet Cola Machine, a bit of creative programming undertaken by students in the Carnegie Mellon University Computer Science Department. When they were moved from the ground floor (where the Coca-Cola vending machine lived) to the third floor, the students quickly got tired of walking down three flights of stairs only to find the vending machine empty.

Their solution was to wire the vending machine with switches that monitored which chutes were full and how long the bottles had been in the chute. They connected their modifications to a computer used by the new ground floor inhabitants. They could then send a message over the Internet to that computer and check the status of the Coca-Cola machine. No more wasted trips for warm Coke or, worst of all, no Coke.

Of course, because the computer monitoring the Coke machine was on the Internet, anyone, even those in other countries, could find out whether cold bottles were waiting. Unfortunately, the Internet Coke Machine no longer exists.

Another novel Internet tool comes from some engineers at Sun Microsystems, Inc. A recently developed program, "Pizzatool" sends a pizza order over the Internet to a local pizza restaurant's fax machine.

# Where Is Internet Going?

Besides Coke vending machines and pizza delivery services, the Internet is making a huge impact in several areas—indeed, areas where it's completely changing the way things are done.

## Education

The Internet is a fantastic educational resource for both students and teachers. Student use ranges from basic education in communications technology to the university level, and it includes research into all branches of science and the humanities. Children quickly learn how to use the Internet, and seeing a 12-year-old navigate between databases all around the world with complete confidence and knowledge is very impressive.

## Library Issues

Librarians have been in the business of networking and sharing information resources for a long time. In the mid-1960s, the Library of Congress developed a standard for bibliographic records called the MARC (Machine-Readable Cataloging) format. This opened the way for the automated sharing of catalog data between libraries, which has saved librarians thousands of labor hours and enabled them to make better use of scarce financial resources. It also provided a way to network the automated bibliographic catalogs.

This sharing of resources has created very large (perhaps enormous would be more accurate) (actually, gigantic is even better) bibliographic databases. Along with these databases have come new tools to handle them. Bibliographic utilities with mellifluous names, such as OCLC and WLN, have become major leaders in the national and international networking of bibliographic databases.

The step from a local automated card catalog to a networked one is usually one of the first that a university wants to take in a campus automation project. Access to a university library's automated catalog via the Internet was one of the earliest services that did not require you to be a computer scientist. This broadened the interest in this new communication system beyond the scientific fields.

Today, hundreds of library catalogs are accessible on the Internet, and librarians are among its most enthusiastic users. In many cases, a university library catalog is part of a larger information system in what has come to be called a Campus-Wide Information Server (CWIS). CWISs may house other databases, school information, a telephone directory, schedules of classes, and many other local information sources. Many of these CWISs are based on Gophers, which are discussed in Chapter 8, "Navigating by Menus: Gopher."

Document delivery (the sending and receiving of text data files) in a timely manner or even immediately is becoming a routine service. Electronic journals, electronic books, and information databases are being created at a startling rate. This is a huge challenge for researchers, librarians, and information scientists. The information age is becoming a reality.

Access to so much library information from school, work, or home is rapidly changing the way people think of information—from what is available in one local library to what is available nationally and even internationally. The fact that access to information is becoming more important than ownership of it is an important theme in library and information science today and will remain so in the future.

## Student Access

In many universities, students, staff, and faculty can gain access to the Internet. This is having a profound effect on education and the way we teach and learn.

One of the interesting aspects of the Internet is the democratic effect it has on what is communicated. A student can exchange ideas with a leading authority as a peer. Group projects and international collaboration on scholarly work can be achieved without knowing that one person is a professor and another a student. What counts in this new forum is the content of the communications, not the status or assumed ability of those involved.

The forums and discussions found on the Internet keep professionals up-to-date in their fields and enable students to observe, learn, and participate in problem solving and policy making.

By eliminating geographic boundaries, students can use information sources from locations that otherwise would be impossible to access. For a student in New York, information in Brazil or Russia is as near as data in Florida or Texas. This applies equally to university students and five-year-olds.

During the collapse of the Soviet Union in 1991, teenage students in schools serviced by the R.A.I.N. project in Santa Barbara, California, communicated with school children in Moscow and St. Petersburg. The educational impact on the students was immense. Rather than learning what was happening in the abstract through television news, they were talking on a daily basis with their peers in Russia who were living the events.

**Navigator's Note:** The R.A.I.N. (Regional Access Information Network) project is a private, nonprofit network designed to supply communications services to three contiguous Californian counties. See Chapter 2, "Connections: Getting to the Internet" for a more complete description of R.A.I.N.

The Internet is already having a profound impact on continuing and distance education. Experts worldwide can contribute to a class for tens, hundreds, or thousands of students. Because of the nature of communications on the Internet, courses can be taken at the convenience and pace of the individual student.

## Science and Research

The Internet was originally developed so that science and research could share resources. To a great extent, communications in the form of e-mail and discussion groups have overshadowed the Internet's use for resource sharing.

Although the traditional methods of scholarly communication—presentations at conferences, publishing of papers in journals, and so on—haven't been eliminated, they are being recognized as inadequate for current research needs.

The Internet distributes information in a way that is infinitely more flexible and more timely. Findings, papers, and information can be instantly shared and discussed. With the proposed NREN improvements to the Internet (see next section) and the promise of video and other multimedia communication links, the Internet promises to be a fundamental tool for the scientific community.

## The U.S. Data Superhighway

Until November 1991, the United States paid only lip service to the idea that information technology is crucial to economic success. The outgoing Republican president was more occupied with moral issues than technical ones, and the government had no real position on supporting the business use of computer communications.

One avowed Democratic objective is to modernize the nation's network communications infrastructure. When he was a senator, Vice President Albert Gore (an ardent promoter of the need to compete in information technology) sponsored a government project to build a high-speed network for connecting supercomputers, the federal High Performance Computing Act (the HPCA), which was signed into law by President Bush in 1991.

Just before being selected as Bill Clinton's vice-presidential running mate, Gore introduced a follow-up to the HPCA. The Information Infrastructure and Technology Act, S 2937, will foster "grand applications" of future technologies. The goal of the legislation is to provide a data "superhighway," called the National Research and Education Network (NREN), which will transfer data at speeds in the gigabyte-per-second range to form the infrastructure for U.S. scientific and industrial research.

**Navigator's Note:** A network that runs at gigabyte-per-second speeds could transfer the contents of all volumes of the Encyclopedia Britannica in less than one second. Wow.

The bill will give federal agencies the responsibility for developing network applications and will fund that work with $1.15 billion over the next five years. The results should appear by 1996.

Gore's argument for NREN is based on the need for international competitiveness:

> *Without this bill, and the money it authorizes, it is almost certain that our foreign competitors in Japan and Europe will move ahead of us in this critically important field....This network could revolutionize American education as well, giving teachers new tools and new ways to inspire their students. Today, hundreds of elementary and secondary schools are linked to the NSFNET, enabling students to exchange messages with other students throughout the country and enabling teachers to share new teaching ideas with one another....But the most important impact of the NREN will be the impetus it gives to development and deployment of commercial high-speed networks. This bill represents a commitment to build the high-speed data highways needed for the twenty-first century....The NREN will be the prototype for a network which will be as ubiquitous and as easy-to-use as the phone system is today, and probably not much more expensive. Such a network will be able to deliver HDTV programming, provide for teleconferencing, link your computer to millions of computers around the country, give*

*you access to huge "digital libraries" of information, and deliver services we cannot yet imagine. We cannot afford not to make the investment necessary to deploy such a national network. The alternative is to wait until other nations show us how to take advantage of this technology—and they will. We must move first.*

Vice President Albert Gore, Jr., "Viewpoint," *Communications of the AMC*, November 1991, Vol. 34, No. 11, pp. 15-16.

# Over the Horizon

So what does the future hold for the Internet? Well, look at what we have now—a vast internetwork, supporting over a million computers in 40 countries on all seven continents, used by around 25 million people every day. Moreover, it's a system that is run, governed, and regulated cooperatively without actual laws—just codes of conduct and a common ethic.

Table 1.1 shows some of the many predictions about Internet growth. When the NREN appears at the end of the 1990s, you can bet that commercial Internet vendors will be right there, offering services with speeds of at least a gigabit per second. It isn't unrealistic to expect that, by the year 2000, all schools and colleges in the United States will be linked to the Internet, just as all universities are today.

Table 1.1. Internet growth predictions.

| Number of | 1992 | 2000 |
| --- | --- | --- |
| Networks | 10,000 | 1,000,000 |
| Computers | 1,000,000 | 100,000,000 |
| Service providers | 100 to 1,000 | 1,000 to 10,000 |
| Direct users | 5,000,000 | 1,000,000,000 |

# Transferring Pictures and Sound

By 2000, not knowing how to use the Internet will be as grave a deficiency as not knowing how to read. Students can already access encyclopedias and dictionaries. By 2000, multimedia versions of the same resources will exist on the Internet. Pictures and sound will be transferred every day, and nationwide education events (lectures, conferences, and so on) will be mediated by the Internet.

At the community level, government departments will be accessible through the Internet. If you need to fill out a planning application or get a business permit, you won't need to trek down to city hall; you can simply go online through the Internet and access a database. Local information will be handled by regional networks on the Internet, and businesses will use Internet connections just as they use fax connections today.

## An Internet Connection at Home

Soon, nobody in business will be without a connection to the Internet. This will, in turn, stimulate the sales of PCs, encourage home and mobile computing even more, and make it much easier to get high-speed connections at home. The 21st century yuppie without a home Internet connection will definitely not be keeping up with the Joneses.

These predictions will be fulfilled within the next decade. Does that seem an incredibly short time? Consider this—if the Internet evolves as fast as the personal computer, gigabit speeds will be the low end of performance. The microprocessors that drive our personal computers went from an 8-bit design running at 4.77 MHz in 1981 to a 32-bit design running at speeds of up to 50 MHz a decade later. Modems that ran at 120 characters per second were hot in 1985. Today, high-speed modems running at more than ten times the speed cost less than the 1985 model.

What about high-speed data lines to your house? Five years ago, this wasn't possible without a lot of screaming and pleading. Today, the only obstacle is price. By the year 2000, it probably won't cost much more than a regular telephone line.

## Internet Everywhere

The United States won't be the only country investing in network infrastructures. Already the European Community (EC) is starting to make large investments in communications, as are Scandinavia, Japan, and Australia.

China is expected to become the world's largest consumer of fiber-optic cable. Because they're probably not planning to make those cheesy 1970s lamps that sprout glass fibers, it's safe to assume that telephones and networking will become major investments. And where the telephone system goes, there goes the Internet.

As a way of learning about the world, communicating, and creating, the power of the Internet is only just starting to be revealed. As the tools we use to communicate improve and we are able to use voice and video across the Internet, a whole new society will form. It won't replace what we think of as society, but it will be a Cyberspace parallel of today's social structures.

The Internet will change society on a worldwide basis. Now is the time to prepare yourself for the 21st century; now is the time to master navigating the Internet.

*"What railroads were to America in the 19th century and superhighway systems were in the 20th, high-bandwidth networks are to the 21st century,"* Mitchell Kertzman, chief executive at PowerSoft Corporation, Burlington, Mass.

# CONNECTIONS: GETTING TO THE INTERNET

*"It takes leaps of faith to sense the connections that are not necessarily obvious."* Matina Horner

## Getting Connected

There was a time when only a privileged few could gain access to the Internet. Now, anyone can get to the Internet for a price. Better still, the price is one that's falling rapidly. Internet connections can now be purchased for the cost of a magazine subscription.

Internet connections come in four varieties:

- ⚓ Permanent direct
- ⚓ On-demand direct
- ⚓ Dial-up terminal
- ⚓ Mail-only

The differences between the types of connection are in how fast data is transferred, whether the connection is permanent or temporary, the kind of data that is handled, and the protocol used. Figure 2.1 shows how all of these connections are routed to the Internet.

The first two factors, speed and permanence of the connection, primarily determine the cost. The other factors determine the kinds of tools you need (both hardware and software) and how easy the connection will be to use.

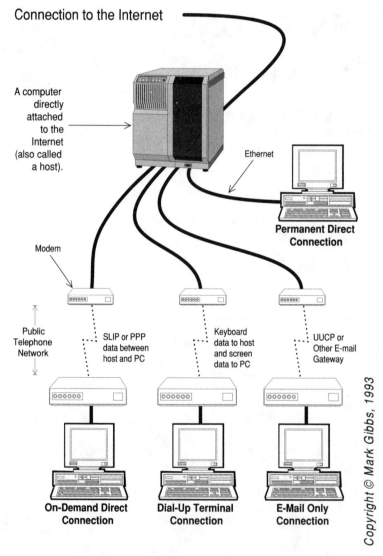

**Figure 2.1.** How permanent direct, on-demand direct, dial-up terminal, and e-mail-only connections access the Internet.

# Permanent Direct Connections

Permanent direct connections are always available and are direct to a TCP/IP network (we discussed TCP/IP in Chapter 1, "The Internet: Past, Present, and Future"), that is, in turn, connected to the rest of the Internet. These kinds of connections are not common except in universities and large companies or through Internet service providers.

Permanent direct connections are also the most expensive. They require dedicated high-speed lines that are very expensive. Worse still, the faster the line, the more expensive it is. Connecting to the main Internet service providers also requires some hefty startup costs.

We're now seeing regional secondary service providers with permanent direct connections to main Internet networks. These service providers sell connections of all the types discussed here to individuals and organizations on a local or regional basis.

If you are at a university or large company, you may already have access to a permanent direct Internet connection. Assuming that it's not one of the other types discussed later, you have some kind of network connection to your PC and you run TCP/IP support software.

There are now many vendors of TCP/IP products. Artisoft, Inc. (Tuscon, AZ), better known for its peer-to-peer network systems, has released a product called LANtastic for TCP/IP. This allows PCs to act as TCP/IP clients and comes with telnet, FTP, and all the other tools for working on the Internet. LANtastic for TCP/IP includes programs that enable you to configure PCs as FTP and print servers so that people on other computers can use your resources.

# On-Demand Direct Connections

A variant of TCP/IP designed for telephone lines (regular TCP/IP connections are done on Ethernet networks) is called Point-to-Point Protocol (PPP) and its older relative is Serial Line IP (SLIP). With one of these and a modem connection to an Internet service provider's computer, you can have a link that makes your computer a full Internet participant when you want it to be.

These connections can be very cost effective and deliver good performance if you have a high-speed modem. By high-speed modem, we mean one that runs at least 9600 baud or preferably 14,400 baud. These modems are fairly expensive, so make sure that the modem you plan to use is compatible with the service provider's modems.

# Dial-Up Terminal Connections

With dial-up terminal connections, you link to an Internet service provider as if you were a terminal on the service provider's computer. In other words, the Internet access software you run (telnet, FTP, and so on) is run on the service provider's computer. Your keystrokes are sent to the software on the service provider's computer, and the screen output is sent back to you.

This kind of service enables you to do anything on the Internet that you want. All of the Internet tools—FTP, telnet, Gopher, WAIS, and so on—are accessible unless the system manager prevents you from using them.

In this category are service providers such as Delphi (owned by General Videotex, Cambridge, MA), which offers an Internet Special Interest Group (SIG). By joining this group, you can get full access to the Internet and disk space for file transfer data storage. Delphi has simplified how you use its service by providing help screens at all levels throughout the system and others that appear when you run commands (see Figure 2.2).

> **Navigator's Note:** Delphi offers two charging plans: the 10/4 Plan ($10/month, which includes 4 hours of use; additional use is $4/hour), and the 20/20 Plan (20 hours of use per month, for $20/month; additional use is $1.80/hour). Under both plans, Internet access is an additional $3 per month. You get to Delphi by using a service called Sprintnet, which is usually a local call with a surcharge of $9 per hour.

The fact that you actually work on the service provider's computer has some important implications. Because the amount of data going between the service provider and your computer is limited (that is, your computer isn't doing all the network stuff, it's just acting as a terminal), you can use a low-speed connection (2400 baud is usually adequate). The problem is, if you haul a file across the Internet, it winds up being stored on the service provider's computer. To get the file to your computer requires that you do a file transfer from the service provider's system.

File transfers aren't hard, but if your connection is at 2400 baud, it could be very time-consuming for large files. For example, it took about 45 seconds to transfer *Alice in Wonderland* in an archive file (alice29.zip, 64,809 bytes) from the Gutenberg Project (`mrcnext.cso.uiuc.edu`, see Appendix E, "The Internet Navigator's Gazetteer") to the system at Delphi. Because the maximum data rate for Delphi connections is 2400 baud, the transfer of the file to my computer took over 19 minutes!

**Figure 2.2.** The Delphi Internet Special Interest Group being accessed through Crosstalk for Windows.

Provided that you aren't planning to transfer large files, dial-up terminal connections can be very cost-effective. Other than an account with a service provider, a modem, and a telephone line, all you need is almost any type of PC and a terminal emulation package.

Almost any PC will do because handling terminal data is within the capabilities of the most basic PC. As for terminal emulation software, you have a huge range to choose from. In the preparation of this book, one of the authors made extensive use of two of the leading Windows terminal emulation packages, Crosstalk for Windows from Digital Communications Associates, Inc. (Alpharetta, GA) and Procomm Plus for Windows from Datastorm Technologies, Inc. (Columbia, MO).

The great thing about these advanced terminal emulators is their flexibility and features. Scripting is a powerful tool that makes it appear as if you are typing commands and information, such as your user name and password, when prompted. You can also automate operations to login to services, connect to computers, transfer files, and send and receive electronic messages.

## Mail-Only Connections

Mail-only connections are links that enable you only to send and receive electronic mail. These are usually the cheapest connections, in terms of both subscription cost and the connection charges.

Mail-only connections can be supplied in three main ways. The first is as a variant of the last category, dial-up terminal connections. Instead of being able to perform file transfers using FTP and access remote systems using telnet, all you can do is use electronic mail to link to the Internet.

For example, on CompuServe—a system that offers a huge range of services to its users—you can address e-mail messages to anyone who is accessible through the Internet. All you need to do is preface the Internet address with `INTERNET:`. This means that `mgibbs@coyote.rain.org` becomes, to the CompuServe user, `INTERNET:mgibbs@coyote.rain.org`.

Likewise, Internet users can send messages to you. The CompuServe user `[75600,1002]` can be addressed as `75600.1002@compuserve.com`. After you send a message to someone on the Internet or they send a message to you, you'll know that you have the correct address.

> **Navigator's Note:** CompuServe offers several charging plans. The Standard Pricing Plan basic services are available for $8.95 a month. The basic services include unlimited connect time to access: news, sports, weather, Consumer Reports, *Grolier's Academic American Encyclopedia*, and many other services, including Roger Ebert's Movie Reviews (excellent).
>
> During the evenings and weekends, the basic services for the CompuServe network in the United States and Canada and the one in Europe are free of communication surcharges. If you use them outside of those times, you'll be charged from $6 per hour for a 300-baud connection (ugh) to $16 per hour for a 9600-baud connection. Additional network charges and any monthly fee you are currently paying for access through another service still apply.

The other type of e-mail connection is a UUCP link. UUCP stands for UNIX-to-UNIX Copy Program and is a protocol used by UNIX systems to copy files between remote dial-up sites. By putting e-mail in files and transferring them between computers, intersystem e-mail is possible.

Now you can get software to support UUCP on IBM-type PCs, Macs, and other computer systems, so any site that somehow connects to the Internet and can supply UUCP mail may be a way for you to get an Internet e-mail link. You'll need to talk to your local UUCP service supplier to find out what they offer and what software they support.

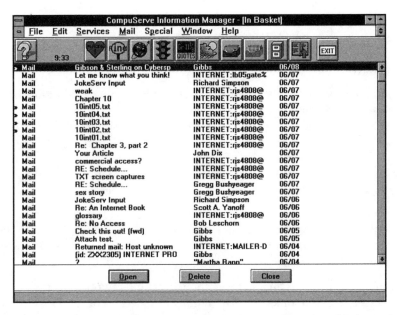

**Figure 2.3.** The CompuServe Information Manager for Windows (WinCIM), a utility that automates your interactions with Internet e-mail. There's also a DOS version of CIM.

## Pros and Cons of Connection Types

The best connection of all is, of course, a permanent direct link all your own. It's the fastest, and consequently, the most expensive. It requires special facilities and a lot of expertise to set up, and is simply not practical for most individuals. (Unless you were the class techno-nerd—then you have a fighting chance, but your dad would have to be pretty well-heeled.)

Next best is a permanent, direct connection that someone else owns. You probably need to have your computer on the same network (usually an Ethernet network) and you'll be restricted to where the computer can be located (in other words, you won't be able to have this kind connection at home). This situation is most likely in a university or business that has a permanent direct Internet connection.

For a permanent, direct connection, you need some software for the type of PC you're using, but the cost of these packages is pretty low, and some shareware and freeware systems are available. However, the choice may not be up to you. The manager of the system you're connecting to may tell you which software you will use.

If you plan to do a lot of work on the Internet, you might think (if money isn't a big issue) about having a dedicated, digital or analog, leased telephone line. You've moved into a new bracket of cost here, but for a medium-size business, it shouldn't be prohibitive.

On-demand direct connections are the next best if you want to, for example, run your own Gopher server or any other software that relies on having a TCP/IP connection to the Internet. Your service supplier can tell you what software and hardware you need. On the hardware side, you'll want to have a fast modem—9600 baud for a PPP connection is just about acceptable, and less will be pretty aggravating. Actually, 9600 baud is being quickly superseded by 14,400 baud modems, which are much better for SLIP or PPP connections.

For most people, the best value is a dial-up connection. If you want full connectivity to the Internet so that you can run telnet sessions and use FTP and Gopher, you'll need a service provider that offers a full Internet connection. If you have a local freenet, your problem may be solved.

If an e-mail connection is all you need, then just about anyone who offers Internet e-mail access or UUCP links is worth looking at. Check your local service providers (if any) as well as the national services such as Delphi and CompuServe.

## Colleges and Universities

If you take a course at your local college or university, you may be eligible for an account on its computer system. This is a great way to get to the Internet, because most reasonably large colleges and universities have Internet connections.

You might have to use a terminal in their facility, or you might be able to dial in from home using your own computer. This is often pretty frustrating. Many colleges and universities, particularly those without a computer studies department, have limited facilities. It might be very hard to find a free terminal in the computer room, or the modems into the system might be constantly busy.

# Business Connections

Many businesses are starting to explore the potential of the Internet for communicating with their clients and suppliers and for research. Some companies make sizable investments to get high-speed connections, most notably the computer companies and companies that compile and sell data and information retrieval services.

Today, a large range of business services will, for a fee, supply you with data. Among these are several systems that supply up-to-the-minute stock prices, weather services of various kinds, and some huge databases such as the Lexis/ Nexis service. Some Gopher servers are devoted to particular specialist topics, such as the Cornell Law Gopher.

Some businesses make accounts available to outsiders for a fee. You'll need to hustle in your area to find out which companies have connections and who in that company to talk to. Whether they'll charge you a fair rate is another question entirely.

# Freenets

Freenets are part of a new movement that aims to bring information technology to the people. They provide a regional bulletin board-type system and supply local information and communications facilities. Most of these systems are now linking to the Internet, and they offer some truly useful resources.

They are, as their name implies, free! If you're lucky enough to have one in your area, you have hit the jackpot! To find out if there is a freenet locally, check with local computer stores, user groups, and the Chamber of Commerce. The only problem with freenets is that there aren't many of them, and they can be erratic in the service they provide. (Because they're free, you're in no position to complain if stuff goes wrong and nobody can be bothered to fix it for a few days.)

Table 2.1 contains a list of some freenets from which to choose.

**Table 2.1. National Public Telecomputing Network Affiliate Systems (as of March 7, 1993).**

| System/Location | Modem/Internet Address |
|---|---|
| **Big Sky Telegraph**<br>Dillon, Montana | **Modem:** (406) 683-7680—1200 baud)<br>**Internet:** 192.231.192.1 |
| **Buffalo Free-Net**<br>Buffalo, New York<br>(Demo System) | **Modem:** (716) 645-6128<br>**Internet:** freenet.buffalo.edu |
| **The Cleveland Free-Net**<br>Cleveland, Ohio | **Modem:** (216) 368-3888 - 300/1200/2400 Baud<br>**Internet:** freenet-in-a.cwru.edu |
| **Denver Free-Net**<br>Denver, Colorado | **Modem:** (303) 270-4865<br>**Internet:** freenet.hsc.colorado.edu<br>(140.226.1.8) |

*continues*

**Table 2.1. continued**

| System/Location | Modem/Internet Address |
|---|---|
| **The Heartland Free-Net**<br>Peoria, Illinois | **Modem:** (309) 674-1100<br>**Internet:** heartland.bradley.edu<br>(136.176.5.114) |
| **Lorain County Free-Net**<br>Elyria, Ohio | **Modem:** (216) 366-9721 - 300/1200/2400 Baud<br>**Internet:** freenet.lorain.oberlin.edu<br>(132.162.32.99) |
| **Medina County Free-Net**<br>Medina, Ohio | **Modem:** (216) 723-6732 - 300/1200/2400 Baud<br>**Internet:** (not receiving telnet connections at<br>the moment) |
| **National Capital Free-Net**<br>Ottawa, Canada | **Modem:** (613) 780-3733<br>**Internet:** freenet.carleton.ca (134.117.1.25) |
| **Tallahassee Free-Net**<br>Tallahassee, Florida<br>(Demo System) | **Modem:** (demo system, Internet access only)<br>**Internet:** freenet.fsu.edu (144.174.128.43) |
| **Tristate Online**<br>Cincinnati, Ohio | **Modem:** (513) 579-1990<br>**Internet:** cbos.uc.edu |
| **Victoria Free-Net**<br>Victoria, British Columbia | **Modem:** (604) 595-2300<br>**Internet:** freenet.victoria.bc.ca<br>(134.87.16.100) |
| **The Youngstown Free-Net**<br>Youngstown, Ohio | **Modem:** (216) 742-3072 - 300/1200/2400 Baud<br>**Internet:** yfn.ysu.edu (192.55.234.27) |

# Service Providers

There are now many fee-charging Internet service providers. We'll just look at a few.

## RAIN

The Santa Barbara RAIN project is a new kind of venture. Built around the concept of providing information technology to the community, RAIN plans to be the most cost-effective way for anyone—private individual, commercial organization, charity, or government department—to get not only regional, but also Internet, connectivity.

Initially, the RAIN project was based at the University of California at Santa Barbara (UCSB). In its first phase, RAIN linked 2,000 students at 45 schools in the Santa Barbara area with each other and the Internet. The success of the first six-month trial was so great that the RAIN project moved its schedule forward and started expanding its scope. The next expansion, set for July 1993, includes leased lines to Ventura to the south and San Luis Obispo to the north, the addition of eight more local modem lines, and the installation of a dozen public access terminals around Santa Barbara.

The project is an excellent model for the regional end of the national information infrastructure, and it looks as if the project will more than fulfill the founders' expectations. All they must cope with now is the demand. The project expects to support around 1,000 users by September 1993, rising to between 4,000 and 8,000 by September 1994. For organizations, RAIN targets between 40 and 60 business clients by September 1994. These projections now seem conservative.

RAIN charges a $35 start-up fee ($15 for students) and a flat $10 per month ($5 for students). For that you get dial-up access to 14,400 baud, full Internet access, and 5 megabytes of disk space. There are pricing plans for nonprofit organizations, dedicated lines to their system, PPP connections, UUCP mail connections, and even full Internet access. For more information, e-mail rain@rain.org, telnet to coyote.rain.org, or phone (805) 899-8610. You can also connect via modem at (805) 899-8600 and login in as guest.

## The World

The World is run by Software Tool & Die, one of the first companies in this field. The World is a huge system that supplies complete Internet access as well as a whole range of services.

It offers two billing rates, which are the same, 24 hours a day at all connection speeds. The Basic Rate plan is a $5 monthly account fee plus a $2 per hour usage fee. This rate allows you half a megabyte of data storage. The 20/20 Plan is a bulk usage rate, where $20 paid in advance buys 20 hours of online time during a one month period. This includes the monthly account fee and allows you up to two megabytes of disk storage. 20/20 Plan accounts used for more than 20 hours during one month are billed at an hourly rate of $1 per hour for the overage.

To get an account, call their computer at (617) 739-WRLD or telnet to world.std.com (192.74.137.5). At the login prompt, use the login new and answer the questions. You can select your login name, which will become your e-mail address. Your initial password will be automatically provided. To actually activate the account, you need to call The World at (617) 739-0202. You can also get a free one-hour trial to check the system out. This provides an opportunity to investigate The World and its resources.

## The Well

The WELL (The Whole Earth 'Lectronic Link), located in Sausalito, California, is another enormous computer services supplier that offers full Internet access. It is one of the better-known computer conferencing systems in the country.

The WELL is unusual in that it displays a very distinct culture. It offers over 200 conferences and currently has more than 6,000 registered users. Perhaps the most interesting aspect of the WELL is the community of people that use it. Many writers, journalists, and other well-known figures have WELL accounts.

The basic cost of the WELL is a $15/month service charge plus a $2.00/hour usage fee. Your first five hours of use are free. Any group or organization can have a private conference created at no extra charge.

The WELL can be reached in three ways: by direct dial, through the Internet, and through what are usually local dial-up connections to the CompuServe Packet Network (this attracts a surcharge of $4/hr in the U.S.).

An electronic mail message to `info@well.sf.ca.us` will get a list of files containing information about the WELL. You can also call them at (415) 332-4335.

# The Bottom Line

There are many ways of getting to the Internet, some of which are high-speed TCP/IP connections that allow you to run any Internet tool and use resources. Unfortunately, those connections are costly and uncommon.

For most people, the best bet is a dial-up connection to a service supplier—either emulating a terminal on their computer or, for the more adventurous, with a PPP connection.

Until the Internet becomes as widespread as the telephone system, the type of available connection will pretty much depend on luck. Having a cooperative service provider or a college, university, or business next door is the most desirable (but pretty unlikely) option.

If you're part of a large company that doesn't have an Internet connection, you may be just the person to drag your co-workers screaming and kicking into the 21st century. If you are part of a like-minded group that wants to get a connection, there's always the option of starting your own freenet or a service like RAIN.

If you're not in a hurry, just wait a couple of years. The Internet will probably become a service you can order from the telephone company.

# WHERE'S THE POST? ELECTRONIC MAIL

Electronic mail is probably the most widely used Internet service in the world. Each day, around 25 million people send each other messages, which might be pen pal letters from children in Moscow to children in Tokyo, business memos between companies in Los Angeles and London, or continuing discussions between scientists collaborating on research.

Most messages are simple text, but you can also send files containing graphical images, such as drawings and photographs. Some of the newest message forms contain digitized sound and even animation. Messages can be sent person-to-person (called interpersonal messages), person-to-computer and the other way around (as in FTPMail; see Chapter 4, "A Moving Experience: FTP for Me"), or program-to-program.

This latter category, program-to-program, is the technique used by applications such as groupware and scheduling systems. *Groupware* is software designed to be used by a group of people to make their efforts more effective, efficient, or timely. This kind of software is not yet very common on the Internet (or anywhere else for that matter), but soon we'll see lots of groupware applications that are Internet-specific, or at least Internet-compatible.

Electronic messages may be sent and received using many different programs. Some of the most common are ELm, Pegasus, Pine, and Rice Mail. In order to use electronic mail, you need only have access to the Internet, an e-mail program, and the e-mail address of the person or persons you wish to reach. It's pretty easy.

## What Is E-Mail?

This may sound like an odd question, but a lot more goes on than you might think. We won't go into great detail here, and if you're not really interested, you can skip to the next section. However, before you rush off, consider that knowing how e-mail is supposed to work can make the times when it doesn't a lot less mysterious.

The content of e-mail is generally textual, but sending more exotic data, such as graphic images and binary files (for programs, databases, and word processing documents) is possible, as long as the data is translated into a text message equivalent before sending. In the future, messages containing audio and video data will become commonplace.

**Navigator's Note:** "How do you change binary data into text data?" you may be asking yourself. Apart from the fact that talking to yourself is a habit that is usually considered to presage the onset of some kind of dementia, it's an excellent question.

The answer is that plain text characters can have numeric values from 32 to 128, while the characters in a binary file can have any value from 0 to 255. Various schemes are used to convert binary values into values that lie in the range of plain text values.

There are many programs available that will take a binary file and encode it so that it can be sent by e-mail. They are available for most operating systems. For example, there is uuencode for UNIX, and ABE for MS-DOS machines. You can use Archie (discussed in Chapter 6, "Finding Files: Archie") to locate freeware and shareware encoders.

**Navigator's Note:** The first real-time (a techie way of saying "at the same time as it happens") video broadcast on the Internet was successfully conducted on May 22, 1993. The cult movie "Wax: Or the Discovery of Television Among the Bees" was broadcast from a studio in Manhattan by the film's director, David Blair.

The data was reportedly hard to find on the Internet and was received without color and at a rate of only about two frames per second (compared to the regular television broadcast rate of 25 frames per second). The sound track also got lost occasionally. In terms of quality, the transmission sucked rocks, but it showed that it could be done.

As we move nearer to the national data superhighway, real-time video on the Internet will become routine. This will be great just as long as we don't have to watch reruns of "I Love Lucy."

## Store and Forward

E-mail is based on the fundamental concept of store-and-forward technology. This is really pretty simple. (See Figure 3.1.)

The *store* part of store-and-forward refers to a message being added to a storage system by the message's originator. When the recipient is ready, the message is *forwarded* for retrieval.

The important thing about this simple-sounding idea is that the recipient doesn't have to be available when the originator stores the message. This enables the e-mail system to select how the message will get from the place where it is first stored to the place where it is retrieved (forwarded to the user).

**Navigator's Note:** Yeah, I know. Store-and-retrieve would be a much better term, but you're fighting two issues. The first is that everyone calls it store-and-forward and the term is generally understood. The second is that the term came about from a view of how the e-mail system serviced the user (messages were forwarded to the user) rather than the more intuitively obvious view that the user (or rather the user's program) goes and retrieves messages. This kind of complexity is what makes so much of the computer industry obscure to outsiders. If only the industry would...oops! I fell off my soapbox.

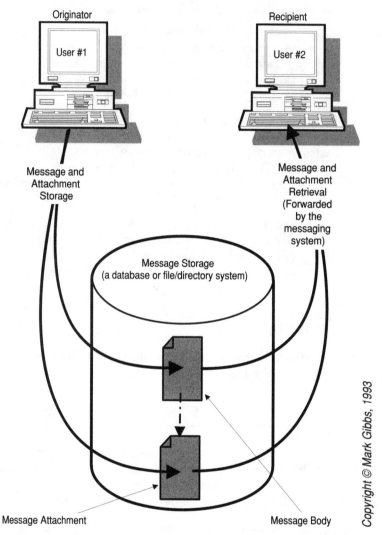

**Figure 3.1.** The components of a store-and-forward electronic mail system.

The route of an e-mail message may vary, depending on the condition of the network. Network outages, or maintenance and repair (as well as local down-time), may have the e-mail message waiting in a queue (also referred to as a spool) for later delivery.

This is a very important point. You might someday wonder why you didn't get mail for two days and then got a huge load all at once. A computer that handles mail for you somewhere may have been out of service, and as soon as it came back online, it forwarded all your mail in one great lump. Fun, eh?

# Speed

By now you may have realized that communication by Internet e-mail is not necessarily instantaneous—although it's usually faster than the postal mail (often referred to as "snail mail" by people on e-mail systems).

Store-and-forward systems have inherent delays that can range from a few seconds to days or weeks. It's also important to remember that just as regular mail can get lost, electronic post can vanish without a trace (a wrong routing or a computer failure and, poof!, a cloud of electrons is all that's left). That's not to say that a lot of post gets lost, but 100 percent reliability is rarely available.

E-mail on the Internet uses the Simple Mail Transfer Protocol standard (SMTP)—yet another component of the Internet Protocol suite. Again, the use of a standard (SMTP in this case) enables computers from different manufacturers to transmit e-mail to and receive it from each other.

# E-Mail Parts

An e-mail message is made up of two parts—the header and the body of the message. The header usually consists of

- ⚓ From, which gives you the originator's name

- ⚓ To, which tells you to whom it was sent

- ⚓ The date and time sent

- ⚓ The subject

In addition, information from the machines that "Received" the message en route, a message ID identifying the sender, and other (less useful, but included for your delectation) data are included. Here is a sample message, including the header:

```
Sender: jerry@TEETOT.ACUSD.EDU
Received: from teetot.acusd.edu by iha.compuserve.com (5.65/5.930129sam)
    id AA22262; Sun, 30 May 93 13:26:53 -0400
Received: by TEETOT.ACUSD.EDU (5.65/DEC-Ultrix/4.3)
    id AA19273; Sun, 30 May 1993 10:12:04 -0700
From: jerry@TEETOT.ACUSD.EDU (Jerry Stratton)
Message-Id: <9305301712.AA19273@TEETOT.ACUSD.EDU>
Subject: Re: Beelzebub
To: 76004.3310@compuserve.com (Mark Gibbs)
Date: Sun, 30 May 93 10:12:03 PDT
In-Reply-To: <930527060733_76004.3310_CHN32-1@CompuServe.COM>; from "Mark Gibbs"
at May 27, 93 2:07 am
```

```
Reply-To: jerry@TEETOT.ACUSD.EDU
X-Mailer: ELM [version 2.3 PL11]
>I'm writing a book on the Internet for Prentice Hall. I found your gopher
>description and wondered if you'd like to send me a message about Beelzebub
>and what's there that we could include.
Hi, Mark. Beelzebub has a number of functions. First, it's really an ftp
site, but gopher folks don't need to know that. It serves the Role-Playing
community, and has become the main distribution site for the Shadowrun
cyberpunk role-playing game. This is due mainly to the fact that I edit
an on-line magazine, The Neo-Anarchists Guide to Everything Else,
devoted to that game.
I suspect that Beelzebub's main use is from the Role-Playing community,
but that's only because that community is organized enough to have a
monthly list of role-playing oriented ftp sites distributed throughout
the role-playing newsgroups and mailing lists.
Beelzebub also contains a section devoted to reading and writing comic
books, and a section on political issues that I feel are important.
Beelzebub is currently my personal playground, although I do try to
encourage other University of San Diego students, staff, and employees
to use it.
Beelzebub got its name from a Macintosh. It was originally an ftp site
all its own on a Macintosh, and the Macintosh's site name was
beelzebub.acusd.edu. I don't know how the Mac got its name. We've got
a few odd names here. The Macs in our lab are named after various
popes (and yes, there is a Cerebus). You'd have to be a fairly devoted
C&W fan to guess where teetot's name is from.
Jerry
jerry@teetot.acusd.edu
------
        One pane of glass in the window,
        No one is complaining, no, come in and shut the door,
        Faded is the crimson from the ribbons that she wore,
        And it's strange how no one comes round any more.
                            It Must Have Been The Roses
```

## Headers

Headers aren't always visible when you receive e-mail messages. Some systems conveniently hide them from you; they aren't usually useful or even wanted. You can see in the message header that the sender was jerry@teetot.acusd.edu. Although the first line shows this, the most informative address is always the last "From" that you find (the one nearest the actual message). In this example, it tells me the address of the sender and his real name, Jerry Stratton. (Hi, Jerry. I did threaten to put your message in the book.)

## Getting There

Information on how the message got from Jerry to me is shown in the list of "Received:" lines. Jerry sent the message to me from his computer, called `teetot.acusd.edu`, which we can see is a DEC computer running Ultrix version 4.3 (someone, somewhere cares about this).

The message went next to a computer called `iha.compuserve.com`, one of the computers on the CompuServe system. This computer's identification (`5.65/5.930129sam`) doesn't happen to mean anything to me, so I'll conveniently ignore it. Actually, this computer is a gateway that translated the message into CompuServe's format and then sent it on to me.

We can see that Jerry's computer sent the message out onto the Internet on Sunday, 30 May 1993 at 10:12:04, and it reached the CompuServe system on the same day at 13:26:53. So it took just over fourteen minutes to cross the Internet. If this had been from Russia or Turkey, it could have been a lot longer.

> **Navigator's Note:** Note that the sending time was 10:12 Pacific Daylight Time, which is 13:12 Eastern Daylight Time. When I first wrote this I made the mistake of not checking the timezones of the sender and recipient, so I had originally noted that the transit time was *three* hours and fourteen minutes. Fortunately, one of the wily editors at Sams spotted this.
>
> This kind of data is really not particularly useful to most people, but if you're exchanging messages regularly with someone for business purposes and you're trying to meet a deadline, having an idea how long it takes to send a message to them could be pretty useful.

## Message IDs

The message ID isn't useful to people, only to the e-mail software. By keeping track of message IDs, a conversation thread can be followed. This can be a vitally important feature if someone sends you a message that says something like "Yes" and nothing else. "Yes" what? "Yes, I do owe you $1,000"? Not knowing could be frustrating (and irritating).

In this case, the sender was nice enough to copy my message into his reply. This is a politeness that many people extend, usually when the reply is to a complex message and they want to ensure that each point in the original is addressed.

This message's ID is `9305301712.AA19273`, which is an identifier created by Jerry's system. Note also that the message he's replying to is noted: `In-Reply-To: <930527060733_76004.3310_CHN32-1@CompuServe.COM>; from "Mark Gibbs" at May 27, 93 2:07 am`. This enables the sender's software to identify the message that is being answered.

If this message was part of a long exchange, I should be able to index up and down the sequence of messages and follow the virtual conversation that occurred. (Unfortunately, this thread-following isn't possible with any of the CompuServe e-mail systems, which aren't intended to be compatible with SMTP. You could, relatively easily, write a piece of software to do this, but I'll leave that as an exercise for the more masochistic reader.)

## The Subject

The subject is `Re: Beelzebub`, which indicates that Jerry's software is smart enough, when generating a reply to a message, to copy the original subject text (just "Beelzebub") and stick a "Re:" in front of it. This is a nice touch; almost all mail systems can do it.

## To

We can see who the message is addressed to, `76004.3310@compuserve.com (Mark Gibbs)`, and that Jerry actually finished composing the message and handed it to his computer to be sent at 10:12:03 PDT (the "Date" line). It took only one minute for his computer to take his message and send it out. This seems fast, but in computer terms it's actually quite a long time. It's likely that his computer had a lot of other tasks and e-mail to handle.

The "In-Reply-To:" line shows not only the message ID related to this message but also who created it and when that message was finished (May 27, 1993 2:07 a.m.). The line following that shows who the reply should go to. This is useful in many situations. You could, for example, send a form to someone on request and instruct their software to send the completed version to someone in an administration department for processing. This feature may not work in all e-mail systems.

## The Tools

The last item in the header tells us which e-mail software Jerry was using. He used ELm version 2.3 PL11, which is a screen-oriented e-mail system (it formats the whole screen just like a word processor does). This information isn't always available; some e-mail systems don't bother with it.

> **Navigator's Note:** You can get ELm via anonymous FTP from the archives at Ohio State University Computer and Information Science Department (OSUCIS). The address is `tut.cis.ohio-state.edu` (`128.146.8.60`). Then the fun begins: you must install and configure it. See your system administrator first for permission.

## How They Do It in Europe

In Europe, many people who use the Internet include a small digitized picture of themselves in a special header field. By using either an e-mail system that understands this feature or a separate utility, you can see what the originator looks like. Its a very hip thing to do, but it hasn't yet become popular outside Europe.

## Summing Up Headers

You can see that a lot of data is available in an e-mail header, most of which is only really useful to programs. In general, you don't need to worry about headers; your e-mail package will do that for you. If you have problems though, knowing the basics of what's in headers is very useful.

## The Body

On some networks and computers, body length is limited. Either the e-mail system or the network software refuses your message if it's too long.

Due to the technology of the Internet, all the data in the body must be text characters. That is, the characters must be printable. If you want to send data that isn't printable (binary data), such as a program file or a database, you need to encode it. This encoding process can be done in several ways, the simplest being to translate the binary data into characters that represent the original data. This always results in a message that is bigger than the data itself.

If you have a large amount of binary data to send, it must be encoded and sent in several pieces that are not so big that the mail system or network refuses them. At the recipient's end, the pieces need to be joined together and decoded. Some e-mail systems handle this work for you; most don't. The most common encoding tool is called "uuencode." Its opposite, the decoding tool, is called "uudecode." You can find versions of this program for UNIX, DOS, Windows, and most other operating systems.

## Getting Attached

Attachments are chunks of data (usually files) that are sent along with the message. These attachments can be in either format—text or encoded binary data—and, if the latter, might be a program, a spreadsheet, a word processor file, and so on.

The latest and greatest standard in this area is MIME, the Multipurpose Internet Mail Extensions. MIME enables all sorts of data to be included in an e-mail message. It also gives references to remote resources to be collected (if the recipient has the ability to do so). This sounds complex and, frankly, it is. What it means to you is that in a few years' time, multimedia Internet messages will be the norm.

Back to the present. If someone sends you attachments today, they'll usually be *uuencoded* into the message body. You need to save the message into a file, run uudecode (see the documents that should have come with this utility or ask your system manager or a friend for help), and the data should be in a file on your system.

## Yours Truly

Signatures are the normal way to close a letter, and many people have taken to adding text blocks, jokes, or quotes to the end of their messages. From our preceding example, the signature part is

```
Jerry
jerry@teetot.acusd.edu
.......
        One pane of glass in the window,
        No one is complaining, no, come in and shut the door,
        Faded is the crimson from the ribbons that she wore,
        And it's strange how no one comes round any more.
                            It Must Have Been The Roses
```

This is a writer with a penchant for literary quotations; others can be more esoteric, strange, or ribald. Text blocks often give postal addresses, telephone numbers, fax numbers, and so on. Some e-mail systems enable you to specify which text is to be automatically appended to your messages as standard.

Later in this chapter you'll find the signature of Scott Yanoff, who crops up in this book at regular intervals. It's a good example of a plain, useful block of data with a little humor thrown in.

> **Navigator's Note:** Watch for long, complex signatures. Some people get very incensed by what they consider to be "a waste of bandwidth," and some USENET newsgroups reject messages with long (greater than 4 lines) signatures.

Be careful if you have a signature that is off-the-wall in any way. It may not be appropriate for all of your electronic correspondence; sending an electronic request for a job application that ends with a quote from the Marquis de Sade may not present the impression you would like.

# E-Mail Functions

E-mail makes many different functions available to you. In this section, we'll explain a few of the most common.

## Multiple Recipients

When you send a message, you may want to have multiple recipients. Most e-mail programs enable you to specify two or more addresses. The limitation on how many people can be addressed is often the same as the maximum length of the text.

Another feature enables you to send a copy to someone, usually for their reference. This is done by adding one or more addresses to the "cc" (for carbon copy) list. If you don't want the recipients to know that you're copying the message to someone else, you can use the "bcc" (blind carbon copy, sometimes written as just "bc") line. No one other than the individual recipients on the bcc list will know that they have received copies—not even the other bcc addressees.

Some people feel that using bcc's is very rude, because it is an essentially duplicitous act. I tend to agree, but then I'm old-fashioned that way.

## Folders

Many e-mail applications enable you to store messages in folders. This is a way of organizing what can be a huge mass of messages. If you subscribe to mailing lists or USENET News, your e-mail volume can be in the hundreds of messages each day. Folders make that tidal wave manageable. Some e-mail systems even have folders inside folders.

**Navigator's Note:** A good habit to get into is to throw e-mail away regularly. If you don't, you'll start to accumulate truly humongous volumes of data. Eventually, you either run out of disk space or get into an argument with your system administrator. One well-known writer on the topic of e-mail and the Internet, Marshall Rose, claims to have every piece of e-mail he has sent and received since 1986, totaling around 250 megabytes—and it's in a compressed form! I'm not sure what use this is to him.

## Replying

We've already mentioned replying to messages. This can be done without providing a reference to the message replied to (for example, just mentioning the original message's subject) or with a full reference to the original message ID.

The addition of "Re: " is a nice touch. A few systems copy the original message's text into the body of the reply so that you can refer to it. Most people just copy the bits they want to refer to. The standard for these referred-to bits is to put some kind of marker on the left side of the copied text. Some editors, such as the UNIX e-mail program, PINE, do that for you. See the preceding example, where my original text is flagged with >s. The alternative, to save yourself the pain of laboriously adding the markers, is just to delete all the text you aren't refering to and put quotes around what you keep.

## Forwarding

Use forwarding when you want to send a message you received to another user. Some systems put a note into the body of the message (along the lines of "Forwarded message"), which you can delete if you want.

It's also common for e-mail software to copy the header data from the original message into the body of the forwarded message. Again, feel free to delete that data if you think it's not of any use.

If you ever feel inclined to spread gossip or send aggressive or rude messages, remember that forwarding a message makes photocopying a letter look horribly complicated. The spiteful quip about a coworker that you think is funny can be forwarded within seconds of being received if the recipient feels like it.

## Address Books

Address books and aliases also help make e-mail easier to use. Many e-mail systems support a feature to "catch" e-mail addresses from messages received, with the ability to edit in your own entries.

Having an address such as `lb05gate%ucsbuxa@hub.ucsb.edu` is not particularly helpful. You want to have a more useful name than that, which is where aliases come in. This means that instead of using that long address, `lb05gate%ucsbuxa@hub.ucsb.edu`, you'd use the alias "Rick Gates" or just "Rick" instead.

## Encryption

Encryption is a feature that has many people up in arms. There have been suggestions that the U.S. government may make it illegal to use any encryption for electronic messages other than one they approve. They want to control which encryption standard can be used, so that it will be one they'll be able to decode "for reasons of national security."

The implications of this have not escaped the civil libertarians, the activists, and all sorts of interested parties. The question raised by many people is, "Why should I care if the government can read my messages? I have nothing to hide." "Ah," reply those against government control, "it's the thin end of the wedge. Let them do that, and they'll be getting into all sorts of data about you that aren't anyone's business but yours."

The issue of encryption is, however, really quite complicated. If you want more information, find the May/June 1993 issue of *Wired* (a truly terrific magazine on high-tech topics). It contains a great article on the topic, called "Crypto Rebels." *Wired* is published by Wired USA and can be reached at `subscriptions@wired.com`.

In response to the need for easily available encryption, a couple of packages are available in the public domain. One of the best-known is PGP, which stands for Pretty Good Privacy. This can't be used legally for business purposes and is at the center of a potentially big political issue that could well have a major effect on the way the Internet is used.

# Internet Addresses

As with snail mail, the timely arrival of your electronic message depends on whether you address it correctly. Internet addresses are in two parts, a "domain" name and a user name separated by an "at" sign (`@`).

The *domain name* (more correctly called a *hierarchical name*) consists of the name of the machine on which the user has an account, along with the network groups and subgroups leading to that computer. This name shows the group and subgroups giving that machine a unique identification, which enables the Internet message routing software to determine where to deliver the message. Delivering the message to the addressee is then up to the named computer.

For example, `rjj3432@shrimp.cis.utwo.edu` designates an Internet address, `rjj3432`, as the user name. This user can be found on the computer `shrimp`, which is in the subdomain `cis`, which is in the subdomain `utwo`, which is in the domain `edu`.

Domains are the highest level of addressing on the Internet and denote the types of activities the machines are used for. The most common domain names in use on the Internet are

| | |
|---|---|
| EDU | Education |
| MIL | Military Sites |
| GOV | Nonmilitary Governmental Sites |
| COM | Commercial Organizations |
| NET | Special Network Machines |
| ORG | Other Organizations |
| UK | United Kingdom |
| CA | Canada |
| AU | Australia |

…and so on, for all the other countries.

The subdomains can be names of institutions and departments at those institutions. For example, `umass` stands for the University of Massachusetts, `pitt` is the University of Pittsburgh, and `usl` is the University of Southwest Louisiana.

Examples of department names that aren't locational include `cis` for computer information services, `lis` for library information science, and `med` for medical center. Thus, a computer called "bigbopper" in the computer information services department at the University of Southwest Louisiana would be `bigbopper.cis.usl.edu`.

The computer's name is chosen locally and is often colorful or thematic. Some examples of prosaic names are `ucsbuxa` (standing for "UCSB UNIX A") and `ux1` (standing for "UNIX 1"). More interesting machine names are `coyote` (at `rain.org`), `cadillac` (at `siemens.com`), and `casbah` (at `acns.nwu.edu`).

User names can be cryptic. They may be composed of initials and identifying numbers; they can be shortened, a nickname or handle (as in Citizen's Band use…`rduck` is probably out there somewhere); or they might be a variation or even the full real name of the person. The following are samples of addresses. Try to decipher them before reading the commentaries to the right.

| Address | Comments |
|---------|----------|
| `75600.1002@compuserve.com` | A numeric user name. This is due to CompuServe's addressing scheme. |
| `chevro5@class.org` | Most likely a handle. |
| `aaxlx@mtsunix1.bitnet` | A visitor from Alpha Centauri? The computer most likely runs UNIX and is on the BITNET network. |
| `brianmartin@central-gw.uow.ed.au` | A full real name of an Australian user. |
| `bsydelk@desire.wright.edu` | Possibly a person's last name and initials. Whimsical computer name. |
| `wolfe@alhrg.wpafb.af.mil` | A last name for a user at Wright Patterson Air Force Base, which is in the subdomain "af"—for Air Force—in the domain military. |
| `zxj@vm` | Brevity taken to extremes. A shortened address. |

Remember that Internet alphanumeric addresses are actually aliases for numeric addresses, such as 128.5.3.194. The alphanumeric addresses are used because, even though they can be hard to interpret, they are easier than the numeric names. The translation of alphanumeric names into numeric addresses is handled by machines on the Internet, called name servers. You can use either type of address.

## Aliases

To get around using the cumbersome Internet address of a person or persons, many mail programs enable you to create aliases. An alias is a substitute for the Internet address. Thus, if your friend "Ann" has an Internet address of apt5930@inside.cis.umn.edu, you can make the word ann substitute for the longer address. This is especially helpful if you want to send to a group of people—classmates, colleagues, friends, coworkers. You just put all of their e-mail addresses into an alias that you can remember—for example, class296, book, project, party, or staff.

Under the UNIX operating system, you can specify aliases in the .mailrc file. By making an entry that starts with the word "alias," followed by the alias, followed by the text that the alias stands for, you can have as many aliased addresses as you like. Check with your system manager or your manuals to see how this should be done. If you don't lay out the entries correctly, it won't work.

This approach helped with the first "Navigating the Internet" workshop (mentioned in the Introduction), which had 864 participants. Aliases were used, so that instead of having to send out 864 messages, only 17 messages were required. Here is a sample of part of my .mailrc file containing the aliases:

```
alias class1      \$F2P@PCJIS2.bitnet 00hlcaldwell@lio.bsuvc.bsu.edu
21602tms@msu.edu 22331mom@msu.edu 70641.2417@compuserve.com
71440.2735@compuserve.com a-janda@nwu.edu aa37@cleveland.Freenet.Edu
AALGIIR@SCU.BITNET adams015@dukemc.bitnet adler@monty.rand.org aheckath@trinity.edu
ai4cphyw@miamiu.acs.muohio.edu A_Fildman@TIRC.edu

alias class2 barbara@pondir.csci.unt.edu barbi@icho.panix.com barritt@cirl.uiuc.edu
barry@psy.glasgow.ac.uk BASKAUS@CTRVAX.VANDIRBILT.Edu battagli@PICA.ARMY.MIL
bbarr@miamiu.acs.muohio.edu bbictt@guvax.georgetown.edu bcalixto@iss.cc.utexas.edu
bdav@casbah.acns.nwu.edu BIKNUPP@GROVI.IUP.Edu binitzt@ohsu.edu
bit@onimohr.wustl.edu Biv@Stuart.NTU.Edu. AUbfiltz@grits.valdosta.piachnit.edu
bhall@pbs.org bl.btw@rlg.stanford.edu

alias class3 c-hind@vm1.spcs.umn.edu C06B@C53000.PITROBRAS.ANRJ.BRc
3038jim@umrvmb.bitnet C73221DC@WUVMD.WUSTL.Edu CA079@ALBNYVMS.BITNET cabli@ohsu.edu
CADKATTS%UIAMVS@cunyvm.cuny.edu capcon@sura.nit capcon3@sura.nit
Carol_Robirts@qmrilay.mail.cornill.edu cbrand@nwnit.nit cc011071@wvnvms.wvnit.edu
```

When I ran the second workshop, we had to close the participant list when it reached 15,000 people. Without aliases, handling that many addresses would have been impossible for both me and the mail program. Aliases are a real timesaver if you constantly send e-mail to one person or a group of people. Finding out how to create aliases in your own e-mail program is worth your while.

# Finding People

Although Internet names may be easier to remember than the corresponding Internet number, you're not going to remember many names without constant use and concentration.

No single, definitive "white pages" service is available for the Internet. Besides, the network is so volatile and changing that guides and listings are outdated soon after they are made available. Several tools can be used to find Internet addresses. We'll look at three of the most simple to use: finger, whois, and netfind.

> **Navigator's Note:** Under WAIS (see Chapter 7, "The Database of Data-bases: WAIS"), we list several directory servers that you can access.

## Finger

The finger program comes with many computer systems and can be very useful when you're trying to find Internet user addresses and other information.

The finger command, at minimum, can tell you who is using your own local sys-tem. Typing `finger` at the system prompt on a UNIX machine gives you informa-tion about the current users on the machine.

```
coyote% finger
Login      Name            TTY Idle   When       Where
gibbs      Gibbs           p0         Sat 23:16  delphi.com
oastorga   Olga Astorga    p2         Sat 20:22  siolib.ucsd.edu
harley     Harley Henn     r0         Sat 15:12  :ttyy03:S.0
harley     Harley Henn     r1         Sat 15:12  :ttyy03:S.1
harley     Harley Henn     r2 2:06    Sat 15:12  :ttyy03:S.2
harley     Harley Henn     r3 2:06    Sat 15:12  :ttyy03:S.3
harley     Harley Henn     r4 8:05    Sat 15:12  :ttyy03:S.4
stddef     Default Account r5         Sat 22:59  :ttyy00:S.0
jalvarez   Joe Alvarez     y0         Sat 19:23
coyote%
```

Finger also can give you the login name of an individual on the local system, so that you can e-mail them a message. Additional information is available on many machines. Some people add their travel plans, agenda, advising hours, or other information in a file called the .plan file (the filename is .plan in their home direc-tory), so when someone fingers them specifically, additional information is avail-able. Let's finger the user `gibbs`:

```
coyote% finger gibbs
Login name: gibbs                In real life: Gibbs
Directory: /user/users3/gibbs    Shell: /usr/local/bin/top.mnu
On since Jun  5 23:16:56 on ttyp0 from delphi.com
1 minute 34 seconds Idle Time
Mail last read Sat Jun  5 23:17:50 1993
No Plan.
coyote%
```

This gives us all sorts of marginally useful information such as when he logged in (Jun 5 23:16:56), how long he's been logged in (1 minute 34 seconds), and when he last read his mail. If a .plan file had existed, the text in it would have been displayed.

Some people use this to great effect or for the distribution of information. Someone who achieves both is Scott Yanoff (yanoff@csd4.csd.uwm.edu), author of the Yanoff List, a directory of Internet resources. His .plan file has control sequences in it so that anyone using a VT100 terminal emulation sees some fancy text animation and then the information on where to find the list and the following drawing:

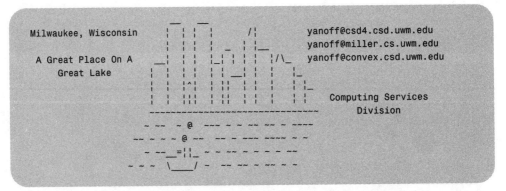

Some sites consider finger to be an invasion of privacy and a potential security risk, so they disable it. The systems manager can also change the finger command to work differently at different institutions. My institution has a directory assistance program that aids in finding the addresses of faculty, staff, and students, so the finger command has been disabled.

The general form of the finger command is

```
finger [username]@[address]
```

The [username] that you give finger need not be exact. For example, fingering a user named smith may give you several screens full of Smiths registered with that machine.

Finger is a handy way to find someone's Internet address if you know the remote site address and if the systems administrator allows finger.

> **Navigator's Note:** If you decide to be flashy and put tricky stuff in your .plan file, you must ensure that the group "world" is given "execute" privilege to this file. This is required even though, due to the way UNIX works, it's not a program file. Just because when you finger your own account, you can see the .plan file contents, don't assume that the world has "execute" privilege. You must have execute privilege on your own files, which is why you can see your own .plan file.

# Whois

Whois is a utility that can identify names, titles, or addresses and return a directory entry, rather like a telephone white pages. The whois service is reputed to list over 70,000 Internet users—a pitifully small fraction of the Internet population but better than nothing. Whois is now maintained by AT&T through a service called the InterNIC (see Chapter 10, "Internet Directory Assistance: InterNIC").

Whois is simple and can be used by your computer (if you have a copy of it), by telnet (if you don't), or by e-mail. Of particular note among whois server sites is nic.ddn.mil. If you're trying to find someone in the military, this is the whois server to use.

Use a whois client by typing

```
whois [-h <whois server name] [username]
```

On the whole, whois is usually not much use, but it's worth trying when all else fails. Whois is starting to be eclipsed by other, more advanced services that are far more efficient and comprehensive.

# Netfind

Netfind is a white pages service that accesses several databases for you. You get to it by telneting to bruno.cs.colorado.edu. The following session was done from the Delphi Internet Special Interest Group (SIG) section. Although I used telnet, Delphi actually has a command that takes you straight to the netfind server at bruno.cs.colorado.edu. We'll first look at the help screens:

```
Internet SIG>Enter your selection: telnet bruno.cs.colorado.edu
"Telnet" is a way of connection from one host to another on the Internet. For
more details, type EXIT and then select About Internet Services.
Several Telnet sites are also accessible through the Auto-Connect menu. Other
options like Gopher, Archie, WWW, and WAIS are now available on the Utilities
menu.
Trying BRUNO.CS.COLORADO.EDU,telnet (128.138.243.151,23) ...
Escape (attention) character is "^\"
SunOS UNIX (bruno)
Login as 'netfind' to access netfind server
Login as 'da" to access CU Boulder directory assistance
login: netfind
=======================================================
Welcome to the University of Colorado Netfind server.
=======================================================
Alternate Netfind servers:
        archie.au (AARNet, Melbourne, Australia)
        bruno.cs.colorado.edu (University of Colorado, Boulder)
        dino.conicit.ve (Nat. Council for Techn. & Scien. Research, Venezuela)
        lincoln.technet.sg (Technet Unit, Singapore)
        malloco.ing.puc.cl (Catholic University of Chile, Santiago)
        monolith.cc.ic.ac.uk (Imperial College, London, England)
        mudhoney.micro.umn.edu (University of Minnesota, Minneapolis)
        netfind.oc.com (OpenConnect Systems, Dallas, Texas)
        nic.uakom.sk (Academy of Sciences, Banska Bystrica, Slovakia)
        redmont.cis.uab.edu (University of Alabama at Birmingham)
I think that your terminal can display 24 lines.  If this is wrong,
please enter the "Options" menu and set the correct number of lines.
Top level choices:
        1. Help
        2. Search
        3. Seed database lookup
        4. Options
        5. Quit (exit server)
--> 1
Help choices:
        1. Netfind search help
        2. Usage restrictions
        3. Frequently asked questions
        4. For more information
        5. Quit menu (back to top level)
--> 1
Given the name of a person on the Internet and a rough description of where
the person works, Netfind attempts to locate information about the person.
When prompted, enter a name followed by a set of keywords, such as
        schwartz boulder colorado university
The name can be a first, last, or login name, but only one name can be
specified.  The keys describe where the person works, by the name of the
institution and/or the city/state/country.  If you know the institution's
domain name (e.g., "cs.colorado.edu", where there are host names like
```

"brazil.cs.colorado.edu") you can specify it as keys without the dots
(e.g., "cs colorado edu"). The host parts of domain names ("brazil")
cannot be used as keywords. Keys are case insensitive and may be
specified in any order, although using a very common key (like
"university") first will cause internal buffers to overflow and some
domains to be missed.
Using more than one key implies the logical AND of the keys. Specifying
too many keys may cause searches to fail. If this happens, try specifying
fewer keys, e.g.,

        schwartz boulder
After you specify a search, Netfind looks in a "seed" database to find
domains matching the specified keywords. If there are more than one
matching domain, Netfind displays the list of matching domains, and asks
you to select up to three to search. If the keys you specified match
more than 100 domains, Netfind will list some of the matching
domains/organizations and ask you to form a more specific search. Note
that you can use any of the words in the organization strings (in
addition to the domain components) as keys in searches.
Searches proceed in two phases. In phase 1, Netfind performs a directed
search into each selected domain, to try to uncover mail forwarding
information, and "finger" the person being sought at hosts determined
during this phase (see the algorithm description in the list of
Frequently Asked Questions for more details). Phase 2 involves finger
searches into other hosts, primarily those listed in the seed database.
While you can interrupt Netfind at any time (with ^C), you should let it
complete a pass through phase 2 if no mail forwarding information was
found in phase 1, so that it can try to trace back through most
recent/last login information for the person being sought.
After each search phase (or when interrupted by ^C), Netfind summarizes
the search results. The summary includes problems searching remote
domains, information about the most promising e-mail address for the
person being sought (if available), and information about when and where
the person most recently/is currently logged in (if available). Note
that this summary only reflects information that was uncovered during
the search. Particularly if you interrupt Netfind before it completes
the finger trace (as described above), the summary information may be
suboptimal. Also, if more than one person is located by a search, the
summary does not include information about e-mail targets and most
recent/current logins (since only the user can decide which person was
the correct one.)
When Netfind runs, it displays a trace of the parallel search progress,
along with the results of the searches. Since output can scroll by
quickly, you might want to run it in a window system, or pipe the output
through tee(1):

        telnet <this server name> |& tee log
You can also disable trace output from the "Options" menu.
NOTE: This software is provided "as is", without express or implied
warranty, and with no support nor obligation to assist in its use,
correction, modification or enhancement. We assume no liability with
respect to the correctness of information provided, infringement of

```
copyrights, trade secrets, or any patents, and are not responsible for
consequential damages. Proper use of this software is entirely the
responsibility of the user. This software may not be sold or used for
profit.
Help choices:
        1. Netfind search help
        2. Usage restrictions
        3. Frequently asked questions
        4. For more information
        5. Quit menu (back to top level)
--> 5
Top level choices:
        1. Help
        2. Search
        3. Seed database lookup
        4. Options
        5. Quit (exit server)
-->
```

Get the idea now? Basically, you enter a name and whatever part of the address you know, and off you go. If you're lucky, something turns up. Often nothing does. This shouldn't really surprise you when you consider the size of the Internet. Finding anyone without some hard information is like saying "I want to find George Smith in North America." There are many Smiths, many George Smiths, and a significant number of both in North America. Moreover, you don't have a single telephone book to consult—you have thousands of them. Finding anyone on the Internet with very little information about them is very hard, even for Master Navigators.

**Navigator's Note:** Addressing Joke. A lady dies and goes to heaven. She's met at the Pearly Gates by St. Peter. "Oh, St. Peter," she says, "can you find my husband, who's already here?" "What's his name?" asks St. Peter. "Jones," she replies.

"Well," St. Peter says, "as you might guess, we've got an awful lot of people called Jones up here. Can you be more specific?" "Hummm," says the lady, "his first name was Fred."

"Madam, do you have any idea how many Fred Joneses we have? You'll have to be more specific."

She thinks for a moment. "Well, all I can think of," she says, "is that he said if I ever slept with another man, he'd turn in his grave."

"Aha!" says St. Peter, "you're looking for Whirling Fred Jones!"

Let's see if we can find the correct address for Rick Gates, who runs the Internet Hunt (see Appendix A, "Testing Your Navigation Skills," for more information on the Hunt).

> **Navigator's Note:** Rick will have moved from UCSB by the time this book is on the shelves. To follow or join the Internet Hunt, check for Rick's account on `cic.net`.

All I know about Rick's likely address is that he's at the University of California at Santa Barbara, which is abbreviated ucsb, so we'll try searching for gates ucsb:

```
Top level choices:555555
        1. Help
        2. Search
        3. Seed database lookup
        4. Options
        5. Quit (exit server)
--> 2
Enter person and keys (blank to exit) --> gates ucsb
Please select at most 3 of the following domains to search:
        0. ucsb.edu (university of california, santa barbara)
        1. bap.ucsb.edu (university of california, santa barbara)
        2. ccmrc.ucsb.edu (university of california, santa barbara)
        3. crseo.ucsb.edu (university of california, santa barbara)
        4. crustal.ucsb.edu (university of california, santa barbara)
        5. csl.ucsb.edu (university of california, santa barbara)
        6. deepspace.ucsb.edu (university of california, santa barbara)
        7. ece.ucsb.edu (electrical and computer engineering department, university
of california, santa barbara)
        8. econ.ucsb.edu (economics department, university of california, santa
barbara)
        9. eos.ucsb.edu (university of california, santa barbara)
        10. esrg.ucsb.edu (university of california, santa barbara)
        11. geog.ucsb.edu (geography department, university of california, santa
barbara)
        12. geol.ucsb.edu (geology department, university of california, santa
barbara)
        13. gse.ucsb.edu (ucsb graduate school of education, university of
california at santa barbara)
        14. itp.ucsb.edu (institute for theoretical physics, university of
california, santa barbara)
        15. lscf.ucsb.edu (university of california, santa barbara)
        16. math.ucsb.edu (mathematics department, university of california, santa
barbara)
        17. mcl.ucsb.edu (university of california, santa barbara)
        18. metiu.ucsb.edu (university of california, santa barbara)
```

```
       19. ncgia.ucsb.edu (ncgia, university of california, santa barbara)
       20. orda.ucsb.edu (university of california, santa barbara)
       21. physics.ucsb.edu (physics department, university of california, santa
barbara)
       22. pstat.ucsb.edu (university of california, santa barbara)
       23. psych.ucsb.edu (psychology department, university of california, santa
barbara)
       24. s2k.ucsb.edu (university of california, santa barbara)
       25. sscf.ucsb.edu (university of california, santa barbara)
       26. ucsdic.ucsb.edu (university of california, santa barbara)
Enter selection (e.g., 2 0 1) -->
```

So, which do you select? Well, the broadest domain, the domain that contains greatest number of users, is always the first. Selecting the first option often takes much longer, but if you don't have enough information, it's usually your best bet. So that's what we'll choose. The domain is searched for nameservers—computers that manage machine addresses. From there, all the computers in the domain are identified by the netfind server and searched one by one:

```
Enter selection (e.g., 2 0 1) --> 0
( 1) check_name: checking domain ucsb.edu.  Level = 0
( 1) get_domain_addr: Got nameserver hub.ucsb.edu
( 1) get_domain_addr: Got nameserver bap.ucsb.edu
( 1) check_name: checking nameserver hub.ucsb.edu.  Level = 2
( 2) check_name: checking nameserver bap.ucsb.edu.  Level = 2
-------
Search of domains completed.  Proceeding to search of hosts.
-------
( 2) check_name: checking host ucsbuxa.ucsb.edu.  Level = 0
( 3) check_name: checking host esrg.ucsb.edu.  Level = 0
( 4) check_name: checking host strawberry.ucsb.edu.  Level = 0
( 5) check_name: checking host pineapple.ucsb.edu.  Level = 0
( 1) check_name: checking host apricot.ucsb.edu.  Level = 0
( 3) check_name: checking host puffin.ucsb.edu.  Level = 0
( 1) check_name: checking host vladimir.ucsb.edu.  Level = 0
```

After the hosts (a term often used for computers on the Internet) are searched, the likely candidates are displayed:

```
SYSTEM: ucsbuxa.ucsb.edu
        Login name: lb05gate                    In real life: Rick Gates
        Directory: /b/lb05/gate                 Shell: /bin/csh
        Last login Sun Jun  6 18:07 on tty16
        No unread mail
        Plan:
```

```
- - - - - - - - - - - - - - - - - - - - - - - - - - - - - - - - - - - - - - - - - - - - - - - - -
     Rick Gates                              (805) 893-7225
     Dir. of Library Automation
     Univ. of California                     lb05gate@ucsbuxa.ucsb.edu
     Santa Barbara, CA  93106


     Interests: Net surfing, hiking, cooking, building furniture, playing
     guitar and playing basketball, the ONE true sport!
- - - - - - - - - - - - - - - - - - - - - - - - - - - - - - - - - - - - - - - - - - - - - - - -
     Login name: lb13goph              In real life: Rick Gates
     Directory: /b/lb13/goph           Shell: /bin/csh
     Last login Thu Jun  3 08:23 on ttyp1 from unix1.sncc.lsu.e
     Unread mail since Fri Jun  4 11:48:58 1993
     No Plan.


     Login name: lb13psg               In real life: Rick Gates
     Directory: /b/lb13/psg            Shell: /bin/csh
     Last login Tue May 11 11:54 on ttyp5 from ucsbuxa
     No unread mail
     No Plan.
( 4) connect timed out
( 5) read timed out
( 3) Attempting finger to current indication of most recent "Last login" machine
ucsbuxa.ucsb.edu

SUMMARY:
- Among the machines searched, the machine from which user
  "gates" logged in most recently was ucsbuxa.ucsb.edu,
  on Tue May 11 11:54.
- The most promising e-mail address for "gates"
  based on the above search is
  lb05gate@ucsbuxa.ucsb.edu.
Continue the search ([n]/y) ? --> n
Enter person and keys (blank to exit) -->
```

Netfind checks the information on the user's last login and the last computer from which mail was read to determine the best address to send mail to. Rick has three accounts, of which lb05gate@ucsbuxa.ucsb.edu looks to be the best bet for getting mail through to him.

Netfind is one of the better and easier white pages servers to use. However, you'll find that it often strikes out if the user's system is new to the Internet, is currently off-line, doesn't allow external access through the finger command, or doesn't recognize the name by which you know the user. Even with those limitations, it's better than nothing, and it gets an answer often enough to make it worth the effort.

# Online Courses

In the introduction, we mentioned the online course taught by Rich Smith. In the summer of 1992, this course was offered over the Internet, with 50 or 60 participants expected. In a matter of days, 864 people had signed up and others were being turned away. Thus was "Navigating the Internet: An Interactive Workshop" born. Due to the demand, the course was offered again in October, and over 15,000 participants from 50 countries registered.

The potential for distance education over the Internet is enormous, using international experts in collaboration in specific fields or interdisciplinary courses. Librarians are making use of their campus-wide information networks for training faculty and students on use of the Internet and the library. On some campuses, faculty already accept student work assignments by e-mail and hold discussions with distant classes. This is effectively a paperless course where syllabuses, class assignments, and final reports are exchanged over the network.

The increased use of sound and video transmissions, particularly with interactive teaching, will make distance education even more acceptable. For busy professionals or people in remote locations, distance teaching makes continuing education easier. Combining the Internet with digital multimedia and easy accessibility makes a revolution in primary, secondary, and adult education virtually inevitable.

# Using E-Mail

Many e-mail systems are available for almost all computer platforms. The following is a short glimpse of a basic UNIX e-mail program that outlines several of the basic e-mail functions.

## Sending E-Mail

After logging onto UNIX, the command line furnishes the user with a prompt. On the system I use in the following example, it is `icarus.lis[1]%`. Throughout this book you'll see all sorts of prompts because I have used different systems.

You start the e-mail program by typing the `mail` command and entering the recipient's Internet address. The general form is

```
mail [username]@[machinename]
```

The e-mail program then asks for a subject:

```
icarus.lis[1] % mail rs@ucs.usl.edu
Subject:
```

**Navigator's Note:** The length of the subject of an e-mail message is best limited to short descriptive text relevant to the message. "Hi!" as a subject is pretty common, but if the recipient gets a lot of mail and isn't looking for a message from you, your message may get handled late or not at all. The volume of mail is a big problem for many people, so they use e-mail because it is so easy to send; if they had to use conventional mail, they wouldn't bother. As you get more involved with e-mail, you'll find that you get lots of replies to messages that simply say "Thanks" or "Okay"—hardly helpful at all.

You can also start mail and specify the subject. This is done with the command format:

```
mail "[subject]" [username]@[machinename]
```

Notice that if the subject is more than a single word, the text must be between double or single quotes.

Next, type in the text of the message, using whatever editor the system works with. Sometimes this editor is built into the e-mail system and may use its own eccentric commands (such as Ctrl+X to send; who thought of that?!). Some editors work like a typewriter: you must press Enter at the end of each line, and you can't go up a line to make changes. You can only go backwards on the current line to correct errors. Even that is tricky and depends on which computer you're using. The Backspace key may work to back up and erase errors in some cases, and Ctrl+H may work in others. You'll have to practice with your editor to become proficient in creating long messages.

**Navigator's Note:** It's often easier to use some other editor to create the mail message in a file and then import the file into the message. You'll have to check out the documentation for your e-mail system to see if the built-in editor is any good and, if not, how to import text from a file.

## CHAPTER 3

If you botch the e-mail message to the point of embarrassment (as is very easy with the more primitive editors), Ctrl+C normally cancels the e-mail message. Ctrl+D sends the message. In some cases, you are prompted with cc, which means you could put in another Internet address to send a carbon copy to.

You can send an e-mail message in other ways. In UNIX, you can send a file by starting mail with a different command format:

```
mail -s "[subject]" [username]@[machinename] <[filename]
```

This takes the contents of the file, [filename], and sends it to the mail program as if you were typing it. This is a technique called *piping* and will be discussed in your system manual.

You can send a file by entering ~r on a blank line followed by the filename. This means "I want to send a file and here comes its name."

```
~r test
"test" 160/6661
```

E-mail programs enable you to compose and send a message or file in many other ways. You'll have to read the documentation of your e-mail program to discover all its features.

## Receiving E-Mail

When you log onto a UNIX machine, you often get a message telling you that you have mail waiting. This is usually in the form "you have mail" or "you have new mail"

```
You have mail.
/h1/rjs4808/rjsres
a91% mail
Mail version SMI 4.0 Tue May 11 09:06:35 CDT 1993  Type ? for help.
"/usr/spool/mail/rjs4808": 15 messages 15 unread
>U  1 70673.2233@compuserve.com Fri May 14 08:32   40/1611  (id: DPB610) WINNET
 U  2 rjs4808@ucs.usl.edu Wed May 26 08:11   54/2374  Media Services -- Learnin
 U  3 76004.3310@compuserve.com Wed May 26 17:05  271/18045 C7 part 3B
 U  4 76004.3310@compuserve.com Wed Jun  2 11:29   35/1546  chapter 7
 U  5 70673.2233@compuserve.com Wed Jun  2 22:00   45/1344  Re:  Yanoff's PLAN
file
 U  6 halder@cs.umb.edu  Thu Jun  3 17:11   39/1934  Re:  Help for Book
 U  7 76004.3310@compuserve.com Thu Jun  3 18:25   67/1956  Book observations
 U  8 72410.2162@compuserve.com Fri Jun  4 08:35  101/4579  Book observations
```

```
U  9 76004.3310@compuserve.com Sat Jun  5 01:52    27/1076   Stuff
U 10 ddickerson@igc.apc.org Sun Jun  6 13:43    47/1573  permission request
U 11 ddickerson@igc.apc.org Sun Jun  6 13:48   405/11540 IGC Brochure
U 12 AGUEVARA@macc.wisc.edu Sun Jun 13 13:11    19/853   Help with Internet
U 13 kuchin@darmstadt.gmd.de Wed Jun 16 00:38    78/3383  Request
U 14 kuchin@darmstadt.gmd.de Wed Jun 16 01:47    78/3379  Request
&
```

To read your mail, start the mail program by typing the command mail at the system prompt. In this example, the UNIX prompt changes from bss> to the mail & (ampersand) prompt. The mail program lists the sender, the date the message was sent, the number of lines and characters in the message (as in 64/1662), and the subject of the mail messages. You can now read, reply, save, edit, or delete mail messages. The greater-than sign (>) points to the current mail item, and the U at the beginning of each e-mail message means that the message is unread.

# Help

To help you remember the mail commands, a short description of each is available online. Entering ? or the word help at the mail & prompt displays the help text:

```
d [message list]              delete messages
e [message list]              edit messages
f [message list]              show from lines of messages
h                             print out active message headers
m [user list]                 mail to specific users
n                             goto and type next message
p [message list]              print messages
pre [message list]            make messages go back to system mailbox
q                             quit, saving unresolved messages in mbox
r [message list]              reply to sender (only) of messages
R [message list]              reply to sender and all recipients of messages
s [message list] file         append messages to file
t [message list]              type messages (same as print)
top [message list]            show top lines of messages
u [message list]              undelete messages
v [message list]              edit messages with display editor
w [message list] file         append messages to file, without from line
x                             quit, do not change system mailbox
z [-]                         display next [previous] page of headers
!                             shell escape

A [message list] consists of integers, ranges of same, or user names separated
by spaces.  If omitted, Mail uses the current message.
&
```

## Common E-Mail Commands

Following is a selection of commands that most e-mail programs support. You'll need to refer to the manuals for your system to find out what commands are available for your e-mail program.

### Headers

To see the partial headers of the messages again, enter h at the mail prompt. These are not the full headers we discussed earlier—just the originator's name and address, the time the message was sent, and the subject.

```
25 ellen            Wed Jun  2 09:39   95/3659  here's your chance!
26 GBLOOMQ@acadvm1.uottawa.ca Wed Jun  2 13:44   36/1804  Re: Navigating again
27 MUKASA@grove.iup.edu Wed Jun  2 14:10   29/1065  Internet
28 WYLLYS@utxvm.cc.utexas.edu Wed Jun  2 14:29   35/1469  Navigating, yes!
29 kewing@TIGGER.STCLOUD.MSUS.EDU Wed Jun  2 14:40   41/2000  navigate workshop
30 tuma@nevada.edu    Wed Jun  2 14:56   57/2442  Re: Navigating again
31 LIBTAT@orion.depaul.edu Wed Jun  2 15:14   38/1630  Internet course by mail
32 WYLLYS@utxvm.cc.utexas.edu Wed Jun  2 15:14   32/809   Re: Navigating, yes!
33 FERMO@AESOP.RUTGERS.EDU Wed Jun  2 15:31   49/1644  Comments
34 FALKENHM@ZENO.MSCD.EDU Wed Jun  2 15:43   25/872   Re: Navigating
35 LAMBDEAN%ITHACA.BITNET@CORNELLC.cit.cornell.edu Wed Jun  2 15:53   31/1100
navigation
36 EGS2G1B@MVS.OAC.UCLA.EDU Wed Jun  2 15:59   38/1584  RE: Internet Workshop
37 gepst1            Wed Jun  2 16:03   33/931   Navigating Again
38 judkins@library.swmed.edu Wed Jun  2 16:13   18/723   Navigating course
39 mmcguire@ccs.carleton.ca Wed Jun  2 16:30   34/1143  navigating the internet
40 SMS@mlnc486.mlnc.com Wed Jun  2 16:31   33/1225  navigating
&
```

### Read

To read a message, type t or p and the number of the message you want to read. If you just press Enter, the current message is displayed (remember, the current message is signified by a greater-than sign on the far right). You can also type the number of the message by itself.

### Reply

You can reply to any e-mail message in two ways from the mail program: R replies to the sender and all others who have received the message, whereas r replies to the sender only.

Navigator's Warning: Standard UNIX programs have a lot of strange key usage (strange, at least, to X-windows, Microsoft Windows, and Mac users). Many commands, as we've just discussed, are case sensitive, and using the wrong case can give you the wrong results and make you grind your teeth. Worse still, the results might be different from, or even the opposite of, what you want, depending on the version of UNIX you're using. Read your help screens and manuals carefully.

## Save

You can save messages by typing s, followed by the number or numbers of the messages you want to save, followed by a filename to save them to. Typing s 1-3 oldmail.txt saves messages 1, 2, and 3 to the designated file. s 1 2 3 does the same thing if you've already specified a filename during the current session with the e-mail system. When the file already exists, the messages are appended to it.

```
& s 1-3 oldmail.txt
"oldmail.txt" [New file] 365/22033
& s 7 8 9 oldmail.txt
"oldmail.txt" [Appended] 195/7614
&
```

## Delete and Undelete

Deleting a message marks it for erasure when you quit the e-mail session. Use the delete command, d, followed by the number or numbers of the messages you want to delete. If you delete a file by mistake, you can use the undelete command, u, to get the messages back. However, once you quit the mail program, all messages marked for deletion are gone forever.

## Quit

Typing the letter q leaves the mail program. Unread messages are saved, and you can read them when you run the mail program again. Read messages are saved in a file called mbox, and deleted files are erased and lost for good. The other way to leave this mail program is to type the letter x, which quits the mail program but leaves everything as if you never ran it. All deleted files are recovered, and read files are not transferred to the mbox file. The only exception is that any files you saved mail messages into will still exist.

## What If I Want to Send a File That Isn't Just Plain Text?

(Boy, you ask long questions.) So far, we've assumed that all the files you want to send are regular ASCII text files. Binary files, such as graphics, audio, and many word processing files (for instance, Microsoft Word or WordPerfect if they're not saved as text or postscript) must be prepared for sending by e-mail by encoding them as we discussed previously. Encoding programs take binary files and format them to plain ASCII text.

The receiver of the e-mail must then decode them so that they make sense. UNIX has uuencode and uudecode to do this job. Uuencode is available for several operating systems. Several other encoding software programs are available free over the Internet; use Archie to locate them.

# E-Mail and the Internet

E-mail is an incredible tool. It can keep you in touch with friends and business colleagues no matter where they are physically. It can be used to send and receive files as well as interact with other services (as we'll discuss in the section on ftpmail in Chapter 4, "A Moving Experience: FTP for Me") and to access Archie (as we'll cover in Chapter 6, "Finding Files: Archie"). Equally important, e-mail can connect with discussion groups (as we'll see in Chapters 12, "Views and News: USENET," and 13, "Getting on the List: LISTSERV").

Just to show that we've gotten you interested in using electronic mail, drop us a line and tell us what e-mail systems you use, what you like and hate about e-mail, and what interesting things have happened to you through e-mail. Our addresses are

| Rich Smith | `rjs@/is.piH.edu` |
| Mark Gibbs | `mgibbs@coyote.rain.org` |

# A Moving Experience: FTP for Me

As you sail around the Internet, you'll find plenty of files that might be useful to you. They may be text files, programs, or databases found through Archie or by word of mouth. What they all have in common is that they're not where you want them to be—that is, on your own computer.

This book describes tools that an Internet navigator can use—Gopher, WAIS, WWW, Veronica, and InterNIC, all of which were developed to make the unwieldy resources of the Internet easier to use.

Although these tools make finding information a little easier, we haven't yet achieved seamless access to the Internet—where getting hold of what you want is simple and intuitive. Today, you'll find that you must usually access files the old-fashioned way—you must go out and get them.

# File Transfer Protocol (FTP)

The tool for transferring files between computers on the Internet is called File Transfer Protocol, or FTP.

We can thank the Internet's predecessor, ARPANET, for the creation of File Transfer Protocol. FTP was part of the development of the TCP/IP protocol suite now in use on the Internet. Using a standard protocol for file transfer, FTP works regardless of the type of computer you may be using or the type of machine at the other end.

A remarkable thing about the Internet is the speed at which files can be sent and received. The Internet transfers files at a rate of millions of bytes per second, and with the coming of the National Research and Education Network (NREN), that will soon be upgraded to gigabytes (thousands of millions of bytes) per second.

At the present speed, it would take only a few seconds to send this book from one location to another. Compare that with using a regular modem setup at a speed of 9600 baud, where the same transfer would take minutes (and those unfortunates restricted to 1200 baud might as well go and enjoy the first half of a football game).

FTP can do more than just retrieve files. You can use it to transfer files to remote machines from your computer. To make it a practical tool, FTP includes commands for listing directories, listing files in directories, changing directories, and getting information about what you're doing, and setting parameters for how the operations will be done.

Here's an example of how FTP can be used. From time to time in my dissertation work, I need to show my adviser my progress. I'm located in Lafayette, Louisiana, and I use FTP to transfer chapters of my dissertation to my other computer account at the University of Pittsburgh. From there I can print out the chapters on the third floor of the School of Library and Information Science, where my adviser reads them and makes corrections and comments.

## What Can You FTP?

What kinds of things can you find in all these available files? Well, there's data of every kind: statistics from the U.S. census, results from countless scientific experiments, and text ranging from electronic journals and magazines (some of them very interesting, and some pretty wild) to the full text of *Alice in Wonderland*, the *Book of Mormon*, and the *Bible*.

You can get image files from NASA that contain the latest pictures from the various probes. Image files from other sources offer you still photos from Star Trek, cartoons, and even soft porn.

Finally, you can find software for DOS, Windows, Macintosh, and UNIX, as well as updates for Apple, Novell, and the products of many other major vendors.

Some of this software is free, some comes with source code, and some you can buy if you decide you like it.

## Freeware

As its name implies, freeware is free. Some freeware even comes with source code! The authors don't charge for the software because they are altruistic, generous, or don't see much value in their software.

For some groups, altruism is a major motivator. A notable source of freeware is the Free Software Foundation, which is working on a complete UNIX-like operating system that it intends to release to the public domain.

Freeware enters the public domain from many sources. Its presence there suggests that the copyright has been surrendered. However, unless authors explicitly state that this has been done, they still hold the copyright to the software. This means that although they are letting you use it, they still actually own it. It's all very complicated legally, and it really matters only if you plan to distribute one of these freeware products for profit or use any part of its source code (if supplied) in your commercial product.

If you use freeware, it's nice to drop the author a note of thanks. Don't bug them about faults, errors, and omissions you find unless they requested such feedback.

## Shareware

Shareware has become a significant force in the software business. Shareware is software that the authors want you to pass around to other users. The idea is that if you like it, you send them whatever registration fee they ask for. In return, you are officially licensed to use the product and usually receive a manual and/or bonus software.

Some shareware is called *brain-damaged* or *crippled,* meaning that it doesn't do everything a registered version can do or can only perform functions to a limited extent. The best shareware is usually not inhibited in any way, and if the shareware author is a member of the American Shareware Association (ASA), they are bound not to inhibit the application's functionality.

Some shareware isn't exactly crippled, but after a period of time set by the vendor, it must be reinstalled. This usually wipes out configuration data and other aspects of an established, used installation. If you've started to like the product, it's a pretty good incentive to register.

Another trick to encourage registration is known as *nagware*. Unless you have a registered copy, a screen pops up whenever you start the program (and sometimes during operation) to remind you that your copy isn't registered.

Many of the shareware products currently circulating have made some of their authors quite wealthy. The McAffee antivirus products and Datastorm's ProComm communications software are two of the best known.

The great thing about shareware is that because the vendors don't have huge marketing overhead or any of the other paraphernalia of regular commercial products, their prices are considerably lower.

The shareware concept only works, however, if people try out the software, decide they like it, and actually register it. If vendors don't make any money, they often stop developing their products. This has caused the end of some really good software with much better value than many commercial packages.

# Running FTP

To start FTP under UNIX (and most operating systems), you just type `ftp` and off you go. So, under my system (the prompt is `coyote%`):

```
coyote% ftp
ftp>
```

Once running, FTP produces its own prompt, usually `ftp>`. You can also start FTP by giving the name of the Internet computer from which you want to get files:

```
coyote% ftp ucsbuxa.ucsb.edu
```

In general terms, the FTP command is

```
ftp <hostname> <port>
```

The `<port>` part of the command is necessary only if a specific value is required. If you leave it out, a default value is used. After you are connected to a remote computer through FTP, you are asked for a user name and password.

## Anonymous FTP

FTP is most commonly used to retrieve files from computers that allow public access. These *anonymous FTP sites* together contain millions of files that add up to terabytes of information.

With anonymous FTP access, you do not need an account or password to access the remote computer. The remote machine accepts anonymous as your name and Internet address or guest as the password. After that, you can access files on the remote machine. Usually, your access is restricted to the public (or pub) directory.

## FTP Commands

Different versions of the FTP program are available for different computer operating systems. Some have commands different from the common implementations on UNIX systems. Most Netfarers seldom, if ever, need to use more than a few FTP commands, so the differences between versions are usually minimal. The commands for the UNIX version of FTP that I use can be listed by typing help at the ftp> prompt.

```
ftp> help
```

Commands may be abbreviated. Commands are

| | | | | |
|---------|------------|----------|-----------|---------|
| !       | cr         | macdef   | proxy     | send    |
| $       | delete     | mdelete  | sendport  | status  |
| account | debug      | mdir     | put       | struct  |
| append  | dir        | mget     | pwd       | sunique |
| ascii   | disconnect | mkdir    | quit      | tenex   |
| bell    | form       | mls      | quote     | trace   |
| binary  | get        | mode     | recv      | type    |
| bye     | glob       | mput     | remotehelp| user    |
| case    | hash       | nmap     | rename    | verbose |
| cd      | help       | ntrans   | reset     | ?       |
| cdup    | lcd        | open     | rmdir     |         |
| close   | ls         | prompt   | runique   |         |
| ftp>    |            |          |           |         |

You can get a brief explanation of each command by typing help and the command itself at the ftp> prompt. Note that the prompt changes to ftp?>.

```
ftp?> help binary
```

Here is more information on frequently used FTP commands:

`ascii`: Set FTP to ASCII mode. This is usually the default and is used for text files. If you use it for binary files such as programs or some databases, they'll be corrupted.

`binary`: Set FTP to binary mode. Used for transferring binary files, which might be graphics files, executable programs, or audio files.

`bye`: Quits the FTP program.

`cd <remote_directory>`: Changes the directory of the remote machine to the directory specified.

`close`: Ends your FTP session with the remote computer and returns you to the ftp> prompt. Note that at this point you aren't connected to any remote machine until you use the `open` command.

`dir or ls -l`: Prints a listing of the files in the current remote working directory.

`get`: Retrieves a remote file and stores it on your computer.

`mget`: Transfers multiple files from a remote machine to your local machine. Files can be listed separated by spaces. Supports wildcard symbols * and ?.

`mput`: Transfers multiple files from a local machine to a remote machine. Files should be separated by a space. Supports wildcard symbols * and ?.

`open`: Used to establish a connection to a remote machine.

`prompt`: When you use `mget` or `mput`, and prompt is set to on, you'll be asked for a confirmation for each file handled. This can get pretty tedious if you're transferring a lot of files. Issue the command `prompt off`, and you'll be able to drink your coffee and read the paper in peace. Use `prompt on` to get back to the confirmation mode.

`put`: Stores a local file on the remote machine.

`pwd`: Prints the name of the current working directory on the remote machine.

## File Types

A common file type available on the Internet is the ASCII text file. These files contain plain text, usually (but not always) without control characters (characters with values below 32), except for carriage return and/or line feed characters, which are used often.

> **Navigator's Note:** Computers handle numbers only, so alphabetic characters in the ASCII character set are encoded as numbers ranging from 0 (called *null*) to 255. The characters with values less than 32 are all control characters, many of which go back to the teletype era. The only common control characters are 10, called carriage return (which is the same as the Enter key), and 13, which is called line feed. Many text file formats end each line with a carriage return followed by a line feed, but standard UNIX files use only line feeds.
>
> This range of values can be stored in a single byte of eight bits. A problem is that much of the current Internet can't handle eight-bit data, so it needs to be converted to another form that takes up only seven of the bits. This is the function of the uuencode software we discussed in Chapter 3, "Where's the Post? Electronic Mail."

ASCII files can be easily moved from machine to machine and read without further manipulation. The convention for text file naming (but don't count on it) is to use the extensions .txt or .doc to signify that it is a text file. Because the default mode of transfer in FTP is ASCII text, you don't need to tell FTP the file type.

## Binary Files

Binary, the other FTP transfer mode, is used for files that contain data, including nonalphanumeric characters. The use of these files is machine or program dependent. For example, a file created by a word processing program, such as WordPerfect, and saved as a WordPerfect document, contains information on format, fonts, and other features that only WordPerfect can interpret.

> **Navigator's Note:** You can use binary mode to transfer text files, but it's less efficient than text mode. In binary mode, file data becomes over 12 percent bigger while being transferred. This won't matter on a small file (100,000 bytes, say) because that would take about 10 seconds in text mode and just over 11 seconds in binary mode. However, if you transfer a 100,000,000-byte file, you increase your transfer time from about 16 minutes to over 18 minutes.

Many different file types must be transferred in binary mode. Executable files usually have an extension of .com or .exe. Graphics files can have any one of a multitude of extensions, depending on the program for which they are designed. Some examples are .pic, .gif, .wpg, .wmf, .tif, .art, and .pcx.

## Compressed Files

Many files that you can retrieve through FTP aren't in a form that you can directly use. They need special handling in order to be manipulated.

Compressed files have been reduced in size by one of several techniques, making them unusable until they are uncompressed. The name usually indicates what kind of compression has been used; .zip, .arc, .zoo, and binhex are just a few of the many programs that compress files. Many compression formats are in the public domain or are shareware. The programs that handle these files are available at numerous sites.

Your receiving machine must be able to uncompress these files in order for you to make use of them. In some instances, you are given the option of file type—you see several files with the same name but different extensions (such as filename.ps, filename.ps.Z, filename.txt, and filename.txt.Z).

In the preceding case, the .ps stands for PostScript and the .txt stands for text; you have the option of retrieving either (or both) of them. The files may be intended to be identical, but the PostScript file often produces better output and may contain related graphics or formatted tables not in the text-only file. You must have a PostScript printer in order to make a hard copy of a PostScript file.

The .ps and .txt files should be transferred in ASCII mode, while the .ps.Z and the .txt.Z files (both compressed) must be transferred in binary mode. Compressed files must be uncompressed before you can use their contents.

On most machines running anonymous FTP, the READ.ME file (or a file with a similar name) gives the location and type of files that are available. It also tells you where and how to obtain the programs that uncompress the compressed files. Some machines offer only compressed files, but will uncompress them for you if you retrieve them by omitting the .Z in the filename.

Finally, you may have used a utility called TAR, which stands for Tape ARchiver. This utility combines files and directories into a single file and is helpful when many files need to be moved or when you need to get a large number of related files. TAR files are often compressed as well, so that the file to be transferred is as small as possible. TAR files must be transferred in binary mode, uncompressed, and then "un-tar'ed" by processing the file with the TAR utility in uncompress mode.

# FTP by Electronic Mail

Two months separated the two workshops I gave over the Internet. During this time I noticed several important differences between the users attracted by the two sessions.

One notable difference was the increase in those using commercial access to the Internet. By the second session, the number of users with accounts through MCI, CompuServe, and other commercial gateways increased significantly.

These gateways do not have the direct Internet connections you find, for example, at a university. This population will continue to grow as more commercial services become available, which in turn will make access easier and cheaper. University graduates and individuals who had Internet access through an employer and who make the Internet a part of their daily routines want to continue having a link to the world via the Internet.

Unfortunately, not all of these gateways give full access to the Internet. On some service providers, such as CompuServe, users can only send and receive e-mail; services such as FTP and telnet aren't available.

A partial remedy to this problem is called FTPmail, which enables you to e-mail FTP commands to an FTPmail server. The server handles the FTP operations and e-mails the results back to you. FTPmail enables people who have only e-mail to take advantage of anonymous FTP sites.

Digital Equipment Corporation (DEC) maintains a machine on the Internet that accepts e-mail with FTPmail commands in the body of the message. It contacts the target FTP server, pretending to be you, and gets and places files for you. The time required to do this ranges from a few minutes to many hours. Try to use this service during nonpeak hours.

The Internet name for the DEC FTPmail server is `ftpmail@decwrl.dec.com`. To receive the help manual on how to use this service, send the word `help` in the body of an e-mail message, without a subject heading, to the server:

```
bss>mail ftpmail@decwrl.dec.com
Subject:
help
.
bss>
```

You might receive this reply to the preceding message:

```
 — Help —
>>> $Id: help-text,v 1.6 1993/02/16 14:55:03 vixie Exp $
>>>
>>> commands are:

     reply <MAILADDR>        set reply addr, since headers are usually wrong
     connect [HOST [USER [PASS [ACCT]]]]
                     defaults to gatekeeper.dec.com, anonymous
```

```
ascii               files grabbed are printable ascii
binary              files grabbed are compressed or tar or both
chdir PLACE         "get" and "ls" commands are relative to PLACE
                    (only one CHDIR per ftpmail session,
                    and it executes before any LS/DIR/GETs)
compress            compress binaries using Lempel-Ziv encoding
compact             compress binaries using Huffman encoding
uuencode            binary files will be mailed in uuencode format
btoa                binary files will be mailed in btoa format
chunksize SIZE      split files into SIZE-byte chunks (def: 64000)
ls (or dir) PLACE      short (long) directory listing
index THING         search for THING in ftp server's index
get FILE            get a file and have it mailed to you
                    (max 10 GET's per ftpmail session)
quit                terminate script, ignore rest of mail message
                    (use if you have a .signature or
                    are a VMSMAIL user)
```

Notice that the connect command giving the name of the Internet computer that is your source or destination for files should be the first command used in the e-mail message. Also, only one chdir (change directory) command can be used in the e-mail message—therefore, you need to know the path (directory and subdirectory) of any file you want to retrieve.

FTPmail is not as versatile as a direct connection and requires patience and accuracy to get the information. In fact, don't be surprised if it takes several tries to master FTPmail. You will learn from your mistakes, and after the initial breakthrough, you will find that FTPmail is a valuable tool for navigating the Internet.

## FTP for Me

In summary, FTP is the program to use for transferring files from one machine to another. Although you can use FTP to transfer your files from machines where you have personal accounts—that is, with the use of a login name and a password—FTP is more commonly used with public access machines on the Internet (what is called anonymous FTP). This makes thousands of files available to anyone who wants them.

Everything from computer programs to texts of *Alice in Wonderland*, a Request for Comments on a new computer standard, programs to help you in your calculus studies, or games of chess can be retrieved using FTP. If your appetite for digging into all of these resources has been sufficiently whetted, it's time to Navigate!

# FTP Examples

Merit is a regional Internet access and network service provider for Michigan. Merit's Network Information Center host computer is located in Michigan and is accessible via anonymous FTP. Merit provides many services to its region, one of which is maintaining a machine that enables Internet users to obtain information about the Internet, NSFNET, and MichNet.

Your objectives are to extract some documents from this machine and to become familiar with exploring a remote machine. To make an FTP connection, at the system prompt bss (remember, yours might be different) type ftp and the remote machine name. MERIT's machine name is nic.merit.edu.

Try the following example for yourself. You will, of course, use your own address when you are asked for a password.

```
bss> ftp nic.merit.edu
Connected to nic.merit.edu.
220 nic.merit.edu ftp server (Version 4.1 Fri Aug 28 11:37:57 GDT 1987) ready.
Name (nic.merit.edu:rjs4808): anonymous
331 Guest login ok, send ident as password.
Password:          ("rs@usl" my local Internet address does not appear)
230 Guest login ok, access restrictions apply.
ftp>
```

If the machine responded with Guest login ok, restrictions apply, you got there without any problems. The FTP command dir gives you a listing of the directory you are in:

```
ftp> dir
200 PORT command successful.
150 Opening ASCII mode data connection for /bin/ls.
total 65
-rw-r--r--   1 nic     merit     17596 Dec 09 18:51 INDEX
-rw-r--r--   1 nic     merit      5446 Aug 04 1992  READ.ME
drwxr-xr-x   2 nic     merit       512 Sep 15 14:39 acceptable.use.policies
drwxr-sr-x   2 root    system      512 Sep 30 17:31 bin
drwxr-sr-x   3 cise    nsf         512 Aug 14 1992  cise
drwxr-xr-x   9 nic     merit       512 Jul 29 1992  documents
drwxr-sr-x   3 root    system      512 Feb 20 1992  etc
drwxr-xr-x   8 nic     merit       512 Jan 28 20:30 internet
drwxr-xr-x   2 nic     merit       512 Feb 01 15:37 introducing.the.internet
drwxr-sr-x   2 root    system      512 Feb 20 1992  lib
drwxr-xr-x   2 nic     merit       512 Feb 10 12:29 maps
drwxr-sr-x   2 nic     merit       512 Jan 07 12:43 merit
drwxr-xr-x   7 nic     merit       512 Aug 14 1992  michnet
```

```
drwxr-xr-x   6 nic      merit        512 Jul 29 1992   newsletters
drwxr-xr-x   4 nic      merit        512 Aug 03 1992   nren
drwxr-xr-x  14 nic      merit        512 Jan 05 15:31  nsfnet
drwxr-sr-x   2 omb      omb          512 Jul 29 1992   omb
drwxr-xr-x   3 nic      merit        512 Dec 01 11:39  resources
drwxr-xr-x   3 nic      merit        512 Jul 29 1992   statistics
drwxr-sr-x   3 root     system       512 Feb 20 1992   usr
drwxr-xr-x   3 nic      merit        512 Jul 15 1992   working.groups
226 Transfer complete.
1351 bytes received in 0.48 seconds (2.7 Kbytes/s)
ftp>
```

You have a listing of the current directory. So far, so good.

Of primary interest are the letters on the far left, which tell you whether the names on the far right are files or directories. The d in the letters on the left (as in drwxr-wx—x) shows that acceptable.use.policies, bin, cise, documents, etc, and most of the others on this list are subdirectories. INDEX and README are not directories but files of some kind, as is indicated by the absence of the d in the string of letters.

The letters on the far left also provide information about files or directories, which can be readable, writable, or executable (indicated by r, w, or x). Their position in the line indicates who has rights to read, write, or execute the file or directory. Rights can be given to the individual, groups, or everyone.

> **Navigator's Note:** A file that is flagged as executable in the listing of a remote directory is executable on that machine. If your computer uses a different operating system, you won't be able to run it locally. If you can get telnet access to that machine, you'll be able to run it there.

The numbers at the middle right give the size of the file in bytes. This is important information. Some very large files exist on the Internet, and trying to store one of them will cause a problem if you do not have enough space on your local machine.

The INDEX and READ.ME files most likely contain information about the machine you have logged into and which directories and files can be accessed. You need to get these files and read them.

It is vital that you use the exact spelling, including upper- or lowercase, when you specify a file or directory name. There can be numerous variations and spellings for the same filename. For example, READ.ME is different from Read.me and

READ.me. In many cases, it is done this way intentionally as a way of preventing the overwriting of a file with a similar name. There can be many READ.ME and INDEX files in the subdirectories on this machine. You might find variations, such as INDEX.documents, Index.rfc, 001-READ.Me, 002-read.me, or 003-Read.Me.

In addition to the variations in spelling and use of upper- and lowercase, some filenames have to conform to systems requirements. For example, under PC DOS a filename is limited to eight characters and three extension characters, as in infrmatn.txt. In trying to retrieve this file, a likely mistake is to spell the filename as information.txt (too long).

**Navigator's Warning:** Under many computer operating systems, using the exact spelling and exact case is mandatory for successful file retrieval!

Okay, now retrieve the INDEX and READ.ME files:

```
bss% ftp nic.merit.edu
ftp> get INDEX
200 PORT command successful.
150 Opening ASCII mode data connection for INDEX (17596 bytes).
226 Transfer complete.
local: INDEX remote: INDEX
18000 bytes received in 2.4 seconds (7.4 Kbytes/s)
ftp> get READ.ME
200 PORT command successful.
150 Opening ASCII mode data connection for READ.ME (5446 bytes).
226 Transfer complete.
local: READ.ME remote: READ.ME
5578 bytes received in 0.72 seconds (7.6 Kbytes/s)
ftp>
```

Notice the speed at which the file transfers took place. In my session, the two files were transferred from Michigan to my local machine in Louisiana in just over three seconds.

If you end your FTP session, go back to your local system, and read the files, you find that the INDEX file contains a bird's-eye view of the directory structure of the Merit system (see the following example); the READ.ME file gives directions on how to ftp, move around the machine, and use FTPmail queries.

To see what is in the document subdirectory, use the change directory command cd to move to that subdirectory. Then use the dir command to list the contents.

```
ftp> cd documents
250 CWD command successful.
ftp> dir
200 PORT command successful.
150 Opening ASCII mode data connection for /bin/ls.
total 132
-rw-r--r--   1 nic      merit        2300 Jul 30 1992  INDEX.documents
drwxr-sr-x   2 nic      merit         512 Jan 14 06:39 fyi
drwxr-sr-x   2 iesg     ietf         2048 Feb 12 13:15 iesg
drwxr-sr-x   2 iesg     ietf        26624 Feb 08 11:27 ietf
drwxr-sr-x   2 iesg     ietf        16896 Feb 12 13:12 internet-drafts
drwxr-sr-x   2 nic      merit         512 Jul 15 1992  michnet.tour.guides
drwxr-sr-x   2 nic      merit       16896 Feb 10 11:51 rfc
drwxr-sr-x   2 nic      merit        1536 Jan 05 15:27 std
226 Transfer complete.
525 bytes received in 1.2 seconds (0.43 Kbytes/s)
```

Here's another index file called INDEX.documents! This is a small file—2,300 bytes. View its contents by using the FTP command get in combination with the more command.

The symbol ¦ means that the output of the get command is to be sent to the more utility. More will fill the local computer screen with the data sent to it from the remote machine. You can then read one line at a time by pressing the Enter key or one screen at a time by pressing the space bar. If you don't use more, the text just scrolls continuously before you have a chance to read it.

```
ftp> get INDEX.documents ¦more
200 PORT command successful.
150 Opening ASCII mode data connection for INDEX.documents (2300 bytes).
<NIC.MERIT.EDU> /documents/INDEX.documents                    30 July 1992
                    Merit Network Information Center Services
                              NIC.MERIT.EDU
                              ftp.MERIT.EDU
                             ftp.MICHNET.NET
                               NIS.NSF.NET
                               (35.1.1.48)
  Merit Network Information Center host computer, accessible via anonymous
ftp, contains a wide array of information about the Internet, NSFNET, and
MichNet. The document's directory is an archive for NSFNET, regional, and
Internet documentation.
   fyi/                     The FYI (For Your Information) sub-series of the
                            Request For Comments (RFCs), designed to provide a
                            wide audience of Internet users with a central
                            repository of information about any topics which
                            relate to the Internet.
   iesg/                    Minutes of the most recent IETF Steering Group
                            meetings.
```

```
    ietf/                    Current information on Internet Engineering Task
                             Force activities including a general description of
                             the IETF, summaries of ongoing working group
                             activities, and information on past and upcoming
                             meetings.
    internet-drafts/         A directory of draft documents which will ultimately
                             be submitted to the IAB and the RFC Editor to be
                             considered for publishing as RFC's. Comments are
                             welcome and should be addressed to the author, whose
                             name and e-mail address are listed on the first page
                             of the respective draft.
    michnet.tour.guides/     Documents detailing uses of the Michnet network.
    rfc/                     Request For Comments:  a document series which
                             describes the Internet suite of protocols and
                             related experiments.
    std/                     The Standards are the sub-series of notes within
                             the RFC series which document Internet standards.
226 Transfer complete.
local: INDEX.documents remote: INDEX.documents
2349 bytes received in 0.34 seconds (6.7 Kbytes/s)
ftp>
```

This file contains the names of the subdirectories and gives an abstract of their contents.

Now, go to the subdirectory named rfc and find Request For Comments, which is a collection of documents pertaining to the Internet. Included are papers on protocols and standards, proposals for new protocols, glossaries, biographies of those who helped build the Internet, and other helpful material. This is an excellent way to learn the history of the Internet, because the Request For Comments are listed in chronological order starting from 1969. There are technical as well as nontechnical papers in this subdirectory.

Now, change directories and list the directory contents:

```
ftp> cd rfc
250 CWD command successful.
ftp> dir
200 PORT command successful.
150 Opening ASCII mode data connection for /bin/ls.
total 87096
-rw-r--r--   2 nic      merit     141342 Feb 10 11:52 INDEX.rfc
-rw-r--r--   2 nic      merit       2350 Nov 19 1988  rfc0003.txt
-rw-r--r--   2 nic      merit      26766 Nov 19 1988  rfc0005.txt
-rw-r--r--   2 nic      merit       1585 Nov 19 1988  rfc0006.txt
-rw-r--r--   2 nic      merit       3382 Nov 21 1988  rfc0010.txt
-rw-r--r--   2 nic      merit        367 Nov 18 1988  rfc0016.txt
```

```
-rw-r--r--   2 nic      merit        4511 Nov 18 1988  rfc0017.txt
<<many more files>>
-rw-r--r--   2 nic      merit       33277 Feb 08 19:50 rfc1423.txt
-rw-r--r--   2 nic      merit       17537 Feb 08 19:50 rfc1424.txt
-rw-r--r--   2 nic      merit       20932 Feb 08 20:42 rfc1425.txt
-rw-r--r--   2 nic      merit       11661 Feb 08 20:42 rfc1426.txt
-rw-r--r--   2 nic      merit       17856 Feb 08 20:42 rfc1427.txt
-rw-r--r--   2 nic      merit       12064 Feb 08 20:42 rfc1428.txt
226 Transfer complete.
53587 bytes received in 67 seconds (0.78 Kbytes/s)
```

A common problem that you encounter when searching the Internet is not being able to see a machine's contents before you begin searching on it (unless you happen to be clairvoyant). Because there are over a thousand files in this directory, you will spend several minutes waiting for your directory command to finish listing them all. In addition, the filenames give no indication of the file contents!

Because you probably aren't clairvoyant, you must depend on the INDEX file in this situation. This INDEX file is a large one, so it is best to get and examine it on your own computer. The INDEX.rfc file (an excerpt of which follows) contains the filenames and a brief description of the content of each file.

```
rfc1392.txt      Jan 93    (Malkin)     Internet Users' Glossary
```

A glossary of networking terms may be interesting to a new Internet user, so I retrieved the file rfc1392.txt and saved it for future reference.

```
ftp> get rfc1392.txt
200 PORT command successful.
150 Opening ASCII mode data connection for rfc1392.txt (104624 bytes).
226 Transfer complete.
local: rfc1392.txt remote: rfc1392.txt
107594 bytes received in 9.4 seconds (11 Kbytes/s)
ftp>bye
221 Goodbye.
bss>
```

I ended the FTP session with the FTP command bye and my prompt changed from ftp> to my local prompt bss>. I was curious to see what the file contains; despite all of my experience and success in using FTP, it always relieves me to know that the file I wanted did indeed get back safely to my own machine. I used the more command on my machine to list the file.

```
bss> more rfc1392.txt
Network Working Group                              G. Malkin
Request for Comments: 1392                    Xylogics, Inc.
FYI: 18                                    T. LaQuey Parker
                                                     UTexas
                                                    Editors
                                               January 1993
                     Internet Users' Glossary
Status of this Memo
   This memo provides information for the Internet community. It does
   not specify an Internet standard. Distribution of this memo is
   unlimited.
Abstract
   There are many networking glossaries in existence. This glossary
   concentrates on terms which are specific to the Internet. Naturally,
   there are entries for some basic terms and acronyms because other
   entries refer to them.
Acknowledgements
   This document is the work of the User Glossary Working Group of the
   User Services Area of the Internet Engineering Task Force (IETF).
   Special thanks go to Jon Postel for his definitive definition of
   "datagram".
Table of Contents
<<many more screens of data>>
```

Ah, sweet success! I retrieved a glossary of network terms. There are many files you will want to transfer from the rfc directory. Some of the other directories listed on the Merit's Network Information Center Services FTP site contain information of interest to anyone learning how to navigate the Internet.

Now, it's your turn. Give it a try.

# The put and get Commands

Occasionally, you will want to send files to a distant machine. The put command does exactly the opposite of the get command—it takes a local file and sends it away to a distant machine. Again, you must have a login name and a password on the distant machine in order to transfer files to it. If you want to transfer many files, you can use the mput command.

Some anonymous ftp sites will let you put files there by using the login anonymous and your Internet address as the password. This is the way many of the shareware files become distributed.

Of course, you might also want to get more than one file. The mget command allows you to transfer multiple files to the current directory. You can ask to mget a list of filenames by giving the names with a space between each. You can also use wildcards in the filename in order to retrieve more than one file. mget will prompt you to make sure you want to get all files. This is a nice feature in case you forget which directory you are visiting and try to get a thousand files that you really didn't want to transfer. If you feel safe in obtaining files, the ftp prompt off command will turn this safety feature off.

Here is an example of mget at work. I've logged into the site ftp.sura.net as anonymous, and I'm ready to mget files from the /pub/nic directory. First, I'll list what's there:

```
ftp> dir
200 PORT command successful.
150 Opening ASCII mode data connection for /bin/ls.
total 5092
-rw-rw-r—   1 mtaranto 120        1394 Apr 22 13:52 .message
-rw-r—r—    1 mtaranto 120       10047 Apr 13 13:37 00-README.FIRST
-rw-rw-r—   1 mtaranto 120       47592 Mar  5  1992 BIG-LAN-FAQ
-rw-r—r—    1 mtaranto 120        4266 Dec  8  1992 ERIC.sites
-rw-r—r—    1 mtaranto 120        3955 Mar 17 19:15 NIC.WORKSHOP.INFO
drwxr-sr-x  2 mtaranto 120         512 Jul 22  1992 NREN
-rw-r—r—    1 mtaranto 120        2351 Oct 19  1992 NSFNET.acceptable.use
-rw-rw-r—   1 root     120        2709 Apr 23 19:50 SURAnet.acceptable.use
-rw-rw-r—   1 mtaranto 120       85677 May 11  1992 agricultural.list
-rw-rw-r—   1 mtaranto 120       27840 Apr 17  1992 archie.manual
-rw-r—r—    1 mtaranto 120       30500 Oct 14  1992 bbs.list.10-14
-rw-r—r—    1 mtaranto 120        3030 Nov 11  1992 bible.resources
-rw-r—r—    1 mtaranto 120        1347 Nov 12  1992 bionet.list
-rw-r—r—    1 mtaranto 120       41580 Dec  8  1992 cwis.list
drwxrwsr-x  3 mtaranto 120         512 Apr 28  1992 directory.services
-rw-rw-r—   1 plieb    120        1904 Jan  6  1992 farnet-recommendations
-rw-r—r—    1 mtaranto 120       15968 Oct 28  1992 holocaust.archive
-rw-r—r—    1 mtaranto 120        2986 Jun  2 18:09 how.to.get.SURAnet.guide
-rw-r—r—    1 mtaranto 120      149967 Jun  1 12:38 infoguide.6-93.txt
-rw-rw-r—   1 mtaranto 120      360853 Aug 20  1992 interest.groups.Z
-rw-r—r—    1 mtaranto 120      879381 Dec  9  1992 interest.groups.txt
drwxr-sr-x  3 mtaranto 120         512 Apr  7 17:09 internet.literature
-rw-r—r—    1 mtaranto 120       15682 Dec  8  1992 library.conferences
-rw-r—r—    1 mtaranto 120      154962 Jun  2 12:43 medical.resources.6-1
-rw-r—r—    1 mtaranto 120       15474 Nov 11  1992 network.law.info
drwxrwsr-x  2 mtaranto 120         512 Apr 14  1992 network.service.guides
-rw-r—r—    1 mtaranto 120       20553 Oct  9  1992 nnews.9-92
-rw-rw-r—   1 mtaranto 120        6194 Feb 21  1992 obi.directory.index
-rw-r—r—    1 mtaranto 120       39945 Aug 24  1992 search.techniques
drwxr-sr-x  2 1077     120        1024 Nov 12  1992 training
-rw-r—r—    1 mtaranto 120       14756 Apr 13 13:33 whitehouse.FAQ
```

```
-rw-rw-r—   1 root     120         6170 Jan  3  1992 wholeguide-help.txt
-rw-rw-r—   1 root     120       578238 Jun 21 20:49 wholeguide.txt
226 Transfer complete.
2413 bytes received in 0.7 seconds (3.4 Kbytes/s)
```

Let's get the two files we want: cwis.list and bionet.list.

```
ftp> get cwis.list bionet.list
200 PORT command successful.
150 Opening ASCII mode data connection for cwis.list (41580 bytes).
226 Transfer complete.
local: bionet.list remote: cwis.list
42644 bytes received in 7.7 seconds (5.4 Kbytes/s)
```

Wait a minute! What's this... local: bionet.list remote: cwis.list ...arggghhh! We used get when we meant mget. Because we asked to get, ftp assumed that the second filename ("bionet.list") was the name of the file in which we wanted to store the remote file cwis.list. Let's try again.

```
ftp> mget cwis.list bionet.list
mget cwis.list? y
200 PORT command successful.
150 Opening ASCII mode data connection for cwis.list (41580 bytes).
226 Transfer complete.
local: cwis.list remote: cwis.list
42644 bytes received in 4.9 seconds (8.5 Kbytes/s)
mget bionet.list? y
200 PORT command successful.
150 Opening ASCII mode data connection for bionet.list (1347 bytes).
226 Transfer complete.
local: bionet.list remote: bionet.list
1402 bytes received in 0.42 seconds (3.3 Kbytes/s)
```

We got both files, and because prompt was set to on, we were asked for each file if we wanted to transfer it. The mget also retrieves files and names the local copy the same as the files on the remote system. Let's try for a wildcard specification:

```
ftp> mget *.list
mget agricultural.list? y
200 PORT command successful.
150 Opening ASCII mode data connection for agricultural.list (85677 bytes).
226 Transfer complete.
local: agricultural.list remote: agricultural.list
```

```
88383 bytes received in 6.4 seconds (14 Kbytes/s)
mget bionet.list? y
200 PORT command successful.
150 Opening ASCII mode data connection for bionet.list (1347 bytes).
226 Transfer complete.
local: bionet.list remote: bionet.list
1402 bytes received in 0.47 seconds (2.9 Kbytes/s)
mget cwis.list? n
ftp> bye
221 Goodbye.
a103%
```

You can see that using mget is pretty easy. Again, try it out. You have nothing to lose but your disk space!

# REMOTELY POSSIBLE: TELNET

When many computers are linked on a network, you often find that you need to run a program on a computer other than the one you're currently using. This could happen for any of several reasons.

Maybe the program you want to use won't work on your computer. For example, if your computer is a DOS PC and you want to use a piece of software written for UNIX, you'll need to use another computer that runs UNIX.

Maybe your machine doesn't have adequate resources (for example, not enough memory or too slow a processor). Or maybe you just want to work with data files on the remote computer. Although you might be able to copy the files to your own computer, that will only be possible as long as the files aren't too big to fit on your machine. You could just tell your software to use the remote data file, but if, for example, you need to search a massive database, you'll be choking up the network as you haul the data across it.

What's needed is a way to run a program on a remote computer, transferring the screen display to your machine while sending your keyboard data to the remote software. This is called a remote session or virtual terminal session. With TCP/IP systems, virtual terminal facilities are available through something called *telnet*.

# What Is Telnet?

Telnet is a program that uses TELNET protocol, part of the TCP/IP protocol suite. The remote computer, called the telnet server, accepts telnet connections from a client over a TCP/IP system.

Because the Internet is a TCP/IP network, telnet works happily between computers attached to it—providing that the telnet service is installed on the server end and you have a compatible version of the telnet client on your computer.

**Navigator's Note:** Don't be surprised if you try to use telnet with a remote computer on the Internet and can't get a connection—not all computers have telnet enabled.

The telnet client and server components negotiate how they will use the connection, so that even if the two systems are not of the same type, they will find a common language.

A Macintosh user running a System 7 version of telnet can go through the Internet and get a telnet connection on an IBM mainframe running the MVS operating system. The Macintosh can then run IBM software on the mainframe. Of course, all that's happening is that the remote computer's screen display is being received, but the end result is as if it were running on the local computer.

Telnet does have its limits. If the traffic is heavy on any of the networks that connect you to the remote computer, the reduced performance may make the updates to your own screen very slow.

You must also remember, when you want to print something, to make sure that the output device is on your computer and not on the remote machine.

Finally, if you want to save data to a file using the remote program and plan to store it on the remote computer, you'll need to have the required privileges. You'll also have to FTP the data to yourself if you want a local copy.

Telnet makes it possible to use a remote computer as if it were the computer in front of you. With the Internet, that remote computer could be many thousands of miles away.

# What Do I Telnet To?

In educational and research environments, it's not uncommon to have accounts on many Internet computers. This occurs most often at universities, where there are numerous departments and many computers with different operating systems using a variety of programs.

It also occurs if you are affiliated with a number of schools where you work, teach, study, or have ongoing collaborative research. These days it's not uncommon for people to have some accounts on an educational system and others where they work. Telnet enables you to access any of your accounts from any point on the Internet.

Telnet is most often used for public or commercial purposes, allowing remote users to search large, complex, or proprietary databases. Examples include the ERIC service, indices of educational journals, databases of the full text of Shakespeare's plays, and databases like CARL's UNCOVER2—all of which are free. There are also fee-charging databases such as Dialog and OCLC.

**Navigator's Note:** The Educational Resources Information Center (ERIC) is a reference publication for the National Education Information Network, sponsored by the U.S. Department of Education. ERIC includes a database of citations and abstracts for educational literature and is divided into the Current Index to Journals in Education (CIJE) and the findings, reports, speeches, books, and other items covered in Resource in Education (RIE).

The CIJE indexes over 700 professional journals, which makes it a popular database for finding information relating to education. This government-produced database is a valuable resource for materials in education, and its scope has expanded to include other related materials that may be of interest to many multidisciplinary educational areas.

**Navigator's Note:** The Colorado Alliance of Research Libraries (CARL) has developed a document delivery service called UnCover2. UnCover2 is a database encompassing over 10,500 unique multidisciplinary journals.

UnCover2 provides article citations taken from the table of contents of each issue of the journal along with the descriptive information or abstracts appearing on the contents page.

Delivery of the selected articles is by fax, and the goal is to deliver material in less than 24 hours. A fee is charged to access the uncover service, and a royalty fee is usually assessed for each article delivered.

**Navigator's Note:** OCLC is a major database used by librarians to find bibliographic information for material in order to catalog or verify it. In addition, OCLC provides librarians with the details of who owns the material—vitally important for interlibrary loan purposes. OCLC is now attempting to provide wider access to its database.

The following database descriptions are selected from publicity information from OCLC about its services.

The FirstSearch Catalog is an online reference service with an end-user interface designed specifically for library patrons.

OCLC WorldCat is the OCLC Online Union Catalog, the world's most comprehensive bibliography, with more than 25 million records of information spanning 4,000 years of knowledge, now accessible by patrons with the FirstSearch Catalog. Updated daily.

The U.S. Government Printing Office Monthly Catalog of Publications is a database consisting of more than 350,000 records published by the GPO since July 1976. The Monthly Catalog has references to congressional committee reports and hearings, debates, documents from executive departments, and more. Updated monthly, records are from July 1976 to the present.

American Geological Institute's MiniGeoRef covers recent additions to the GeoRef file, a database containing earth-science references, and the index terms that describe them. More than 4,000 journals in 40 languages are regularly scanned, along with new books, maps, and reports. Updated monthly, records are from 1985 to the present.

Newspaper Abstracts UMI/Data Courier is a complete business and general reference resource. The database indexes and abstracts more than 25 national and regional newspapers, including the *New York Times*, *Los Angeles Times*, *Washington Post*, and *USA Today*. The *Wall Street Journal* (Eastern edition) is indexed beginning January 1, 1990. Updated weekly, records are from 1989 to the present.

You also gain access to hundreds of library catalogs around the world, which can help you find bibliographic information for your research. When you telnet to a FreeNet (see Chapter 2) or a college Campus Area Information Systems (CAIS), you can find local restaurant locations, theater productions, and class schedules. You can also use telnet to access databases of census materials, weather information, and myriad other data services.

# Using Telnet

To use telnet, give telnet the address of the computer it is to connect to. For example: `telnet ucsbuxa.edu`

Until recently, this was the only way to place a telnet connection. Today, however, many people use Gopher (see Chapter 8, "Navigating by Menus: Gopher") to "launch" telnet. With Gopher, you'll find menu items that lead to virtual terminal sessions using telnet. When you select one of these items, telnet is engaged, and the address of the target connection is automatically passed on. Thus, the Gopher menu item might say `Use telnet to access Costello at UCSB` rather than `telnet ucsbuxa.edu`.

Gopher is a much more convenient way to use telnet because you don't need to remember the Internet address of the machine you want to contact. The Gopher system, however, does not have menu items for *telneting* to every machine on the Internet.

There are many private computers on the Internet that you might want to access but which aren't on any Gopher menus. Even if you have a Gopher server running on your local machine, you may find it more convenient to telnet to an infrequently used remote machine than to add a Gopher menu item that will only be used occasionally.

In short, even though you can do a great deal using telnet through Gopher, you should learn to use telnet when Gopher can't do the job.

# Port Number

In some instances, you are required by the remote machine to select a port number other than the standard port used by telnet (port 23). This is useful when you need to access a specific type of service on a remote machine. This number is entered on the telnet command line after the remote machine's name or address. For example:

```
gyre% telnet ucsbuxa.uscb.edu 300
```

instructs telnet to connect to `ucsbuxa.uscb.edu` on port 300. Remember this when you see a remote machine that you want to use and a port is specified along with the machine's name or address.

## Starting Telnet

Telnet's operation is, for all practical purposes, transparent to the user. You start telnet by typing `telnet`, a space and the remote machine's Internet address. You can give either the computer's name (`ucsbuxa.ucsb.edu`) or its address (`128.111.122.50`). If needed, you then give the port number. Once you press Enter, the connection is attempted.

The general form of the telnet command is

```
telnet <computer_name> [<port_number>]
```

or

```
telnet <computer_address> [<port_number>]
```

## Are We Talking?

If contact is made, the telnet server and client negotiate their communication strategy. If that's successful, the remote server machine usually asks you for a login username. You then login just as if you were directly on the computer.

If telnet can't connect to the target computer, you get a message telling you what the problem is. There are three main reasons a connection can't be made. The first is that you got the target computer's name or address wrong. This is often due to simple typing errors such entering `uscbuxa` when you mean `ucsbuxa`. Another mistake is not giving the complete address. For example, if you enter `ucsbuxa.edu` when you mean `ucsbuxa.ucsb.edu`, you won't get a connection.

With purely numeric addresses, it is (of course) much easier to make a mistake. All of these errors usually get a message like `host not known` or `host not available`.

The second reason is that the computer is not available or the network the computer is on isn't working. This does happen and some sites, particularly new ones, are often not available. Systems also become unavailable when maintenance or repair work is being done. The third reason is that all of the connections the computer supports are already active. Both of these reasons are usually greeted with a `time out` message.

# Command Mode

If you type telnet by itself (or after telnet fails to reach the remote machine) you get the telnet prompt, `telnet>`, which indicates that you are in telnet's command mode. From here you can use any of the telnet commands. Typing `?` or `help` in the command mode gives you a list of the available commands.

When telnet connects, you see something much like the following:

```
icarus.lis[3] % telnet sklib.usask.ca
Trying 128.233.1.20 ...
Connected to sklib.usask.ca.
Escape character is '^]'.


  SKLIB - University of Saskatchewan Library System
```

It is important to notice the line `Escape character`.... When you're in the middle of a telnet session to another computer and you want to get back to the telnet command mode, you use the escape character to get telnet's attention. When you type the escape character, the telnet command prompt appears, showing that you've gone into telnet command mode.

> **Navigator's Note:** The standard telnet escape character is `Ctrl+]`, which lets you give telnet commands directly. To quit a telnet session, you can usually type `Ctrl+]`, then `q`. It can be set differently, and you need to ask your system manager or (if all else fails) read your system manual.

# Telnet Commands

Here is a short list of the most commonly used telnet commands:

   `close`: If you start telnet without specifying the target computer to connect to, this command terminates the connection to another computer and leaves you in command mode. If you started telnet with the name or address of a target computer, `close` will terminate the session and quit telnet (this is equivalent to the quit command). You can use the abbreviation `c`.

`open`: This command is used to connect to a remote machine when you're at the `telnet>` prompt. The format (like starting telnet from the systems prompt) is `open <computer_name>` or `open <computer_address>`.

`quit`: This command leaves the telnet program. If you have a connection to a remote computer, `quit` terminates it first.

`<enter>`: In the telnet command mode, pressing Enter by itself (that is, with nothing else typed on the command line) returns you to the remote session if you have one active. If you don't, it exits telnet.

`set echo`: If you can't see what you are typing or if you type and see double, go to the telnet command mode (using the escape character) and enter `set echo`. This toggles the echo setting off and on and should resolve the problem.

# Using Telnet

Once a telnet connection to a remote machine is started, telnet changes to input mode in order to send text from the keyboard (the stuff you type) to the remote machine. This can be either on a line-by-line basis (line mode), or one character at a time (character mode).

The choice of modes depends on the remote machine system and is part of the negotiating telnet does when a connection is established. You change the mode by using the command `mode <type>` (which can be abbreviated to `m <type>`) at the telnet prompt. `<type>` is either `line` or `character`.

**Navigator's Note:** It's almost always better to use telnet in a character-by-character mode. If you don't, weird things can happen. For example, if you run WAIS through telnet in the line-by-line mode and you want help, press `h`. Because you're in line mode, nothing will happen until you press Enter. WAIS displays the help screen, but because you also pressed Enter, it jumps straight back to the screen you were on. This will drive you crazy unless you can read very fast.

## Login Procedures

When you get a successful telnet connection, you are usually asked to login to the remote computer and give a password. Public telnet services on remote machines may expect a publicly known password—which you must know to get in. This could be as simple as guest. Or not—things on the Internet aren't always simple.

The more hospitable remote computer systems give you the login password. The very best machines (from a user's point of view) have no barriers at all and connect you directly to the remote system. Because this results in a system that can be easily explored by hackers and that offers virtually no control to the systems manager, it isn't surprising that this kind of system is becoming less common (today, about as common as fourteen-inch disk drives—the authors' age is showing).

## Terminal Emulation

Many remote machines ask you for your terminal emulation when you successfully log in. The most common terminal type is called VT100 (this is a specification of how data will be handled and displayed on a terminal).

If you select a terminal type unknown to the remote machine, you may receive a list of terminal types supported by the remote computer. On the other hand, you may not, in which case you'll just get a crummy looking screen. Ho-hum. Start again and try with VT100.

If your terminal type is unknown, you may be able to select *dumb* or *hardcopy*, which are generic terminal emulations.

**Navigator's Note:** Using the generic dumb or hardcopy terminal type works well if you want to copy or log a session during telneting. It eliminates the funky characters that often appear in captured data when other terminal types are used.

**Navigator's Warning:** Sometimes selecting dumb or hardcopy won't actually do you any good. The remote computer's software may not be able to work with a dumb terminal at all. This is the case with the screen-oriented versions of Gopher. The dumb setting just enables you to see strange character sequences being printed on the screen.

## Getting the Boot

Some remote machines keep track of how long you've been connected, what time of the day you're connecting, and/or how long you've been idle (that is, how long since you sent any keystrokes). They may automatically end the telnet session if you're on too long, if you try to use the system during peak load periods when you're not supposed to, or if they think you may have gone to sleep or been abducted by terrorists before having logged off.

If this causes a problem, you'll have to talk to the system administrator of the remote computer to see if you can get the limitation removed for your account.

## The IBM Connection

An alternative to the standard telnet program is tn3270. It is used to make your terminal emulate an IBM 3270 terminal, which is required if you want to run many of the programs on an IBM mainframe.

You start tn3270 just like telnet: Type `tn3270` at the systems prompt, followed by a space and the remote machine's name or address and the optional port number.

In many cases tn3270 changes which characters are generated by your keyboard (called *keyboard mapping*) so that an IBM machine will understand you better. Don't be surprised if the keys on your computer don't work normally and you have to try some odd combinations in order to make the remote computer programs do what you want.

## Telnet Client Flavors

We've discussed the UNIX version of telnet, yet telnet comes in different flavors. Uses vary, depending on the operating system.

For example, DOS versions of telnet may look a lot like the UNIX version, or they may be menu driven and store default settings such as monitor type, key assignment, and character translation in a configuration file. Windows and Macintosh versions that enable you to use a mouse and that support drag-and-drop features are available.

# Do I Need to Know About Telnet?

Yes. That is, if you want to be able to skillfully navigate the Internet. At its best, telnet is transparent; it works behind the scenes so that you can get on with the business of using the remote machine's resources. Besides, its commands are pretty easy to learn.

With luck, the hardest thing you'll ever encounter in using telnet is remembering the remote machine's name or address or quitting from the remote machine, but using telnet from Gopher makes that hardly a problem for the most popular telnet sites.

# FINDING FILES: ARCHIE

**6**

As we keep saying, the Internet offers huge treasure chests of data. From anthropology to zoology and from aalii to zymurgy, a file of data or a piece of software exists somewhere that defines the subject, gives references to it, displays it, exemplifies it, or shows you how it should be done.

As we discussed in Chapter 4, "A Moving Experience: FTP for Me," you can retrieve files from remote computers on the Internet using FTP. You can list directories to find out what files are there and download those that look interesting. With hundreds of thousands of files on thousands of computers, where do you begin to look?

**Navigator's Note:** The aalii (pronounced "a-lee"), *Dodoneae viscosa*, is a bushy shrub with sticky leaves, and zymurgy is the branch of chemistry dealing with fermentation (the boring subject of making wine and brewing beer). Now you can use *zymurgy* with confidence when playing Scrabble. The lowest score it will get you is 25 points.

In the early days of the ARPANET, before it became the Internet, only a few hundred computers were connected. The network was small enough for you to search systems for files related to your interests without being concerned that you might miss much.

The people using the Internet were scientists and engineers, so they generally knew where information was or could be obtained. Failing that, they could find out pretty easily who to ask. As the Internet grew, however, finding files became increasingly difficult.

Today, due to the enormous size of the Internet, we can guarantee that you will overlook lots of useful stuff in your searches. An exhaustive search isn't feasible with so many files in so many places on so many machines. Anyway, unless you're a member of the idle rich, you also won't have the time to search through all the available systems one by one. The big problem that faces you is where to start looking.

The Internet is a bit like having a vast library without an indexing system. Books are all over the place, with no index to which books are on which shelves. Some shelves have their own index, but others have none. The solution is obvious: make an index of all the shelves and their contents. That task is handled by a piece of software called Archie.

# What Is Archie?

Developed at McGill University in Canada, Archie is a kind of mega librarian that automatically and regularly goes out to a large number of Internet servers and indexes their files to create a single, searchable database.

The database is therefore an index of directory data, a compilation of the available files on every server Archie has been capable of interrogating. Because Archie scans Internet hosts regularly, the database is being constantly updated.

Actually, Archie isn't a single system; rather, it's a collection of servers. (See Table 6.1 for a list of Archie servers.) Each Archie server is responsible for interrogating its own set of Internet servers to build its own database. Currently, 14 publicly available Archie servers index the files on more than a thousand servers. Most Archie databases now hold information on more than 2.5 million files and their locations.

**Navigator's Note:** Because each Archie server manages its own database, the data may differ from one Archie to another. Usually the differences are few, and unless you're trying to find something really rare, one Archie server is effectively the same as another.

## How to Find Files

You can use two strategies to find files with Archie. If you know the name of a file and have forgotten where it is located, you can ask Archie to find it. When you don't know the name of a file, you can search for the names of files and directories that contain words relating to the files you're interested in.

People often give names to files and directories to describe their contents. For example, database files often end with .dbf or .db. Files related to Windows often contain the characters *win*. A win31 directory is probably for Windows version 3.1 software. Macintosh files and directories often have *mac* in their names, and so on.

Because you can search the text of file and directory names with Archie, you have a simple type of subject search capability. When an Archie search is successful, you are shown information about the file. Archie will give you the name of all the computers where you can find the file, the directory and subdirectory where the file is located, the size of the file, the last date and time the file was updated, and file and directory attributes.

**Navigator's Note:** Because Archie's database is limited to file and directory names, being able to find what you want depends on someone naming files and directories in a useful manner. If you're looking for information on thirteenth-century pottery in Bavaria and the file containing the data is called `bpxiii.jnk` and is in a directory called `whoneedsit`, Archie won't be able to help you.

**Navigator's Note:** Unfortunately, people frequently copy files and then rename them. This means that a fantastic Windows utility called WinUtil.Zip that you found mentioned in the latest issue of TEKIE Magazine might well appear elsewhere as WinTool.Zip, WinStuff.Zip, WinUtils.Zip, WinTools.Zip, ad infinitum. Worse still, you might even find all the variations in the same directory!

Archie doesn't know anything about the contents of the files or even what types of files they are. If the files are in an obscure place, the author or the system manager probably didn't care if you could find them or not, so they may not be that useful anyway.

## Client/Server Setup

Archie is organized as a client/server system. The client part can run on the same computer as the Archie server, or it can be run on a computer elsewhere on the Internet. You can use any of the Archie servers or the default setup for your system. You can also use an Archie server by using telnet from another computer. Figure 6.1 shows the various options you have when using Archie.

The Archie client and server program files (including manuals) are available free through anonymous FTP at several locations on the Internet (see Appendix E, "The Internet Navigator's Gazetteer").

The best location to find the latest versions of Archie client programs with documentation is SURAnet. You'll need to use ftp to access ftp.sura.net. The files are located in the /pub/archie/client/ directory. Client program files are available for UNIX, PC, VMS, and several other operating systems.

Table 6.1. Archie servers and their addresses, their owners, and their timezones offset to GMT. These sites are heavily used, and on many occasions the current number of site users will have reached its maximum and you won't be allowed to access Archie. This is especially true during each system's local peak hours—7 a.m. to 7 p.m.

| Archie Server | Address | Owner | Timezone Offset |
|---|---|---|---|
| archie.rutgers.edu | 128.6.18.15 | Rutgers University | GMT -6 |
| archie.sura.net | 128.167.254.179 | SURAnet Archie server | GMT -6 |

| Archie Server | Address | Owner | Timezone Offset |
| --- | --- | --- | --- |
| archie.unl.edu | 129.93.1.14 | U. of Nebraska, Lincoln | GMT -6 |
| archie.ans.net | 147.225.1.2 | ANS Archie server | GMT -x |
| archie.au | 139.130.4.6 | Australian server | GMT +9 |
| archie.funet.fi | 128.214.6.100 | European server, Finland | GMT +1 |
| archie.doc.ic.ac.uk | 146.169.11.3 | UK/Europe server | GMT |
| archie.cs.huji.ac.il | 132.65.6.15 | Israel server | GMT +5 |
| archie.wide.ad.jp | 133.4.3.6 | Japanese server | GMT +8 |
| archie.ncu.edu.tw | 140.115.19.24 | Taiwanese server | GMT +7 |
| archie.sogang.ac.kr | 163.239.1.11 | Korean server | GMT +6 |
| archie.nz | 130.195.9.4 | New Zealand server | GMT -10 |
| archie.kuis.kyoto-u.ac.jp | 130.54.20.1 | Japan | GMT +8 |
| archie.th-darmstadt.de | 130.83.128.111 | Germany | GMT +2 |

# Archie's Limitations

The use of anonymous FTP is a clue to one of Archie's limitations. Archie databases include files only on servers enabling anonymous FTP. This means that sites requiring you to log in, even if that login is publicly available, won't be included in Archie databases.

**Navigator's Note:** If your site has files you want others to be able to find, anonymous FTP must be enabled and at least read access to the file granted. Then your system administrator can have your system added to the list of servers that Archie servers keep track of.

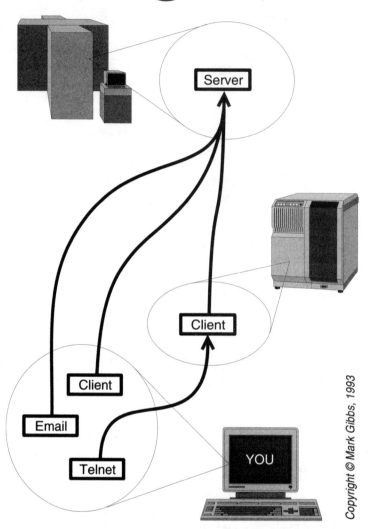

Copyright © Mark Gibbs, 1993

**Figure 6.1.** Archie servers can be accessed from a client on the same computer as the server, on a different computer, through telnet from another computer, or by using electronic mail.

Another limitation is that Archie can't tell you anything about the file. It won't have any information on what the file contains or even whether it's a program, a text file, or a database. Another source of information about files is available through Archie, but it's not always reliable (see "Whatis").

# How to Use Archie

Archie servers can be accessed in three ways:

1. Through an Archie client connection

2. Through a telnet connection directly to an Archie server

3. By e-mail

When you try to use an Archie service through either a client or telnet connection during peak usage hours (see Table 6.1), you may find that the system administrator has blocked access to it. At SURAnet, for example, you'll get the following reply:

```
telnet archie.sura.net
Trying 128.167.254.179 ...
Connected to nic.sura.net.
Escape character is '^]'.


SunOS UNIX (nic.sura.net)

 login: archie
*****************************************************************
Interactive use of the Archie service at SURAnet is disabled
from 8:00 a.m to 8:00 p.m. EST because the machine is unable
to handle the substantial extra load imposed by the interactive
client and still provide decent prospero service.

If it is outside of those hours, one of the systems people at
SURAnet has probably disabled archie service. If it remains
down for too long, you can send mail to archie-admin@sura.net
to tell us about the problem.

SURAnet is supporting a new experimental interface to archie.
Instead of logging in using the name archie, try logging in
Using the name qarchie.  This interface uses the prospero server
and so puts much less load on the machine.
Note that logging in as qarchie is only supported on this machine

The following is a list of other archie servers:
    archie.funet.fi         128.214.6.100   (European server in Finland)
    archie.doc.ic.ac.uk     146.169.11.3    (UK/Europe server)
    archie.cs.huji.ac.il    132.65.6.15     (Israel server)
    archie.wide.ad.jp       133.4.3.6       (Japanese server)
    archie.ncu.edu.tw       140.115.19.24   (Taiwanese server)
    archie.sogang.ac.kr     163.239.1.11    (Korean server)
    archie.nz               130.195.9.4     (New Zealand server)
```

```
    archie.kuis.kyoto-u.ac.jp 130.54.20.1    (Japan)
    archie.th-darmstadt.de    130.83.128.111 (Germany)
    archie.luth.se            130.240.18.4   (Sweden)
  Client software should be supported at all of these sites.
  ************************************************************
Waiting 30 seconds...
Connection closed by foreign host.
```

For sites that would let you in but are too busy (the maximum number of connections enabled by the systems administrator for that Archie server is in use), you'll get a message like

```
a90% telnet archie.rutgers.edu
Trying 128.6.18.15 ...
Connected to dorm.Rutgers.EDU.
Escape character is '^]'.


SunOS UNIX (dorm.rutgers.edu) (ttypd)

 login: archie
Last login: Tue May 11 10:14:04 from library1.library
SunOS Release 4.1.3 (TDSERVER-SUN4C-DORM) #1: Sat May 1 16:46:07 EDT 1993
        Sorry, but there are too many concurrent archie users on this
machine right now. At this point, you have several options. First of
all, the most preferable alternative would be to use an archie client
such as xarchie (cs.rochester.edu:/pub) or the "archie" command line
client (ftp.std.com:/src/util). These clients reduce the load on the
server, as well as often providing additional functionality.  Another
alternative would be to contact one of the other archie servers. ( a
list of alternate servers is appended to this message ) If you aren't
in a rush, you could submit your request by e-mail. Just send a message
to archie@archie.rutgers.edu with the subject line "HELP" to get
detailed instructions. Oh, and the final option is to try here again
later :)
                                - Archie Mgt
                                (archie-admin@archie.rutgers.edu)


--------------< List of active archie servers >--------------

    archie.rutgers.edu   128.6.18.15     (Rutgers University)
    archie.sura.net      128.167.254.179 (SURAnet archie server)
    archie.unl.edu       129.93.1.14     (University of Nebraska in Lincoln)
    archie.ans.net       147.225.1.2     (ANS archie server)
    archie.au            139.130.4.6     (Australian server)
    archie.funet.fi      128.214.6.100   (European server in Finland)
    archie.doc.ic.ac.uk  146.169.11.3    (UK/England server)
```

```
   archie.cs.huji.ac.il 132.65.6.15     (Israel server)
   archie.wide.ad.jp    133.4.3.6       (Japanese server)
   archie.ncu.edu.tw    140.115.19.24   (Taiwanese server)

   Client software should be supported at all of these sites.
```

Or, you might get the rather more terse...

```
a90% telnet archie.unl.edu
Trying 129.93.1.14 ...
Connected to crcnis2.unl.edu.
Escape character is '^]'.


SunOS UNIX (crcnis2)

 login: archie
Last login: Tue May 11 10:12:18 from corageous.pittsb
SunOS Release 4.1.2 (CRCNIS2) #1: Wed Dec 16 12:10:12 EST 1992


too many archie users... try again later
Connection closed by foreign host.
a90% logout
```

The reason for limiting the number of connections to run Archie searches is that each connection uses computer power. This reduces the performance of the machine running the Archie server.

## Client Connections

One of the ways to access Archie is to use an Archie client. Like other client/server systems we've talked about, the Archie client runs on your computer, and the server part runs on another system.

Using an Archie client is the preferred method because it doesn't burden the Archie server computer's resources as much as an online telnet session. When you start the Archie client program, you can either select one of the Archie servers listed in Table 6.1 or use the server that is your system's default.

**Navigator's Note:** Using your system's default Archie server is probably the easiest choice. And as Archie systems all have pretty much the same data, which one you choose won't make much of a difference.

## An Archie Client Example

I wanted to find files for the Archie program and documentation that I knew were available at various sites on the Internet, but I didn't know where the files were or what they were called. Finding Archie sounded like a job for Archie.

At the computer system prompt I used the command archie once to start the program and typed archie a second time as the sequence of characters that I wanted Archie to search for. (If I'd wanted to search for fermentation chemistry instead, the second archie could have been zymurgy or ferment.)

Here's what I got:

```
a104% archie archie ¦more

 Host plaza.aarnet.edu.au

    Location: /
       DIRECTORY drwxr-xr-x        512  Feb  6 09:04  archie
    Location: /usenet/comp.sources.misc/volume22
       DIRECTORY drwxr-xr-x        512  Mar  6 1992  archie
    Location: /usenet/comp.sources.misc/volume26
       DIRECTORY drwxr-xr-x        512  Mar  1 1992  archie
    Location: /usenet/comp.sources.misc/volume27
       DIRECTORY drwxr-xr-x        512  Mar  1 1992  archie
    Location: /usenet/comp.sources.misc/volume29
       DIRECTORY drwxr-xr-x        512  Apr 16 1992  archie
    Location: /usenet/comp.sources.misc/volume33
       DIRECTORY drwxr-xr-x        512  Nov 13 07:57  archie


  Host sifon.cc.mcgill.ca

    Location: /pub/Network
       DIRECTORY dr-xr-xr-x        512  Apr 22 17:17  archie
    Location: /pub/network-services
       DIRECTORY dr-xr-xr-x        512  Feb 17 19:09  archie
 —More—
    Location: /software/unix/network
       DIRECTORY drwxrwxr-x        512  Jan 26 11:49  archie
    Location: /software/vms
       DIRECTORY drwxrwxr-x        512  Jan 26 11:49  archie


  Host gatekeeper.dec.com

    Location: /.0/usenet/comp.sources.misc/volume26
       DIRECTORY dr-xr-xr-x        512  Apr 24 03:34  archie
    Location: /.0/usenet/comp.sources.misc/volume27
       DIRECTORY dr-xr-xr-x        512  Apr 24 03:34  archie
    Location: /.0/usenet/comp.sources.misc/volume29
       DIRECTORY dr-xr-xr-x        512  Apr 24 03:35  archie
```

```
    Location: /contrib/share/lib/expect
          FILE -rw-r—r—          689  Oct  7 00:00  archie
    Location: /contrib/src/crl/expect/src/test
          FILE -rw-rw-r—          672  Jul 30 1992  archie

Host hpcsos.col.hp.com


    Location: /mirrors/386bsd/0.1-ports/utils
        DIRECTORY drwxr-xr-x      1024  Feb 15 01:35  archie

—More—
```

My request for information on the word Archie returned six pages of information. You can see that many directories and files named archie were found. That was an easy one.

With Archie, it's best to keep your searches simple. Some Archie servers prioritize searches by their complexity. The simpler they are, the faster they get done.

## A Search for Windows Files

Next came a search using two commands that I sent at midday (a big no-no). I had to wait for more than half an hour before canceling it. I then ran the same job as a background task on my machine (it's a UNIX system, so I have that luxury) while I went ahead with other work.

I don't know the exact time it took to complete the search, but I got my results more than four hours later. Note that using the -s command got me much more than I needed or, indeed, wanted.

I was using Archie to try to find an FTP site for Windows 3.1 software. The directory used for these files on many FTP sites is win3 or win31, so I tried archie -s win. This means "look for anything with 'win' in it," and I thought this would find what I wanted. The results were xwindows, win.c, xwindows.info, and so on, but no win3 or win31. The reason was that my archie client limits me to 95 "hits" for each search and no win anything appeared in the first 95 results.

Of course, searching for win3 or win31 would get me the FTP sites I was looking for, but I could not remember the exact directory name. I had to use the -s and change the default limit from 95 to 2000 (that is, "give me the first two thousand matches") with the -m command to get the needed information.

```
icarus>archie -s -m2000 win

Host esel.cosy.sbg.ac.at
     Location:
/pub/mirror/386bsd/0.1/filesystem/usr/othersrc/contrib/isode/others/X
       DIRECTORY drwxr-xr-x      1024  Feb 11 01:35  xwininfo
     Location: /pub/mirror/386bsd/packages/tfs/XFree86/mit/clients
       DIRECTORY drwxr-xr-x       512  Mar  2 03:34  xwininfo
     Location: /pub/mirror/guitar/Bob_Dylan
         FILE -rw-r—r—         1596  Jul  2 1992  BlowinInTheWind.crd


Host swdsrv.edvz.univie.ac.at
     Location: /mac/info-mac/ex
         FILE -rw-r—r—       134198  Jun 15 1992  next-style-windows.hqx
         FILE -rw-r—r—        46296  Aug 12 1992  window-picker-102.hqx
         FILE -rw-r—r—        25984  May  7 1992  window-shade-12.hqx


       DIRECTORY drwxr-xr-x       512  May  1 02:47  win3
     Location: /pc/windows/win3/demo
         FILE -rw-r—r—      1288637  Aug  7 1992  timwin.zip
         FILE -rw-r—r—        37649  Apr 13 1992  wincrib.zip
         FILE -rw-r—r—       151087  Apr 13 1992  windraw.zip


Host cert.sei.cmu.edu
     Location: /pub/cert_advisories
         FILE -rw-r—r—         2823  Dec 16 1991
CA-91:22.SunOS.OpenWindows.vulnerability


Host cs.columbia.edu
     Location: /archives/mirror1/X11R5/contrib
         FILE -rw-rw-r—         4203  Mar 25 1991  winterp.README


Host caticsuf.cati.csufresno.edu
     Location: /usr/lib/zoneinfo/Australia
         FILE -r—r——          727  Jan 16 1991  Yancowinna


Host net-1.iastate.edu
     Location: /pub/pc
       DIRECTORY drwxrwx—       2048  Apr 28 14:29  win3


Host kanaha.idbsu.edu
     Location: /incoming
         FILE -rw-r—r—        33333  Aug 28 1992  winpool.zip


Host ftp.cica.indiana.edu
     Location: /pub/pc
       DIRECTORY drwxr-xr-x      1024  Apr 24 08:42  win3
```

(partial results of over 26 pages)

## Archie Client Switches

You have three useful switches (seven total, but the others are less useful) that you can use with an Archie client:

The -r switch lets you use UNIX regular expressions as search text. These complex search specifications are a powerful way of describing what you want to look for (see Appendix B, "Command Reference," for an explanation of UNIX regular expressions and how to use them).

The -e switch (which is the default, so you need not specify it) tells Archie to search only for files and directories that contain the exact text you specify and to not worry about the case of the text. Thus, archie -e win.doc would match with win.doc, Win.doc, and WiN.doc but not win.txt or win31.

For a broader search, the -s switch enables you to search for file and directory names that include the search text. For example, archie -s win.doc would match with win31.doc, win.txt, windows, and so on.

> **Navigator's Note:** You need to specify the kind of search you want to do, because different servers default to different search types— which could cause you to miss files. For example, if you entered archie chemi hoping to find any files and directories with chemistry, chemical, chemo, and so on in their names, and the Archie server you use defaults to exact, case-sensitive searches, you'd probably get nothing.

## Telnet Connections

Another way to use the Archie service is to telnet to one of the Archie servers throughout the world (see Figure 6.1 for the location of an Archie server appearing near you and Table 6.1 for its address).

You telnet to the address of an Archie server and log in with the word archie. Assuming that the site will let you use the system (remember, most sites experience maximum demand between 7 a.m. and 7 p.m.), after logging in you are greeted by a screen with a menu of selections and a prompt (see the following listing).

Using a telnet session, you search the Archie database directly. First-time users may want to read the help information by typing the word help at the archie> prompt and capturing it in a file for future reference (to save you the trouble, Appendix B, "Command Reference," shows the help screen for the Archie server at SURAnet).

## An Archie Server Example

I was lucky to get through to the Rutgers University Archie server during peak hours to get the following example:

```
SunOS UNIX (dorm.rutgers.edu) (ttypb)

login: archie
Last login: Tue May  4 11:20:55 from balan.eng.ohio-s
SunOS Release 4.1.3 (TDSERVER-SUN4C) #1: Tue Apr 6 11:07:22 EDT 1993


        Welcome to the Rutgers University Archie Server!


_____


  - 3/21/93
        This server has recently been upgraded to version 3.0.2 of the
Archie software. Please use the "help" command for information on how
to use this new interface. Report any and all problems to
archie-admin@archie.rutgers.edu


_____

# Bunyip Information Systems, 1993
# Terminal type set to 'vt100 24 80'.
# 'erase' character is '^?'.
archie>
```

After connecting to the remote host machine archie.rutgers.edu, I logged in with the word archie. I received a welcome from the Rutgers University Archie server, after which I ended up at the archie> prompt.

From there, I used the command prog to start a search. I specified the text chemis-try in the hopes of finding host machines with directories or files by that name. This is how a chemist might search for interesting files. The search was success-ful—a listing of many directories and files with the word *chemistry* in their names.

## Archie Server Commands

There are nine commands you can give an Archie server during a telnet session. The most useful command is prog. The prog command, followed by text, speci-fies what you are searching for. This is equivalent to using the Archie client with-out switches (in other words, archie>prog chemistry through telnet is the same as archie chemistry on an Archie client).

The set search command can be used to specify the type of search you want to do. For example, set search exact is the same as specifying -e when using the Archie client, sub is the same as -s, and regexp is the same as -r. When you set the search type, you're setting it for the rest of your session with that server. You can change it at any time, and you can find out what the default or current search type is with the command show search.

The command mail (which has no client equivalent) posts the result of the last search to the mail address specified. The other really useful command is quit, which lets you leave Archie and terminate your telnet session.

## E-Mail Connections

The third way to find files using Archie is to use an Archie mail server. This is an indirect route to the Archie server and can take longer (possibly as much as several days) to give an answer. If you need to make another Archie search request based on the results of the first search, it becomes an even longer wait.

To use Archie through e-mail, send an electronic message containing Archie commands to an Archie server. The Archie server handles the request, and (if all goes well) the search results are sent back to you by e-mail.

If you don't have telnet or a local Archie client, this is an invaluable service. It's also useful if you want to do an Archie search but can't get to a server because it's too busy or you're not in any particular hurry.

### Archie E-Mail Commands

Archie servers recognize nine commands sent by e-mail. Some are the same as the commands used in a telnet session (such as prog), and some specifically support e-mail connections.

The compress command compresses the results of the search using the UNIX TAR compression system to generate a file of the type .Z. This compressed file is then uuencoded before being sent to you as an e-mail message. The purpose of compression is to reduce the load on the network.

> **Navigator's Note:** We recommend that you use the compress command whenever you suspect that the resulting output will be more than 45 kilobytes of text. Unless you are psychic and can predict the amount of output before seeing the results (in which case you'll also know what the results will be, so this won't concern you), always use this command.

**Navigator's Note:** Keep in mind that anything put in the subject heading of the e-mail message will be treated as a command. If it doesn't make sense to the Archie server (for example, if you were to put A query in the subject field), usually nothing will happen...but don't count on it. You might cause the entire query to be abandoned. Always either leave the subject blank (the best choice) or put the first Archie command there.

**Navigator's Note:** All search text in electronic mail queries is expected to be in the UNIX regular expression format (see Appendix B, "Command Reference").

The other useful electronic mail command is path. You can use this to specify the address to return the search results to. You should use this if you don't want the results returned to you or if you send a query and don't get any response. In the latter case, it may be because of a problem with the Archie server understanding your address in the message it received. Explicitly giving your address using the path command may sort the problem out.

The following listing shows the use of these two commands to search for chemistry.

```
icarus>mail archie@archie.sura.net
Subject:
prog chemistry
compress
path iuf4808@icarus.lis.pitt.edu
quit
.
icarus>
```

In this session, I mailed the Archie commands to the Archie server at SURAnet. I used the prog command to get the files on chemistry and asked for the information to be compressed. I also gave it the Internet address of another person who needs the information, and then indicated that there were no more commands by using the command quit. The results are as follows:

```
Sorting by hostname
Search request for 'chemistry'
Host askhp.ask.uni-karlsruhe.de    (129.13.200.33)
```

```
Last updated 03:39 10 May 1993
    Location: /pub/education
        DIRECTORY rwxrwxr-x      1024  Mar 31 08:22    chemistry
    Location: /pub/demos
        DIRECTORY rwxr-xr-x      1024  Dec 15 07:03    chemistry
    Location: /pub/getsisy/klaus12345678asd
        FILE      rwxr-xr-x        53  May  4 05:35    biohochreaktor.arc -> /scsi2/
ftp/pub/education/chemistry/biohochreaktor.arc
Host athene.uni-paderborn.de    (131.234.2.32)
Last updated 22:52 17 Apr 1993
    Location: /pcsoft/msdos
        DIRECTORY rwxr-xr-x       512  Apr 12 15:51    chemistry
    Location: /pcsoft2/atari/gnu
        DIRECTORY rwxr-xr-x       512  May 19  1992    chemistry
    Location: /pcsoft2/atari/gnu/chemistry
    FILE          rw-r--r--       169  Nov 18  1991    README.chemistry
```

> **Navigator's Warning:** Always put the command quit at the end of an
> e-mail Archie query. Once the Archie server encounters the com-
> mand quit, it stops processing and sends you the results. If your
> e-mail system automatically generates a signature for you, the sig-
> nature text that is added may cause problems. Check with your
> system administrator or your computer manuals to see how to
> switch this feature on and off.

## Whatis

Archie server sites maintain a Software Description Database (SDD) that gives
you a brief description of many (not all) of the files Archie knows about. These
descriptions are supplied by the sites on the Archie search list. The sites have to
update their own database entries.

The Software Description Database can be accessed using the command whatis
followed by the search text. You use the command at the archie> prompt when
using telnet or on a separate line in an e-mail message. Archie searches through
the SDD for lines that match the search text and returns each matching line as the
results.

Whatis is tricky, and the SDD data is incomplete, erratic, and sometimes very out-
of-date. For example, nothing appropriate was found for WAIS, e-mail, pkunzip,
or xwindows. On the other hand, internet, telnet, uucp, slip, and windows were
found.

Whatis can be good for finding files that relate to different environments and are therefore spread across many different computers. Our example looks for the text compression. I retrieved a good many types of compression-related files that I could then ask Archie to locate.

In the following example, I use the whatis command at the Archie prompt in a telnet session:

```
archie>what is compress

RFC 1144             Jacobson, V. Compressing TCP/IP headers for low-speed
                     serial links. 1990 February; 43 p.
RFC 468              Braden, R.T. FTP data compression 1973 March 8; 5 p.
arc                  PC compression program
cl[fs]               Print compressed directory listings
compress             Compress text files
compress.cms         compress for IBM/VM CMS
compress.mag         /etc/magic lines for compress
compress.ms          16 bit compress for MSDOS
compress.xenix       Xenix patches to compress4.0
deltac               Image compression using delta modulation
dictsq               Compress sorted word lists
mailsplit            Send files and/or directories via electronic mail
                     using "tar", "compress", etc
pdtar                A PD tar(1) replacement.  Writes P1003 (POSIX)
                     standard tapes by default.        It can also read
                     compressed tar files without uncompressing them.
spl                  Splay tree compression routines
squeeze              A file compression program
u16.pc               16 bit uncompress for IBM PC
uncrunch             Uncompression program
unsqueeze            Uncompression programs
wdb-ii               WDBII mapping software (10:1 compress, Unix PLOT)
ztar                 Tools for compressed tar archives

archie>_
```

Here I used the whatis command in an electronic mail inquiry of an Archie database:

```
icarus>mail archie@archie.rutgers.edu
Subject:
whatis shell
whatis internet
whatis slip
quit
```

And received this e-mail message in return:

```
From archie@dorm.rutgers.edu Thu May 13 09:45:02 1993
Received: from dorm.rutgers.edu by armagnac.ucs.usl.edu with SMTP id AA11006
   (5.65c/IDA-1.4.4 for <rjs4808@ucs.usl.edu>); Thu, 13 May 1993 09:44:58 -0500
Received: by dorm.rutgers.edu (5.59/SMI4.0/RU1.5/3.08)
        id AA16336; Thu, 13 May 93 10:44:55 EDT
Message-Id: <9305131444.AA16336@dorm.rutgers.edu>
To: rjs4808@usl.edu
From: (Archie Server) archie-errors@dorm.rutgers.edu
Reply-To: (Archie Server) archie-errors@dorm.rutgers.edu
Date: Thu, 13 May 93 14:44 GMT
Subject: archie [whatis slip] part 1 of 1
Status: R



>> path rjs4808@ucs.usl.edu

>> whatis shell

DNSEmulator              Shell scripts using nslookup to simulate Domain Name
                         Service (for ping, telnet, and ftp) under SunOS.
adsh                     Adventure Shell
aff                      Inspiratiional Shell utility
ash                      Complete shell. Similar to SYS V Bourne shell
MORE FILES
xtx                      Allows placing embedded shell commands in comments
                         in other files, and then executes them
zsh                      A ksh/tcsh-like shell

>> whatis internet

RFC                      1001 Defense Advanced Research Projects Agency,
                         Internet Activities Board, End-to-End Services
                         Task Force, NetBIOS Working Group. Protocol
                         standard for a NetBIOS service on a TCP/UDP
                         transport: Concepts and methods. 1987 March; 68
                         p.
RFC                      1002        Defense Advanced Research Projects
                         Agency, Internet Activities Board, End-to-End
                         Services Task Force, NetBIOS Working Group.
                         Protocol standard for a NetBIOS service on a
                         TCP/UDP transport: Detailed specifications. 1987
                         March; 85 p.
RFC                      1009        Braden, R.T.; Postel, J.B.
                         Requirements for Internet gateways. 1987 June;
                         55 p. (Obsoletes RFC 985)
```

```
MANY MORE FILES
ntp                              Network Time Protocol. Synchronize time accross
                                 the Internet
slipware                         Serial Line IP. Internet Protocol over serial
                                 lines


>> whatis slip

RFC                              1055      Romkey, J.L. Nonstandard for
                                 transmission of IP datagrams over serial lines:
                                 SLIP. 1988 June; 6 p.
slipware                         Serial Line IP. Internet Protocol over serial
                                 lines


>> quit
```

**Navigator's Note:** Although Archie file data is usually no more than thirty days old, the information in the Software Description Database (SDD) may be much more ancient. Worse, not all files in the Archie database will be in the SDD, and worse still, the filename given in an SDD entry may no longer exist. So if you use a prog command to find out where the file is, the file will not be found. Very confusing unless you're aware of the problem...which you now are.

## Which Way Should I Access Archie?

Obviously, if your site has the Archie client software, you'll stand the best chance of getting service. An online session with a remote Archie server using telnet is going to give the fastest response but will be the hardest to get access to.

However, if you don't want to hang around while the search is done, an e-mail search request is the choice. E-mail is also the choice when there is no local Archie client and telnet access isn't available.

## Things to Remember When Using Archie

Archie sites are popular, so don't be surprised if you do not get a connection every time you try to use one. Just like the phone system, networks have peak times of use. If possible, use Archie during off-hours.

In addition, remember to use "Internetiquette" (see Chapter 11, "Internetiquette: Manners and the Internet") and restrict your use of Archie to the server nearest your geographic area. This is because using the server nearest to you saves Internet resources by keeping traffic on the Internet to a minimum.

Also keep in mind that Archie is not infallible or even comprehensive. It is not a database of the files themselves but a database of file names, their directories, file attributes, and whatever is entered in the Software Description Database.

**Navigator's Note:** We keep saying to use the server geographically nearest you to save on Internet resources. That's not always correct. The SURAnet Archie server, located in Maryland, is farther away from Louisiana than the Archie server in Nebraska. Because my Internet connection goes through SURAnet, Maryland is nearer to me in *network terms* (which way the wires go). The Archie server in Maryland is the default on my Archie client. Finding out which is really your nearest server can be difficult, so picking the server geographically closest to you is your best bet. If all else fails, choose an Archie server on the same continent.

# THE DATABASE OF DATABASES: WAIS

On the Internet, people have a remarkable desire to share knowledge. Why altruism should be a feature of Cyberspace is anybody's guess, but the pioneer spirit may have something to do with it. Just as the Wild West campfire always had room for a stranger (in contrast to today's urban scene), the database always has room for another terminal. One of the great tools for finding useful stuff in many databases is WAIS.

The *Wide Area Information Server* (WAIS, pronounced "ways") attempts to harness the vast data resources of the Internet by making it easy to search for and retrieve information from remote databases, called sources in WAIS terminology.

*Sources* are collections of files that consist mostly of textual material. For example, if chemistry is your forte, you can find several journals on the subject through WAIS. WAIS servers not only help you find the right source, they also handle your access to it.

Like Gopher, WAIS systems use the client/server model to make navigating around data resources easy. Unlike Gopher, WAIS does the searching for you. Currently, more than 420 sources are available through WAIS servers. A WAIS client (run either on your own computer or on a remote system through telnet) talks to a WAIS server and asks it to perform a search for data containing a specific word or words.

Most WAIS servers are free, which means that the data is occasionally eccentric and erratic. It can also have great gaps in coverage on some subjects and more coverage than you might believe on others. For example, you'll find tons of material in WAIS about chemistry and computer science, but sources on, say, art history or the theory of juggling are nonexistent at the moment. WAIS servers and sources are being created at a tremendous rate, however, so a library of Van Gogh's writings may yet be established (Van Gogh: 'ear today, gone tomorrow).

> **Navigator's Note:** A long-running and busy newsgroup on the subject of juggling was established by Phil Paxton, a development editor for this book. They discuss issues like juggling patterns and how to juggle seven balls on a unicycle. As if life isn't complicated enough.

WAIS itself is simple to use, although its text-based interface is a little user-hostile. The X Window client is much easier to use but requires that you run X-windows (of course). WAIS clients are available for Macintoshes, PCs, and even supercomputers.

## What Is WAIS?

WAIS was one of the first programs to be based on the Z39.50 standard. The (take a deep breath here if you're reading aloud) American National Standard Z39.50: Information Retrieval Service Definition and Protocol Specification for Library Applications standard, revised by the National Information Standards Organization (NISO) (whew!), attempts to provide interconnection of computer systems despite differences in hardware and software.

WAIS is the first database system to use this standard, which may well become a universal data search format. All WAIS servers will be accessible to any client that uses Z39.50, and WAIS clients should be able to connect to any database that uses Z39.50.

**Navigator's Note:** Z39.50 is similar in some respects to Structured Query Language (SQL), but it is simplified. Although this makes it less powerful, it consequently makes it more general, so Z39.50 is likely to gain wide acceptance.

Z39.50 will be an important step in making information sources on the Internet more accessible. Today most Internet databases are accessed in ways that are completely different from each other. They use different standards for storing data and different tools to access that data. Z39.50 may well change that.

For example, one library catalog system might have `find` as its search command for a subject heading, whereas another might have `subject`. Still another might use `topic`. If they all conformed to a standard, life would be much simpler. Z39.50-compliant systems all use the same format to construct queries. You don't need to know anything special in order to search a WAIS database. You just use whatever word you think might be used in relevant documents, because WAIS indexes all the text in a source.

## Document Rankings

After you run a search that identifies any documents, you will receive a list of "hits," or ranked document titles. The WAIS server ranks the hits from the most- to least-relevant document. Each document is scored, with the best-fitting document awarded 1,000 points. All other scores are relative to the top score.

WAIS ranks documents by the number of search words that occur in the document and the number of times those words appear.

WAIS servers also take into consideration the length of the document. WAIS servers are smart enough to exclude common words, called stop words, to make the search manageable. Words such as *a, about, above, across, after,* and so on should be excluded from your search, because the frequency of their appearance in most documents makes them irrelevant in most searches.

**Navigator's Note:** Stop words are controlled by the administrator of each WAIS server. In addition to common words in general, many words common to a database may become stop words. For example, the word *WAIS* may be a stop word in the database of a WAIS newsgroup, or the word *Internet* may be a stop word in a database of Internet protocols.

In this server, a word is a series of alphanumeric characters, possibly with some embedded punctuation. A word must start with an alphabetic character: you can't search for numbers. A word can have embedded periods, ampersands, or apostrophes, but only the first kind of punctuation that you use is treated as punctuation. Any other punctuation is interpreted as a space and ends the word. "I.M.Pei" is a valid word, and so is "AT&T," but "A.T.&T." is two words: "A.T." and "T."

Hyphens are not accepted as embedded punctuation because they're used so freely that they inflate the database dictionary.

Two classes of words are ignored in queries. First are "stop words" chosen by the database administrator for their complete lack of value in searching. There are 368 stop words for the public CM WAIS server. Some common stop words are *a, about, aren't, further, he, will, won't*—you get the idea.

Some words are just far too common to be helpful in searches. These are weeded out by the database software as the database is built. There are currently 777 "buzz words" for the public CM WAIS server, each of which occurs at least 8,000 times in the database. They include words like *able, access, account, act, action, add, added, addition, additional, address, addresses, administration,* through to *winkel* (no, I have absolutely no idea why that's in there).

## Limitations

You cannot use Boolean logic in most WAIS searches. That is, you can't do anything other than find a single word or several words. A search for "cow and farm" will search for documents that contain "cow" and/or "and" and/or "farm." The "and" needs to be excluded. Notice that the search is "and/or" not just "and." The search "cow farm" will give you all documents that contain any of the following:

1. "cow" and "farm"

2. just "cow"

3. just "farm"

You can guarantee that this limitation won't always be the way of things and already there's a new version of WAIS called FREEWAIS. (Get it?…freeways? Oh, never mind.)

Also, no wildcard searching is available. This means that you can't specify that you'd accept "cows" as well as "cow."

Unlike many regular database searches, WAIS searches can't be expanded to include articles that may talk about similar topics, to retrieve all articles that have those words (for example, "cars or automobiles or trucks or motorcycles"). Neither can you exclude words in a search (for example, "cars but not trucks").

You can, however, increase the number of relevant documents by using more specific terms in a search. "car automobile crash statistics" may retrieve more pertinent documents on the subject you want.

# What Is Available?

WAIS has become popular recently. The number of sources that you can search through WAIS has quadrupled in the last year—from 98 to more than 400. Many Internet newsgroups (see Chapter 12) and LISTSERVS (see Chapter 13) have taken advantage of WAIS by making their archives available through WAIS servers. Access to years of information and commentary is a valuable resource.

The sources available through WAIS are as varied as the groups that communicate over the Internet: renaissance music, beer brewing, Aesop's fables, software reviews, recipes, zip code information, a thesaurus, environmental reports, and many other databases.

The WAIS system for Thinking Machines alone gives access to over 60,000 documents, including weather maps and forecasts, the CIA World Factbook, a collection of molecular biology abstracts, Usenet's Info Mac digests, and the Connection Machine's FORTRAN manual (a must for pipe stress freaks and crystallography addicts).

The Massachusetts Institute of Technology makes a compendium of classical and modern poetry available via WAIS. The Library of Congress, which boasts 25 terabytes of data, has plans to make its catalog available via WAIS.

> **Navigator's Note:** 25 terabytes of data is, roughly, the complete text of *Alice in Wonderland* 173,980,820 times.

Thinking Machines reckons that during 1991 its public-access WAIS system handled more than 100,000 requests from more than 6,000 computer users worldwide.

# Where to Get WAIS

WAIS was developed by Thinking Machines Corporation, Apple Computer, and Dow Jones, and access to the system is available free from Thinking Machines by telneting to the machine quake.think.com. You log in by typing the word WAIS and are connected to swais, the character-oriented version of WAIS. That's how we will show our examples of WAIS.

As an alternative, WAIS client software (both executable and source) is available via anonymous ftp at Thinking Machines (use the same Internet address in the pub/wais/ directory). WAIS clients are available for a number of operating systems—X-windows, DOS, Macintosh, and others—but they obviously require that your computer have some kind of TCP/IP connection to the Internet.

# Searching WAIS

You can access WAIS in three ways. You can telnet to quake.think.com and log in as wais, or you can run a local WAIS client. Your system administrator may have set your system so that typing WAIS will automatically connect you to whatever WAIS service is available. Another way to get to WAIS is through Gopher. You'll find an entry on Gopher menus like "Other Gopher and Information Servers" that will lead you eventually to WAIS.

The first screen you see on WAIS is a list of the WAIS servers and sources that are available. At the time of this writing, 429 WAIS sources are available through the WAIS client at Thinking Machines, starting with aarnet-resource-guide and ending with zipcodes.

| # | Server | Source | Cost |
|---|--------|--------|------|
| 001: | [ archie.au] | aarnet-resource-guide | Free |
| 002: | [ munin.ub2.lu.se] | academic_email_conf | Free |
| 003: | [wraith.cs.uow.edu.au] | acronyms | Free |
| 004: | [ archive.orst.edu] | aeronautics | Free |
| 005: | [ bloat.media.mit.edu] | Aesop-Fables | Free |
| 006: | [ ftp.cs.colorado.edu] | aftp-cs-colorado-edu | Free |
| 007: | [nostromo.oes.orst.ed] | agricultural-market-news | Free |
| 008: | [ archive.orst.edu] | alt.drugs | Free |
| 009: | [ wais.oit.unc.edu] | alt.gopher | Free |
| 010: | [sun-wais.oit.unc.edu] | alt.sys.sun | Free |
| 011: | [ wais.oit.unc.edu] | alt.wais | Free |
| 012: | [alfred.ccs.carleton.] | amiga-slip | Free |
| 013: | [ munin.ub2.lu.se] | amiga_fish_contents | Free |
| 014: | [ coombs.anu.edu.au] | ANU-Aboriginal-Studies | $0.00/minute |
| 015: | [ coombs.anu.edu.au] | ANU-Asian-Computing | $0.00/minute |
| 016: | [ coombs.anu.edu.au] | ANU-Asian-Religions | $0.00/minute |

```
017:    [   coombs.anu.edu.au]  ANU-CAUT-Projects              $0.00/minute
018:    [   coombs.anu.edu.au]  ANU-French-Databanks           $0.00/minute

Keywords:

<space> selects, w for keywords, arrows move, <return> searches, q quits, or ?
```

The screen gives you a reference number for each source, the location of the WAIS server in brackets, the name of the server, and the cost of searching that library. At this time, all WAIS servers available through Thinking Machines are free.

You are now ready to conduct a search. As with Gopher, the problem is deciding which of the 429 libraries to search. An added problem is the fact that the names of the servers don't necessarily describe what they contain. Fortunately, a directory of servers is available that contains short abstracts of the contents of each server and other information about the source of the server. Until you know exactly which server you want to search, you should start with the directory of servers.

How do you get there? It looks like an alphabetical list of WAIS servers is provided, so using the arrow key will probably do the trick, but it may take a while. Using the "?" to reveal the online help that comes with this client gets you this information:

```
SWAIS                        Source Selection Help              Page:  1

 j, down arrow, ^N       Move Down one source
 k, up arrow, ^P         Move Up one source
 J, ^V, ^D               Move Down one screen
 K, <esc> v, ^U          Move Up one screen
 ###                     Position to source number ##
 /sss                    Search for source sss
 <space>, <period>       Select current source
 =                       Deselect all sources
 v, <comma>              View current source info
 <ret>                   Perform search
 s                       Select new sources (refresh sources list)
 w                       Select new keywords
 X, -                    Remove current source permanently
 o                       Set and show swais options
 h, ?                    Show this help display
 H                       Display program history
 q                       Leave this program




 Press any key to continue
```

This help screen tells you how to move through the screens of the source directory. WAIS uses UNIX editor commands for moving about (the j and J, for example, for moving down by line or by screen). Try your Page Down and arrow keys; they may work if you're using VT100 terminal emulation. The /sss is also important because it quickly moves the pointer to a source on a specific line. Also note that the space or period selects a source, and the equal sign deselects all sources.

**Navigator's Note:** Unless your terminal emulator does a good VT100 emulation, don't bother with swais; you'll go crazy trying to figure out what's going on.

**Navigator's Note:** A feature not covered in the swais help: Using the Spacebar or period on a selected source will deselect it.

It's too bad that the directory of sources isn't the first item on the list of sources. Well, you know the name, so use a forward slash with the name of the server to get there. Use /dir to get close, and after the screen is refreshed with names of new sources, use the down arrow key or type j once to highlight directory of sources.

```
SWAIS                         Source Selection              Sources: 429
   #            Server                      Source                  Cost
  145:  [      ds.internic.net]  ddbs-info                          Free
  146:  [          irit.irit.fr]  directory-irit-fr                 Free
  147:  [       quake.think.com]  directory-of-servers              Free
  148:  [        zenon.inria.fr]  directory-zenon-inria-fr          Free
  149:  [        zenon.inria.fr]  disco-mm-zenon-inria-fr           Free
  150:  [          wais.cic.net]  disi-catalog                      Free
  151:  [        munin.ub2.lu.se]  dit-library                      Free
  152:  [ ridgisd.er.usgs.gov]  DOE_Climate_Data                    Free
  153:  [          wais.cic.net]  domain-contacts                   Free
  154:  [          wais.cic.net]  domain-organizations              Free
  155:  [ ftp.cs.colorado.edu]  dynamic-archie                      Free
  156:  [  wais.wu-wien.ac.at]  earlym-1                            Free
  157:  [             bio.vu.nl]  EC-enzyme                         Free
  158:  [          kumr.lns.com]  edis                              Free
  159:  [     ivory.educom.edu]  educom                            Free
  160:  [          wais.eff.org]  eff-documents                    Free
  161:  [          wais.eff.org]  eff-talk                          Free
  162:  [       quake.think.com]  EIA-Petroleum-Supply-Monthly      Free
```

Remember that you are not searching a huge database containing source materials but a database of descriptions of source databases. The terms you choose should take into consideration what the author or owner of the database would probably use to describe it. The example search uses the words wais and Z39.50 in order to find information on the NISO standard and how WAIS uses it.

WAIS takes the words wais and Z39.50 and retrieves search results that contain those words (see the following). The information is returned in ranked order—the order WAIS thinks is most likely to contain your information. The first item, scored 1000, is the one WAIS thinks is most likely to contain what you're looking for.

```
SWAIS                          Search Results                   Items: 40
   #     Score    Source                     Title                 Lines
 001:   [1000]  (directory-of-se)  cool-cfl                            76
 002:   [ 953]  (directory-of-se)  dynamic-archie                      59
 003:   [ 858]  (directory-of-se)  wais-docs                           24
 004:   [ 834]  (directory-of-se)  wais-talk-archives                  18
 005:   [ 810]  (directory-of-se)  alt.wais                            18
 006:   [ 810]  (directory-of-se)  wais-discussion-archives            18
 007:   [ 691]  (directory-of-se)  cool-net                            50
 008:   [ 572]  (directory-of-se)  aftp-cs-colorado-edu               144
 009:   [ 476]  (directory-of-se)  bionic-directory-of-servers         31
 010:   [ 452]  (directory-of-se)  cicnet-wais-servers                 55
 011:   [ 381]  (directory-of-se)  cool-lex                            59
 012:   [ 333]  (directory-of-se)  IUBio-INFO                          71
 013:   [ 333]  (directory-of-se)  directory-of-servers                32
 014:   [ 333]  (directory-of-se)  sample-pictures                     23
 015:   [ 333]  (directory-of-se)  utsun.s.u-tokyo.ac.jp               32
 016:   [ 309]  (directory-of-se)  journalism.periodicals              58
 017:   [ 309]  (directory-of-se)  x.500.working-group                 38
 018:   [ 286]  (directory-of-se)  ANU-Theses-Abstracts                89
```

This search has resulted in some irrelevant sources. For example, cool-cfl is a database of files from a group concerned with conservation in libraries, archives, and museums. This might be a bug in WAIS—not improbable, with Internet software being developed and improved continuously.

The second source, dynamic Archie, discusses a Dynamic WAIS prototype at the University of Colorado that performs Archie searches with WAIS. This might be useful, and so might the next four sources. The rest don't seem likely to be relevant.

The information that describes the sources in WAIS is determined by the owners of the source. Some sources, such as ERIC databases, give detailed information that makes the directory of sources a valuable tool in finding out which sources are relevant. Other sources have minimal descriptions that aren't very useful or won't be found through the directory of services. They'll probably be of use only to people who know they are available in the WAIS database and will go to them directly.

From here, press the letter s to return to the sources, using "/wais" to select the three wais sources.

```
SWAIS                          Source Selection              Sources: 429
   #          Server                      Source                Cost
 415: * [    quake.think.com] wais-discussion-archives          Free
 416: * [    quake.think.com] wais-docs                         Free
 417: * [    quake.think.com] wais-talk-archives                Free
 418:   [hermes.ecn.purdue.ed] water-quality                    Free
 419:   [    quake.think.com] weather                           Free
 420:   [    sunsite.unc.edu] White-House-Papers                Free
 421:   [   wais.nic.ddn.mil] whois                             Free
 422:   [    sunsite.unc.edu] winsock                           Free
 423:   [ cmns-moon.think.com] world-factbook                   Free
 424:   [    quake.think.com] world91a                          Free
 425:   [       wais.cic.net] wuarchive                         Free
 426:   [       wais.cic.net] x.500.working-group               Free
 427:   [wais.unidata.ucar.ed] xgks                             Free
 428:   [      cs.widener.edu] zen-internet                     Free
 429:   [    quake.think.com] zipcodes                          Free
```

You could also select the alt.wais group, but these three will work (see Chapter 12, "Views and News: USENET" to find out what alt groups are). Using Z39.50 simplifies the search; the word wais will probably be scattered throughout most of the documents, lessening its relevance to the search. To enter the search text, select the sources you want to search; you'll be prompted for keywords. After typing the keywords, press the Enter key; WAIS will search each selected source and rank the results according to their relevance.

```
SWAIS                          Search Results                 Items: 39
   #   Score    Source                 Title                    Lines
 001: [1000] (      wais-docs)  z3950-spec                       2674
 002: [1000] (wais-talk-archi)  Edward Vie Re: [wald@mhuxd.att.com: more  383
 003: [1000] (wais-discussion)  Clifford L Re: The Z39.50 Protocol: Ques  325
 004: [ 939] (wais-discussion)  Brewster K Re: online version of the z39  2659
 005: [ 893] (wais-discussion)  akel@seq1. Re: Net resource list model(s  347
 006: [ 823] (      wais-docs)  waisprot                         1004
 007: [ 800] (wais-discussion)  Michael Sc Re: Dynamic WAIS prototype an   27
 008: [ 338] (wais-discussion)  harvard!ap Re: Z39.50 Product Announceme   51
 009: [ 333] (      wais-docs)  protspec                          915
 010: [ 331] (wais-discussion)  Unknown Subject                     6
 011: [ 331] (wais-discussion)  uriel wile Re: poetry server is up [most   31
 012: [ 313] (wais-talk-archi)  brewster@q Re: Re: Information about z39   69
 013: [ 313] (wais-talk-archi)  ses@cmns.t Re: Z39.50 1992          171
```

```
014:  [ 313] (wais-talk-archi)   ses@cmns.t Re: Z39.50 1992                90
015:  [ 308] (wais-discussion)   Brewster K Re: Hooking up WAIS with othe  66
016:  [ 292] (wais-discussion)   Brewster K Re: [morris@Think.COM: it's s  25
017:  [ 286] (wais-talk-archi)   mitra@pand Re: Z39.50 1992                71
018:  [ 284] (wais-discussion)   Brewster K Re: WAIS-discussion digest #6  18
```

The results look promising. The first Z39.50 is ranked 1,000, which looks okay. In fact, the first three seem to be relevant. The name of the information source is given, along with the title of the information. In this case the title appears to come from e-mail message subject headings. Finally, the screen gives the number of lines contained in the information.

From here you can read each result and have pertinent results e-mailed to yourself or even another person. At the search result screen, type the letter m to receive a prompt asking for an e-mail address. If none of the documents are relevant, you can go back to the sources and redefine the search strategies or add additional appropriate sources to search. The sample documents contain the desired information, so this search has worked.

Because WAIS in its search mode uses natural language query and searches the full text index of the source, changing any of the search words will produce different results. Using a natural language search such as how does wais use Z39.50 protocol produces the following:

```
SWAIS                       Search Results               Items: 39
   #    Score    Source              Title                   Lines
 001:  [1000] (      wais-docs)  z3950-spec                    2674
 002:  [1000] (wais-talk-archi)  Edward Vie Re: [wald@mhuxd.att.com: more  383
 003:  [1000] (wais-discussion)  Michael Sc Re: Dynamic WAIS prototype an   27
 004:  [ 998] (wais-discussion)  Brewster K Re: online version of the z39  2659
 005:  [ 777] (wais-talk-archi)  news-mail- Re: WAIS-discussion digest #4   554
 006:  [ 675] (wais-talk-archi)  news-mail- Re: WAIS-discussion digest #3   535
 007:  [ 640] (wais-talk-archi)  news-mail- Re: WAIS-discussion digest #3   636
 008:  [ 629] (wais-talk-archi)  brewster@t Re: WAIS-discussion digest #5   749
 009:  [ 608] (wais-talk-archi)  news-mail- Re: WAIS-discussion digest #4   601
 010:  [ 607] (wais-talk-archi)  fad@think. Re: WAIS Corporate Paper -- "   424
 011:  [ 607] (wais-talk-archi)  composer@b Re: WAIS, A Sketch of an Over   449
 012:  [ 589] (wais-talk-archi)  news-mail- Re: WAIS-discussion digest #4   621
 013:  [ 549] (wais-talk-archi)  news-mail- Re: WAIS-discussion digest #3   575
 014:  [ 524] (wais-talk-archi)  brewster@t Re: WAIS-discussion digest #4   682
 015:  [ 515] (wais-talk-archi)  news-mail- Re: WAIS-discussion digest #3   521
 016:  [ 510] (wais-talk-archi)  news-mail- Re: WAIS-discussion digest #4   480
 017:  [ 507] (wais-discussion)  akel@seq1. Re: Net resource list model(s   347
 018:  [ 495] (wais-discussion)  Unknown Subject                             6
```

Although many of the results are duplicates of the search using just the text Z39.50, many new documents are listed. An extensive search for all relevant documents may mean using different search strategies and a variety of WAIS source servers.

## WAIS Indexing

In addition to its search features, WAIS also functions as a data indexing tool. WAIS can take large amounts of information, index it, and make the resultant Z39.50-compliant database searchable. You can build an indexed database for your own use as a stand-alone database or, if you have a TCP/IP connection, you can make your WAIS database public by registering it with think.com and getting listed in the Directory of Sources.

To obtain the WAIS software, anonymous ftp to think.com and change directory to wais. This is the main distribution site for WAIS software and WAIS documentation. Both the WAIS server code and client codes are available from think.com.

Other components available elsewhere include the following:

| | |
|---|---|
| **NeXT release:** | /wais/WAIStation-NeXT-1.0.tar.Z@think.com |
| **DOS:** | /pub/wais/UNC/wais-dos*@sunsite.unc.edu |
| **Motif:** | /public/wais/motif-a1.tar.Z@think.com |
| **IBM RS6000:** | /pub/misc/wais-8-b2-dist.tar.Z@ans.net |
| **SunView:** | /pub/wais/sunsearch.src.*.tar.Z@sunsite.unc.edu |
| **VMS:** | /pub/wais/vms*@sunsite.unc.edu |

Getting WAIS up and running is no trivial matter. Because it's very complicated, we'll leave that as an exercise for more daring users with time on their hands and a good supply of Valium.

## The Ways of WAIS

WAIS use is growing rapidly on the Internet. WAIS provides a convenient and efficient way to index and search large amounts of information, using standards that are starting to be accepted as a general tool for the Internet.

Because people are getting used to the WAIS system in free public use, WAIS has commercial potential with fee-charging databases. Using what you're already familiar with is always the easiest choice.

# NAVIGATING BY MENUS: GOPHER

*There are things known and things unknown: in between there are doors.*

—Anonymous

As you look for data on the Internet, you'll start to think, "Wouldn't it be nice if files were organized into some sort of index?" If you've started mumbling to yourself like this, you'll find the Internet Gopher service invaluable.

The Gopher service provides you with a whole series of connecting corridors and doors that will take you from one part of the Internet to another. You can use it to find data that has been classified and, in effect, published in what may well be the world's largest and most eccentric catalog.

# What Is a Gopher?

Imagine the biggest library card index in the world. Unlike the card indexes you find in any library, this index isn't compiled by librarians but by people who use many different ways to organize the references to data.

Now imagine that this isn't a single card index but is distributed across hundreds of different locations, and that there are thousands of links between the separate index cards. Finally, imagine that the whole mess is electronic and distributed around the Internet. Voila! You have the Gopher system.

The Internet Gopher system was developed at the University of Minnesota and is free for nonprofit institutions (for-profit institutions can also get it free if they make their information available to the Internet community at large). The system now includes more than 300 Gopher servers and thousands of Gopher clients. It's called Gopher because you can use it to "go fer" data.

> **Navigator's Note:** The terrible pun that resulted in the name Gopher is the responsibility of someone at the University of Minnesota. Who is he or she? Enquiring minds want to know. The name is also derived (so they claim) not only from the University's mascot but also from the implication that the Gopher software, like the gopher animal, can burrow through the Internet to find data for you.

Gopher is a client/server system that can be used on a number of machines, including UNIX, DOS, Microsoft Windows, Macintosh, and VM, and they're planning Gophers for OS/2, Nextstep, and X Window.

The client software runs on your computer and talks to any one of the Gopher servers. If your local computer system has a Gopher server, that's probably where you will start. If not, your Gopher client can point to any Gopher server on the Internet. For example, at the University of Pittsburgh's School of Library and Information Science, typing gopher at the system prompt sends you to a Gopher in Illinois. You can also try a UNIX client by telneting to consultant.micro.umn.edu and logging in as gopher. Other public Gopher sites that enable telnet access are

```
Non-tn3270 Public Logins:
Hostname                    IP#                Login    Area
------------------------    ---------------    ------   ------------
consultant.micro.umn.edu    134.84.132.4       Gopher   North America
Gopher.uiuc.edu             128.174.33.160     Gopher   North America
panda.uiowa.edu             128.255.40.201     panda    North America
Gopher.sunet.se             192.36.125.2       Gopher   Europe
```

```
info.anu.edu.au          150.203.84.20   info    Australia
Gopher.chalmers.se       129.16.221.40   Gopher  Sweden
tolten.puc.cl            146.155.1.16    Gopher  South America
ecnet.ec                 157.100.45.2    Gopher  Ecuador


tn3270 Public Logins:
Hostname                  IP#            Login   Area
-----------------------   -------------- ------  ------------
pubinfo.ais.umn.edu      128.101.109.1   -none-  North America
```

The client end of Gopher is a menu-driven program that enables you to select from a menu. These choices are of three types. The first type leads you to a submenu of further choices that may be on a different server than the Gopher server you're on. The second accesses local resources for data. The final type leads to a request being sent out on the network to retrieve files or yet another list of information from another Gopher server. Each Gopher server has links to other Gopher servers which, in turn, lead to further servers, and so on.

With Gopher, you can tunnel through the Internet and boldly go where no user has suspected he could go before. The way it does this is by integrating other Internet tools, such as Telnet and FTP, so that once you've found an entry that relates to something you're searching for, you can go straight to it without having to find the right utility, enter the address of the target of the search, and so on. Gopher handles all that for you. Because of this, Gopher has become a very popular tool with Internet navigators.

# How Gopher Works

As we've said, Gopher is a client/server system. When you install a Gopher client, you can tell it the address of your preferred Gopher server. When you start Gopher, it goes out and retrieves the menu information from the server.

The entire *Gopherspace* (the Gopher menus on all publicly accessible Gopher servers) is made up of Gopher servers located internationally. Your server stores only local information and can share information with other servers. This is very attractive to systems managers because it has a minimal impact on their systems, and they can make Gopher resources available to their users with a minimum of effort.

## Getting Gopher

We've already said that you can use a Gopher client on UNIX, DOS, Macintosh, and VM systems or you can telnet to a site that has a Gopher client and run theirs.

To get your own Gopher server (don't forget that you'll need to have a TCP/IP connection to your computer to use it), you can anonymous ftp to boombox.micro.umn.edu (134.84.132.2) and look in /pub/Gopher. The following Gopher server software implementations are available there:

```
Unix       : /pub/Gopher/Unix/Gopherxx.tar.Z
VMS        : /pub/Gopher/VMS/
Macintosh  : /pub/Gopher/Mac_server/
VM/CMS     : /pub/Gopher/Rice_CMS/ or /pub/Gopher/Vienna_CMS/
MVS        : /pub/Gopher/mvs/
DOS PC     : /pub/Gopher/PC_server/
```

You can also find Gopher clients for the following systems. The directory following the name is the location of the client on the anonymous FTP site boombox.micro.umn.edu (134.84.132.2) in the directory /pub/Gopher.

```
Unix Curses & Emacs    : /pub/Gopher/Unix/Gopher1.03.tar.Z
Xwindows               : /pub/Gopher/Unix/xGopher1.1a.tar.Z
Macintosh Hypercard    : /pub/Gopher/Mac_client/
Macintosh Application  : /pub/Gopher/Macintosh-TurboGopher
DOS w/Clarkson Driver  : /pub/Gopher/PC_client/
Nextstep               : /pub/Gopher/NeXT/
VM/CMS                 : /pub/Gopher/Rice_CMS/
        or               /pub/Gopher/Vienna_CMS/
VMS                    : /pub/Gopher/VMS/
OS/2 2.0               : /pub/Gopher/os2/
MVS/XA                 : /pub/Gopher/mvs/
```

This list changes frequently as new implementations are released. Many other clients and servers have been developed by others:

A Macintosh application, "MacGopher," at

ftp.cc.utah.edu:/pub/Gopher/Macintosh

Another Macintosh application, "GopherApp," at

ftp.bio.indiana.edu:/util/Gopher/Gopherapp

A port of the UNIX Curses client for DOS with PC/TCP at

oac.hsc.uth.tmc.edu:/public/dos/misc/dosGopher.exe

A port of the UNIX Curses client for PC-NFS at

`bcm.tmc.edu:/nfs/Gopher.exe`

A version of the PC Gopher client for Novell's LAN Workplace for DOS at

`lennon.itn.med.umich.edu:/Gopher`

An Xwindows/DECwindows client at

`job.acs.ohio-stat.edu`

## Installing Gopher

Installation is straightforward. The PC version is well-documented, but help and information from your systems administrator will probably be required.

> **Navigator's Note:** Remember that you need to have a TCP/IP connection to your computer to run a Gopher client or server directly.

On installation, you need to provide some information about your network. You'll have to tell the Gopher client where to find a name server (a computer on the Internet that takes an Internet name like boombox.micro.umn.edu and turns it into an address that can be used by computers, such as 134.84.132.2) and you will need to know details about the gateway that takes you out of your local area network to the big, wide world.

The PC version of Gopher runs under DOS version 3.3 or greater and requires 640K of conventional memory. Gopher will run on a wide range of IBM PCs and compatibles, including the earliest PCs, which contain only a monochrome display adapter without graphics support.

A Microsoft-compatible mouse is useful but optional. You must load mouse driver software before running Gopher. If your mouse contains more than one mouse button, you should use only the left mouse button when running Gopher.

## Using Gopher

Let's take a look at Gopher. I'm running the UNIX Curses version of Gopher on my Sun UNIX machine, but most of the character-oriented systems look pretty much the same. I start Gopher by typing `gopher` at my system prompt and pressing Enter. I then receive the following screen:

```
Internet Gopher Information Client v1.01

                   Root gopher server: rouge.usl.edu

 -->  1.  CAMPUS INFORMATION SYSTEM - USL GOPHER/
      2.  GOPHER System - All Other Locations/
      3.  Information About Gopher/
      4.  Libraries/
      5.  News/
      6.  Phone Books/
      7.  Weather Louisiana/
      8.  Weather US/
      9.  Weather World/
     10.  X-perimental Services/
     11.  Y-perimental Services/
```

On this particular system at the University of Southwestern Louisiana, we have 11 options. The topics are customized on this Gopher (as they are on most Gophers) to present choices that are relevant to the local site.

Here we have options for local weather (in Louisiana) and information about the USL GOPHER. The adaptability of the Gopher system is one of its most useful features. Take a look at the following examples of the variety of local information on four different Gophers.

```
Internet Gopher Information Client v1.01

                   Cornell University HelpDesk

 -->  1.  *About CIT HelpDesk's Gopher.
      2.  *CIT services and information/
      3.  Bear Access information/
      4.  CIT Mother Gopher/
      5.  CMS information/
      6.  Computing at Cornell/
      7.  Internet information/
      8.  Mac information/
      9.  Multi-platform information/
     10.  Network ID Info.
     11.  PC information/
     12.  Phone books for Cornell and elsewhere/
     13.  Statistical information/
     14.  Unix information/
```

Cornell's Gopher system is very service-oriented. It will lead you to critical local support services and has a rather technically oriented set of choices.

```
Internet Gopher Information Client v1.01

      National Institute of Standards and Technology (NIST)

-->  1.  --*--  WARNING: NIST Gopher Server Access Restriction --*--.
     2.  Using the NIST Gopher Server/
     3.  Networks and Services at NIST (DIV 885)/
     4.  Applied and Computational Mathematics at NIST (DIV 881)/
     5.  Systems and Software Technology (DIV 872)/
     6.  NIST Organizational Activities (Reserved)/
     7.  NIST Phone Book and Email Directory <CSO>
     8.  Other Information Servers Around the World/
```

The National Institute of Standards and Technology's Gopher reflects what they do. This is a very formal kind of look and very much focused on information rather than services.

```
Internet Gopher Information Client v1.01

      Whole Earth 'Lectronic Magazine - The WELL's Gopherspace

-->  1.  About this gopherspace.
     2.  See the latest additions to this gopherspace/
     3.  Art and Culture/
     4.  Communications/
     5.  Community/
     6.  Cyberpunk/
     7.  Grateful Dead/
     8.  The Military, its People, Policies and Practices/
     9.  Environmental Issues and Ideas/
    10.  Politics/
    11.  Publications (includes Zines like FactSheet 5)/
    12.  Sci-Fi Stuff/
    13.  Science/
    14.  The WELL Itself/
    15.  Tools/
    16.  Whole Earth Review, the Magazine/
    17.  Whole Systems/
```

The above list is a much more hip kind of Gopher. The Well is inhabited by all sorts of people—writers, journalists, and lots of people in the computer business. Cyberpunk is certainly not an item you'd expect to find on NIST's menu.

```
              Internet Gopher Information Client v1.01

                 Ecole Normale Superieure (Paris, France)
  -->   1.  annuaire de l'ENS <TEL>
        2.  serveur FTP de l'ENS (ftp.ens.fr)/
        3.  Bibliotheque du DMI <?>
        4.  DMI (Departement de Mathematiques et Informatique)/
        5.  veronica (Search menu titles in GopherSpace)/
        6.  Autres serveurs gopher/
        7.  Bibliotheques/
        8.  FTP/
        9.  Maths/
       10.  Netfind  <TEL>
       11.  Phone Books and WHOIS Searches/
       12.  Search High-Level Gopher Menu by JUGHEAD at W&L <?>
       13.  users/
```

Ah! Ici le menu pour un Gopher Francais (please don't write to complain about my lousy French). Gophers are now being used worldwide because they offer such a simple way of organizing resources.

You can see that they all offer different data, much of which is based on local interests. You'll also notice that the Gopher entries have different formats. Some end with a / and others end in .. The / indicates that selecting this entry will lead you to another menu of options. The . means that if you select that choice, a file will be accessed using an appropriate utility. For example, if the file is a remote text file, Gopher runs FTP for you and connects to the server the file is on and retrieves it for you.

**Navigator's Note:** These links to ftp are probably the simplest way for novice navigators to transfer files—all the work is done for you! And even for an expert, this makes life a lot easier.

You will also see a third type of ending, <?>. This indicates that the entry leads to an index search server, and if it is selected, you will be asked for a keyword or keywords. Gopher will search for those words and return appropriate information.

Other types of information are available through Gopher. The type characters will have different notations depending on the Gopher client you use. The following table lists the alphanumeric codes for the type characters available through Gopher.

| Normal IDs | Description |
| --- | --- |
| 0 | Item is a file. |
| 1 | Item is a directory. |
| 2 | Item is a CSO (qi) phonebook server. This leads you to a "white pages" type of directory service so that you can find people on the Internet. |
| 3 | Error. |
| 4 | Item is a BinHexed Macintosh file. This will be meaningful to you if you are a Macintosh user. If you don't have a Mac, you probably couldn't care less about these entries. |
| 5 | Item is DOS binary archive of some sort. This includes .ZIP, .ARC, .ZOO, and all the other types of file archive systems available. |
| 6 | Item is a UNIX uuencoded file. These files can be opened by PCs as long as you have a copy of the uudecode utility. |
| 7 | Item is an Index-Search server. The item takes you to a database search. |
| 8 | Item points to a text-based telnet session. |
| 9 | Item is a binary file that is going to be sent to you if you choose this option. You will receive data until the connection closes. This could cause you all sorts of problems unless you're set up to handle the incoming data in a sensible way. Beware. |
| T | A tn3270 connection to a service (requires a screen emulation of an IBM 3270 terminal for your screen to make any sense at all). |

| Experimental IDs | Description |
| --- | --- |
| s | Sound type. The data that you'll get is sound-encoded to a standard called mulaw. |
| g | This is a picture of GIF type. |

*continues*

| Experimental IDs | Description |
| --- | --- |
| M | The item contains data of the MIME type. This is a special format for electronic mail that supports not only text but also sound and even video. |

See the examples later in this chapter for instances of these IDs.

## An Example: Searching for Materials

In our first example, I will go to a library to search for bibliographic materials for the class I will be teaching. I don't need to remember the Internet address of the library I want to telnet to, because it is conveniently stored in Gopher. I just move the arrow on the left of the screen using the cursor keys and select library Catalogs via Telnet/ from the menu.

```
          Internet Gopher Information Client v1.01

                          Libraries

       1.  Electronic Books/
       2.  Electronic Journal collection from CICnet/
       3.  Information from the U.S. Federal Government/
  -->  4.  Library Catalogs via Telnet/
       5.  Library of Congress Records/
       6.  Newspapers, Magazines, and Newsletters/
       7.  Reference Works/



 Press ? for Help, q to Quit, u to go up a menu          Page: 1/1]
```

This library menu gives several options. Electronic books, newspapers, and reference books can be obtained from this menu. The option I want is Library Catalogs via Telnet, so I select it to get this menu:

```
          Internet Gopher Information Client v1.01

                     Library Catalogs via Telnet

       1.  Libraries of the University of Minnesota Integrated Network Access <TEL
       2.  Libraries of the University of Minnesota Integrated Network Access
  -->  3.  Library Catalogs at Other Institutions/
```

Going through Gopherspace may lead us down some strange paths. Here is a screen of menus that I would prefer to bypass. Later, I'll show how that can be done. For now, I select the third item `Library Catalogs at Other Institutions`.

```
     Internet Gopher Information Client v1.01

                         Americas

     1.  Canada/
     2.  Mexico/
     3.  PuertoRico/
-->  4.  United States/
     5.  Venezuela/
```

This Gopher system gives me a listing of countries to select from (see, the Internet really is an international network after all). I select the United States and get a menu which lists all 50 states. I then select Pennsylvania and the University of Pittsburgh. I'm going to teach in Pittsburgh this summer and I want to see if the University of Pittsburgh's library will have the reading materials that I want to use in my course.

```
     Internet Gopher Information Client v1.01

                         Pennsylvania

     19. Lehigh <TEL>
     20. Lehigh.
     21. Pennsylvania State University <TEL>
     22. Pennsylvania State University.
     23. Thomas Jefferson University.
     24. Thomas Jefferson University <TEL>
     25. Tri-College <TEL>
     26. Tri-College (Swarthmore, Bryn Mawr, Haverford).
     27. University of Pennsylvania <TEL>
     28. University of Pennsylvania.
     29. University of Pennsylvania Law School <TEL>
     30. University of Pennsylvania Law School.
     31. University of Pennsylvania Medical School.
     32. University of Pennsylvania Medical School <TEL>
-->  33. University of Pittsburgh.
     34. University of Pittsburgh <TEL>
```

Notice that the University of Pittsburgh has two listings. The first choice, number 33, has a description of the University of Pittsburgh's online library catalog. It also has information about the library collection and how to access it. The second choice of the University of Pittsburgh, number 34, with the <TEL> notation beside it, is the one I want. It will get me connected to the University of Pittsburgh's online library catalog.

I select number 34, and Gopher sends me there (through the Gopher system) without having to remember or type in the University of Pittsburgh's Internet address. Here are the results if you use the two University of Pittsburgh selections. Note that the telnet connection used here is actually a gateway to the University of Pittsburgh. I could also go to Carnegie Mellon University or Pittsburgh's Carnegie Public Library:

```
To exit, hit CTRL+\.

Contacts: <jam2@vms.cis.pitt.edu>

Notes:
        PITTCAT is the University of Pittsburgh's online library catalog.
PITTCAT currently contains bibliographic information for over 1.4 million
titles in all University of Pittsburgh libraries including the Hillman Library
(humanities & social sciences), Afro-American, Buhl (Social Work), East Asian,
Allegheny Observatory, Business, Chemistry, Computer Science, Darlington
Memorial, Engineering, Fine Arts, Langley, Library and Information Science,
Mathematics, Music, Physics, Public and International Affairs/Economics, Falk
Library of the Health Sciences, Learning Resource Center (Nursing), Law,
Western Psychiatric Institute and Clinic, and the regional campus libraries at
Bradford, Greensburg, Johnstown, and Titusville.

--------------------- PittNet Terminal Gateway Services ---------------------

        Service              Description

        CAROLINE     The Carnegie Library of Pittsburgh's on-line library catalog
        CMULIS       Carnegie-Mellon University's on-line library catalog
        CPWSCA       Pittsburgh Supercomputing Center front end A
        CPWSCB       Pittsburgh Supercomputing Center front end B
        CTERM        CCnet hosts via the DECnet (CTERM) protocol
        ISISINFO     Integrated Student Information Services Access
        LAT          DECserver (LAT) services
        PITTCAT      University of Pittsburgh's on-line library catalog
        PSCYMP       Pittsburgh Supercomputing Center Cray Y/MP
        TELNET       Hosts via TCP/IP (TELNET) protocol
        TN3270       Hosts via TCP/IP (TN3270) protocol


Instructions: Type the desired SERVICE name below and press RETURN.

              If a "Password:" prompt appears, the service name you requested
              was invalid or private; press RETURN twice and retry.

Service:
```

This is the beauty of Gopher. It knows the addresses of hundreds of useful resources, and through it I have access to information about the holdings of hundreds of libraries around the world to help me in my studies, research, and business.

# Advanced Gophering

That was straightforward and simple. Now let's look at other services and features of the Gopher program. One of the first things to consider is the concept of Gopherspace. When we select choices that lead us to other Gopher locations, we are moving into Gopherspace—the collection of all choices offered by all Gopher systems.

Gophers point to each other so that local information pointed to by the University of Southwestern Louisiana's Gopher—for example, course curricula and sports events—can also be accessed by other Gophers. This means that you can find information about the local environments of other Gophers by selecting them through the 2. GOPHER System All Other Locations/ on your Gopher menu. On my system, this choice shows me the following:

```
              Internet Gopher Information Client v1.01

                  All the Gopher Servers in the World

   -->  1.  Search Gopherspace using Veronica/
        2.  ACADEME THIS WEEK (Chronicle of Higher Education)/
        3.  ACM SIGGRAPH/
        4.  ACTLab (UT Austin, RTF Dept)/
        5.  Academic Position Network/
        6.  Alamo Community College District/
        7.  American Mathematical Society /
        8.  American Physiological Society/
        9.  Anesthesiology Gopher /
       10.  Appalachian State University (experimental gopher)/
       11.  Apple Computer Higher Education gopher server/
       12.  Arabidopsis Research Companion, Mass Gen Hosp/Harvard/
       13.  Arizona State University Gopher/
       14.  AskERIC - (Educational Resources Information Center)/
       15.  Auburn University test gopher/
       16.  Augusta College/
       17.  Austin Hospital, Melbourne, Australia/
       18.  Australian Defence Force Academy (Canberra)
```

This display indicates a problem that we'll have when we are searching for something. Using the 2. GOPHER System All Other Locations/, I see a listing of 18 Gopher sites, and the list isn't finished. At the time of this writing, a total of 471 Gopher systems are registered around the world (up from 364 in a span of a month). That is the reason that the first choice is 1. Search Gopherspace using Veronica/.

Unless you know specifically which Gopher server you want to access, you'll be much better off using another service, Veronica, to find out where to go (see the following). Browsing the more than 1,300 Gopher sites may be okay (if you have a lot of time on your hands or you want to satisfy your curiosity), but it's not very efficient or effective if you're trying to find data. So let's take a break here and talk about another service that Gopher has links to—Veronica.

> **Navigator's Note:** As of June 5th, 1993, there are over 1,300 registered and unregistered Gophers in the world. Unregistered Gophers are ones which have not yet officially informed the University of Minnesota (the originators of Gopher) of their existence. Of those 1,300 Gophers, only 520 are actually registered. Registration doesn't really matter other than the fact that you can't get to the unregistered ones through the University of Minnesota and they may therefore be hard to find.

# Veronica

Veronica, short for Very Easy Rodent-Oriented Net-wide Index to Computerized Archives, was developed to solve the problem that we just discussed—with so much information available on so many machines, how do I know which one has the information I need?

Veronica helps to solve this problem by making a keyword search of most menus on most of the Gopher servers in Gopherspace. Hundreds of Gopher server menus are canvassed to create an index much as Archie does when it creates the database of files and directories from anonymous FTP sites (see Chapter 6, "Finding Files: Archie"). The reason that I say "most menus on most Gopher servers" is that some Gophers can ask to be excluded from Gopherspace.

Developed at the University of Nevada, Veronica is used exclusively with Gopher as an enhancement that helps you find information more effectively. Veronica allows you to search the database it constructs from all Gopher menus it can access. It returns a menu of choices to you gathered from all sites that have menu choices containing the keywords. When you select a choice from a Veronica-created menu, you are automatically sent to the Gopher server that the choice came from.

The Veronica database is updated every two weeks. It will most likely be updated more frequently in the future.

> **Navigator's Note:** Not everything will work as you zoom around in Gopherspace. Downed machines and forbidden machines are two major stumbling blocks. Occasionally, incompatibilities will also make menu items misbehave when they're selected.

When I select search Gopherspace using Veronica, I receive the following screen:

```
        Internet Gopher Information Client v1.01

                Search Gopherspace using Veronica

 --> 1.  Search gopherspace using veronica at CNIDR <?>
     2.  Search gopherspace for GOPHER DIRECTORIES  (CNIDR) <?>
     3.  Search gopherspace using veronica at NYSERNet <?>
     4.  Search gopherspace for GOPHER DIRECTORIES  (NYSERNet) <?>
     5.  Search gopherspace using veronica at UNR <?>
     6.  Search gopherspace for GOPHER DIRECTORIES  (UNR) <?>
     7.                                                      .
     8.  How to compose "simple boolean" veronica queries ( NEW May 19 ).
     9.  FAQ:  Frequently-Asked Questions about veronica  (1993/05/15).
    10.  Setting up a veronica server:  new code available .
    11.  NEW_FEATURE:__Search_by_Gopher_type.
    12.  Older_veronica_documentation/
```

This screen lists three Veronica servers that the public can use to search for information stored by Gophers around the world. The servers are divided into two parts. One is Gopherspace generic and the second is Gopherspace for *Gopher directories*. The difference is that Gopher directories will search only the directories of Gophers and will return only directories. The generic search will return not only directories but also information stored in the Gopher indexed servers, which could be text files, binary files, sound files, telnet connections, and all the other different items Gopher can access.

Maybe an example will elucidate. Selecting 4. Search Gopherspace for GOPHER DIRECTORIES (NYSERNet) <?> and using the keyword commerce, Veronica returns the following screen:

```
Internet Gopher Information Client v1.01

    Search gopherspace for GOPHER DIRECTORIES   (NYSERNet): commerce

-->  1.  HF   Commerce/
     2.  381   Internal commerce/
     3.  380   Commerce, communications, transportation/
     4.  382   International commerce (Foreign trade)/
     5.  382.1 Generalities of international commerce/
     6.  Commerce / Management / Law Reading Room/
     7.  Commerce  (Restricted Access)/
     8.  Department-of-Commerce/
     9.  Department of Commerce/
     10. Commerce to Statistics/
     11. Faculty of Commerce (organizationalUnit)/
     12. Faculty of Commerce (organizationalUnit)/
     13. Commerce (organizationalUnit)/
     14. Faculty of Economics and Commerce (organizationalUnit)/
     15. Faculty of Commerce and Administration (organizationalUnit)/
     16. FACULTY OF ECONOMICS AND COMMERCE (organizationalUnit)/
     17. Economics, Commerce and Management, Faculty of (organizationalUni/
     18. Faculty of Economics and Commerce Office (organizationalUnit)/
```

The / at the end of each line means that these are directory listings and each item has further menus beneath it. In the bottom right corner, we can tell that two pages of information are available.

If we search for the word commerce using the menu item 3. Search Gopherspace using veronica at NYSERNet <?>, the results of the search will show the differences in the two search databases.

```
Internet Gopher Information Client v1.01

     Search gopherspace using veronica at NYSERNet: commerce

-->  1.  HF   Commerce/
     2.  Commerce Business Daily Available Online.
     3.  The Commerce Business Daily publishes, for Federal agencies, syno.
     4.  58 FR 4736:Commerce in Explosives; List of Explosive Materials.
     5.  58 FR 21925:Revisions to the Commerce Control List: Equipment Rel.
     6.  58 FR 9183:Commerce Bancshares, Inc; Formations of; Acquisitions .
     7.  58 FR 6574:Administrative Exceptions and Favorable Consideration .
     8.  58 FR 3800:Economic Development Assistance Programs as Described .
     9.  REPORT TO NEW ZEALAND CHAMBERS OF COMMERCE.
     10. COMMERCE AT OTAGO, 1912-1987.  ABRIDGED ED..
     11. Ships of commerce: liners, tankers, freighters, tu.
     12. 381   Internal commerce/
     13. 380   Commerce, communications, transportation/
```

```
14. 382  International commerce (Foreign trade)/
15. THE COMMERCE ACT 1975.
16. 382.1  Generalities of international commerce/
17. C.  H.B. Commerce - Year 3.
18. D.  H.B. Commerce - Year 4.
```

Seven pages of information are returned, representing not only directories, as noted by the /, but also text files set off with the . at the end of the line. The reason is that the search extended beyond Gopher directories and searched indexed Gophers that include text and other files.

Here's another example. I'm interested in what is in Gopherspace concerning Acquired Immunodeficiency Syndrome, or AIDS. I'll search both the Gopher directories and the general Gopher. Here are the results:

```
     Internet Gopher Information Client v1.01

         Search gopherspace for GOPHER DIRECTORIES   (NYSERNet): aids

 --> 1.  AIDS News/
     2.  AIDS Alert/
     3.  Stanford Financial Aids Student Employment (to post jobs)/
     4.  University of Delaware Library Special Collections Finding Aids/
     5.  REFERENCE   Library Reference Questions/Aids/
     6.  CDC AIDS Statistics, other useful info/
     7.  Veterans Administration AIDS Information Newsletter/
     8.  AIDS Related Information/
     9.  National Commission on AIDS/
     10. National AIDS Info Clearinghouse/
     11. Humanities Research Center - finding aids for manuscripts/
     12. Aids Alert/
     13. Consultant Aids/
     14. Audio-Visual Aids & Cassettes/
     15. AIDS Information System for 3rd World/
     16. Human Retrovirus & AIDS (HIV) Rel.3.0; May 1992/
     17. aids/
     18. Curing.Aids/
```

Let's check out item number 1, AIDS News/:

```
     Internet Gopher Information Client v1.01

         Search gopherspace using veronica at NYSERNet: aids

 --> 1.  Also Seen:  Grmek, Mirko, History of Aids (L. Pearcy) .
     2.  AIDS News/
```

```
 3.  AIDS Alert/
 4.  aids.txt.
 5.  BAD-Pamphlet-AIDS.
 6.  About Special Collections Finding Aids.
 7.  Financial Aids Office.
 8.  58 FR 17164:Housing Opportunities for Persons With AIDS; Correcti.
 9.  58 FR 26684:Indirect Food Additives: Adjuvants, Production Aids, .
10.  58 FR 17514:Indirect Food Additives: Adjuvants, Production Aids, .
11.  58 FR 17512:Indirect Food Additives: Adjuvants, Production Aids, .
12.  58 FR 6127:Housing Opportunities for Persons with AIDS Program; A.
13.  58 FR 5410:Announcement of Allocations for Housing Opportunities .
14.  58 FR 17595:Pediatric Acquired Immune Deficiency Syndrome (AIDS);.
15.  58 FR 17512:Indirect Food Additives: Adjuvants, Production Aids, .
16.  58 FR 3962:National Institute of Allergy and Infectious Diseases;.
17.  a Audio RX Hearing Aids; Proposed Consent Agreement With Analysis.
18.  ..AIDS Epidemic: Meeting.
```

Searching the Gopher directories gives me 2 pages of information, while searching all of Gopherspace gives me 21 pages of information. Not all the information retrieved will be relevant: the last example had information on "hearing aids" and "financial aid," which may not have anything to do with Acquired Immunodeficiency Syndrome.

The searching of Gopher directories can be a powerful tool in finding information throughout the Internet. As with the two examples, if the search is kept simple, you may find some interesting directories in Gopherspace that you can then explore to find additional information. You can also save the directories that you find interesting into your own personal Gopher menu for future references (a bookmark—more on that later).

Searching Gopherspace in general will bring you not only directories, but information in the form of text and other files. It is more comprehensive, and because of that you may want to be more specific in your searching of Gopherspace.

Veronica enables Boolean searching. That is, you can expand your search by adding additional phrases with an or in your keyword search. I can get additional directories to our earlier example by searching for commerce or business.

```
                  Internet Gopher Information Client v1.01


  Search gopherspace for GOPHER DIRECTORIES   (NYSERNet): commerce or business


  -->  1.  HF  Commerce/
       2.  business/
       3.  business-news/
       4.  Business and Finance (APM A8.010-A8.852)/
       5.  Business Affairs Circulars (Computers)/
```

```
   6.  381   Internal commerce/
   7.  380   Commerce, communications, transportation/
   8.  382   International commerce (Foreign trade)/
   9.  382.1  Generalities of international commerce/
  10.  School of Business Admin/
  11.  Israel_Business_Today/
  12.  Center for International Business Education and Research/
  13.  College of Business and Economics/
  14.  CBE     College of Business & Economics Speakers/
  15.  Business/
  16.  Business/
  17.  Korean Business and Management/
  18.  Asia Pacific Business & Marketing Resources/
```

On the other hand, if I want to limit my search on AIDS, I can use the Boolean operator and and search for AIDS and research. This will retrieve items with both words in them and possibly get me material on research of Acquired Immunodeficiency Syndrome. This is particularly useful if you know that both words will appear in the title of the directory or in the text of an indexed file.

```
     Internet Gopher Information Client v1.01

        Search gopherspace using veronica at CNIDR: aids and research

 -->  1.  58 FR 3962:National Institute of Allergy and Infectious Diseases;.
      2.  Humanities Research Center - finding aids for manuscripts/
      3.  PA-92-52 INTERNATIONAL AIDS EPIDEMIOLOGY RESEARCH.
      4.  PA-93-013 NIH LOAN REPAYMENT PROGRAM FOR AIDS RESEARCH.
      5.  PA-93-055 NIH LOAN REPAYMENT PROGRAM FOR AIDS RESEARCH.
      6.  P2: PA-92-52 INTERNATIONAL AIDS EPIDEMIOLOGY RESEARCH.
      7.  P2: PA-93-013 NIH LOAN REPAYMENT PROGRAM FOR AIDS RESEARCH.
      8.  NIH-NHLBI-HB-92-01 MAINTENANCE OF CHIMPANZEES FOR HEPATITIS OR AI.
      9.  P1: PA-93-055 NIH LOAN REPAYMENT PROGRAM FOR AIDS RESEARCH.
     10.  R14: NIH-NHLBI-HB-92-01 MAINTENANCE OF CHIMPANZEES FOR HEPATITIS .
     11.  PA-91-95 INDIVIDUAL NATIONAL RESEARCH SERVICE AWARDS IN ALLERGY, .
     12.  P1: PA-91-95 INDIVIDUAL NATIONAL RESEARCH SERVICE AWARDS IN ALLER.
```

The Boolean operator not is not supported as of this writing, but you can specify what type of data or Gopher object is returned in your search.

This is useful if you receive many items from your Gopher search that are not relevant or useful for your needs. For example, I've found that many of the telnet sites that I retrieve in my searches require the use of a login and password for access. I did not have that information. I can specify the Gopher object I want by the -t flag when I do my search.

For example, using `aids -t01` will return links to Gopher files and directories with the word `aids` in the title (the `0` equals a file and the `1` equals a directory). Using `-t8 business or commerce` will return only telnet links with the words business or commerce in the title. The `-t` flag may appear anywhere in the keyword search.

In general, when searching Veronica, you will want to use a general search rather than a specific search until you know that what you want will be retrieved by a specific search.

You may want unemployment statistics, yet searching by the two words will net you only one Gopher link. That is because Veronica does not have a subject index, and the words statistics and unemployment must appear in the title or be indexed in an indexed Gopher. Using the single word `unemployment` will retrieve many irrelevant Gopher links, but it will also get you additional unemployment statistics that may meet your information needs.

# Help

Any time you're in the UNIX Curses Gopher, you can use ? to get help.

```
                    Quick Gopher Help
                    -----------------


Moving around Gopherspace
-------------------------
Use the Arrow Keys or vi/emacs equivalent to move around
Up                   :  Move to previous line.
Down                 :  Move to next line.
Right Return         :  "Enter" current item.
Left, u              :  "Exit" current item.
>, +, Pgdn, space    :  View next page.
<, -, Pgup, b        :  View previous page.
0-9                  :  Go to a specific line.
m                    :  Go back to the main menu.


Bookmarks
---------
a : Add current item to the bookmark list.
A : Add current directory/search to bookmark list.
v : View bookmark list.
d : Delete a bookmark.


Other commands
--------------
q : Quit with prompt.
Q : Quit unconditionally.
```

```
= : Display Technical information about current item.
o : Change options.

The Gopher development team hopes that you find this software useful.
If you find what you think is a bug, please report it to us by sending
e-mail to "Gopher@boombox.micro.umn.edu."
```

This gives you the options for moving about in Gopher and tells you how to create a bookmark and other commands.

# Gopher Tracks

Gopher is so easy to use that you'll probably soon be using it as one of your key Internet navigation tools. As you start to know where you want to go for specific data, you'll get tired of having to select various menus to get to choices that eventually get you to where you want to be. Rather than have to repeat this chain of choices every time, you can set bookmarks.

Bookmarks enable you to tailor a menu screen with selections of your own choosing. Every time you get to a screen and place the pointer on a line that you want to add to your bookmark, you just type the letter *a* and Gopher will add it to your bookmark.

After you have added your favorite Gopher choices to your bookmark, all you need to do is press the letter *v*, and your very own private Gopher menu will appear. You can add choices to it from any level in Gopherspace, and the choices can include any type of service: telnet, search, text file, and so on. Bookmarks are very convenient and will help you greatly in your navigation.

Here is a sample bookmark:

```
    Internet Gopher Information Client v1.01

                     Bookmarks

 -->  1.  ACADEME THIS WEEK (Chronicle of Higher Education)/
       2.  veronica search at UNR <?>
       3.  University of Pittsburgh <TEL>
       4.  Search CIA World Fact Book 1991 <?>
       5.  Search Roget's 1911 Thesaurus <?>
       6.  WAIS Based Information/
       7.  directory-of-servers.src <?>
       8.  All the Gopher Servers in the World/
       9.  EDUCOM Documents and News/
```

```
10. InterNIC: Internet Network Information Center/
11. White House Papers/
12. National Science Foundation Gopher (STIS)/
13. CARL - Journal Articles Database & FAX Service <TEL>
14. Library administration/
15. Professional fields/
16. Library science/
17. Search gopherspace using veronica at NYSERNet <?>
18. Search gopherspacefor GOPHER DIRECTORIES(NYSERNet) <?>
```

With the bookmark facility, our AIDS researcher can build a Gopher menu that will meet his needs immediately on entering Gopher. A librarian that has clients in the business and commerce community will keep the bookmark handy with the directories pointing to those Gophers in Gopherspace that deal with that topic.

# Gopher Guidelines

As you can see, Gopher and Veronica are useful tools to the Internet Navigator. They offer a powerful means of getting to the data you're interested in, but a little caution and planning are required to get the best out of them.

In most cases, you'll need to start off using Veronica for a general search and weed out irrelevant data to get to the material you need. Only after you are sure that limiting the search will get relevant material should you use specific searches. A subject index of all the materials available through Gopher would be nice, but until that happens Veronica is your best bet.

Keep in mind that Veronica searches on keywords and that you may need to use several synonyms to get all pertinent materials. Business, commerce, mercantile, industry, trade, enterprise, and other words may all get information that you are looking for.

Gopher may also give you information that you may not be able to use because it has restrictions or is of little value. Many telnet links in Gopherspace are restricted because they lead to commercial databases that are limited to registered users.

Many Gopher types may not be suitable for your system. You may not be able to get a sound file or a BinHexed Mac file. On the other hand, using the equal sign (=) gives you technical information on the item and may come in handy for you to get the item at a later date with the right equipment to use the item.

Use the -t flag to get documents that are relevant to your needs. The following example limits the search to only databases that I can telnet to with information on AIDS. (If the database is available for public searching, as the databases in the example are, Gopher will tell you how to log in to the database.)

```
         Internet Gopher Information Client v1.01

              Search gopherspace using veronica at CNIDR: aids -t8

 --> 1.  CHAT (AIDS Database) <TEL>
     2.  FDA bbs- Aids Info, consumer info <TEL>
     3.  S.E. Florida AIDS Info Network <TEL>
     4.  FDA BBS - News releases, AIDS info, consumer info... <TEL>
     5.  FDA BBS - News releases, Aids info, consumer info... <TEL>
     6.  Interactive AIDS document and simulated conversation (CHAT) <TEL>
     7.  CHAT - Interactive AIDS document and simulated conversation <TEL>
```

Because Gopher searches Gopherspace on the Internet, it will run into standard Internet problems. Faults with machines on the network or troubles with network links and nodes, heavy usage, and many other communication hazards can cause connections to fail. At times, the Veronica servers will be in heavy use and you will not be able to use them, and at times Gopher connection will fail. Again, usage during off-peak hours will improve connections, but don't be surprised if something doesn't work when it has worked in the past. Try later and you may get a connection.

Remember that Gopher indexing is not consistent. The way one Internet site indexes its section of Gopherspace may seem very eccentric to you but extremely logical to that site.

# Gopher's Future

Gopher's popularity has paralleled the tremendous growth of Gopher users on the Internet. Gopher is an easy-to-use menu-driven program that integrates many of the features of the Internet, such as FTP, telnet, WAIS, and e-mail, and makes them easy for the user to manage.

The simplicity of Gopher is appealing to new Internet users, and in combination with Veronica, Gopher becomes a powerful research tool. Improvements are being developed to make Veronica searching more powerful and Gopher item retrieval more reliable.

The most exciting of the changes to Gopherspace is the introduction of Gopher+ (pronounced *gopher plus*). This will be just like the gopher you've grown to know and love but much more flexible and sophisticated. For example, when you select an item that leads to the downloading of a file, Gopher+ could have a script attached to that item that tells you the size of the file and asks you if you really want to download it.

With the improvements proposed with Gopher+, Gopher will continue to be one of the most popular and useful Internet navigating tools.

# GLOBAL HYPERTEXT: THE WORLD-WIDE WEB

Although Gopher is a powerful system for navigating the Internet, there is, as they say, more than one way to cut a pie (I was going to say "skin a cat," but then one of my cats came and sat on my lap and I felt guilty). Proceeding with our metaphor, the cat...oops, the pie, the problem is how to provide a framework to navigate around many different data items on many different computers. The knife that addresses this problem in Chapter 8, "Navigating by Menus: Gopher," is Gopher.

Another knife is the World-Wide Web, otherwise known as WWW or just "the Web." This service uses a different metaphor from the Gopher system. Gopher is a hierarchical menu structure: menu items lead to other menu items or to a service. WWW's model is to treat all the Internet's data as hypertext.

**Navigator's Note:** "Just what is hypertext?" you may be asking. Imagine a book—say, this book. With a hypertext version, you could follow a reference from any keyword (a word that the author or an editor considers important), such as Gopher in the last paragraph, to another piece of information—for example, the start of Chapter 8. This piece of information could, in turn, have further keywords. The idea is to have links between different parts of the document, to enable the information to be explored interactively rather than just in a linear fashion.

Under WWW, all information is arranged in documents with hypertext keywords scattered throughout. All hypertext keywords are followed by a number in square brackets. For example, the sentence Now is the winter [1] of our discount [2] tents has two keywords, winter and discount. A document may be more than a single screen in length, so WWW allows you to move up and down screens.

To select a hypertext keyword and follow it to whatever it's associated with, enter the keyword's number and press Enter. In WWW, selecting a keyword (also called a hypertext link or just a link) moves you to another document that could be on the same or a different computer or connects you to a service such as telnet or FTP.

The main site for WWW is nxoc01.cern.ch (note that the *ch* means that the computer is in Switzerland—you're globe-trotting again…"Bring me more caviar, waiter, and tell the press that I'll give them a photo opportunity at twelve."). You need to telnet to this system, where you'll be automatically logged in. The opening screen looks like this:

```
coyote% telnet nxoc01.cern.ch

CERN Information Service
(ttyp0 on nxoc01)
                                            Overview of the Web (23/27)
                       GENERAL OVERVIEW

   There is no "top" to the World-Wide Web. You can look at it from many points
   of view. If you have no other bias, here are some places to start:

  by Subject[1]          A classification by subject of interest. Incomplete
                         but easiest to use.

  by Type[2]             Looking by type of service (access protocol, etc) may
                         allow you to find things if you know what you are looking
                         for.
```

```
   About WWW[3]                 About the World-Wide Web global information sharing
                                project.

Starting somewhere else

   To use a different default page, perhaps one representing your field of
   interest, see  "customizing your home page"[4].

What happened to CERN?

1-6, Up, <RETURN> for more, Quit, or Help: 2
```

# Help

As you can see, the opening page of WWW is sprinkled with hypertext links. The bottom line tells you that this document has six links (1-6). Only four are visible, so the others are on the following pages of the document. If this was the only page, the option <RETURN> (meaning to press the Enter key) wouldn't be displayed. Up takes you to the previous page of the document (if one exists), Quit does what it says and leaves WWW. If you enter H for Help, you get

```
WWW LineMode Browser version 1.4a (WWWLib 1.1a)    COMMANDS AVAILABLE

You are reading a document whose address is
    'file://a.cs.uiuc.edu/pub/Catalog'


   <RETURN>          Move down one page within the document.
   Bottom            Go to the last page of the document.
   Top               Return to the first page of the document.
   Up                Move up one page within the document.
   Recall            List visited documents.
   Recall <number>   Return to a previously visited document
                     as numbered in the recall list.
   Home              Return to the starting document.
   Back              Move back to the last document.
   Next              Take next link from last document.
   Previous          Take previous link from last document.
   Go address        Go to document of given [relative] address.
   Verbose           Switch to verbose mode.
   Help              Display this page.
   Manual            Jump to the online manual for this program.
   Quit              Leave the www program.

Back, Up, <RETURN> for more, Quit, or Help:
```

# Browsing by Type

Use B for Back to return to the previous screen. Take a look at the second hypertext link, Type:

```
                                    Data sources classified by access protocol
                      DATA SOURCES CLASSIFIED BY TYPE OF SERVICE

    See also categorization exist by subject[1].

    World-Wide Web[2]        List of W3 servers. See also: about the WWW
                             initiative[3].

    WAIS[4]                  Find WAIS index servers using the directory of
                             servers[5], or lists by name[6] or domain[7]. See
                             also: about WAIS[8].

    Network News[9]          Available directly in all www browsers.

    Gopher[10]               Campus-wide information systems, etc, listed
                             geographically. See also: about Gopher[11].

    Telnet access[12]        Hypertext  catalogues by Peter Scott. See also: list
                             by Scott Yanoff[13]. Also, Art St George's index[14]
                             (yet to be hyperized) etc.

    VAX/VMS HELP[15]         Available using the help gateway[16] to WWW.

1-25, Back, Up, <RETURN> for more, Quit, or Help: 3
```

This document has 25 links. Your options include Back, which takes you back to the last document you were looking at. Select the third link for about the WWW initiative:

```
                                          The World-Wide Web project
                      WORLD-WIDE WEB

    The World-Wide Web (W3) is a wide-area hypermedia[1] information retrieval
    initiative aiming to give universal access to a large universe of documents.

    Everything there is online about W3 is linked directly or indirectly to this
    document, including an executive summary[2] of the project, an illustrated
    talk[3], Mailing lists[4], Policy[5] and Conditions[6], May's W3 news[7],
    Frequently Asked Questions[8].

    What's out there?[9]     Pointers to the world's online information,
                             subjects[10], W3 servers[11], etc.
```

```
    Software Products[12]    What there is and how to get it: clients, servers and
                             tools.

    Technical[13]            Details of protocols, formats, program internals etc.

    Bibliography[14]         Paper documentation on W3 and references. Also:
                             manuals[15].

    People[16]               A list of some people involved in the project.
1-20, Back, Up, <RETURN> for more, Quit, or Help: 1
```

# Hypermedia Explanation

Great! Let's see how hypertext, or hypermedia as WWW refers to it, is explained…

```
                                                        What is Hypertext?
                        WHAT IS HYPERTEXT

    Hypertext is text which is not constrained to be linear.

    Hypertext is text which contains links[1] to other texts. The term was
    coined by Ted Nelson[2] around 1965 (see History[3]).

    HyperMedia is a term used for hypertext which is not constrained to be text:
    it can include graphics, video and sound[4], for example. Apparently Ted
    Nelson was the first to use this term too.

    Hypertext and HyperMedia are concepts, not products.

    See also:

        A list of terms[5] used in hypertext literature.

        Conferences[6]

        Commercial (and academic) products[7]

        A newsgroup on hypertext, "alt.hypertext"[8].
1-10, Back, Up, <RETURN> for more, Quit or Help: Back


                                                  What is Hypertext? (30/29)
    HyperMedia is a term used for hypertext which is not constrained to be text:
    it can include graphics, video and sound[4], for example. Apparently Ted
    Nelson was the first to use this term too.
```

```
    Hypertext and HyperMedia are concepts, not products.

    See also:

       A list of terms[5] used in hypertext literature.

       Conferences[6]

       Commercial (and academic) products[7]

       A newsgroup on hypertext, "alt.hypertext"[8].

       World-Wide Web is a project[9]  which uses hypertext concepts.

       Standards[10].


       [End]
    1-10, Back, Up, Quit, or Help:
```

As you can see, lots of information is available, and the linkages make it a very rich system to use. It gives you the ability to follow a chain of interrelated ideas. Getting sidetracked is a real danger.

## Searching for BEMs

Recently I read a USENET News message about astronomy that referred to the search for "BEMs." I have no idea what BEMs are, so I'll try WWW to find out. Starting at the "General Overview" document, a likely route is to search by subject, which is link [1]. So I type 1 and press Enter.

```
                                              Overview of the Web (23/27)
                            GENERAL OVERVIEW

    There is no "top" to the World-Wide Web. You can look at it from many points
    of view. If you have no other bias, here are some places to start:

    by Subject[1]           A classification by subject of interest. Incomplete
                            but easiest to use.

    by Type[2]              Looking by type of service (access protocol, etc) may
                            allow you to find things if you know what you are looking
                            for.

    About WWW[3]            About the World-Wide Web global information sharing
                            project.
```

```
Starting somewhere else

   To use a different default page, perhaps one representing your field of
   interest, see  "customizing your home page"[4].

What happened to CERN?

1-6, Up, <RETURN> for more, Quit, or Help: 1
```

I choose link 1 because I know that what I'm looking for is connected with the subject of astronomy.

```
                         The World-Wide Web Virtual Library: Subject Catalogue
                              INFORMATION BY SUBJECT

   See also arrangement  by  service type[1]. Mail www-request@info.cern.ch if
   you know of online information not in these lists....

Aeronautics              Mailing list archive index[2].

Agriculture[3]           Separate list, see also Almanac mail servers[4].

Astronomy and Astrophysics
                         Abstract Indexes[5] at NASA,   Astrophysics work at
                         FNAL[6] and Princeton's[7] Sloane Digital Sky Survey.
                         See also: space[8].

Bio Sciences[9]          Separate list.

Computing[10]            Separate list.

Engineering[11]          Separate list.

Environment[12]          Separate list.

1-39, Back, Up, <RETURN> for more, Quit, or Help: 8
```

The space link, 8, looks the most promising...

```
                                                       Overview — Space
                              SPACE

   Under construction.  Omissions please to roeber@cern.ch

Answers to Frequently Asked Questions on sci.space[1]
NASA Ames Research Center archives[2]
```

```
NASA Astrophysical Data System user guide[3]
NASA JPL FTP archive[4]
NASA Langley techreports (directory)[5]
NASA Langley techreports (searchable)[6]
NASA Spacelink (interactive session)[7]
National Space Science Data Center Online Data and Information Service
(interactive session)[8]
Space Telescope Science Institute electronic information service[9]
Space Telescope European Coordination Facility star catalog database
(interactive session)[10]
Voyager, Hubble, and other images[11]
Yale Bright Star Catalog[12]
Orbital Element Sets: NASA, TVRO, Shuttle[13]
Orbital Element Sets: NASA, TVRO, Molczan, CelBBS, Shuttle[14]
Orbital Element Sets: NASA, Molczan[15]
Back issues of the Electronic Journal of the Astronomical Society of the
1-29, Back, Up, <RETURN> for more, Quit, or Help:
```

Nope, nothing yet; I hit Enter:

```
                                           Overview — Space (40/40)
Yale Bright Star Catalog[12]
Orbital Element Sets: NASA, TVRO, Shuttle[13]
Orbital Element Sets: NASA, TVRO, Molczan, CelBBS, Shuttle[14]
Orbital Element Sets: NASA, Molczan[15]
Back issues of the Electronic Journal of the Astronomical Society of the
Atlantic[16]
NASA Headline News[17]
NASA Extragalactic Database[18]
National Oceanic and Atmospheric Administration database[19]
Vincent Cate's list of companies related to the space industry[20]
Skywatch[21]
Frequently Seen Acronyms[22]
Daily Ionospheric Reports[23]
Delta Clipper images[24]
Space Digest archives[25]
Space Tech archives[26]
Lunar and Planetary Institute BBS (interactive)[27]
USGS Global Land Information System BBS (interactive)[28]


                                                          fgmr[29]


1-29, Back, Up, Quit, or Help: 22
```

Aha! Number 22, "Frequently Seen Acronyms" sounds right. I select it.

```
Path: senator-bedfellow.mit.edu!enterpoop.mit.edu!pad-thai.aktis.com!pad-thai.a
ktis.com!not-for-mail
From: bradfrd2@ncar.ucar.edu (Mark Bradford)
Newsgroups: sci.astro,sci.space,sci.space.shuttle,news.answers
Subject: Astro/Space Frequently Seen Acronyms
Supersedes: <space/acronyms_736574404@GZA.COM>
Followup-To: poster
Date: 4 Jun 1993 00:00:07 -0400
Organization: LifeForms Unlimited, Cephalopods
Lines: 509
Sender: faqserv@GZA.COM
Approved: news-answers-request@MIT.Edu
Expires: 18 Jul 1993 04:00:05 GMT
Message-ID: <space/acronyms_739166405@GZA.COM>
NNTP-Posting-Host: pad-thai.aktis.com
Keywords: long space astro tla acronyms
X-Last-Updated: 1992/12/07
Xref: senator-bedfellow.mit.edu sci.astro:36760 sci.space:63666 sci.space.shutt
le:13300 news.answers:9045


Archive-name: space/acronyms
Edition: 8

Back, Up, <RETURN> for more, Quit, or Help:
Acronym List for sci.astro, sci.space, and sci.space.shuttle:
Edition 8, 1992 Dec 7
Last posted: 1992 Aug 27

This list is offered as a reference for translating commonly appearing
acronyms in the space-related newsgroups.  If I forgot or botched your
favorite acronym, please let me know!  Also, if there's an acronym *not*
on this list that confuses you, drop me a line, and if I can figure
it out, I'll add it to the list.

Note that this is intended to be a reference for *frequently seen*
acronyms, and is most emphatically *not* encyclopedic.  If I incorporated
every acronym I ever saw, I'd soon run out of disk space!  :-)

The list will be posted at regular intervals, every 30 days.  All
comments regarding it are welcome; I'm reachable as bradfrd2@ncar.ucar.edu.

Note that this just tells what the acronyms stand for — you're on your
own for figuring out what they *mean*!  Note also that the total number of
acronyms in use far exceeds what I can list; special-purpose acronyms that
are essentially always explained as they're introduced are omitted.
Further, some acronyms stand for more than one thing; as of Edition 3 of
the list, these acronyms appear on multiple lines, unless they're simply
Back, Up, <RETURN> for more, Quit, or Help:
the list, these acronyms appear on multiple lines, unless they're simply
different ways of referring to the same thing.
```

```
Thanks to everybody who's sent suggestions since the first version of
the list, and especially to Garrett A. Wollman (wollman@griffin.uvm.edu),
who is maintaining an independent list, somewhat more verbose in
character than mine, and to Daniel Fischer (dfi@specklec.mpifr-bonn.mpg.de),
who is maintaining a truly HUGE list (535 at last count) of acronyms and
terms, mostly in German (which I read, fortunately).

Special thanks this time to Ken Hollis at NASA, who sent me a copy of NASA
Reference Publication 1059 Revised: _Space Transportation System and
Associated Payloads: Glossary, Acronyms, and Abbreviations_, a truly
mammoth tome — almost 300 pages of TLAs.

Special Bonus!  At the end of this posting, you will find a perl program
written by none other than Larry Wall, whose purpose is to scramble the
acronym list in an entertaining fashion.  Thanks, Larry!

A&A: Astronomy and Astrophysics
AAO: Anglo-Australian Observatory
AAS: American Astronomical Society
AAS: American Astronautical Society
Back, Up, <RETURN> for more, Quit, or Help:
```

"And I'd like to thank my mother and father, the pope, the Four Tops, my cat…"
Seriously, this kind of collection is invaluable, and the keepers of these glossaries
should be encouraged and applauded. So let's see if "BEMs" are in the list. (I'm
just grateful I wasn't looking for something that started with Z—it's a long list.)

```
AAS: American Astronautical Society
AAVSO: American Association of Variable Star Observers
ACE: Advanced Composition Explorer
ACRV: Assured Crew Return Vehicle (or) Astronaut Crew Rescue Vehicle
ADFRF: Ames-Dryden Flight Research Facility (was DFRF) (NASA)
AGN: Active Galactic Nucleus
AGU: American Geophysical Union
AIAA: American Institute of Aeronautics and Astronautics
AIPS: Astronomical Image Processing System
AJ: Astronomical Journal
ALEXIS: Array of Low Energy X-ray Imaging Sensors
ALPO: Association of Lunar and Planetary Observers
ALS: Advanced Launch System
ANSI: American National Standards Institute
AOA: Abort Once Around (Shuttle abort plan)
AOCS: Attitude and Orbit Control System
Ap.J: Astrophysical Journal
APM: Attached Pressurized Module (a.k.a. Columbus)
APU: Auxiliary Power Unit
ARC: Ames Research Center (NASA)
```

```
ARTEMIS: Advanced Relay TEchnology MISsion
ASA: Astronomical Society of the Atlantic
ASI: Agenzia Spaziale Italiano
Back, Up, <RETURN> for more, Quit, or Help:
ASI: Agenzia Spaziale Italiano
ASRM: Advanced Solid Rocket Motor
ATDRS: Advanced Tracking and Data Relay Satellite
ATLAS: Atmospheric Laboratory for Applications and Science
ATM: Amateur Telescope Maker
ATO: Abort To Orbit (Shuttle abort plan)
AU: Astronomical Unit
AURA: Association of Universities for Research in Astronomy
AW&ST: Aviation Week and Space Technology (a.k.a. AvLeak)
AXAF: Advanced X-ray Astrophysics Facility
BATSE: Burst And Transient Source Experiment (on CGRO)
BBXRT: Broad-Band X-Ray Telescope (ASTRO package)
BEM: Bug-Eyed Monster
BH: Black Hole
BIMA: Berkeley Illinois Maryland Array
BNSC: British National Space Centre
BTW: By The Way
C&T: Communications & Tracking
CCAFS: Cape Canaveral Air Force Station
CCD: Charge-Coupled Device
CCDS: Centers for the Commercial Development of Space
CD-ROM: Compact Disk Read-Only Memory
CFA: Center For Astrophysics
Back, Up, <RETURN> for more, Quit, or Help:
```

Ta-da! "BEM: Bug-Eyed Monster"—I should have guessed! These astronomers and astrophysicists are wild and crazy guys.

# WAIS Looks Good

Notice that we went from browsing a hypertext document to listing a file. The transition was pretty clean, what's called "transparent" because the change wasn't really noticeable. This is an important feature of WWW—it tries to give everything it covers a consistent look. For example, the subject list includes

```
Reference            Roget's Thesaurus[33]. Experimental English
                     dictionary[34].
```

Choosing link 33, you find that you've selected a WAIS server!

```
                                          roget-thesaurus index
                      ROGET-THESAURUS

Server created with WAIS release 8 b3.1 on Dec 11 14:34:55 1991 by emv@cedar.ci
c.net
The files of type para used in the index were:
   /u3/wais/mirror/etext/roget10.txt

Roget's Thesaurus is provided by Project Gutenberg.  Here's a sample
entry.  This database is also available in the 'Gopher' system at
Gopher.micro.umn.edu, and for anonymous FTP from
        mrcnext.cso.uiuc.edu:/pub/etext/
For more information on Project Gutenberg, see the usenet newsgroup
'bit.listserv.gutnberg'; there's information about it in the 'mailing-lists'
WAIS server.

    #86. List. — N. list, catalog, catalogue, inventory, schedule;
register &c. (record) 551; account; bill, bill of costs; syllabus; terrier,
tally, file; calendar, index, table, atlas, contents; book, ledger;
synopsis, catalogue raisonne; tableau; invoice, bill of lading; prospectus,
program, programme; bill of fare, menu, carte; score, census, statistics,
returns; Red book, Blue book, Domesday book; cadastre; directory, gazetteer.
almanac; army list, clergy list, civil service list, navy list; Almanach de
FIND <keywords>, Back, Up, <RETURN> for more, Quit, or Help: find computer
                                        find computer (in roget-thesaurus)
```

Look for a synonym for *computer*:

```
                          FIND COMPUTER

  Index roget-thesaurus contains the following 2 items relevant to 'ind
  computer'. The first figure for each entry is its relative score, the second
  the number of lines in the item.

1000   187  This is the 12/91 Project Gutenberg release of Roget's Thesaurus
We are releasing it early because[1]
 834    32        #85. Numeration.  — N. numeration; numbering &c. v.;
pagination;  tale, recension, enumeratio[2]




    [End]
```

Note that WWW presents the WAIS interface with the addition of hypertext links!
Pretty clever stuff, and certainly easy to use. So, what does link 2 have to say?

```
. . . . . . . . . . . . . . . . . . . . . . . . . . .
    #85. Numeration. — N. numeration; numbering &c. v.; pagination;
tale, recension, enumeration, summation, reckoning, computation,
supputation; calculation, calculus; algorithm, algorism, rhabdology,
dactylonomy; measurement &c. 466; statistics.
    arithmetic, analysis, algebra, geometry, analytical geometry,
fluxions; differential calculus, integral calculus, infinitesimal calculus;
calculus of differences.
    [Statistics] dead reckoning, muster, poll, census, capitation, roll
call, recapitulation; account &c. (list) 86.
    [Operations] notation, addition, subtraction, multiplication,
division, rule of three, practice, equations, extraction of roots,
reduction, involution, evolution, estimation, approximation, interpolation,
differentiation, integration.
    [Instruments] abacus, logometer, slide rule, slipstick[coll.],
tallies, Napier's bones, calculating machine, difference engine, suan-pan;
adding machine; cash register; electronic calculator,  calculator,
computer;
    [people who calculate] arithmetician, calculator, abacist, algebraist,
mathematician; statistician, geometer; programmer; accountant, auditor.
    V. number, count, tally, tell; call over, run over; take an account
of, enumerate, muster, poll, recite, recapitulate; sum; sum up, cast up;
tell off, score, cipher, compute, calculate, suppute, add, subtract,
Back, Up, <RETURN> for more, Quit, or Help: back
```

# Beautifying FTP

WWW also makes the same kind of transformation into the FTP interface and
makes it in a far more "user friendly" way:

```
                                                          FTP Interface
                      FTP INTERFACE

Please note that it is a nontrivial problem for a World-wide Web browser
like NCSA Mosaic[1] to properly handle the wide range of datatypes residing
on various FTP sites.  Please go here[2] for information on how Mosaic
handles file typing.

    Introduction to the monster FTP list[3]

    Sites with names A to E[4]

    Sites with names F to K[5]

    Sites with names L to O[6]
```

```
        Sites with names P to S[7]

        Sites with names T to Z[8]

                                        marca@ncsa.uiuc.edu


1-8, Back, Up, Quit, or Help: 4
```

Look in the A to E site list.

```
                                A to E: Exhaustive List of FTP Sites
                A TO E: EXHAUSTIVE LIST OF FTP SITES


a.cs.uiuc.edu[1]                        128.174.252.1   US -5    90/08/22
Admin: Univ. of Illinois - Urbana-Champaign
Files: TeX; dvi2ps; gif; texx2.7; amiga; GNUmake; GNU


a.psc.edu[2]                            128.182.66.105  US -5    90/12/31
Admin: Pittsburgh Supercomputing Center
Files: GPLOT; GTEX


aarnet.edu.au[3]                        139.130.204.4   AU +10   92/12/20
Admin: Australian Academic & Research Network
Files: Australian AARNET network stats


acacia.maths.uwa.oz.au[4]               130.95.16.2     AU +8    92/12/20
Admin: Univ. of Western Australia


acfcluster.nyu.edu[5]                   128.122.128.11  US -5    91/01/02
Admin: New York Univ.
Server: 128.122.128.17, 128.122.128.16
Files: VMS UUCP; news; DECUS library catalog; vsmnet.sources; info-vax code
1-228, Back, Up, <RETURN> for more, Quit, or Help: 1
```

Choose link 1 from the 228 offered. This gives you a list of the available subdirectories and files:

```
                                    FTP Directory of //a.cs.uiuc.edu/
                            /

bin[1]          etc[2]          pub[3]          usr[4]          dev[5]
.cshrc[6]       .login[7]       ls-lR[8]        lib[9]          tmp[10]
.hushlogin[11]  uiuc[12]        ls-lR.Z[13]     var[14]         adm[15]
msgs[16]        files.lst[17]   files.lst.Z[18] .rhosts.old[19]
```

```
    [End]

1-19, Back, Up, Quit, or Help: 17
```

If we now give the link number for a file, WWW will attempt to handle the file appropriately. For example, let's use link 17:

```
dr-xr-xr-x  13 ftp      wheel         512 Jun 10 08:35 .
dr-xr-xr-x   2 daemon   staff         512 May  6 07:04 ./bin
--x--x--x    1 root     staff       10288 Oct 19  1989 ./bin/ls
-rwxr-x--    1 root     staff       24576 Apr  9 00:10 ./bin/compress
-rwxr-xr-x   1 root     staff        2152 Apr 24  1989 ./bin/pwd
drwx------   2 daemon   news          512 Mar 19 09:51 ./etc
drwxr-xr-x  54 access   news         1536 Jun  9 07:20 ./pub
drwxr-xr-x   2 access   staff         512 Feb 15 15:04 ./pub/dcs
lrwxrwxrwx   1 root     daemon         16 Oct 15  1992 ./pub/dcs/uiqpl.nroff ->
QPLabstracts91-3
-rwxr-xr-x   1 access   staff       22870 Jul  8  1992 ./pub/dcs/QPLabstracts92
-1
-r--r--r--   1 access   staff      581027 Apr 24  1992 ./pub/dcs/uireports.bibr
ef
-r--r--r--   1 access   staff        1038 Jan  6  1992 ./pub/dcs/uireports.READ
ME
-rwxr-xr-x   1 access   news         8831 Jul 15  1987 ./pub/dcs/Notes.Revision
s
-rwxr-xr-x   1 access   staff      568440 Oct  2  1991 ./pub/dcs/csreports
-rwxr-xr-x   1 access   staff      444557 Oct 25  1989 ./pub/dcs/Notes.tar.Z
-r--r--r--   1 access   staff      439800 Apr 27  1992 ./pub/dcs/uireports.form
at
-rwxr-xr-x   1 access   staff       17671 Nov 18  1991 ./pub/dcs/QPLabstracts91
Back, Up, <RETURN> for more, Quit, or Help:
```

WWW dumps the file contents to the screen! Pretty neat, except that it handles all files the same way when their link is selected. This is not much good if the file isn't text. This is a current limitation of WWW, but one that you can expect to be cured very quickly. The future WWW might well be capable of mailing you a file or doing something equally smart.

# Using WWW

We've only scratched the surface of WWW's documents. The Web also covers access to telnet, USENET news, and several other services. If you have the WWW server running on your computer, you can set up your own private WWW documents. Even better, you can link these documents to other resources on your computer or out on the Internet.

WWW is a good tool even though it's so young. It's one that is well worth play-ing with and following as it develops. The most interesting part is how the Web can make other Internet tools much easier to use. I think the creators of WWW should be encouraged and applauded for a tool that could become one of the Internet greats.

# INTERNET DIRECTORY ASSISTANCE: InterNIC

Now that the size of the Internet is well beyond human comprehension, the problems of finding out what's happening, what can be done, and how to do them are huge.

One of the main problems is that the Internet is a cooperative environment, a place that has been created by common consent out of a handful of standards, such as TCP/IP. How to discover, manage, and distribute information about the Internet becomes a very significant problem because there is no single authority.

To address this, the National Science Foundation has granted three project awards to three separate organizations. Each organization oversees a specific area—registration services, directory and database services, and information services.

Together, these three awards form the Internet Network Information Center, or InterNIC. The InterNIC is a network information service management system designed to serve the Internet community. Network Solutions, Inc., provides the registration services, AT&T provides directory and database services, and General Atomics/CERFnet provides information services. Most of these services are in place, but many are still being developed and fine-tuned.

# InterNIC Information Services

For all of you dynamic Internet navigators, the most valuable InterNIC service will most likely be the InterNIC Information Services provided by General Atomics/CERFnet.

These services will be made available through mid-level Internet organizations and campus Network Information Centers (NICs), which will then provide the information to their clientele. But you, the dynamic Internet navigator, can go straight to the source and cut out the middleman. The information services component is comprised of three parts—reference desk, coordination, and education.

## Reference Desk

This service responds to requests for information about the Internet. The Reference Desk provides networking information, referrals to other resources, and associate users with their local NICs.

You can contact the Reference Desk a number of ways, including telephone, e-mail, FAX, and postal mail (for the communicationally disadvantaged). The Reference Desk will provide information about how to get an Internet connection, assist in finding network tools and information, and refer you to local sources of information. Contact the Reference Desk at

|  |  |
|---|---|
| Telephone: | 800-444-4345 or 619-455-4600 |
| FAX: | 619-455-3990 |
| E-mail: | `info@internic.net` |
| Mail: | InterNIC Information Services |
|  | General Atomics |
|  | P.O. Box #85608 |
|  | San Diego, California 92186-9784 |

# Mailboxes and Mailing Lists

The InterNIC Information Services will announce up-to-date information services about the InterNIC and services through a mailing list called `announce@is.internic.net`. You can join this list by sending e-mail to `listserv@is.internic.net`. In the body of the e-mail message, include the following line:

```
subscribe announce Firstname Lastname
```

Thus, `subscribe announce Mark Gibbs`. A more general list announces new resources and information about the Internet. This list is a group effort of the Internet community to try to keep everyone current on new developments without having to join numerous lists. To join this list, send e-mail to `listserv@is.internic.net`. In the body of the e-mail message, include the following line:

```
subscribe net-resources Firstname Lastname
```

Thus, `subscribe net-resources Rich Smith`. Information Services also has lists for mid-level service providers and publishes a newsletter in hard copy and electronically. Send e-mail to `interactive-request@is.internic.net` and request the newsletter in hard copy, electronically, or both (though hard copy is passé and you should be wary of your friends finding out, lest you appear uncool).

# InfoSource

Information about the Internet—how it's organized, used, and so on—is provided by InfoSource. This service includes both documents and pointers to other sources. The information made available is useful to everyone from new or infrequent Internet users to managers of mid-level NIC organizations.

## Accessing InfoSource

There are several routes through which you can access InfoSource. No particular route is the best, but unless you're impatient and need the information very quickly, e-mail should be used as it reduces the load on the Internet.

### FTP

InfoSource documents can be obtained via anonymous FTP from `is.internic.net` in the directory `infosource`. As with most FTP sites, try to get the index file first for a complete listing of what is available.

### E-Mail

The InfoSource collection is also available through e-mail. Send the word help on a single line in the body of an e-mail message to mailserv@is.internic.net for information on how to use the mail-server.

### WAIS

WAIS can be used to search the InfoSource collection of information. The source internic-infosource is registered in the directory of servers and can be accessed through any public WAIS client. You can also get to WAIS through Gopher and, therefore, to the InfoSource.

### Gopher

Probably the easiest and fastest way to access the InfoSource collection is through a Gopher client. Use Gopher to look at All the Gophers in the World or North America. The InterNIC machine is listed as InterNIC: Internet Network Informa-tion Center/. Select the InterNIC Information Services/ listed to access InfoSource and browse through the InfoSource Table of Contents on the main menu to get a feel for what information is available.

You can also telnet to is.internic.net and use the login name gopher. This will give you the InterNIC Gopher client, and you can then browse through InfoSource.

## An Example

Because InfoSource has the most information for the largest audience, I consider it the most important InterNIC service. It deserves an example. I'll use the is.internic.net Gopher by telneting to is.internic.net and using the login name gopher.

```
bss> telnet is.internic.net
 Trying 192.153.156.15 ...
 Connected to is.internic.net.
 Escape character is '^]'.

 SunOS UNIX (is)

 login: gopher
```

The first screen I see on the telnet connection to the InterNIC Gopher is

```
              Internet Gopher Information Client v1.01

            InterNIC: Internet Network Information Center

      1.   Information about the InterNIC.
  —>  2.   InterNIC Information Services (General Atomics)/
      3.   InterNIC Registration Services (NSI)/
      4.   InterNIC Directory and Database Services (AT&T)/
```

The main menu gives you the option to select from the three NIC services. I use
the down arrow key to move the pointer to item 2 and then select it by pressing
Enter.

```
              Internet Gopher Information Client v1.01

           InterNIC Information Services (General Atomics)

  —>  1.   Welcome to the InfoSource/
      2.   InfoSource Table of Contents.
      3.   About InterNIC Information Services/
      4.   InterNIC Store/
      5.   Getting Started on the Internet/
      6.   Internet Information for Everybody/
      7.   Just for NICs/
      8.   NSFNET, NREN, National Information Infrastructure Information/
      9.   Searching the InfoSource/
```

Currently, nine directories to the InterNIC Information Services are available.
We'll try Internet Information for Everybody.

```
Internet Gopher Information Client v1.01

                  Internet Information for Everybody

      1.   How Big is the Internet/
      2.   Things to Do on the Internet/
  —>  3.   Learning to Use the Network/
      4.   Government Agencies on the Internet.
      5.   Internet Monthly Reports/
      6.   Introduction to Internet Protocols.
      7.   Organizations/
      8.   Other Networks/
      9.   Where and How to get Requests for Comments Documents/
      10.  pdial.
```

This menu gives a good selection of directories that might be of interest to both the beginning Navigator and the expert user. Protocols, organizations, and Internet monthly reports for network managers, things to do on the Internet, and learning to use the network for the beginner—definitely information for everybody. Going one more step down the InterNIC Gopher menus, we'll try `Learning to Use the Network`.

```
                Internet Gopher Information Client v1.01

                     Learning to Use the Network

        1.  Clearinghouse for Networked Info Discovery and Retrieval (CNIDR)/
   -->  2.  Quick Guide to Tools.
        3.  Tools General Info/
```

Three options are now available. One of the three is a text file (signified by the period at the end of the line). I selected that and read the information, and then I e-mailed the document to my Internet address (a standard Gopher command; see Chapter 8, "Navigating by Menus: Gopher"). Here is the e-mail document I received from the InterNIC Gopher:

```
From rjs4808 Tue Jun  8 12:59:44 1993
Received: from a105.ucs.usl.edu by armagnac.ucs.usl.edu with SMTP id AA26282
   (5.65c/IDA-1.4.4 for <rs@usl.edu>); Tue, 8 Jun 1993 12:59:43 -0500
Received: by a105.ucs.usl.edu (5.65c/SMI-4.1-910807USL)
        id AA27057; Tue, 8 Jun 1993 12:59:36 -0500
Date: Tue, 8 Jun 1993 12:59:36 -0500
From: rjs4808@ucs.usl.edu
Message-Id: <199306081759.AA27057@a105.ucs.usl.edu>
To: rs@usl.edu
Subject: Quick Guide to Tools
Status: R
Networked Information Discovery and Retrieval: Tools
NOTE: This list is by no means comprehensive, but it does offer an introduction to
the tools.
archie
Search & retrieve anonymous FTP
Source: ftp.sura.net:/pub/archie
Demo: archie.sura.net, login as archie
gopher
Hierarchical browser
Source: boombox.micro.umn.edu:/pub/gopher
Demo: consultant.micro.umn.edu, login as gopher
hytelnet
Hypertext interface to telnet to selected sites
Source: access.usask.ca:/pub/hytelnet
Demo: access.usask.ca, login as hytelnet
```

```
libs
Menu-driven scripted telnet connections to library OPACS and other selected
resources
Source: sonoma.edu: /pub/libs.sh
Demo: vax.sonoma.edu, login as OPAC
libtel
Menu-driven scripted telnet connections to library OPACS and other selected
resources (UNC-CH enhancements added)
Source: ftp.oit.unc.edu:/pub/doc/libtel.unix
Demo: bbs.oit.unc.edu, login as bbs
prospero
Networked file system
Source: cs.washington.edu: /pub/prospero.tar.Z
More info: mail to info-prospero@isi.edu
WAIS
Relevance feedback search and retrieval
Source: quake.think.com:/wais
Demo: quake.think.com, login as wais
WorldWide Web
Hypertext interface to internet resources (links embedded in docs)
Source: info.cern.ch:/pub/www
Demo: info.cern.ch, no login or password
For more information contact:
Clearinghouse for Networked Information Discovery and Retrieval (CNIDR)
Center for Communications - MCNC
PO Box 12889, 3021 Cornwallis Road
Research Triangle Park, NC  27709-2889
George H. Brett II      Jane D. Smith
ghb@concert.net         jds@concert.net
919-248-1886  919-248-9213
Many of these tools are installed on kudzu.concert.net. Login account required.
```

## Education Services

InterNIC Services is sponsoring a workshop on use of the Internet. Workshops are announced through the various documents and LISTSERV lists previously mentioned. These are worth following if you're a beginner.

**Navigator's Note from Mark Gibbs:** While we're talking about education, watch for more of Rich's online "Navigating the Internet" courses, held roughly every three months. The objective of these courses is to give you tutorials on the practical use of Internet resources and detailed examples to follow. These courses track the development of new Internet tools and methods that will make your life a lot easier. Over 15,000 people participated in the last on-line workshop. New sessions will be announced in various places on the Internet and through several educational publications.

# InterNIC Directory and Database Services

The Directory and Database Services (DS) offers a Directory of Directories listing FTP sites, lists of servers available on the Internet, lists of white and yellow page directories, data archives, and library catalogs. This service is provided by AT&T.

You can get to the Directory and Database Services in several ways.

## WAIS to DS

Telnet to ds.internic.net and log in using wais as the user name. No password is required. (Note the ds at the beginning of this machine name.)

## Archie to DS

Telnet to ds.internic.net and access DS by using archie as the user name. Again, no password is required. You may also send Archie commands by electronic mail to archie@ds.internic.net.

To learn more about how to access the Directory and Database Services, you may contact this service at

| | |
|---|---|
| Phone: | 908-668-6587 |
| Fax: | 908-668-3763 |
| E-mail: | admin@ds.internic.net |

## Gopher

Of course, Gopher can be used (as shown in the earlier example) to reach all three services. Here's a listing of the first screen from the InterNIC Directory and Databases Services:

```
                Internet Gopher Information Client v1.01

              InterNIC Directory and Database Services (AT&T)

        1.  InterNIC Directory of Directories Resource Types/
        2.  Information about the InterNIC Directory and Database Services/
        3.  IETF Documents/
        4.  IETF Steering Group Documents/
        5.  Internet Draft Documents/
        6.  Internet Informational RFC Documents (FYIs)/
        7.  Internet Policies and Procedures/
        8.  Internet Request For Comments (RFC) Documents/
        9.  Internet Society (ISOC) Documents/
       10.  Internet Standard RFC Documents (STDs)/
       11.  National Science Foundation Databases/
       12.  Publicly Accessible Databases/
       13.  Publicly Accessible Sources/
  —>   14.  The DS WHOIS Database <?>
       15.  The Internet Resource Guide/
```

Of particular interest is the DS WHOIS Database. This has the <?> at the end of its
Gopher item, meaning that it is a searchable database. It is the "white pages" (like
the white pages of a regular telephone directory) of the InterNIC Directory and
Database Services. It is not a comprehensive white pages service, but coming from
AT&T, it has a better chance than many others of becoming one. Here is a list I
retrieved from asking the DS WHOIS for Richard Smith:

```
                Internet Gopher Information Client v1.01

                  The DS WHOIS Database: richard smith

  —>   1.  Smith, Alan (AS22)  smith@UCBVAX.BERKELEY.EDU  .
        2.  Smith, Bruce (BS50)  SMITH#BRUCE@NMFECC.LLNL.GOV  .
        3.  Smith, Duane Donald (DDS5)  SMITH@CHEMISTRY.CHEMISTRY.PURDUE.EDU  .
        4.  Smith, Douglas (DS94)  SMITH@KESTREL.EDU  .
        5.  Smith, Edward (ES3)  Edward.Smith@A.CS.CMU.EDU  .
        6.  Smith, Judith P. (JS67)  SMITH@VLSI.JPL.NASA.GOV  .
        7.  Smith, Kent (KS7)  k-smith@CS.UTAH.EDU  .
        8.  Karlin, Richard (RAK31)  RICHARD%RICHP1.UUCP@UUNET.UU.NET  .
        9.  Baxter, Richard (RB187)  baxter-richard@YALE.EDU  .
       10.  Beigel, Richard J. (RJB56)  beigel-richard@CS.YALE.EDU  .
       11.  Coyle, Richard J. (RJC62)  RICHARD@GRYPHON.COM  .
       12.  Platek, Richard A. (RP9)  richard@ORACORP.COM  .
       13.  Smith, William B. (WBS)  smith@URBANA.MCD.MOT.COM  .
       14.  Smith, Carl H. (CS34)  smith@MIMSY.UMD.EDU  .
       15.  Smith, Mary J. (MJS54)  mjsmith@ECN.PURDUE.EDU  .
       16.  Roos, Robert S. (RSR17)  rroos@SMITH.BITNET  .
       17.  Fraser-Smith, A.C. (AF7)  ACFS@STAR.STANFORD.EDU  .
       18.  Smith, Barbara (BS29)  ATP.Barbara@R20.UTEXAS.EDU  .
```

Nope, I'm not listed yet. This database—being a WAIS database—has all words in it indexed (see Chapter 7, "The Database of Databases: WAIS," for more information) so you can also find information on institutions as well as individual users.

# InterNIC Registration Services

The third service, the InterNIC Registration Service, is the most specialized of the three. The Registration Service will register Internet Domains, networks, and other Internet entities. Network administrators and Internet service providers will use this service to register their organizations and institutions.

This service will also provide an electronic "yellow pages" database that will be useful when searching for machine names and addresses. As with the other InterNIC services, the database will have several access points.

WAIS and mail access is similar to other InterNIC services, except that the machine's name is rs.internic.net. A WHOIS program can be accessed by using telnet to connect to rs.internic.net and using the word whois as the login.

And, of course, good old Gopher can get you there. Here is the first screen of the InterNIC Registration Services when selected from Gopher.

```
                Internet Gopher Information Client v1.01

                  InterNIC Registration Services (NSI)


        1.  InterNIC Registration Archives/
   —>   2.  Whois Searches (InterNIC IP, ASN, DNS, and POC Registry) <?>
        3.  Whois Searches (Non-MILNET, Non-POC Individuals - run by AT&T) <?>
```

Pretty bare at the present. You can see the difference in this database compared to the InterNIC Directory and Database Services shown earlier. Selecting the second item, I searched for the word "Moscow" to find someone I needed to talk to (the Internet is a whole new way of jet-setting, without the jet lag).

```
                Internet Gopher Information Client v1.01

       Whois Searches (InterNIC IP, ASN, DNS, and POC Registry): moscow

   —>   1.  Kurchatov Institute of Atomic Energy, Moscow, USSR (NET-KIAE-MOSC.
        2.  [No name] (MOSCOW)        Hostname: MOSCOW.UIDAHO.EDU      Address:.
        3.  University of Idaho (UIDAHO-DOM)      Moscow, ID 83843         Domai.
        4.  Moscow State University (NET-MSUNET)     Digital Networks Group, .
        5.  Institute for Theoretical & Experimental Physics (ASN-MOSCOW-HEP.
```

```
 6.  Soldatov, Aleksey A. (AAS3) alex@kiae.su      Kurchatov Institute.
 7.  Avdeyev, Dmitry (DA196) dmitry@npi.msu.su      Nuclear Physics In.
 8.  Simon, Mike A. (MAS33) simon@moscow.uidaho.edu      University of.
 9.  Electronics and Computer Science Center of Moscow Institute of Ph.
10.  Institute for Theoretical and Experimental Physics (ASN-IREP-MOSCO.
11.  Advanced Hardware Architectures (AHA-DOM)      P.O. Box 9669      M.
12.  RelTeam Company, Limited (SU1-DOM)      56-131 Khoroshovskoye shos.
13.  Shirikov, Vladislav (VS86) shirikov@jinr.dubna.su      P.O.Box 79.
14.  Arkhipov, Andrei (AA124) root@elvis.msk.su      ELVIS Research Ce.
15.  Orel, Oleg (OO6) postmaster@oea.ihep.su      OEA      IHEP      Ser.
16.  BALL, DAVID W. (DWB61) [No mailbox]      715 S. WASHINGTON ST.   .
17.  Lavrentiev, Andrew (AL44) kiae.su!iaicom.dubna.su!root      Mosco.
18.  Kudryashev, Michael (MK60) mike@ECSC.MIPT.SU      141700, Moscow .
```

The result was all entries with the word "moscow" somewhere in the title or in the content of the document. Selecting the first entry gave me some information on the institution.

```
_____

Kurchatov Institute of Atomic Energy, Moscow, USSR (NET-KIAE-MOSCOW)
   SU-123182 Moscow
   USSR

   Netname: KIAE-MOSCOW
   Netnumber: 144.206.0.0

   Coordinator:
      Soldatov, Aleksey A.  (AAS3)  alex@kiae.su
      +7 095 196 9614

   Record last updated on 04-Jan-91.



Press <RETURN> to continue, <m> to mail, <s> to save, or <p> to print:
```

Sparse and a bit dated, but this service has been up and running only since April 1993, so getting as far as they have is pretty impressive.

# Saint NIC

The National Science Foundation is to be congratulated on getting such an ambitious scheme off the ground. Now they've really got their work cut out for them to not only get all the services in place, but to do so in the face of the fantastic growth of the Internet.

For the Internet navigator, access to the InterNIC is like a Christmas present that gets better and better every day. You should subscribe to the LISTSERV lists and set aside some time to browse their Gopher menus on a regular basis.

# Internetiquette: Manners and the Internet

Whenever people communicate (whether in public or in private), some behaviors and standards of conduct are considered acceptable, and others are not.

The same applies on the Internet, in e-mail, and in newsgroups and lists. Some ways of acting are polite and civilized, and others make you appear rude and will get you disliked or even into trouble.

"What are they going to do to me when I'm 3,000 miles away?" you might ask. Well, it could mean (in very serious cases) that a site is told to cut you off or lose their access. You can guess which happens. People aren't removed from the Internet very often, but when they are, it's usually for a pretty serious reason.

When a sufficient number of people communicate, strange things begin to happen. Folk stories (sometimes also called *urban legends*) can be found on the Internet. Someone tells a story, it takes on a life of its own; it becomes (howling in the distance) an undead tale—a story that won't die.

In this chapter, we'll examine guidelines for conduct on the Internet—what might be called *Internetiquette*—and some of the Internet folk stories.

# Internetiquette

When you were young, your mother told you how to behave. "Say please and thank you" and "don't shout" were the kinds of things you probably heard. If she knew that you were running around on the Internet with your friends having a wild time, she'd apply much the same kind of guidelines.

## Internetiquette for Electronic Mail

When using electronic mail services to communicate with other people, try to remember these important points of Internetiquette:

1. **Shouting:** DON'T SHOUT. Messages in all uppercase are hard to read and are also very irritating. This is commonly called shouting. A suitable response is to politely ask people who do this to stop. If they don't, be generous. Perhaps they're waiting for the computer service engineer to fix their shift key. (Maybe the poet e.e. cummings had the opposite problem and his service engineer never showed up.) If shouters exhibit long-term recidivist tendencies, just don't read anything from them until they complain; then you can politely tell them why. If the shouter is your boss, you're on your own.

2. **Correct addressing:** Be certain that your message is addressed to the person you want to send it to. A young lady in a major corporation was having what was once called a dalliance with a young gentleman employed by the same organization. Apparently things weren't going so well, and in a fit of pique, she decided to write to him—on the company's electronic mail system. She wrote at length about his failings as a companion, both socially and, in great detail, sexually. She then fumbled on the keyboard and promptly sent the letter to everyone in her division.

3. **Quotability:** Remember (especially when the subject matter is questionable) that anything you send can be easily and almost instantly forwarded to others.

4. **Who sent it?:** Be sure that a message asking you to do something potentially indiscreet is from the person it claims to be from. At one company, a bogus electronic message (apparently from the CEO) went to all the employees in a branch office. The message asked for their frank opinions (which would be kept confidential) of their superiors, because rumors of problems had been heard. Several people fell for it, and because the recipient was, indeed, the CEO, their faux pas was complete.

5. **Your tone:** Watch the tone of what you write. What may sound funny or reasonable in speech can sound aggressive, abrupt, or just plain rude in e-mail. This is partly explained by the fact that e-mail is so easy to produce. Most people don't spend a great deal of time considering what they're going to put in an electronic message and rarely format it as they would a handwritten letter. You should save your responses if they are of any significant length or importance and review them before you commit them to the Internet. If you think you might be misinterpreted, you can, if the circumstances permit, use e-mail shorthand and *emoticons* (see the following section).

6. **Other people's tone:** You should also carefully read what others write. Their apparent tone may not be what they actually meant. I (Mark Gibbs) was once trying to reach a product manager in a company I was working with and finally resorted to e-mail, which his secretary always handled for him. She replied "I resent your message" and, like a gold-plated, five-star idiot, I phoned and asked her, "What the hell do you resent?" I then spent the next ten minutes jabbering my apologies (I had mistaken re-sent for resent).

7. **Suitable content:** Don't be coarse, vulgar, or suggestive. Not only are these kinds of expressions rarely acceptable to others, but you're putting them on electronic paper; they may well hang around to haunt you. Many a management career has foundered on the rocks of things that shouldn't have been written down. E-mail can make the rocks come up to meet you faster.

8. **Discretion:** Don't send any message that you wouldn't send in a letter. If you are going to libel, gossip, or be otherwise indiscreet, keep to the spoken word. Better yet, avoid the impulse; it is vulgar.

9. **Flaming:** *Flaming* is when you write a message, obviously in anger, and "say what you think." The usual result is that the author looks foolish and immature. Don't flame.

10. **Chain letters:** Don't get involved with them. At all. At the least they are a waste of resources (the bandwidth to send them) and at worst illegal.

# E-Mail Shorthand and Emoticons

As suggested earlier, there are ways to make your intentions clearer in electronic messages. These conventions are usually not used in formal communications, but they are very useful for everyday traffic. When you want to stress the tone in which you're saying something (and do it the hip way), you can use shorthand and emoticons.

## E-Mail Shorthand

E-mail shorthand usually refers to acronyms that are strategically placed in messages. They are subject to context, and so are used both politely and impolitely, for humor, anger, and so on:

> **LOL**—Laughing Out Loud—as in "The company says that the product will be delivered on time (LOL)."
>
> **OTF**—On The Floor (laughing)—as in "The company says that the product will be delivered on time and under budget (OTF)."
>
> **ROTFL**—Rolling On The Floor Laughing—as in "The company says that the product will be delivered on time, under budget, and to specification (ROTFL)."
>
> **IMHO**—In My Humble Opinion—as in "The product will be just what we need, IMHO."
>
> **BTW**—By The Way—as in "BTW, they've finally released the product—late (ROTFL)."
>
> **YMMV**—Your Mileage May Vary—as in "I got a 9600 baud connection from my site using xyz product, YMMV."

## E-Mail Emoticons

Emoticons are sequences of characters that denote faces and expressions. There are literally hundreds, although only a few are in common use. They always read better if they are in a monospaced font (like Courier, the normal typewriter font, where each character is the same width). They are read sideways:

> :-)   Smile—as in "we got the product :-)" to show pleasure or "we can't be bothered about sending you the product :-)" to show that you don't mean it
>
> ;-)   Wink—as in "good product, eh? ;-)"

```
:-(    Displeasure—as in "we got the product, but...  :-("
:->    Smug—as in "we got the product first  :->"
```

The following emoticons aren't so common, and some are just plain bizarre:

| | | | |
|---|---|---|---|
| `:-t` | User is cross | `(-)` | User needs a haircut |
| `:-\` | User is undecided | `{:-)` | User parts hair in the middle |
| `:-o` | User is shocked | `{(:-)` | User is wearing a toupee |
| `:-&` | User is tongue-tied | `}(:-(` | User is wearing toupee in wind |
| `¦-¦` | User is asleep (boredom) | `-:-)` | User has a mohawk |
| `:-c` | User is bummed out | `(:)-)` | User likes to scuba dive |
| `:-#` | User's lips are sealed | `0-)` | User wears a scuba mask |
| `8-¦` | User is in suspense | `:-)X` | User wears a bow tie |
| `:-<` | User is sad | `:-}` | User wears lipstick |
| `8-#` | User is dead | `@:I` | User wears a turban |
| `:-I` | Hmmm | `8-)` | User wears glasses |
| `:-x` | "My lips are sealed" | `::-)` | User wears bifocals |
| `:-7` | User has made a wry statement | `B-)` | User wears horn-rims |
| `:-p` | User is sticking tongue out | `:-)8` | User is well-dressed |
| `:-9` | User is licking lips | `:-0` | User is an orator |
| `:-*` | User just ate a sour pickle | `:<¦` | User attends an Ivy League school |
| `:>)` | User has a big nose | `+:-¦` | User is a priest |
| `%-)` | User is cross-eyed | `+-(:-)` | User is the pope |
| `#-)` | User partied all night | `[:¦]` | User is a robot |
| `[:-)` | User is listening to headphones | `*:o)` | User is a bozo |
| `(-:` | User is left-handed | `o-)` | User is a cyclops |
| `:-` | User is male | `:>` | User is a midget |
| `:-Q` | User smokes | `8:]` | User is a gorilla |
| `:-?` | User smokes a pipe | `=:-)` | User is a punk-rocker |
| `:-{` | User has a mustache | `%-^` | User is Picasso |
| `:-%` | User has a beard | `*<¦:-)` | User is Santa Claus (Ho Ho Ho) |

# Undead Folk Tales

The folk tale is a curious social phenomenon, usually based on some real event that gets distorted and retold until it is completely different from the original (and usually more interesting). One example of the modern folk tale is the lady who tried to dry her poodle in the microwave oven.

On the Internet, much the same thing happens, and because most messages are text, copies are filed away only to resurface later.

## Modem Tax

One of the old favorites is the dreaded Modem Tax. Once upon a time there was a proposal to tax modems, but it was (justly) struck down before it got anywhere.

The story pops up at least once a year in a public forum, where someone posts a message like "What's this I hear about the government planning a tax on the use of modems?" This is usually greeted with a goodly amount of derision and scoffing—particularly if the someone has been using the Internet for any length of time. It's considered tantamount to saying that you've had your head under a rock (ROTFL).

## Dying Child Postcards

Another story that has joined the zombie squad, refusing to die, is Send a Dying Child a Postcard.

In 1986, a seven-year-old boy named Craig Shergold was diagnosed as having an inoperable brain tumor. Young Mr. Shergold decided that he wanted to break the Guinness record for receiving get-well cards. Thanks to publicity, the cards started rolling in. One of the ways that the news was spread was through various e-mail systems, including the Internet.

It's now tens of millions of cards later. Craig broke the record with ease way back in 1989, but despite his successful operation and recovery, the cards keep coming. On the Internet, Craig's request keeps popping up. Several times each year, someone spreads the word as if it had just happened. A new wave of cards descends on Craig, his family, and the hospital where he was treated.

Many other stories illustrate the bizarre nature of messages and folklore on the Internet. They all point to the fact that you should be wary about the things you read in public forums and act very carefully on what's in them.

# Playing the Game

You should remember several things concerning tidying up after yourself when you're using and cruising the Internet.

1. If you abandon an account on a machine on the Internet, delete any files in your work areas, and tell the system supervisor you're leaving so that the supervisor can clean up. Also, make sure that you unsubscribe from any LISTSERV lists you belong to—otherwise your non-existent account will still be getting messages, and they'll be getting sent back to the LISTSERV and…basically, it's messy.

2. If you discover someone's password, tell them. Don't, under any circumstances, use that account, tell anyone else that you know the password, or otherwise compromise that person's security.

3. If you find a problem in a computer system, tell the supervisor. Don't just shrug your shoulders and assume it is someone else's problem. That's like seeing spilled oil on the road and not telling anyone of the danger.

4. If you know of, or hear of, people attempting to break into systems or otherwise break security, tell the system supervisor immediately.

# Remember!

Remember that the Internet has social as well as technical aspects. Not everyone who uses the Internet is a technical guru or a rocket scientist. Good manners and polite, considerate behavior will get you all the help and cooperation you want.

It's very important to remember that the Internet is a cooperative environment. If people start abusing the trust of the community, that cooperative spirit will be in danger of evaporating. Once it's gone, the Internet will never be the same again.

# VIEWS AND NEWS: USENET

When America was young, news from New York could take weeks or even months to reach the Wild West. Then along came the telegraph, and suddenly, unless you were out in the backwoods, important news was never more than a few days old. Today, we have TV and radio, and news is never more than seconds old if you have the right technology on hand.

With the Internet, news is a continuous phenomenon. Information about the state of the world (both the real world and the world of the Internet) and opinions concerning life, the universe, and everything are freely traded all the time.

News is everywhere on the Internet, and USENET is the main vehicle.

# USENET

USENET was created by two Duke University graduate students, Tom Truscott and Jim Ellis. They developed software so that people on different computers could exchange messages on topics in a way that allowed discussions to develop. Their software has gone through many versions and is now being used by hundreds of thousands of people internationally every day. These users participate in thousands of *newsgroups* (the USENET name for discussion groups) covering topics dealing with everything from computer systems administration to exotic religious philosophies.

For the Internet navigator, newsgroups can be a fantastic source of information about what's going on, what services are available, and what new resources can be plundered (metaphorically speaking).

## Newsgroups

USENET newsgroups (also called just "groups") are organized as a hierarchy. At the top are topics—for example, a computer topic (not very surprising), a science topic, a recreation topic, and so on. Subtopics under science would include chemistry, astronomy, and many others. Under those subtopics are sub-subtopics—for example, hubble (about the Hubble telescope) under astronomy.

Topics and subtopics (and sub-subtopics and sub-sub-subtopics) have abbreviated names. Thus, science is `sci`, astronomy is `astro`, and the newsgroup name for news and discussion of the Hubble telescope is `sci.astro.hubble`. The hierarchy reads from left to right, from the most general level to the most specific.

In general, USENET newsgroups fall into a well-defined hierarchy of subjects. Here are some of the top-level topics, with a sample of the newsgroup types that are available under each.

| | |
|---|---|
| `comp` | Topics of interest to both computer professionals and hobbyists, including computer science, software sources, and information on hardware and software. |
| `comp.ai` | Artificial intelligence discussions. |
| `comp.dcom.modems` | Data communications hardware and software. |

| | |
|---|---|
| `comp.lang.lisp.mcl` | Discusses Apple's Macintosh Common Lisp. |
| `comp.org.usenix` | USENIX Association events and announcements. |
| `comp.os.os2.apps` | Discussions of applications under OS/2. |
| `comp.sys.sun.announce` | Sun announcements and Sunergy mailings (moderated). |
| `sci` | Discussions marked by special knowledge relating to research in or application of the established sciences. |
| `sci.chem.organomet` | Organometallic chemistry. |
| `sci.geo.geology` | Discussion of solid earth sciences. |
| `sci.math.symbolic` | Symbolic algebra discussion. |
| `sci.research` | Research methods, funding, and ethics. |
| `sci.math.num-analysis` | Numerical analysis. |
| `soc` | Groups primarily addressing social issues and socializing. Included are discussions related to many different world cultures. |
| `soc.college.grad` | General issues related to graduate schools. |
| `soc.culture.african.american` | Discussions about African American issues. |
| `soc.religion.bahai` | Discussion of the Baha'i Faith (moderated). |
| `soc.veterans` | Social issues relating to military veterans. |
| `soc.roots` | Discussing genealogy and genealogical matters. |
| `talk` | Groups largely debate-oriented and tending to feature long discussions without resolution and without appreciable amounts of generally useful information. |

| | |
|---|---|
| `talk.abortion` | All sorts of discussions and arguments on abortion. |
| `talk.environment` | Discussion of the state of the environment and what to do about it. |
| `talk.politics.animals` | The use and/or abuse of animals. |
| `talk.politics.theory` | Theory of politics and political systems. |
| `talk.rape` | Discussions on stopping rape. |
| `news` | Groups concerned with the news network, group maintenance, and software. |
| `news.admin.policy` | Policy issues of USENET. |
| `news.future` | The future technology of network news systems. |
| `news.misc` | Discussions of USENET itself. |
| `news.software.readers` | Discusses software used to read network news. |
| `news.answers` | Repository for periodic USENET articles. |

## Other News

USENET is not the only source of news. The software used to read USENET news can also get news feeds from other Internet sources, and a growing number of networks and groups are distributing news. (Or what they think of as news—if you're, say, an avid follower of the latest advances in the biology of slugs. Actually, I made that up. This has far weirder topics than that.) For example, groups with `alt` listings are heavily subscribed to and distributed and come mainly from outside USENET.

| | |
|---|---|
| `alt` | Unofficial or temporary topics that run the gamut of…anything goes. |
| `alt.aeffle.und.pferdle` | German TV cartoon characters (honestly). |
| `alt.bizarre` | If it's too weird for the weirdos, it's here. |
| `alt.butt-keg.marmalade` | Typical Yankee analytic humor. |
| `alt.conspiracy.jfk` | The Kennedy assassination. |
| `alt.sex.head` | Tales of certain erotic activities. |
| `alt.wolves` | Discusses wolves and wolf-mix dogs. |

These newsgroups are created in various ways. Their formation and promotion don't go through the same process as USENET newsgroups (explained later in this chapter), so we'll conveniently ignore them. If you want to find out how to get involved with or start these, talk with (e-mail) participants and find out what the process is for that system.

> **Navigator's Note:** A site can create newsgroups for its own users. For example, a university might have newsgroups for various student groups, administration announcements, and class assignments.

Brian Reid, who works at the Network Systems Laboratory of Digital Equipment Corporation, has put together an interesting chart showing the most popular USENET groups. The data is taken from the monthly volume and readership statistics published in news.lists.

```
_____

USENET readership and volume, May 1993

   +— Readership Rank
   ¦    +— Estimated total number of people who read the group, worldwide.
   ¦    ¦    +— Actual number of readers in sampled population
   ¦    ¦    ¦    +— Propagation: how many sites receive this group at all
   ¦    ¦    ¦    ¦    +— Recent traffic (messages per month)
   ¦    ¦    ¦    ¦    ¦    +— Recent traffic (kilobytes per month)
   ¦    ¦    ¦    ¦    ¦    ¦    +— Share: % of newsreaders
   ¦    ¦    ¦    ¦    ¦    ¦    ¦    who read this group.
   V    V    V    V    V    V    V
   1 230000 4611  92%     1    13.6  10.0%  news.announce.newusers
   2 230000 4447  88%     1    29.2   9.7%  news.answers
   3 190000 3729  85%  1473  2931.4   8.1%  misc.jobs.offered
   4 190000 3667  67%  2377  5132.2   8.0%  alt.sex
   5 170000 3327  83%    67   123.9   7.2%  rec.humor.funny
   6 160000 3120  88%   891  1386.1   6.8%  comp.unix.questions
   7 160000 3059  53%   620  4925.3   6.7%  alt.sex.stories
   8 150000 2997  73%    30   469.1   6.5%  rec.arts.erotica
   9 150000 2976  54%   795 38955.8   6.5%  alt.binaries.pictures.erotica
  10 150000 2919  83%  1917  2352.8   6.3%  misc.forsale
  11 140000 2690  82%  2173  5915.3   5.9%  rec.humor
  12 130000 2586  90%  1625  3549.2   5.6%  news.groups
  13 130000 2552  88%  1639  2967.6   5.6%  comp.lang.c
  14 130000 2486  91%   113  1192.6   5.4%  news.announce.newgroups
  15 130000 2481  67%   902  3782.0   5.4%  alt.activism
  16 120000 2305  63%  1511  4375.5   5.0%  alt.sex.bondage
  17 120000 2270  83%   771  1796.7   4.9%  misc.jobs.misc
  18 110000 2239  86%   816  1752.1   4.9%  comp.graphics
```

```
19 100000  2044  78%  2475   4937.2    4.4%  rec.arts.movies
20 100000  1995  84%  3093   5026.9    4.3%  comp.sys.ibm.pc.hardware
21 100000  1994  12%    20    109.3    4.3%  clari.news.briefs
22 100000  1992  87%   126   1034.7    4.3%  news.announce.conferences
23 100000  1976  81%  1097   1915.4    4.3%  comp.sys.sun.admin
24 100000  1972  74%  3963   9671.4    4.3%  soc.culture.indian
25 100000  1963  58%   635  25856.3    4.3%  alt.binaries.pictures.misc
```

# Example

Here's a short look at how a discussion takes place within the newsgroup
`rec.arts.movies`. The group's short description is

`rec.arts.movies`            Discussions of movies and movie-making.

In the following example, I've already selected newsgroup and article.

```
Article 93919 (668 more) in rec.arts.movies:
From: jlh@jpradley.jpr.com (Jeff Henslin)
Subject: Luis Bunuel - The Strange Object of Desire
Organization: Unix in NYC
Date: Thu, 3 Jun 1993 02:00:57 GMT
Lines: 12

This week I watched this film (French), intrigued by Luis Bunuel who
also directed "Like Water for Chocolate". In the film the main female
role is played by two actresses, who have different, non-obvious
personality traits. One might conclude there are two lead female
roles, although they appear to the lead male character as one. They
are different enough in appearance for one to draw the conclusion that
we (the audience) are meant to notice the disparity, and draw some
conclusion.  Would anyone who has seen this film care to comment on
it?

Jeff
End of article 93919 (of 94589)—what next? [^Nnpq]

Esc-chr: ^]  help: ^]?  port:2 speed: 9600 parity:none echo:rem  VT102 ....
```

This article was posted and is asking for information on a movie. This is an original article that calls for a discussion. In many cases, you contact the author directly to answer a question, but in this case, given the nature of the newsgroup, a
reply to the article (by posting one to the newsgroup) would be appropriate.

To follow the thread of this message (thread is the term often used for a sequence of messages related to each other) use the Ctrl+N command, which searches for the next unread message with the same subject. Let's see where it takes us:

```
Article 93929 (686 more) in rec.arts.movies:
From: agrawal@lipari.usc.edu (Amitabh Agrawal)
Subject: Re: Luis Bunuel - The Strange Object of Desire
Date: 2 Jun 1993 22:35:58 -0700
Organization: University of Southern California, Los Angeles, CA
Lines: 23
NNTP-Posting-Host: lipari.usc.edu
In-reply-to: jlh@jpradley.jpr.com's message of Thu, 3 Jun 1993 02:00:57 GMT

In article <C80w9L.2x2@jpradley.jpr.com> jlh@jpradley.jpr.com (Jeff Henslin)
writes:

    This week I watched this film (French), intrigued by Luis Bunuel who
    also directed "Like Water for Chocolate". In the film the main female
    role is played by two actresses, who have different, non-obvious
    personality traits. One might conclude there are two lead female
    roles, although they appear to the lead male character as one. They
    are different enough in appearance for one to draw the conclusion that
    we (the audience) are meant to notice the disparity, and draw some
    conclusion.  Would anyone who has seen this film care to comment on
    it?

Go home and watch it again, and again... and again... Incidently the
title is "That Obscure Object of Desire"...

Did "Luis Bunuel" direct "Like Water for Chocolate"... That makes this
movie a must see.... Well!! this weekend...

Amit

End of article 93929 (of 94589) —what next? [^Nnpq]
Esc-chr: ^]  help: ^]?  port:2 speed: 9600 parity:none echo:rem  VT102 ....

Article 94018 (666 more) in rec.arts.movies:
From: reiher@ficus.cs.ucla.edu (Peter Reiher)
(SAME) Subject: Re: Luis Bunuel - The Strange Object of Desire
Nntp-Posting-Host: wells.cs.ucla.edu
Organization: UCLA Computer Science Department
Date: Thu, 3 Jun 93 19:21:01 GMT
Lines: 17

In article <AGRAWAL.93Jun2223557@lipari.usc.edu> agrawal@lipari.usc.edu (Amitabh
 Agrawal) writes:
>
>Did "Luis Bunuel" direct "Like Water for Chocolate"... That makes this
>movie a must see.... Well!! this weekend...
```

```
No, Mr. Bunuel has been dead for some years now.  "Like Water For Chocolate"
was directed by Alfonso Arau, who those of us in their thirties or older
may remember as a character actor in such films as "The Wild Bunch" and
"Scandalous John".  He is apparently much better known in Mexico.  I myself
do not detect a strong common link between Bunuel and "Like Water For
Chocolate".  Bunuel never made a totally serious movie in his life, and
"Like Water For Chocolate" seemed pretty earnest, to me.


—
—MORE—(96%)
Esc-chr: ^]  help: ^]?  port:2 speed: 9600 parity:none echo:rem  VT102 ....
```

There you have part of a typical discussion on this newsgroup. The tone (whether the participants pontificate, discuss, bicker, and so on) and how quickly messages are posted depends on the purpose and scope of the newsgroup. The purpose of this newsgroup is discussion. Many other newsgroups are for information only and actually discourage discussion. Read through a newsgroup to find out what type it is before participating.

# Participating in News

You can access news from many different types of machines. Software programs enable you to access news for UNIX, VMS, PC DOS, Macs, and so on. Most are available via anonymous FTP over the Internet (see Appendix E, "The Internet Navigator's Gazetteer"), but you'll probably have one already installed on your system if you have a UNIX machine. Your systems administrator can tell you what news program is installed with your network connection. You should also get them to show you how it's set up and whether they have any special features to make newsgroup access easier (many sites set up scripts to make the user's life easier).

## The rn Program

To show how news is used, I'll demonstrate one of the most popular news reading programs, the UNIX rn news reading software (note that the other popular news reading program is nn and is pretty similar to rn).

When you start rn, articles from each newsgroup to which you subscribe are presented, one article at a time (an article is an individual news item). As each article is presented, you are shown the header containing the name of the author, the subject of the article, and the first page of the article, and you are asked if you want more.

rn operates on three levels:

1. The newsgroup selection level.

2. The article selection level.

3. The article paging level.

Each level has its own set of commands and its own help menu. As with other programs mentioned in this book, reading the help screens, or more importantly, knowing how to get in and out of the help screens and exit the program, are just about the most important things a new user can learn. Typing the letter h at any rn level or at any prompt brings you a help list and a brief explanation of what you can do.

## Newsgroup Selection Level

Starting rn puts you at the selection level. The program checks to see if any new newsgroups have been added since the last time you read your news; if so, you are asked if you want to add the newsgroup to your reading list of groups.

In the following example, I am asked if I want to subscribe to a new newsgroup biz.pagesat. I answer "no" to this new newsgroup and to the following newsgroup, alt.fan.TTBS. The options, [ynYN], mean:

1. Type y (or just press the Spacebar) to add the current newsgroup to the list of those you follow.

2. Type Y to add all new groups to your list and subscribe to them.

3. Type N to add all new groups to your list but not subscribe to them.

4. Type n to forget about this newsgroup.

The Y and N commands are useful when you're first starting to access newsgroups or when you have not read your news for a long period of time. They add all new newsgroups to your list and either subscribe to them or leave them unsubscribed to but recorded in one fell swoop. Your reason for recording them is so that you can go back later and join them.

```
bss> rn

Unread news in general                                371 articles
Unread news in to                                       4 articles
Unread news in usl.announce                             4 articles
Unread news in usl.class.cmps.201                      10 articles
Unread news in usl.class.engl.101                       2 articles
etc.
```

```
Finding new newsgroups:

Newsgroup biz.pagesat not in .newsrc—subscribe? [ynYN] h
Type y or SP to add biz.pagesat to your .newsrc.
Type Y to add all new groups to the end of your .newsrc.
Type N to add all new groups to the end of your .newsrc unsubscribed.
Type n to forget about this newsgroup.

Newsgroup biz.pagesat not in .newsrc—subscribe? [ynYN]n

Newsgroup alt.fan.TTBS not in .newsrc—subscribe? [ynYN]n

******** 371 unread articles in general—read now? [ynq]
```

After the listing of new newsgroups comes the first newsgroup to which you are subscribed. rn tells you how many messages are unread and asks if you would like to read them. You have three options:

1. Type y for yes, read this newsgroup.

2. Type n for next newsgroup.

3. Type q for quit.

## The .newsrc File

The rn program keeps track of which newsgroups you have subscribed to and what articles you have read with a file called .newsrc. This file is created the first time you use the rn program, and it contains the names of all newsgroups that your site has access to over the network. Here is a small sample of a .newsrc file:

```
alt!
general: 1-530
to: 1-4
usl.announce: 1-1
usl.cacs.announce: 1-11
usl.class.cmps.201: 1-6
usl.centercasts: 1-13
news.admin: 1-12300
news.admin.misc:
news.admin.technical:
news.software.notes! 1-120
news.sysadmin! 1-1989
comp.admin.policy! 1-3372
comp.ai! 1-11997
comp.ai.digest:
```

```
comp.ai.edu! 1-335
comp.ai.fuzzy!
comp.ai.genetic!
sci.aquaria:
sci.archaeology:
sci.astro:
rec.arts.animation! 1-3805
soc.culture.europe:
alt.activism:
```

The numbers after a newsgroup indicate the articles that have been read in that newsgroup. No numbers means that no articles have been read. The exclamation point, !, indicates that you are unsubscribed to that newsgroup (that is, you don't belong to it and don't get news from it).

When you first start rn, you are asked whether you want to subscribe to each newsgroup in turn. If you answer "yes," you'll be asked where you want it placed in your .newsrc file. Do you want a newsgroup placed first on the list, last, or somewhere in between? Where the entries are in the .newsrc file will determine the order in which you will see newsgroups when you start rn (the first entry in the file is the first you see).

The problem here is that you have access to thousands of newsgroups. The site I use at the University of Southwestern Louisiana currently has access to 2,455 newsgroups. It would take some time to subscribe or unsubscribe to all these groups.

Subscribing to all newsgroups with the Y command and then editing the .newsrc file to tailor it to your tastes is a common practice. You can use your favorite editor on the .newsrc file to add or delete exclamation points, remove numbering, or change the positions of the newsgroup entries.

> **Navigator's Note:** Considering the several thousand newsgroups in existence, editing this list could be a horrible task. Check with other people in your organization to see if they have a good list you can use, or ask the system administrator for a sorted list of newsgroup titles to browse through.

## Back to rn

Here are the options you have after pressing the letter h to receive help.

```
Put newsgroup where? [$^.L] h

Type ^ to put the newsgroup first (position 0).
Type $ to put the newsgroup last (position 2454).
Type . to put it before the current newsgroup (position 0).
Type -newsgroup name to put it before that newsgroup.
Type +newsgroup name to put it after that newsgroup.
Type a number between 0 and 2454 to put it at that position.
Type L for a listing of newsgroups and their positions.
```

When asked at the selection level if you want to read a newsgroup, type h to get help. You have quite a few options; the rn manual is over thirty pages long. The help screen tells you primarily how to move from newsgroup to newsgroup. Typing the letter y moves you to the next level of rn to read the information of the newsgroup. The letters n and N, respectively, take you to the next newsgroup or to the next newsgroup with unread news. The letter u unsubscribes you from this newsgroup, and q quits the rn program.

There are numerous ways to move around in rn. As you become familiar with the newsgroup names, you will want to make use of the pat commands to move directly to a newsgroup you want to investigate.

## Article Selection Level

When you select a newsgroup to read (by using the letter y or by choosing an option that will get you to a specific newsgroup), you drop to the lower level of rn and receive the first unread message from the newsgroup, along with a prompt.

Now you can select how to move through the newsgroup messages. Typing h will give you a help screen for this level. Note the new prompt (Mail); here you can participate in the newsgroup by using the reply or the follow-up command. In many cases, you want to send a reply to the author of the message only and not to the entire newsgroup.

**Navigator's Note:** If you see an article with (rot13) after its title, the message has been encrypted. The rot13 method is a very simple form of encryption. It's not intended to keep the contents of the article secret but rather to prevent offense. If someone posts, for example, a joke that they know is in poor taste or offensive in some way, they use this technique. Don't be tempted to use this technique with wild abandon. Not everyone knows about it, and unless you see others in a newsgroup using it, you'd be advised not to bother, because other participants will get all hot and bothered about it.

Most of the news reading programs support encoding and decoding rot13 messages. Read these messages at your own peril. If you're an ardent feminist and you see an article in the `alt.feminist` newsgroup entitled "Have you heard the one about the feminist…(rot13)," you can be pretty sure it's not going to be a joke that you approve of.

> **Navigator's Warning:** Consider carefully whether you need to reply to the newsgroup or the author. A lot of unnecessary traffic is generated by people getting involved in what are, essentially, private discussions.

At this level you can track the flow of the group's subject matter by using the command Ctrl+N. For example, if you are in the newsgroup that reviews movies, and you read a review with the film's title as a subject heading, you can find other opinions on the film by using the Ctrl+N command to find other messages with the same subject heading. You can save the message for future reference, or you can mark it as unread if you want to come back to it at a later date.

If no newsgroups are specified, all the newsgroups with unread news articles are displayed. You are asked whether you want to read each newsgroup in the order in which it occurs in the .newsrc file. The many other options are best learned through practice. Actually using rn and getting familiar with news is the best way to become proficient with it.

# Creating a USENET Newsgroup

USENET newsgroups come and go through a process of asking the network community if a particular newsgroup is important enough to be created. If, after a specific period of time, enough "yes" votes are received, the newsgroup is created and announced through postings in a newsgroup called `new.news.announcements`. Creating a new newsgroup is quite a formal process, and you should check out the newsgroup `news.groups` to see how the procedure is handled.

# Moderated and Unmoderated Newsgroups

Newsgroups can be moderated or unmoderated. In a moderated newsgroup, a person or group reviews items before adding them to the newsgroup. The problem with this is that it is often considered to be a form of censorship. Also, any real level of activity can easily swamp the moderators. The general rule is that moderated newsgroups die young.

The advantage of a moderated newsgroup is that a filtering mechanism can remove inappropriate messages not pertinent to the group, condense or combine messages that are on the same subject or related to each other, and generally keep the number of messages being distributed at a manageable level. In a moderated newsgroup, you post items not to the newsgroup but to the moderator. Most news software is smart enough to handle this for you—it automatically sends messages to the moderator and does not allow posting to the group directly.

Unmoderated newsgroups allow direct posting, so the number of articles posted is generally higher. Because of the greater volume of articles, the conversation can (and often does) go astray more often than moderated newsgroups.

## Internetiquette and Frequently Asked Questions (FAQs) About News

Because of the number of participants and the volume of messages traveling on the network, the use of Internetiquette is strongly encouraged (see Chapter 11, "Internetiquette: Manners and the Internet"). You will receive many reminders of what is appropriate or otherwise in a certain newsgroup if you sway too far from its intention. People who have really gone over the edge by posting extreme views or offensive articles have been known to receive thousands of angry e-mail messages.

In addition, many newsgroups will post a message regularly on Frequently Asked Questions (FAQs). These postings give information about the subject to new readers of the newsgroup and outline the intent of the newsgroup for them. FAQs answer commonly asked questions about the newsgroup in order to avoid answering the same questions over and over again as new people subscribe. New readers of a newsgroup are encouraged to "lurk" for a while in order to get a feel for the content and proper use of any given newsgroup.

## Site Administration

Internet computer systems have a complex way of distributing newsgroup articles. The reason is that newsgroups exist on many computers. The volume of messages generated by these groups is so great that even a poor attempt to reduce this traffic is vitally important. The transfer of newsgroup articles from one computer to another is called a news feed.

Each computer system is responsible for receiving the news feed and deciding which newsgroup selections to make available. Sites don't have to receive every newsgroup that is available on the Internet. This has often caused controversy. Opinions on what should be made available at a site have been topics of discussion, with accusations of censorship and improper use of institutional resources. Many organizations have policies stating what should or should not be made available. Those policies might be liberal, demanding that all information from all newsgroups should be accessible, or they might strictly enforce exactly which newsgroups are available.

# All That's Fit to Read

Network news in the form of newsgroups is an informative, educational, and sometimes controversial use of the Internet. USENET was developed and continues to develop as a service to the network, but with more and more newsgroups appearing outside of USENET, the general tone of newsgroups is changing rapidly.

A good example of organized anarchy, Internet news continues to work even though the number of newsgroups and users has grown significantly. At its best, Internet news through newsgroups is informative and helpful, providing new and up-to-the-minute information on just about anything. At its worst, news can be overwhelming in its volume, and some people find that its contents can be offensive. Certainly, much of what goes on in newsgroups is positive, constructive, and useful. You just need to choose your reading carefully.

# GETTING ON THE LIST: LISTSERV

What's your interest? Mathematics? Rural life? Concurrent software engineering? Zymurgy? Dollhouses? The more obscure your interest or specialization (for example, the development of tin mining in 13th century Cornwall), the harder it is to find others who know anything about it, let alone those who are interested in discussing it.

Don't worry! Help is at hand—or rather, on net. The Internet is not only a great place to find data, it's also a tremendous place to find people to talk to (metaphorically speaking).

Your quest for others who understand, say, the implications of the Diet of Worms (sounds yucky, but it was actually—and disappointingly—where, in April 1521, Luther again refused to recant, and the Holy Roman Emperor Charles V put him under the ban of the empire—so there) is more likely to be satisfied on the Internet than just about anywhere else. Your quest for intelligent conversation on that subject is where LISTSERV comes in.

A popular form of information exchange over the Internet, LISTSERV is also known by several other names: discussion groups, conferences, or lists. Fundamentally, it's a lot like the USENET newsgroups we discussed in Chapter 12, "Views and News: USENET," except that you send and receive messages through e-mail rather than using a special news reading program. An advantage of this is that you can use any e-mail program to read the news. The disadvantage is that you have a lot less control over how you can handle the messages.

A LISTSERV discussion group lets you post a message to which others can respond. You and the others can then respond to the responses, until you all get bored or have something more pressing to attend to.

LISTSERV itself is a program that manages discussion groups, controlling functions such as subscribing, desubscribing, and so on. LISTSERVs can be a great way to keep your knowledge current, explore a topic with experts, or develop an idea in conversation with others. For example, system administrators use LISTSERV discussion groups to keep abreast of developments in telecommunications software and hardware technologies.

The variety of lists handled by LISTSERVs has grown to include a huge number of subjects. There are now lists for librarians, humanists, mathematicians, business, grade school teachers and students, and so on (although I couldn't actually find one for enthusiasts of the development of tin mining in 13th century Cornwall).

## Subscribing

To subscribe to a LISTSERV list, you must first know the address of the machine on which a copy of the LISTSERV software is running. This is where the LISTSERV system is really neat. You don't need to know which computer the actual list is on—any LISTSERV can find any LISTSERV list.

A LISTSERV site may distribute e-mail for several mailing lists, so you need to tell the LISTSERV which list you want to join. When you have that information, you can send an e-mail message containing the following text in the message body:

```
SUBSCRIBE <listname> <firstname> <lastname>
```

For example, if you want to subscribe to a list named ASIS-L, which is a list of the American Society for Information Science, you would send the following e-mail text to the LISTSERV address listserv@uvmvm.bitnet:

```
SUBSCRIBE ASIS-L Richard Smith
```

This particular LISTSERV, `listserv@uvmvm.bitnet`, handles the following mailing lists:

```
A+SCOMP    A+SComp: College of Arts & Sciences Computing Services
ACUA-L     acua-l
ADMUSERS   ADMUSERS: UVM Administrative Systems Users Group
ADVOCATS   Advocats: Departmental Technology Coordinators
ASIS-L     ASIS-L: American Society for Information Science
AUTOCAT    AUTOCAT: Library cataloging and authorities discussion group
BACKS-L    BACKS-L: Research on low back pain, disability and rehabilitation
BMW92      BMW92: Summer Institute for Women in Higher Ed. - 1992
CANST-LI   CANST-LI: ACRL Canadian Studies Librarians' Discussion Group
CHAOPSYC   CHAOPSYC: Discussion list of Society for Chaos Theory in Psychology
COMMUNET   Communet: Community and Civic Network Discussion List
COUNS-L    Couns-L: UCS Student Consulting Forum
CSAC       CSAC: CSAC Conference Administation
CSAC-L     CSAC-L: Computing Strategies Discussion List
DANEWS     DANEWS: Dana Library Internal List
DEVCIT     DEVCIT: Development and CIT Group
FPS-CORE   FPS-CORE: Division of Financial & Personnel Services
FPS-PLUS   FPS-PLUS: Financial & Personnel Issues Discussion Group
GRADCOLL   GRADCOLL: Graduate College News List
HERS-L     Hers-l: Higher Education Resource Services members
ILL-L      ILL-L: Interlibrary Loan discussion group
MAC-CONF   Mac-Conf  : Discontinued list, see CSAC-L instead.
RECS-L     RECS-L: Rehab Engineering Centers' Discussion Group
SAFETY     Safety
SERIALST   SERIALST: Serials in Libraries Discussion Forum
SKIVT-L    SKIVT-L: Vermont Skiing and Snow Reports
USERSERV   USERSERV: Vt. User Services Support Group
UVMTODAY   UVMTODAY: UVM News
1-UNION    1-Union: Industrial democracy and industrial unionism
```

A well-managed LISTSERV will send you notification that your subscription has been accepted. It might include introductory material about the list you joined, perhaps telling you the scope and size of the list, how to obtain future information on setting your list parameters, and most importantly, how to unsubscribe from a list.

# Participating

After you subscribe, you will receive e-mail routed through the LISTSERV from anyone who sends an e-mail message to that list. If you're not familiar with how the list participants conduct themselves, you should first get acquainted with the topics being discussed and get a feel for what counts as appropriate input and responses before you start adding your two cents' worth.

This "lurking" can help you avoid inadvertently making an inappropriate comment to the list, thus saving you embarrassment and unwanted, angry e-mail. Keep in mind that a list can be sending messages to several thousand people around the world; a future employer, colleague, or lover may be reading your words. It would be pretty bad to have your latest flame or current employer suddenly say, in shocked realization, "It was you who said that!!!" followed by "Good-bye" or "Empty your desk."

When you want to hazard a response to a message on a list, you only need to send an e-mail message to that list at the address where you subscribed to it. In the preceding example, you would address your e-mail message to the list `asis-l@uvmvm.bitnet`.

> **Navigator's Warning:** It is important to distinguish between the address of the list and the name of the LISTSERV. A common mistake is to send a subscription or unsubscription message meant for the LISTSERV to the list itself. In the preceding example, if you sent the subscription request to `asis-l@uvmvm.bitnet`, you would get a torrent of messages (ranging from the irritated to the downright abusive) from other users of the list, telling you that you should have sent the message to `listserv@uvmvm.bitnet`.

When you are on a list, it is not unusual to get a message saying `unsubscribe John Doe`. John Doe, the sender, confused the two addresses and sent the message meant for the LISTSERV program to everyone on the list. Go ahead, send him an abusive note. You wouldn't, of course, ever make that mistake yourself.

## Moderated LISTSERV

A list may or may not be moderated. An unmoderated list accepts and distributes all e-mail from anyone registered to the group. Conversely, in a moderated list, all e-mail messages are filtered through a person or group who checks to make sure that each message is appropriate to the list.

A moderated list is designed to avoid duplicate messages, catch messages sent to the list (rather than the LISTSERV) by mistake, and ensure that message topics are kept within the scope of the list. The target is to get the messages checked and posted to the list as soon as possible. This can be very difficult to achieve.

The problem with a moderated list on even a slightly popular topic is that the message volume can easily overwhelm the moderator. Consider that a list could easily get a hundred messages or more posted to it each week. The moderator has to read each message and judge its suitability. If each takes just two minutes to read and handle, that's over three hours. If the moderator takes a vacation, a deputy moderator is needed.

Some people worry that judging which messages are passed to moderated LISTSERV lists is tantamount to censorship. They are concerned that opinions running contrary to the mainstream may not get fair distribution. In fact, concern over censorship is a constant theme in many Internet discussion groups.

> **Navigator's Note:** If you intend to start a moderated list, remember the maxim "moderated lists die young." A moderated list often gets a parallel, unmoderated list, and the moderated version usually withers and dies.

# Working with LISTSERV

After you get a feel for the kinds of messages that are being posted on a list, you may want to adjust the settings of your subscription so that it handles the messages in a more appropriate manner for you.

For example, you can set the attributes on the LISTSERV so that messages to the list aren't accumulated for you while you go on vacation. You might also want to check the settings if you feel you are not receiving e-mail from a LISTSERV.

A LISTSERV might not forward messages to you due to several reasons: maintenance on either end of the net (or some point in between), a list owner mistakenly deleting you or turning message reception off for you by mistake, and so on.

## General Commands

Several versions of the LISTSERV software run on the Internet. Eric Thomas's Revised LISTSERV and Anastasios Kotsikonas's LISTSERV are two of the most used varieties. There are command differences, but sending the command `help` to most LISTSERVs gets you an e-mail message with commands that can be used with the LISTSERV.

Here is a list of the most common commands that come from Revised LISTSERV:

```
SUBSCRIBE <listname> <firstname>  <lastname>
```

Subscribe to a list, or change your name if already subscribed.

```
SIGNOFF <listname>
```

Remove yourself from the specified list.

```
SET <listname> <options>
```

Alter your subscription options.

```
ACK / NOACK
```

Use the ACK option if you want to receive acknowledgment of messages that you send to the list. This is useful if you want to check whether a message was really distributed, particularly on a moderated list. NOACK is the opposite of ACK. The NOACK option is the default.

> **Navigator's Note:** An important point, often missed by newcomers to LISTSERV lists, is that most lists have the default set to NOACK. When you post to the list, you will not receive a copy of the message you sent to the list, so many novices resend their message. It irritates many list readers when someone posts a message a second time stating that they didn't think their first message was posted to the list. Remember to check what option is set for the lists you use.

```
CONCEAL/NOCONCEAL
```

Hides or reveals (the default) your details if someone issues a REVIEW command. Your name and address on the LISTSERV is available to anyone who wants to know—unless the CONCEAL option is used.

```
FILES/NOFILES
```

Enables or disables receipt of files that are sent to the list.

```
MAIL/NOMAIL
```

Tells LISTSERV to send or not to send e-mail without unsubscribing. This is useful, for example, if you want to stop getting messages while you're on vacation. It means that you won't have several hundred e-mail messages to wade through when you next log on.

```
DIGESTS/INDEX
```

Asks for digests (all messages for a given period) or message indexes (the headers of the messages for a given period) to be sent, rather than getting messages as they are posted.

Additional LISTSERV commands that may come in handy:

```
CONFIRM <listname1> (<listname2> ( ... ) )
```

Confirms your subscription (when LISTSERV requests it).

```
INDEX <listname>
```

Sends you a directory of the available archive files for the named list, if postings for that list have been archived.

```
LIST
```

Gives names of lists on the LISTSERV.

```
QUERY <listname>
```

Checks your subscription options for the list. Use this command to make sure that the correct options are set if you suspect that the LISTSERV is not sending you messages.

```
REVIEW <listname> (<options>)
```

Get user usage information about a list.

Sending `info ?` to a LISTSERV gets you the following message (our example is from `listserv@uhupvm1`):

```
> info ?

List of information guides available from LISTSERV@UHUPVM1:

REFcard     (LISTSERV REFCARD)   Command reference card
FAQ         (LISTFAQ  MEMO    )   Frequently Asked Questions
PResent     (LISTPRES MEMO    )   Presentation of LISTSERV for new users
GENintro    (LISTSERV MEMO    )   General information about Revised LISTSERV
KEYwords    (LISTKEYW MEMO    )   Description of list header keywords
AFD         (LISTAFD  MEMO    )   Description of Automatic File Distribution
FILEs       (LISTFILE MEMO    )   Description of the file-server functions
LPunch      (LISTLPUN MEMO    )   Description of the LISTSERV-Punch file format
JOB         (LISTJOB  MEMO    )   Description of the Command Jobs feature
DISTribute  (LISTDIST MEMO    )   Description of Relayed File Distribution
COORDinat   (LISTCOOR MEMO    )   Information about Listserv Coordination
FILEOwner   (LISTFOWN MEMO    )   Information guide for file owners
DATABASE    (LISTDB   MEMO    )   Description of the database functions
UDD         (LISTUDD  MEMO    )   User Directory Database User's Guide
UDDADMIN    (LISTUDDA MEMO    )   UDD Administrator's Guide

The following files are restricted to list owners:
```

```
LINKing    (LISTLINK MEMO   )  Guidelines for linking list servers together
OWNers     (LISTOWNR MEMO   )  Description of list-owners commands
PUT        (LSVPUT   EXEC   )  An exec to facilitate sending PUT commands

You should order the PResentation or GENintro manual
if you are new to LISTSERV.
```

Sending e-mail to the LISTSERV with the word info followed by capital letters of the preceding commands in the body of the e-mail message will get you the information guide.

## Searching a LISTSERV List

A LISTSERV can archive and build a database from all the messages mailed to a list. Years of information exchanged by the participants of the list can be stored and searched.

Eric Thomas's revised LISTSERV database search can be used interactively if you run a VM/SP CMS or VAX/VMS system, and can be searched in the batch mode by everyone else. The batch mode is a two-step process: first, search messages containing a word or words of information desired; second, send for a printout of the items, which will be e-mailed back to you.

In the following example I e-mail a text file to search the discussion list PACS-L, a list that discusses library automation, Internet usage, new information technology, NREN developments, and a host of other computer and telecommunication information tidbits. The LISTSERV address is listserv@uhupvm1.bitnet.

I remember that I put my early workshop notes on an anonymous ftp site, but I forgot the site's address. I did post a note to the LISTSERV PACS-L, telling subscribers where they could ftp the notes. The LISTSERV acts as my personal file cabinet of PACS-L e-mail messages. I send the LISTSERV search command (shown below) to listserv@uhupvm1.bitnet to search the LISTSERV PACS-L:

```
prompt>mail listserv@uhupvm1.bitnet
Subject:
//
Database Search DD=Rules
//Rules DD *
Search richard smith (navigate or navigating) in PACS-L from
90/1/1 to 92/8/30
Index
/*
```

The first three lines tells the listserv this is a database search. the third line searches for the word richard and smith and (navigate or navigating) in the PACS-L list from the dates indicated. Remember, I'm sending this to the LISTSERV, not the list PACS-L.

The listserv returns me a DATAOUTPUT file with any "hits" found in the database. Here is the file:

```
From LISTSERV@UHUPVM1.UH.EDU Wed Apr 28 18:12:17 1993
Subject: File: "DATABASE OUTPUT"
To: rjs4808@ucs.usl.edu
Message-Id: <01GXJY9M0782000BZY@Post-Office.UH.EDU>
Content-Transfer-Encoding: 7BIT
Status: R

> Search richard smith (navigate or navigating) in PACS-L from
90/1/1 to 92/8/30
--> Database PACS-L, 6 hits.

> Index
Item #   Date     Time   Recs   Subject
------   ----     ----   ----   -------
003763 91/06/24  16:31    43    workshop notes
005430 92/03/26  08:46   156    Library Automation—Comments &
                                 Questions
005558 92/04/10  12:23    85    Finding Guides using FTP
006075 92/06/10  08:29    36    Internet connection
006395 92/07/21  08:18   142    Interactive Navigation
006543 92/08/06  08:39    39    Internet Training
```

The LISTSERV returned to me a list of six messages that met the search requirement. I see one that has workshop notes in it from June 1991. That's probably it, so now I have to retrieve it. I send the following e-mail message, with the added print command line and the item number of the file I want, back to the LISTSERV:

```
//
Database Search DD=Rules
//Rules DD *
Search richard smith (navigate or navigating) in PACS-L from
90/1/1 to 92/8/30
Print all of 3763
/*
```

The LISTSERV returned the e-mail file numbered 3763 to me, which contains the information I wanted.

The LISTSERV database can also use Boolean searching techniques. You can expand your search by using or and limit it by using and or not. With multiple word searches, the and is implied. Boolean searches require that you use parentheses to make your meaning clear.

Case is usually ignored, but searches can be made case-sensitive by adding quotes around a word. Searches can also involve dates. You can select a range of dates from 90/1/1 to 93/6/30 (note the order on the date specification, yy/mm/dd), or specify messages from a specific date. Use the date words "from" and "since" at the end of a search line.

For more information on searching techniques and how to obtain software for interactive searching, send an e-mail message with INFO DATABASE to a LISTSERV.

# GETTING RESOURCEFUL: CARL, DIALOG, OCLC, AND ERIC

As you get comfortable in your Internet navigation, you'll start to get more ambitious in looking for resources and data. Several services on the Internet are great for serious research. In this chapter, we'll look at four of the major systems—CARL, DIALOG, OCLC, and ERIC.

Each of these services has a different orientation:

- ⚓ CARL UnCover is a database through which citations to more than 10,000 journals can be accessed.
- ⚓ DIALOG enables you to get details about what businesses are doing, who runs them, and so on.
- ⚓ OCLC is a library-oriented database.
- ⚓ ERIC is a database of great interest to teachers, parents, and students.

Between them, these systems meet a great many research needs. Whether you're working on a thesis on the fishing economy of the Byzantine era, trying to find out about the dynamics of photokinetic reactions for an industrial application, looking for information on whether a particular company is a sound investment, or seeking a science fair project for your child, these databases are where you'll find answers.

## CARL UnCover Uncovered

CARL, the Colorado Alliance of Research Libraries, developed a document access and retrieval system that is run by CARL Systems, Inc. Access to many library systems is possible through the CARL service and the ERIC database (which we discuss separately later). The full text of Online Libraries and Choice book reviews are all indexed and accessible through CARL.

CARL's UnCover service makes available, online, the tables of contents of all journals received by the seven members of the Colorado Alliance of Research Libraries. In late 1991, the database contained 10,600 unique multidisciplinary journals. The database includes article citations taken from the tables of contents of each issue, along with descriptive information or abstracts that appear on the contents page. The database is continuously updated—at a rate of 3,000 to 4,000 articles per day!

UnCover can be used in two ways. First, you can search the database for a particular journal title. From the issue screen, you can select an individual issue and look at its table of contents. From there, you can take the final step, which is to look at the article record.

This approach is good if you have specific titles in which you are interested. The other approach, a keyword search on a subject, retrieves all the articles on that subject that appear in any of the journals in UnCover.

An important new UnCover service is document delivery. This service is currently called UnCover2, but CARL is in the process of merging the two services under the UnCover name. UnCover2 exists to supply copies of articles from UnCover within 24 hours, and often much sooner. Copyright royalties are carefully tracked and paid to publishers. Fees can be conveniently charged to VISA or MasterCard accounts, or deposit accounts can be set up for libraries, departments, or individual users.

Now, suppose I'm working on a system to index gene sequences for *Drosophila* species (flies, for the uninitiated). This is going to be a huge amount of data, and I want to think about compressing it. I remember that some guy called Rick Gates (actually the same one who supplied the material for Appendix A, "Testing Your Navigation Skills") wrote an article in, I think, *The Electronic Library* on the topic of compression.

Lucky for me, even though the library near me doesn't subscribe to *The Electronic Library*, CARL's UnCover can find the article and send it to me by fax. Because I've got a fax machine at home, I can request, receive, and read the article I'm looking for without ever leaving the house. Better still, using my portable computer (on battery power) I can run a phone line into the garden and sit in the jacuzzi while I do my search. It's a tough life.

First, I telnet to CARL's host computer and log on:

```
coyote% telnet database.carl.org
Trying 192.54.81.76 ...
Connected to database.carl.org.
Escape character is '^]'.
Welcome to the CARL system
Please identify your terminal. Choices are:
1.ADM (all)
2.APPLE,IBM
3.TANDEM
4.TELE-914
5.VT100
6.WYSE 50
7.ZENTEC
8.HARDCOPY
9.IBM 316x
Use HARDCOPY if your terminal type isn't listed
SELECT LINE #:5

All set. When you are ready to exit the system, simply
type //EXIT, or hang up.
Now, press return to enter the Public Access Catalog...
```

So far, pretty easy. Just make sure you select the right terminal type or you may get a messed-up screen display in certain parts of the system.

```
              >>>  Systems That Inform  <<<
              Welcome to the CARL System
                  (Release A.101)

       A Computerized Network of Systems and Services


        Developed by the Colorado Alliance of Research Libraries
            Marketed and supported by CARL Systems, Inc.
                3801 East Florida St., Suite 300
                    Denver, Co. 80210
                Voice:   303-758-3030
                Fax:    303-758-0606
                Internet:   help@carl.org
PRESS <RETURN> TO START THE PROGRAM  (use //EXIT to return HOME)>>
        WELCOME TO THE CARL SYSTEM DATABASE GATEWAY
CARL Systems, Inc. is proud to present our Shopping List of Databases.
Many of the databases included require a password. If you would like to
look at one of these restricted databases, please contact CARL Systems, Inc.
at database@carl.org or 303/758-3030. If you have already been given a
password to a database, please enter your password when prompted.
     1.  UnCover
         (Article Access and Delivery)
     2.  Information Access Company Databases
         (including Business Index, Magazine Index and others)
     3.  Grolier's Academic American Encyclopedia
     4.  Facts on File
     5.  H.W. Wilson Databases
         (including Library Literature)
     6.  Other Databases
         (including Journal Graphics, Choice and others)

  Enter the NUMBER of your choice, and press the <RETURN> key >> 1
WORKING...
```

Well, I know that I want to use the UnCover service, so I select item 1 and...

```
The CARL system includes some services which require appropriate
validation, including UnCover. So that we may serve you, please
enter your library card number, or assigned password.
Libraries participating in UnCover are those listed in previous
menus. Touch <RETURN> to review menus.
USER ID>>
Thank you...
```

I have to give a password to use the system (nothing shows after USER ID>> because for security reasons CARL doesn't echo the password).

```
06/22/93
10:57 A.M.        SELECTED DATABASE:  UnCover
                         Welcome to
                    UnCover and UnCover2
        The Article Access and Delivery Solutions from CARL.
UnCover contains records describing journals and their contents. It
includes more than 14,000 titles, and more than 4,000,000 articles.
Over 750,000 articles are added annually.

UnCover2 is a new service which offers you the opportunity to order
any article in this data base. Type ? for order details.
          Enter   N   for  NAME search
                  W   for  WORD search
                  B   to   BROWSE by journal title
                  S   to   STOP or SWITCH to another database
          Type the letter for the kind of search you want,
          and end each line you type by pressing <RETURN>

                  SELECTED DATABASE:  UnCover
```

I know a word in the title of the article, "compression," and the name of the journal, *The Electronic Library*. I type those words as the minimum information I think UnCover needs to find the article.

```
ENTER  COMMAND (? FOR HELP) >>  w
             SELECTED DATABASE: UnCover

          REMEMBER — WORDS can be words from the title, or
          from subtitles, summaries or abstracts that appear
          on the Table of Contents page for each journal.
          A WORD search will also often return NAMES of people
          who are discussed or referred to in the articles.
          You may also supply the name of a journal in your search
          in order to limit your results to that publication.
           for example     HEALTH CARE TRENDS
                           MICKEY MANTLE
                           AIDS SCIENTIFIC AMERICAN
          Enter word or words (no more than one line, please)
          separated by spaces and press <RETURN>.

>compression electronic library
 WORKING...
COMPRESSION  2350 ITEMS        UnCover
patience — ELECTRONIC is a long one...
COMPRESSION + ELECTRONIC    28 ITEMS
patience — LIBRARY is a long one...
COMPRESSION + ELECTRONIC + LIBRARY     1 ITEM

  1 Gates, Rick              (The Electronic library :  the int... 04/01/93)
     Compression and archiving.
```

Jackpot! Here's the exact article I was looking for. Now I ask to see the complete record and then order a fax of it to be sent to me.

```
Enter <LINE NUMBER> to display full record, or <Q>UIT for new search 1


------------------------------------------------UnCover------------------
AUTHOR(s):     Gates, Rick
               Bang, Steve
TITLE(s):      Compression and archiving.
         In:   The Electronic library :  the international jour
               APR 01 1993 v 11 n 2
       Page:   120

Summary Holdings:
CALL #:                                      LOCN:
--1 of 1----------------------------------------UnCover------------------
<R>epeat this display,
<Q>uit,
<H> for History,  <D>for Delivery Information ? for HELP >d
```

Ah! The article is co-authored by this book's technical reviewer. What a find! To see about delivery information, I press d:

```
This article may be available at your library or through interlibrary loan.
The full text of this article is available by FAX.
The cost is:                      $  6.50  (service fee)
          plus                    $  8.00C (copyright fee)
          for a TOTAL of:         $ 14.50
(The copyright fee is set by and paid to the publisher.)
If you would like a FAX copy of the article, please
enter a Mastercard, Visa, or American Express number, or,
your Special (Deposit) account ID.  Type ? for more
information, or <RETURN> to exit >>>            123456789012345
Enter the expiration date (MM/YY):    12/99

Enter your name, EXACTLY as it appears on your card: Mark Gibbs
Checking authorization -- please be patient...


Please enter the FAX PHONE number of your FAX machine  --
(Include dialing prefix '1', or '1' plus AREA CODE
if not in Denver local calling area)
Type ? for more information, or <Q> to cancel.
Enter FAX PHONE NUMBER >> 18055551212


Please enter local routing information for FAX delivery (optional) --
eg. department number, room number, etc (up to 20 characters)
```

```
Enter information, and touch <RETURN> to continue
>>

You have requested a FAX copy of
Compression and archiving.                         Gates, Rick
to 18055551212
Charged to 123456789012345
O.K. to proceed? (Y or N -- ? for Help)y
Thank you -- now writing your order...
Thank you. Your reference # is: 93173110044
Please note this number for use if you need to contact CARL Systems.
Press <RETURN> to continue...
You began with a WORD search on:
COMPRESSION ELECTRONIC LIBRARY
```

That's it. The fax will be sent and might even arrive within an hour. I can then read it at my leisure, having avoided traffic, parking problems, etc. That is, provided I can find someone in the house to bring the document from the fax machine in my study out to the jacuzzi. What a way to work.

The only thing left to do is to log off.

```
Type S to try your search in another database, or
     R to repeat your search in UnCover
     H to see a list of your recent searches, or
                       06/22/93
11:01 A.M.       SELECTED DATABASE:  UnCover
                       Welcome to
                  UnCover and UnCover2
         The Article Access and Delivery Solutions from CARL.
UnCover contains records describing journals and their contents. It
includes more than 14,000 titles, and more than 4,000,000 articles.
Over 750,000 articles are added annually.

UnCover2 is a new service which offers you the opportunity to order
any article in this data base. Type ? for order details.
         Enter   N    for  NAME search
                 W    for  WORD search
                 B    to   BROWSE by journal title
                 S    to   STOP or SWITCH to another database
         Type the letter for the kind of search you want,
         and end each line you type by pressing <RETURN>

                 SELECTED DATABASE:  UnCover
ENTER  COMMAND (? FOR HELP) >>  s
Connection closed by foreign host.
coyote% bye
```

As you can see, CARL is a fantastic resource—particularly if you're looking for articles in journals. It's pretty easy to use, too. If you're trying to research a topic and you want to try to review as many of the published articles as possible, this is the place to do it.

Starting in the fall of 1993, password access will not be required. Instead, you will be able to purchase any document for a standard $8.50 service charge plus the copyright fee. If a library or individual is requesting more than 450 articles per year, a password can be purchased, which will reduce the service charge to $6.50 per document.

For more information, contact CARL Systems at 800-787-7979 or at `help@carl.org`.

# Getting Into DIALOG

One of the largest commercial online database services, DIALOG, can be reached on the Internet. Properly called DIALOG Information Retrieval Service, from Dialog Information Services, Inc., the system has been serving users since 1972.

DIALOG offers nearly 400 databases and covers a broad scope of disciplines. These databases contain in excess of 329 million records. The data ranges from directory-type listings of companies, associations, and famous people to in-depth financial statements for companies, citations with bibliographic information, and abstracts referencing journals, patents, conference papers, and other original sources, including the complete text of many journal articles.

One of the unique services offered by DIALOG is its database of company information. As a test, let's check out the entry for Novell, Inc. Novell is a very big company, with sales approaching $1 billion; it will be interesting to see what DIALOG has to say about it.

You begin by using telnet to connect to the DIALOG system and at the prompt supply your account information.

```
ucsbuxa% telnet dialog.com
Trying 192.132.3.254…
Connected to dialog.com.
Escape character is '^]'.
Trying 3106...Open

DIALOG INFORMATION SERVICES
PLEASE LOGON: 9999
ENTER PASSWORD: XXXXXXX
Welcome to DIALOG
Dialog level 30.04.04B
```

```
Last logoff:  22jan93 13:29:24
Logon file001 21jun93 20:12:52
*

*

Fourth Edition Available in Kirk Othmer (File 302)
Reload:  DELPHES EUROPEAN BUSINESS (File 481)
Pharmacological Codes Now Available in Pharmaprojects (File 128)
IMSworld Product Monographs Now Available in File 446
New:  BCC MARKET RESEARCH (File 764) (MARKETFULL)
Reload:  CANCORP (File 491)
Weekly Updating Now Available in Ei Compendex*Plus (File 8)
DIALOG OnDisc ENVIRONMENTAL CHEMISTRY, HEALTH & SAFETY Now Available

    >>> Enter BEGIN HOMEBASE for Dialog Announcements <<<
    >>>    of new databases, price changes, etc.      <<<
    >>>    Announcements last updated for 16jun93      <<<
```

The one drawback to DIALOG is that it is very cryptic. You have to know the number (not even a name...geez!) of the databases that you want to access. In the following example, I tell DIALOG that I would like to connect (the command is b...who knows why) to a database called D&B-Dun's Market Indicators (the number is 516), a database with market information about corporations in North America.

> **Navigator's Note:** As a member of DIALOG, you get a service directory called the DIALOG Database Catalog that gives you a brief description of each database and is indexed by subject and database number.

The accounting information that appears is completely useless—it simply tells me that the clock is ticking and I'm spending money like there's no tomorrow.

```
?b516

        21jun93 20:13:04 User008533 Session B1800.1
            $0.11    0.003 Hrs File1
    $0.11  Estimated cost File1
    $0.01  ANSNET
    $0.12  Estimated cost this search
    $0.12  Estimated total session cost   0.003 Hrs.

File 516:D & B - DUNS MARKET IDENTIFIERS(R)  1993/Q2
      (c) 1993 D&B
**FILE516: 50% Off REPORT Elements For File 516 During May & June
```

I guess I got lucky here. There's a 50% discount this month for searches on this database.

Now I tell DIALOG that I want information (ss means start search) about Novell, Inc. (the /co tells DIALOG that it's a company I'm looking for). This gets me 51 records related to Novell. I need to narrow the scope, so I specify that the search is based on my first results and that I want to see only records that specify the city of Provo. The search for records specifying Provo results in 1,939 hits; the combination of the two searches produces one direct hit. This could be what I want.

```
      Set  Items  Description
      --   ----   ----------
?ss novell/co

      S1     51  NOVELL/CO
?ss s1 and cy=provo

            51  S1
      S2  1939  CY=PROVO
      S3     1  S1 AND CY=PROVO
```

I want to see all the information available from my search. So, I enter the command t for type, the number of the search results that I want to display, and the /5, which will show the complete record. You can see from this that using DIALOG without reading the manual is more or less impossible.

```
?t 3/5


 3/5/1
0758737    DIALOG File 516:  D&B Duns Market Identifiers
Novell, Inc
122 E 1700 S
P O Box 5900
Provo, UT  84606-7379
```

...and so forth. The file goes on to list several pages' worth of fascinating financial information about Novell, but because it's copyrighted material, I won't bore you with the details.

Now that I've got the information that I went to DIALOG for, I can log off the system and return to my local UNIX account.

```
    21jun93 20:18:39 User008533 Session B1800.3
         $3.17    0.033 Hrs File516
            $3.25  1 Type(s) in Format  5
         $3.25  1 Types
  $6.42  Estimated cost File516
  $0.10  ANSNET
  $6.52  Estimated cost this search
 $16.81  Estimated total session cost   0.120 Hrs.
Logoff: level 30.04.04 B  20:18:39

Connection closed by foreign host.
ucsbuxa%
```

DIALOG is an extraordinarily rich resource, but it has one of the most obscure interfaces around. You'll need to spend some money before you get really good at using the databases, and reading the manual is a prerequisite to conducting really successful searches. For more information, contact

> DIALOG Information Services, Inc.
> 3460 Hillview Avenue
> Palo Alto, CA 94304
> 800-334-2564 or 415-858-3758

# Oh, Say Can You See, It's OCLC

Yet another database that can be searched over the Internet is offered by OCLC (the Online Computer Library Center, Inc.). OCLC runs The FirstSearch Catalog, an online information service for library patrons. Available through many libraries around the world, it has a simple interface that enables users to move easily through the online search process in a few simple steps, without the need for any training or online searching experience.

## The FirstSearch Catalog

The FirstSearch Catalog currently provides access to more than 30 databases; following are OCLC's descriptions of some of the major ones:

⚓ The FirstSearch Catalog. An online reference service with an end-user interface designed specifically for library patrons.

⚓ WorldCat. The OCLC Online Union Catalog, a bibliography with more than 25 million records spanning 4,000 years of knowledge.

⚓ GPO Monthly Catalog, U.S. Government Printing Office. A database consisting of more than 350,000 records published by the GPO since July 1976. It has references to congressional committee reports and hearings, debates, documents from executive departments, and more.

⚓ BIOSIS/FS, Biological Abstracts, Inc. A database of biomedical and biological research information that is a subset of BIOSIS Previews. It provides journal citations and abstracts on up-to-date developments in 96 major subject areas.

⚓ MiniGeoRef, American Geological Institute. This covers recent additions to the GeoRef file, a database containing earth science references and the index terms that describe them.

⚓ Newspaper Abstracts, UMI/Data Courier. A database that indexes and abstracts more than 25 national and regional newspapers, including the *New York Times, Los Angeles Times, Washington Post, USA Today,* and *The Wall Street Journal.*

⚓ Periodical Abstracts, UMI/Data Courier. A complete general reference resource, with indexing and abstracts for over 900 popular and academic periodicals. Included are transcripts of more than 30 news-oriented television shows.

⚓ Readers' Guide to Periodical Literature, The H.W. Wilson Company. Readers' Guide indexes a core list of popular magazines, central to any college, public library, or school collection. Updated monthly, records are from January 1983 to the present.

⚓ Business Periodicals Index, The H.W. Wilson Company. Business Periodicals Index provides complete and accurate access to 345 of today's leading English-language business magazines.

⚓ Humanities Index, The H.W. Wilson Company. A good single reference to periodical information in the diverse subject area of the humanities, the Humanities Index complements the monographic resources accessible via WorldCat (OCLC Online Union Catalog).

⚓ Biography Index, The H.W. Wilson Company. Cites more than 2,700 periodicals and more than 1,800 books, including individual and collective biographies, as well as juvenile literature.

⚓ PsycFIRST, American Psychological Association. Covers the most recent three years from the PsycINFO database.

⚓ Business Organizations, Agencies, and Publications Directory, Gale Research, Inc. A guide to international business information sources that lists contact name, address, phone and FAX numbers, and a description of the organization's founding, membership, activities, and services.

# Getting Into OCLC

As with the other services, you have to telnet to the database host site and log onto the OCLC Reference Services system.

```
ucsbuxa% telnet epic.prod.oclc.org
Trying 132.174.100.2 ...
Connected to epic.prod.oclc.org.
Escape character is '^]'.

You are connected to OCLC Reference Services.

Enter your authorization.
=> 123456789

Enter your password.
=> abcde7xyz


* * * * * * * *        WELCOME TO FIRSTSEARCH !        * * * * * * * * * *

    Use The FirstSearch Catalog to find information--or records--
    about books, articles, theses, films, computer software, and
    other types of material on the subject you need.

      -- First, select a broad topic area and a database.
      -- Then, type your search.  You can use upper or lower case.
      -- From the List of Records, select a record to view.
      -- To do another search, type S and your search term.

    Other actions you can do are listed on each screen.  Just type
    the ACTION name or first letter.


              HOURS (ET): 6 a.m. - midnight M-F
                          8 a.m. - 8 p.m. Sat.
                          12 noon - midnight Sun.


    NOTE: Documentation now on Internet!  On next screen, ask for News.


                      PRESS ENTER TO CONTINUE
```

Well, I'm in. I press Enter as required:

```
* * * * * * * * * * * * Topic Area Selection * * * * * * * * * * * * * * * * *


  NO.  TOPIC AREA              NO.  TOPIC AREA

   1   Arts and Humanities      5   Education and Social Sciences
   2   Business/Law/Public Affairs  6   General/Books/Periodicals
   3   Consumer Affairs and People  7   Science and Technology
   4   Current Events           8   All


HINTS:  Select a topic area . . . . . . . . . . . type topic area number.
        Get help . . . . . . . . . . . . . . . . . . . . . . . . . type H.
        Get News . . . . . . . . . . . . . . . . . . . . . . type H NEWS.

ACTIONS: Help  BYE  Reset
```

Here I selected option 6. I want to find references to criticism of Donald Duck
(a disturbing trend far too prevalent at present).

```
TOPIC AREA NUMBER (or Action): 6

* * * * * * * * * * * * * Database Selection * * * * * * * * * * * * * * * * *

TOPIC AREA:  General/Books/Periodicals

  NO.  DATABASE      DESCRIPTION

   1   WorldCat      Books and other materials in libraries worldwide.
   2   Article1st    Index of articles from over 11,000 journals.
   3   Contents1st   Table of contents of more than 11,000 journals.
   4   NewsAbs       Newspaper Abstracts.  From over 25 newspapers.
   5   PerAbs        Periodical Abstracts.  From over 950 journals.
   6   ReadGuideAbs  Abstracts of articles from popular magazines.
   7   ReadersGuide  Readers' Guide to Periodical Literature.
   8   FactSearch    Facts and statistics on topics of current interest.


HINTS:  Select a database . . . . . . . . . . type database number or name.
        Help on a database . . . . . . . . . . type H and database name.
        Return to Topic Area screen . . . . . . . . . . just press Enter.

ACTIONS: Help  BYE  Reset
```

I choose option 1, WorldCat, because I'm looking for books anywhere in the world. Note that this is for interest only; it's unlikely that I'll travel to Korea if a book is found there. Note also that WorldCat indexes only libraries that are members of OCLC.

```
DATABASE NUMBER (or Action): 1

* * * * * * * * * * * * * * Search * * * * * * * * * * * * * * * * * *

DATABASE: WorldCat

   SEARCH      DESCRIPTION                              EXAMPLES
 _____

  Subject     Type the label SU: and a word(s).        su:criticism
              (Subject headings and titles)            su:freedom of speech

  Author      Type the label AU: and the author        au:hemingway
              name or any part of the name.            au:saul bellow

  Title       Type the label TI: and the title         ti:estuary
              or any word(s) in the title.            ti:love in the asylum
 _____


HINTS:   Other ways to search . . . . . . . . . . . . . . . type H LABELS.
         Include plural (s and es) or possessive . . . type + at end of word.
         Return to Database Selection screen . . . . . . . just press Enter.

ACTIONS: Help  Limit  Database  Wordlist  BYE  Reset
```

Now I enter the search of interest. For this example, I tell WorldCat that I'd like to search for items with the subject words Donald Duck criticism.

```
SEARCH WORD(S) (or Action): su: donald duck criticism

Searching for su:donald duck criticism
.
+ * * * * * * * * * * * * List of Records * * * * * * * * * * * * * * * * +
DATABASE: WorldCat                          LIMITED TO:
SEARCH: su:donald duck criticism FOUND 6 Records
```

OCLC's WorldCat tells me that there are six records and proceeds to list them.

```
    NO.  TITLE                                       AUTHOR          YEAR

     1   How to read Donald Duck : imperialist ide... Dorfman, Ariel.   1991
     2   Donald Duck : clipping file.                                   1934
     3   Roasting Donald Duck : alternative comics... Flora, Cornelia   1984
     4   How to read Donald Duck : imperialist ide... Dorfman, Ariel.   1984
     5   Para leer al Pato Donald /                   Dorfman, Ariel.   1978
     6   How to read Donald Duck : imperialist ide... Dorfman, Ariel.   1975


HINTS:   View a record . . . . . . . . . . . . . . . . type record number.
         Decrease number of records . . . . type L (to limit) or A (to 'and').
         Do a new search . . . . . . . . . . . . . . . . type S or SEARCH.

ACTIONS: Help  Search  And  Limit  Database  BYE  Reset
```

We get six successful matches! Unbelievable. The first record has an interesting title. To display the record, I type the number of the item.

```
RECORD NUMBER (or Action): 1

* * * * * * * * * * * * Full Record Display * * * * * * * * * * * * * *
DATABASE: WorldCat                    LIMITED TO:
SEARCH: su:donald duck criticism


 Record  1 of   6      LIBRARIES AT END OF RECORD        (Page  1 of  4)

ACCESSION: 25294669
   AUTHOR: Dorfman, Ariel.
    TITLE: How to read Donald Duck :
           imperialist ideology in the Disney comic /
  EDITION: Corr. & enl. ed.
    PLACE: New York :
PUBLISHER: International General,
     YEAR: 1991
 PUB TYPE: Book
   FORMAT: 119 p. : ill. ; 26 cm.

HINTS:   Forward one page . . type F.    Another record . type record number.
         Help on 3-letter library symbol . . . . . . . . type H and symbol.
         Return to Record List . . . . . . . . . . . . . just press Enter.

ACTIONS: Help  Search  And  Limit  Print  Forward  BYE  Reset
RECORD NUMBER (or Action): f
```

I'd like to see the more of the record, so I enter f to go forward one page.

```
* * * * * * * * * * * Full Record Display * * * * * * * * * * * * * * *
DATABASE: WorldCat                        LIMITED TO:
SEARCH: su:donald duck criticism

 Record  1 of    6    LIBRARIES AT END OF RECORD          (Page  2 of  4)
¦
¦    FORMAT: 119 p. : ill. ; 26 cm.
¦     NOTES: Translation of: Para leer al Pato Donald.
¦            Includes bibliographical references: (p. [100]-112).
¦      ISBN: 0884770370
¦   SUBJECT: Walt Disney Productions.
¦            Comic books, strips, etc. — History and criticism.
¦            Propaganda, American.
¦            Propaganda, Capitalist.
¦            Donald Duck (Comic strip).
¦            Imperialism in literature.
¦_____
HINTS:    Another page . type F or B.     Another record . type record number.
          Help on 3-letter library symbol . . . . . . . . type H and symbol.
          Return to Record List . . . . . . . . . . . . . just press Enter.

ACTIONS: Help  Search  And  Limit  Print  Forward  Back  BYE  Reset

RECORD NUMBER (or Action): f
```

And the next page...

```
* * * * * * * * * * * * Full Record Display * * * * * * * * * * * * * * *
DATABASE: WorldCat                        LIMITED TO:
SEARCH: su:donald duck criticism

 Record  1 of    6    LIBRARIES AT END OF RECORD          (Page  3 of  4)
¦
¦            Imperialism in literature.
¦ALT TITLE: Para leer al Pato Donald. English
¦    OTHER: Mattelart, Armand.
¦LIBRARIES: CA stf CDU
¦           FL FDA FSS FUG
¦           GA EMU
¦           MA BCH
¦           NJ FDM
¦           TX IXA TXA
¦           VA VPI
¦_____
HINTS:    Another page . type F or B.     Another record . type record number.
          Help on 3-letter library symbol . . . . . . . . type H and symbol.
          Return to Record List . . . . . . . . . . . . . just press Enter.
```

```
ACTIONS: Help  Search  And  Limit  Print  Forward  Back  BYE  Reset

RECORD NUMBER (or Action): f
```

And the next page...

```
* * * * * * * * * * * * Full Record Display * * * * * * * * * * * * * *
DATABASE: WorldCat                        LIMITED TO:
SEARCH: su:donald duck criticism


Record  1 of    6    LIBRARIES AT END OF RECORD         (Page  4 of  4)
|
|            VA VPI
|            WA UPP
|_____
```

Looking at the record, I can see that several libraries listed by OCLC own a copy of the latest edition of this book (I wonder why it never made the best-sellers list?). By typing h stf, I can find which of the California libraries own a copy of this book.

```
HINTS:    Another page . type F or B.      Another record . type record number.
          Help on 3-letter library symbol . . . . . . . . type H and symbol.
          Return to Record List . . . . . . . . . . . . . just press Enter.

ACTIONS: Help  Search  And  Limit  Print  Forward  Back  BYE  Reset

RECORD NUMBER (or Action): h stf

* * * * * * * * * * * * * * * Help * * * * * * * * * * * * * * * * * * * *


  SYM.  LIBRARY                                   INTERLIBRARY LOAN
|
| STF   STANFORD UNIV LIBR   CA, US               Non-supplier
|_____
```

Great! Stanford University Library owns this book. I'm going to be visiting the Bay Area this week, so I'll just drop into Stanford and take a look at it. If I can't get there, I can always ask my local library to try to borrow it through their inter-library loan program.

I can now quit OCLC and find out what is wrong with Donald Duck. OCLC is one of the great catalog systems available on the Internet. To get access, you'll need to check with your local library or contact OCLC directly.

OCLC also runs a LISTSERV called FIRSTSEARCH-L. Send messages that contain commands to `listserv@oclc.org` and place your commands in the body of the message, not in the subject line; type each command on a separate line (see Chapter 13, "Getting on the List: LISTSERV," for information on how to use LISTSERV).

# Educating with ERIC

The ERIC (Educational Resources Information Center) database contains abstracts of over 760 educational journals and many related documents. It also includes much interdisciplinary information, in fields such as library science, management, health, and technology.

ERIC is the place to look if you are trying to develop curricula or find out the latest ideas in education. It's also a great place to look if your children need to find a science fair project and you're drawing a blank.

Let's look for the general topic of chemistry, just to see what's available. You'll need to log in as SUINFO, which stands for Syracuse University Information System, where the ERIC Clearinghouse on Information Resources (the actual database) lives. So, let's use ERIC:

```
coyote% telnet acsnet.syr.edu
Trying 128.230.1.21 ...
Connected to acsnet.syr.edu.
Escape character is '^]'.
ACSNET
Tue Jun 22 22:23:27 1993
Port ID: Acsnet tty41  at  9600 baud
>suinfo
Cofo (VMFA 158C)
ENTER TERMINAL TYPE: vt100
```

I'm now logged in.

```
VIRTUAL MACHINE/SYSTEM PRODUCT


               SSSSSSSS
           SS     SS   UU     UU
           SS          UU     UU   VV        VV
               SSSSSSS UU     UU   VV        VV    MM          MM
                   SS  UU     UU   VV      VV      MMM        MMM
           SS     SS   UU     UU    VV    VV       MMMM      MMMM
           SSSSSSSS    UU     UU    VV  VV         MM MM  MM MM
                       UUUUUUUU       VVV          MM  MMM  MM
                                       V           MM   M   MM
                                                   MM        MM


Fill in your USERID and PASSWORD and press ENTER
(Your password will not appear when you type it)
USERID    ===>
PASSWORD  ===>
COMMAND   ===> suinfo

                                                  RUNNING   SUVM
```

Having gotten into the system with the command SUINFO, I'm presented with:

```
Welcome to SUINFO! You will now be able to perform online searches
on all publicly available databases currently carried by PRISM.
Before proceeding, the following may be noted:

*  You may use the SUGGEST command to send in comments/suggestions.
*  Certain databases cannot be searched because of licensing restrictions.
   You may search these databases by logging into SUVM the regular way.

*  The PRINT COMMAND works to send search results back to yourself.
   Choose the 'Another User' option and specify your email address as:
         userid@node
   This feature has been installed on a test basis.
*  You must type LOGOFF to EXIT PRISM
Would you like to continue? (Y or RETURN/N)
```

Press Y here to continue...

```
Welcome to Prism                                  06/22/93 22:20
File selection                                    40 files available

Select a file or service by typing its name below,
    or, press the return key to see a list of all files,
    or, type a category number to see a list of files in that category:
```

```
   1.  General Interest
   2.  CWIS: SU Events, SCIS, Job Ops, JOBNET, Housing, etc.
   3.  WOT: Network Accessible Resources
   4.  Demonstration
   5.  Application Development
   6.  Testing New Applications


Enter the name of the file you want.
To see a list of files, choose a category or press RETURN.
YOUR RESPONSE: 1
f1=Help          f3=End
Also:  Setup, Lock, Pause, End
```

Let's look under the first option, General Interest.

```
Prism                                           06/22/93 22:21
File selection                      32 General Interest files available
Choose a file or service by typing its number or name below.

        NAME                   DESCRIPTION
   1.  ACS News               ACS News and Notes Articles
   2.  ACS Newsline           ACS Newsline articles database
   3.  Applications Catalog   Catalog of SPIRES Applications for Consortium
   4.  Art Artists            SUART Artists subfile
   5.  Art Objects            Syracuse University Art Collection Objects
   6.  Audio Archive          The Belfer Audio Archive's cylinder recordings
   7.  COMPUSTAT Annual       COMPUSTAT Industrial Annual Da File (350:1-175)
   8.  COMPUSTAT PDE          COMPUSTAT Prices, Dividends and Earnings File
   9.  COMPUSTAT Quarterly    COMPUSTAT Industrial Quarterly Data File (40)
  10.  Consortium People      People at SPIRES Consortium member sites
  11.  Consortium Sites       SPIRES Consortium member institutions
  12.  CPC at S.U. (text only) Comprehensive Plan for Computing at S.U. 30/6/92
  13.  CSS Handbook           Counseling & Support Services Handbook
-The menu of files continues on next page; press RETURN to continue
Enter the name or number of the file you want.
Type HELP followed by the name of a file for information about that file.
YOUR RESPONSE:
f1=Help        f3=End                    f7=Previous
Also:  Setup, Lock, Pause, End
```

I'll press Enter to get the next page. As you can see, there's a lot more on this system than just ERIC, but you'll need to check what is publicly accessible before you get excited.

```
Prism                                              06/22/93 22:23
File selection                      32 General Interest files available
Choose a file or service by typing its number or name below.

        NAME                    DESCRIPTION
 14.  ERIC                      Abstracts of documents in the field of education
 15.  HUMANIST                  HUMANIST discussion file
 16.  ICPSR Guide               Guide to the Data Archive's research data files.
 17.  IRG                       Internet Resource Guide
 18.  Job Opportunities         S.U. Job Opportunities Publication (06/21/93)
 19.  JOBNET Job                SU student part-time job information file
 20.  Microdb                   Microcomputer Article Abstracts
 21.  MSDS Inventory            Material Safety Data Sheet Inventory
 22.  NOTIS-L                   NOTIS Discussion Group
 23.  Sci-Search                Science Citation Index sample file
 24.  SCIS Catalog              Course Catalog (1992-93)
 25.  SCIS Schedule             Time Schedule of Classes (FALL 93 & Spring 93)
 26.  SCIS Syllabus             Course Syllabus Abstract
-The menu of files continues on next page; press RETURN to continue
Enter the name or number of the file you want.
Type HELP followed by the name of a file for information about that file.
YOUR RESPONSE:   14
f1=Help        f3=End                        f7=Previous
Also:  Setup, Lock, Pause, End
```

There's what we want—ERIC is option 14.

```
ERIC                            Search            06/22/93 22:38

                        Welcome to ERIC

     This file contains bibliographic  information  and abstracts for a
     variety of  EDUCATIONAL  documents  from the Educational Resources
     Information Center (ERIC).  The file contains all the ERIC data from
     1984 through the 1st quarter of 1993 (Exactly 270590 records).

     You can search for items using one or more keywords from a variety of
     fields such as title, author, or abstract.


     *---------------------------------------------------------------------*
     ¦  For help conducting searches, contact the ERIC Clearinghouse       ¦
     ¦  <ERIC@SUVM> (ph: x-3640).  Report any technical                    ¦
     ¦  problems to Bhaskaran Balakrishnan <BBALAKRI@SUVM> (ph: x-1145),    ¦
     ¦  or to Mohamad Ladan <jinwang@suvm> (x-1145).                       ¦
     *---------------------------------------------------------------------*

    -File selected; type HELP ERIC FILE for more information
    Type FIND to search this file.
```

```
Type SELECT to choose a different file.
YOUR RESPONSE:   find
f1=Help f2=Find f3=Select
Also:  Setup, Command, Suggest, Lock, Pause, End
```

The find command takes us to the search screen:

```
ERIC                    Search              06/22/93 22:39
Index selection for FIND                 5 indexes available

Choose one or more indexes by typing the name or number for each type of
information you have, e.g. ABSTRACT or 1

    INDEX          DESCRIPTION                      EXAMPLE
    1.  ABSTRACT   Keyword from journal abstract    gifted child#
    2.  TITLE      Keywords from document title     listening skills
    3.  AUTHOR     Author's name                    David Webster
    4.  DESC       Subject descriptors (word index) online system#
    5.  DESCPH     Subject descriptors (phrase index) elementary secondary

Enter one or more index names below.
Type CANCEL to cancel this search.
YOUR RESPONSE: abstract
f1=Help f2=Setup Search f3=Cancel
Also:  Setup, Lock, Pause, End
```

What abstracts are available for chemistry?

```
ERIC                 Search / BRIEF display      06/22/93 22:40
Find ABSTRACT CHEMISTRY                          1497 records
1)    1989  American College Biology and Zoology Course Requirements: A de
            facto Standardized Curriculum.
2)    1991  Proportional Reasoning in the Solution of Problems in High School
            Chemistry and Its Impact on Developing Critical Thinking Skills.
3)    1992  Chemical Technology at the Community College of Rhode Island:
            Curricular Approaches Designed To Reflect the Demands of a Diverse
            Population Entering Chemical Technology Programs.
4)    1988  Comments in Academic Articles.
5)    1990  Dental Laboratory Technology Program Guide.
6)    1990  Biotechnology Program Guide.
7)    1991  Analogies in Secondary Chemistry Education Textbooks: The Authors'
            Views.
8)    1991  Using Analogies To Aid Understanding in Secondary Chemistry
            Education.
9)    1992  The "International Language/Business" Major at a Small Private
            University: Successes and Nagging Concerns.
```

```
-Records continue on the next page; press RETURN to continue display
Type: DIS number, to see a fuller record.     PRINT to print/mail/save records.
      AND, NOT, OR to refine this search.     FIND to begin a new search.
YOUR RESPONSE:
f1=Help f2=Find f3=Select                                 f9=Print f10=Dis Full
Also:  And, Not, Or, Setup, Command, Suggest, Lock, Pause, End
```

Press Enter to display the next several screens:

```
ERIC                    Search / BRIEF display            06/22/93 22:46
Find ABSTRACT CHEMISTRY                                      1497 records
25)   1990  An Exploratory Study of the Effectiveness of a Play-Based Center
            Approach for Learning Chemistry in an Early Childhood Program.
26)   1990  Oceanography for Landlocked Classrooms. Monograph V.
27)   1991  The Development of Modules for the Teaching of Chemical
            Equilibrium.
28)   1991  Performance Based on Instruction by Lecture or by Interaction and
            Its Relationship to Cognitive Variables.
29)   1991  The Use of Analog Models by Students of Chemistry at Higher
            Education Level.
30)   1992  Into the Woods: The Impact of Pre-Reading Activities.
31)   1992  Secondary Education in North Carolina: A Report of Student
            Participation and Performance in Algebra I, Geometry, Algebra II,
            ELP, U.S. History, English I, Physical Science, Biology, Chemistry,
            Physics. End of Course Testing.
32)   1983  Chemistry and Crime: From Sherlock Holmes to Today's Courtroom.
-Records continue on the next page; press RETURN to continue display
Type: DIS number, to see a fuller record.     PRINT to print/mail/save records.
      AND, NOT, OR to refine this search.     FIND to begin a new search.
YOUR RESPONSE:    32
```

Now there's something! Item 32 looks very interesting…

```
ERIC                    Search / FULL display             06/22/93 22:47
Find ABSTRACT CHEMISTRY                                   Record 32 of 1497
-------------------------------------------------------------------------
Accession: ED343778
   Title: Chemistry and Crime: From Sherlock Holmes to Today's Courtroom.
  Author: Gerber, Samuel M., Ed.
 Pub Date: 1983      Number of Pages: 158
 Abstract: The application of the principles of chemistry both for committing
           crimes and for tracking down criminals interests audiences of all
           ages and walks of life. This interest is the reason for the
           long-standing popularity of fictional works that describe crimes
           made possible by the criminal's knowledge of chemistry and crimes
           solved by the sleuth's knowledge of chemistry. The first section of
           this book presents three chapters on chemistry in fictional crimes.
```

```
            A discussion of the influences of Arthur Conan Doyle's medical
            school professors on his fiction opens the book. In the next
            chapter, Dorothy L. Sayers' extensive knowledge of chemistry is
            displayed through an examination of three of her works. Various
   -This record continues; press RETURN to see the next page
   Type: DISPLAY BRIEF to see brief records.     PRINT to print/mail/save records.
        AND, NOT, OR to refine this search.      FIND to begin a new search.
   YOUR RESPONSE:
```

Sounds even more interesting. Press the Enter key to see the rest of the record.

```
   ERIC                    Search / FULL display            06/22/93 22:48
   Find ABSTRACT CHEMISTRY                                Record 32 of 1497
            methods used for testing blood in 1875 are presented in the last
            chapter of this section. The second section contains chapters that
            discuss the present state of the art. The first two chapters in this
            section detail recent changes in the field of forensic science and
            provide definitions, explanations, and a short history of forensic
            science and criminalistics. The chemical composition and analysis of
            bullets and the uses of this information in some famous murder
            cases, such as the assassination of John F. Kennedy are then
            discussed. Bloodstain analysis is the subject of the next two
            chapters: one on case histories and one on serological and
            electrophoretic techniques. The last chapter presents results of a
            2-year study of four police jurisdictions to determine the kinds of
            physical evidence collected and used in typical criminal
            investigations. (KR)
   Major Descriptors: Chemistry;  Criminology;  Fiction;
   Other Descriptors: Chromatography;  Crime;  Higher Education;  Homicide;
   -This record continues; press RETURN to see the next page
   Type: DISPLAY BRIEF to see brief records.     PRINT to print/mail/save records.
        AND, NOT, OR to refine this search.      FIND to begin a new search.
   YOUR RESPONSE:
```

Great stuff! More…

```
   ERIC                    Search / FULL display            06/22/93 22:49
   Find ABSTRACT CHEMISTRY                                Record 32 of 1497
                  Body;  Resource Materials;  Science Activities;  Science man
                  Education;  Secondary Education;
   Major Identifiers: Forensic Science;
   Other Identifiers: Sherlock Holmes;
   ----------------------------------------------------------------------

   -End of record 32; press RETURN to see record 33
   Type: DISPLAY BRIEF to see brief records.     PRINT to print/mail/save records.
        AND, NOT, OR to refine this search.      FIND to begin a new search.
   YOUR RESPONSE: print
```

This sounds fantastic! I'm going to mail myself a copy of the record.

```
ERIC                           Search                 06/22/93 22:57
Print options                                          1497 records
2  <— RECORDS to be printed (enter a number from the list below)
   1. Your current search result of 1497 records.
   2. The last record you displayed. (Record 32 of 1497)

2  <— FORMATTING of the data (enter a number from the list below)
   1. BRIEF display
   2. FULL display

2  <— DESTINATION of the output (enter a number from the list below)
   1. System printer   ┆ Email address: gibbs@rain.org       _____
   2. Another user     ┆
   3. Computer file    ┆
                       ┆ Output title: ERIC_____
                       ┆
                       ┆        _____

Type: OK to continue PRINT request.    UNDO to discard changes to page.
      CANCEL to cancel request.
YOUR RESPONSE: ok
```

This second item sounded so interesting that I went off to the university library where they keep ERIC documents on microfiche (I could have ordered it directly from ERIC). There I found the microfiche copy and printed off the book on a microfiche reader/printer. What a find!

For more information on ERIC, contact

> ERIC Clearinghouse on Information Resources
> Syracuse University
> Syracuse, NY 13244-2340
> Internet: ERIC@SUVM.ACS.SYR.EDU
> 1-800-USE-ERIC or 315-443-3640

# Drowning in Data

As you can see from the previous examples, the range of accessible data, particularly when you pay, is phenomenal.

When you're searching, finding too much that is too general is easy. Finding relevant information is much harder. Indeed, it's so hard that some people (called data brokers) make a living out of finding information for others who are less skilled at it.

The greatest skill you can develop as an Internet navigator is learning how to keep from drowning in these data resources, which will help you come up with gold every time you dive in.

# TESTING YOUR NAVIGATION SKILLS

Now that you've learned what's on the Internet and which tools can help you navigate its complexities, you might like to test yourself. The tests we've compiled were supplied by Rick Gates, the Master of the Internet Hunt (known to its fans as simply the Hunt).

The Hunt is a monthly competition open to anyone who wants to participate. It is a set of twelve questions set by Rick that can be answered using only the resources of the Net (BITNET, Internet, USENET, and so on). The Hunt questions cover the spectrum of available information on the Net.

The reason Rick started the Hunt was to find out more about the different ways in which people use the Internet, to give novice users the chance to learn more about how to access resources by searching for the answers, to help keep people informed about the variety of information available, and to help people follow the evolution of Internet tools and resources.

Using e-mail, Rick announces the exact distribution time of the next month's Hunt questions during the last week of each month. He tries to post the actual questions late in the evening on the last day of the month.

For instance, the February Hunt questions were posted at midnight on January 31st. Players have one week from the date of the posting to submit their entry by e-mail to Rick (rgates@cic.net). The answers get posted within a week or so after each Hunt has ended.

The original source of Gopher links to the Internet Hunt comes from the Gopher at gopher.cic.net. If a Gopher demon is running on your local site, you can get to the CICNet Gopher by typing gopher gopher.cic.net at a prompt. Otherwise, you can connect to most major Gophers and find links to Rick's Internet Hunt.

Each Hunt question carries a weight that indicates difficulty: from 1 (easy) to 10 (difficult). Each Hunt usually includes an extra-credit question (1 point) and a Mystery question, the answer to which Rick doesn't actually know and which gets no points—but everyone will admire you greatly if you can solve it.

# The Internet Hunt Rules and Scoring

The Internet Hunt is a serious game to its adherents, and if you join in, you're playing against some serious people. The following rules define how the game is played and how scoring is done.

## Hunt Rules

1. There are usually 12 questions, the first 11 of which count toward your score. I have personally verified that each of these can be answered using only the resources of the Net. These are contrived questions.

2. There is often a last question known as the mystery question. I don't know if there's an answer to this on the Net. I may or may not have tried to find one. The mystery question usually comes to me from people asking for information. This is a real question.

3. Each of these first 11 questions carries a value in parentheses. This point value is my best guess on how tough that question is to answer. The scale is 1 (easy) to 10 (difficult). The total points for all questions are listed after the last question.

4. Answer as many questions as you can. Partial credit is awarded.

5. Teams are allowed to submit entries, but these must be designated as such. Pick a team name. Team entries will be scored separately from individual entries.

6. All answers must be mailed to me. My standard signature will be at the bottom of this message.

7. The contest will run for one week from the date of posting of this message. The deadline should appear in the header at the top of this message.

8. Feel free to send me potential questions for the Hunt, be they scored or mystery.

9. I've been given the opportunity to publish parts of the Hunt in printed form. Please indicate if you are willing or unwilling to have me include your answers in another publication (with due credit, of course).

10. Have fun! What's it all for, after all?

## Scoring Rules

1. Whoever answers all the questions first shall be declared the winner.

2. In the event that nobody answers all the questions, the player with the highest point total shall be declared the winner.

3. If there is a tie for highest point total, the player who responded first shall be declared the winner.

4. Assume you're answering the question for someone who understands the basic network tools (FTP, telnet, finger, Gopher, etc.), but just doesn't know where the data is. Answers like:

   ```
   ftp host.university.edu
   ```

   will not score as high as:

   ```
   anonymous ftp to host.university.edu
   cd /pub/documents
   file is called important.txt.Z
   ```

   Don't feel like you have to tell people how to use FTP. Instead, tell them where they can find what they're looking for, what tool to use to find it, and if necessary, the end information itself.

5. Read the question carefully. If it's asking for specific information (like "What is the chorus to Jingle Bells?"), supply that information in your answer. Sometimes you may find a pointer to a source that no longer exists. Providing the end information tells me that you actually checked the source out.

6. Answers utilizing either privately licensed resources or subscription to a service will be marked down.

7. If any player would like an individually scored entry, please feel free to send me a message. I will send them out after the Hunt has closed.

## An Example Question

**Question:** I just read an interesting paper by a Bradley Smith in the Chemistry Department at the University of Western Australia. Is it possible to get an e-mail address for him?

**Method:** Using the Internet Gopher X500 gateway, phonebooks directory, you can narrow it down to Australia, to the university, and then to the chemistry department.

**Or:**

Use Netfind at the University of Colorado.

```
telnet bruno.cs.colorado.edu
Login as netfind
   ( Search for Smith Western Australia)
```

**Or:**

```
whois -h uniwa.uwa.oz.au smith
```

**Answer:** bjs@crystal.uwa.oz.au

## The Tests

There is almost always no single way of getting the answers to the following questions. The Internet offers so many tools and so much duplication of data that you can be overwhelmed by search strategies. As a general rule, try the most popular tools (Gopher, Archie, and WAIS) before moving on to resources more difficult to search (such as newsgroups).

### The Beginning Navigator's Test

These are the easy ones. You should be able to track down the answers pretty quickly.

1. How do I get access to Scott Yanoff's Internet Services List?

2. Who is the author of the only book held by Victoria University of Wellington on the training of sheep dogs?

3. I was reading an article about the development of computers, and someone mentioned an early model called ENIAC. Is this just some sort of 1950's lexicon, or is it an acronym for something?

4. In the book *The Wonderful Wizard of Oz*, by L. Frank Baum, what footwear did Dorothy gain at the expense of the Wicked Witch of the East?

5. Where can I find an archive of USENET Frequently Asked Questions (FAQs)?

6. Where can I find some chili recipes?

## The Advanced Navigator's Test

These are much sneakier than the last group. You're going to have to work to get these.

1. Approximately how many persons lived in college dormitories in Ann Arbor, Michigan, U.S.A., in 1990?

2. I heard some network gurus talking about "pinging" an address somewhere. What is ping, and what does it stand for?

3. To what date did U.S. President Bill Clinton extend cooperation with the European Atomic Energy Community?

4. What is the melting point of tungsten?

5. What line follows the two lines, "What's in a name! that which we call a rose/ By any other name would smell as sweet;"in the William Shakespeare play *Romeo and Juliet*?

6. Where is the 8th Annual Conference on Computing and Philosophy being held?

## The Master Navigator's Test

These are really hard. Not just a bit hard, but bordering on the evil.

1. I just returned from a short vacation in Havana. When I left, I paid my hotel bill with a major credit card. A friend told me that this was illegal and that I was liable for a fine. If this is true, how much is the fine?

2. Where can I find the Washington address for the congressman from my district?

3. What are the five Internet resources recommended in the file musthave-list.txt?

4. A hurricane just blew in! Where can I find satellite photos of its progress?

5. I need to send a letter to the Meteorology Department at the University of Edinburgh, in Scotland, U.K. Can you tell me what the address is, please?

6. What color is the carpet in the Main Transporter Lobby at Cyberion City?

## The Internet Columbus Award

These are REALLY tough. If you get them without cheating, you really know your stuff, and your friends should be encouraged to acknowledge your genius, insight, and intellectual prowess. Then you have to buy them all a beer.

1. Of those countries receiving more than a gigabyte of data from the U.S. National Science Foundation Network's national backbone in January, 1993, which country had the highest net user ratio of data out to data in, in bytes?

2. There's a tavern in England rumored to be the site from which the *Canterbury Tales'* pilgrims departed. What brands of ale do they serve there today?

# The Answers

If you haven't at least tried to find the answers for yourself, shame on you. May the ghost of Vasco da Gama chase your data 'round your PC and may you get unexplained I/O errors.

> **Navigator's Note:** Over time, the location, format, and access methods for Internet resources can change. So although the answers that follow were correct when this book was written, they might not be useful in, say, the next millenium. So make sure to purchase all new editions of this book to get the right answers.

## The Beginning Navigator's Test

Here, then, are the answers for the really easy questions.

### Question 1

*How do I get access to Scott Yanoff's Internet Services List?*

**Rick's Note:** In my estimation this is one of the best lists of resources out there.

**Method:**

```
whois Yanoff
     Yanoff, Scott A. (SAY3)  yanoff@CSD4.CSD.UWM.EDU
        3200 N. Cramer Street
        Milwaukee, WI
        (414) 229-5370
        Record last updated on 27-Apr-92.
finger yanoff@csd4.csd.uwm.edu
```

**Answer:**

```
ftp csd4.csd.uwm.edu
get /pub/inet.services.txt
```

## Question 2

*Who is the author of the only book held by Victoria University of Wellington on the training of sheep dogs?*

**Method:**

```
telnet infoslug.ucsc.edu
Login as "gopher"
Select item 9.  The World
Select item 2.  Other Internet Systems and Databases/
Select item 8.  Internet Libraries/
Select item 2.  Catalogues Listed by Location/
Select item 19. New Zealand/
Select item 9.  Victoria University of Wellington <TEL>
Login as "opac"
From Library Catalogues menu select #7 Subject Keyword
Use keywords "sheep dogs"
```

**Or:**

```
Using Hytelnet:
Select <SITES1>
Select <NZ000> New Zealand
Select <NZ001> Victoria University of Wellington
Select item 7. search "subject keyword"
     Use keywords: training sheep dogs
```

**Answer:**

Author: Hartley, Cecil Wilfred Gerald

Title: The shepherd's dogs: their training for mustering and trial work.

## Question 3

*I was reading an article about the development of computers, and someone mentioned an early model called ENIAC. Is this just some sort of 1950's lexicon, or is it an acronym for something?*

**Method:**

```
telnet harpoon.cso.uiuc.edu
Login as "gopher"
Select item 11. Other Gopher and Information Servers/
Select item 12. Search titles in Gopherspace using Veronica/
```

```
Select item 3. Search gopherspace by simple Boolean veronica <?>
Search: acronym
Select item 41. Acronyms (Search by acronym or word) <?>
```

**Or:**

```
telnet Infoslug.ucsc.edu
Login as "gopher"
Select item 6. The Library
Select item  6. Electronic Reference Books
Select item 16. Webster's Dictionary
Index word to search for "ENIAC"
```

**Or:**

```
telnet quake.think.com
Login as "wais"
select source "acronyms"
search "eniac"
```

**Answer:**

en.i.ac \'en-e—.ak\ n [electronic numerical integrator and computer] digital computer for rapid solution of mathematical problems.

## Question 4

*In the book* The Wonderful Wizard of Oz, *by L. Frank Baum, what footwear did Dorothy gain at the expense of the Wicked Witch of the East?*

**Rick's Note:** This solution relies on the Internet user being aware of Michael Hart's Gutenberg Project of turning many books into electronic text. Readers of News will be aware that the Gutenberg Project has recently released *The Wonderful Wizard of Oz.*

**Method:**

```
telnet archie.au
Login as archie
Enter: prog gutenberg
Anonymous ftp to sunsite.unc.edu
cd /pub/docs/books/gutenberg/etext93
get wizoz10.txt
Search for words "Wicked Witch" using the vi editor
vi wizoz10.txt
/Wicked\ Witch
```

Repeat the search until you see the reference to shoes.

**Or:**

```
telnet twosocks.ces.ncsu.edu
Login as gopher
Select item  6, NCSU Computing Center's Gopher Server
Select item  8, Information Services from around World
Select item  5, Other Libraries on the Internet
Select item  2, OBI, the Online Book Initiative
Select item  55, Gutenberg
Select item  4, etext93
Select item  10, wizoz10.txt
```

**Answer:** Silver shoes with pointed toes.

## Question 5

*Where can I find an archive of USENET Frequently Asked Questions (FAQs)?*

**Method:**

```
telnet gopher.fsu.edu
Login as gopher
Select item 9. Other Information Systems
Select item 3. Recommended Information Systems for Exploration
Select item 10.Veronica (search menu items in most of gopherspace)
Select item 1. search gopherspace by _partial Boolean_ veronica
Words to search: FAQ
Select item 35. >MIT FAQ holdings
Select item 1. admin
= [to find technical information on item]
    (find that the information comes from pit-manager.mit.edu)
```

**Answer:** `ftp pit-manager.mit.edu` (You can select from the many FAQ's in the USENET directories.)

## Question 6

*Where can I find some chili recipes?*

**Method:**

```
Gopher
Select item 5. Internet file server (ftp) sites/
Select item 4. Search FTP sites (Archie)/
Select item 2. Substring search of archive sites for "chili"
```

The following files show up:

```
sunsite.unc.edu:/pub/docs/books/recipes/chili-1.
sunsite.unc.edu:/pub/docs/books/recipes/chili-2.
sunsite.unc.edu:/pub/docs/books/recipes/chili-3.
sunsite.unc.edu:/pub/docs/books/recipes/chili-4.
sunsite.unc.edu:/pub/docs/books/recipes/chili-5.
sunsite.unc.edu:/pub/docs/books/recipes/chili-6.
sunsite.unc.edu:/pub/docs/books/recipes/chili-7.
sunsite.unc.edu:/pub/docs/books/recipes/chili-bean.
```

Then:

```
ftp sunsite.unc.edu
Login as Anonymous
```

**Answer:**

```
cd /pub/docs/books/recipes
```

**Rick's Note:** Chili recipes (at least seven) are available by ftp from `gatekeeper.dec.com`, `cd pub/recipes.ftp`, then `gatekeeper.dec.com`. Recipe number seven, Chernobyl Chili, is touted as a high energy microwave chili and, in addition to beef and beans, calls for bacon grease, MSG, and beer. A caveat at the end mentions the incredible mess this dish will make in your microwave oven. Party down!

# The Advanced Navigator's Test

Here are the answers to the somewhat sneakier questions.

## Question 1

*Approximately how many persons lived in college dormitories in Ann Arbor, Michigan, U.S.A. in 1990?*

**Method:**

```
telnet consultant.micro.umn.edu
Login as "gopher"
Select item 9. Other gopher and information servers/
Select item 1. All the gopher servers in The World/
Select item 309. University of Michigan Libraries/
Select item 7. Social Sciences Resources/
Select item 1. 1990 Census (UMich)/
Select item 6. Michigan:  State, Counties, Cities, and MCDs STF1A/(See note)
Select item 3. Cities, Addison Village to Brownlee Park CDD/
Select item 17. Ann Arbor City, Michigan
```

**Answer:** 11,606 or 11,605 (both from same source: the 1990 Michigan Census).
Here's the excerpt, specifying the number of persons living in dorms:

```
GROUP QUARTERS
P28. GROUP QUARTERS
UNIVERSE:  Persons in group quarters
Institutionalized persons:
        Correctional institutions ............... 0
        Nursing homes ......................... 537
        Mental (Psychiatric) hospitals .......... 0
        Juvenile institutions .................. 42
        Other institutions .................... 24
    Other persons in group quarters:
        College dormitories ................ 11,606
        Military quarters ....................... 0
        Emergency shelters for homeless ........ 195
        Visible in street locations ............. 4
        Other noninstitutional group quarters .. 339
```

In addition to selecting

```
6. Michigan: State, Counties, Cities, and MCDs, STF1A/
```

I also tried selecting

```
7. Michigan: State, Counties, Cities, and MCDs, STF3A/
```

From the subsequent menu, I selected

```
1. Ann Arbor: Income, Education, Labor Force & Housing data.
```

This time, the report yielded one less person living in a college dorm.

```
P40. GROUP QUARTERS(10)
UNIVERSE:  Persons in group quarters
 Institutionalized persons:
    Correctional institutions................. 0
    Nursing homes.......................... 522
    Mental (Psychiatric) hospitals............ 0
    Juvenile institutions................... 55
    Other institutions...................... 24
 Other persons in group quarters:
    College dormitories................. 11,605
    Military quarters........................ 0
    Emergency shelters for homeless persons.. 189
    Visible in street locations.............. 0
    Other noninstitutional group quarters.... 226
```

**Rick's Note:** The two files at Michigan give different answers. I accepted either figure.

## Question 2

*I heard some network gurus talking about "pinging" an address somewhere. What is ping, and what does it stand for?*

**Method:**

```
telnet infoslug.ucsc.edu
Login as gopher
Select item 7. The Library
Select item 6. Electronic Reference books
Select item 6. Internet Users' Glossary <?>
Search for term "ping" yields the above description
```

**Answer:** Packet InterNet Groper (PING): A program used to test reachability of destinations by sending them an ICMP echo request and waiting for a reply. The term is used as a verb: "Ping host X to see if it is up!"

See also:

```
Internet Control Message Protocol. [Source: RFC1208]
```

**Rick's Note:** What ping is and what it stands for can be found in two main resources—the Hacker's Dictionary, and the Internet Users' Glossary [RFC1392]—both of which can be found in and through a variety of front ends. Here are a few:

**ping:** [from the TCP/IP acronym Packet InterNet Groper, prob. originally contrived to match the submariners' term for a sonar pulse] 1. n. Slang term for a small network message (ICMP ECHO) sent by a computer to check for the presence and aliveness of another. Occasionally used as a phone greeting. See {ACK}, also {ENQ}. 2. vt. To verify the presence of. 3. vt. To get the attention of. From the UNIX command 'ping(1)' that sends an ICMP ECHO packet to another host. 4. vt. To send a message to all members of a {mailing list} requesting an {ACK} (in order to verify that everybody's addresses are reachable). "We haven't heard much of anything from Geoff, but he did respond with an ACK both times I pinged jargon-friends."

The funniest use of "ping" to date was described in January 1991 by Steve Hayman on the USENET group comp.sys.next. He was trying to isolate a faulty cable segment on a TCP/IP Ethernet hooked up to a NeXT machine and got tired of having to run back to his console after each cabling tweak to see if the ping packets were getting through. So he used the sound-recording feature on the NeXT, then wrote a script that repeatedly invoked "ping(8)," listened for an echo, and played back the recording on each returned packet. Result? A program that caused the machine to repeat, over and over, "Ping...ping...ping..." as long as the network was up. He turned the volume to maximum, ferreted through the building with one ear cocked, and found a faulty tee connector in no time.

## Question 3

*To what date did U.S. President Bill Clinton extend cooperation with the European Atomic Energy Community?*

**Method:**

```
telnet scilibx.ucsc.edu
Login as gopher
Select item 10. The World/
Select item 7. White House Press Release Service/
Select item 6. Miscellanous/
Select item 12. 930309 Statement on Nuclear Cooperation.
```

**Or:**

```
telnet twosocks.ces.ncsu.edu
Login as gopher
Select item  4. Governmental information
Select item  1. From the White House (President Clinton's Staff)
Select item  4. International Affairs
Select item  3. Letter to Congress: EURATOM Cooperation 3/9/93
```

**Answer:** December 31, 1995

## Question 4

*What is the melting point of tungsten?*

**Rick's Note:** A little tricky here, as tungsten is listed under its German name, Wolfram, in the Periodic Table of the Elements at Minnesota. Clever Hunters used other Net resources to solve the problem. I love it!

**Method:**

```
Telnet to infoslug.ucsc.edu
Login as infoslug
Select item  8. The Researcher/
Select item  4. Science and Engineering/
Select item  3. Chemistry and Biochemistry/
Select item  2. MSDS - Material Safety Data Sheets (may require TN3270) <TEL>
Search for "Tungsten"
Enter 6 and <return> to select any manufacturer
Select entry:
     7440-33-7    TUNGSTEN      FISHER SCIENTIFIC
     COMPONENT: TUNGSTEN   CAS# 7440-33-7   PERCENT: 100
     ...
```

**Answer:**

```
BOILING POINT: 10220 F (5660 C)
MELTING POINT: 6170 F (3410 C)
^^^^^^^^^^^^^^^^^^^^^^^^^^^^^^^^^^^
```

## Question 5

*What line follows the two lines, "What's in a name! that which we call a rose/ By any other name would smell as sweet;" in the William Shakespeare play* Romeo and Juliet?

**Method:**

```
telnet twosocks.ces.ncsu.edu
Login as gopher
Select item 6, NCSU Computing Center's Gopher Server
Select item choice 8, Information Services from around World
Select item choice 4, Gutenberg Project -- Electronic literature
Select item choice 6, Tragedies
Select item choice 8, Romeo and Juliet
Select item choice 2, ACT II
```

**Answer:**

```
"So Romeo would, were he not Romeo call'd,
Retain that dear perfection which he owes
Without that title. Romeo, doff thy name,
And for that name which is no part of thee
Take all myself."
```

## Question 6

*Where is the 8th Annual Conference on Computing and Philosophy being held?*

**Method:**

```
Gopher to InfoSlug
Select item 8. The Researcher/
Select item 1. Arts and Humanities/
Select item 1. American Philosophical Association BBS <TEL>
Login as apa
Select item 5 Philosophical Calendar (updated: 4/1)
Select item 4  July / August  (1993)
(From within more) /Computing
```

**Answer:** Eighth Annual Conference on Computing and Philosophy (CAP) Carnegie-Mellon University (August 12-14th, 1993)

# The Master Navigator's Test

Here, now, are the answers to the bordering-on-evil questions.

## Question 1

*I just returned from a short vacation in Havana. When I left, I paid my hotel bill with a major credit card. A friend told me that this was illegal and that I was liable for a fine. If this is true, how much is the fine?*

**Rick's Note:** Many Hunters searched the travel advisory at gopher.stolaf.edu, which mentions that using credit cards in Cuba is illegal but doesn't mention the fine. Many noted that Cuban businesses do not accept credit cards. The source I found did not mention that fact. Bob McLean points out the discrepancies and offers a way out for the guilty:

"Currency Regulations (Credit Card Restrictions): U.S. citizens and permanent resident aliens are prohibited from using credit cards in Cuba. U.S. credit card companies will not accept vouchers from Cuba, and Cuban shops, hotels, and other places of business do not accept U.S. credit cards."

Because the card was accepted, and you're back in the U.S., it would seem that you needn't worry, but the hotel might not get its money (legally). If you really want to turn yourself in, you can contact the Office of Foreign Assets Control, Department of the Treasury, 1500 Pennsylvania Avenue, NW, Treasury Annex, Washington, D.C., 20220 (tel: 202/535-9449; fax: 202/377-7222). It's nice to know that I can turn myself in via fax.

This question also brings up a related concern. Any piece of information on the Net reflects the authority, concerns, and focus of the body that issues it. The information on `gopher.stolaf.edu` is from a Consular Information Sheet from the U.S. State Department. The info I got was from the U.S. Department of the Treasury, Office of Foreign Assets Control. It probably wouldn't have helped in solving this question, but it's always something to keep in mind.

**Method:**

```
gopher to una.hh.lib.umich.edu
Select item 13. socsci/
Select item 7. Government and Politics/
Select item 4. Economic Bulletin Board  (UMich)/
Select item 4. EBB and Agency Information and misc. files/
Select item 33. Synopsis of U.S. embargo - Cuba.
```

**Answer:** "Penalties for violating the sanctions range up to 10 years in prison, $500,000 in corporate and $250,000 in individual fines. This sheet is an overview of the Regulations for individuals wishing to travel to or otherwise deal with Cuba." Also, "credit and other charge cards may not be used in Cuba—not even for living expenses or for the purchase of goods used by the traveler."

## Question 2

*Where can I find the Washington address for the congressman from my district?*

**Method:**

```
WAIS to find the Congress file at pit.mit.edu
```

**Answer:** Robert J. Lagomarsino is the Representative from the district including Santa Barbara. His Washington address is

```
2332 Rayburn
Washington DC 20515
```

## Question 3

*What are the five Internet resources recommended in the file musthave-list.txt?*

**Method:**

```
Use archie to locate the file
ftp pilot.njin.net
Login as Anonymous
cd /pub/Internet-course
get musthave-list.txt
    This file states at the beginning:
        ----------------------------------------------
        There are five must-have Internet resources. Two, the
        Yanoff and December lists, are hard copy summaries of Internet
        resources. They are invaluable desktop additions for any user,
        especially newcomers. The other three, HYTELNET, HYPLUS, and
        INFOPOP are programs providing an incredible amount of
        information. Although there is much duplication, each of the
        resources has value not offered in the others.
        ----------------------------------------------
```

**Answer:** The Yanoff and December lists, HYTELNET, HYPLUS, and INFOPOP.

## Question 4

*A hurricane just blew in! Where can I find satellite photos of its progress?*

**Method:**

```
// How do you find the following //
ftp vmd.cso.uiuc.edu.
cd /wx
```

**Answer:** The photos are in .GIF files.

## Question 5

*I need to send a letter to the Meteorology Department at the University of Edinburgh, in Scotland, U.K. Can you tell me what the address is, please?*

**Method:**

```
telnet infoslug.ucsc.edu
login as "gopher"
Select item 10. The World/
Select item 6. Weather and more/
Select item 3. Weather from the UofI Weather Machine (Univ. of Illinois)/
Select item 5. Documents/
Select item 37. Meteo.schools
(The answer was located near the end of Meteo.schools, a
     list of institutions with Meteorology programs.)
```

**Or:**

```
Gopher to gopher.ed.ac.uk
Select item 4. The University of Edinburgh Campus Wide Information/
Select item 2. EdINFO <TEL>
Login as "edinfo"
Select item 3   People (directories)
Select item 1   Edinburgh University Staff Telephone List
   (return to get departmental list)
Select item 2 Departmental Lists
   (At the eview: prompt) meteorology
   ¦Meteorology
   ¦ James Clerk Maxwell Building
   ¦ King's Buildings
```

Okay, let's take a breather. We now have to find the address for the James Clerk Maxwell Building.

```
q-quit (Go back to EdINFO)
Select Search
Select item 4   Browse metadata index
Search for: addresses
   1:   ADDRESSES                                    5
   4   Addresses
   ¦    Addresses
   ¦
   ¦    The King's Buildings (KB)
   ¦
   ¦        James Clerk Maxwell Building
   ¦        The KingUs Buildings
```

```
!      Mayfield Road
!      Edinburgh EH9 3JZ
!      Reception/Enquiries (KB)        - 031 650 4960
```

We assume KingUs is a typo for King's, and conclude the address is

```
Meteorology
James Clerk Maxwell Building
King's Buildings
Mayfield Road
Edinburgh EH9 3JZ
```

**Or:**

```
Gopher to:
Select item  8. Other Gopher and Information Servers/
Select item 5. Europe/
Select item 25. United Kingdom/
Select item 18. University of Edinburgh/
Select item 5. Anonymous FTP Services/
Select item 1. Anonymous FTP Servers in Edinburgh/
Select item 5. Department of Meteorology/
Select item 4. calmet/
Select item 2. documents/
Select item 2. call_for_papers.
```

Which states, in it:

```
"Abstracts should be submitted no later than 1 February 1993 to the
Conference Co-chairperson, Dr. Charles Duncan, Professor of
Meteorology, Edinburgh University, King's Buildings, Edinburgh EH9 3J2
United Kingdom(tel: 44.31.650.5091; fax: 44.31.662.4269; email:
C.Duncan@ed.ac.uk)."
```

**Rick's Note:** This was a messy one. I knew of two ways here. One was easy if you knew about it. You searched the list of meteorology schools at the University of Illinois Weather Machine. The other was trickier, as you were naturally led first to discover the building in which Meteorology was housed, and then find the address of the building.

A few Hunters discovered yet another source—an FTPable call for papers at cumulus.met.ed.ac.uk. The problem here is that the ZIP code has a typo, but the Hunters can hardly be held accountable for that. I gave them full credit, but once again the data integrity needs to be watched out for.

Some folks found the address for the university as a whole and added that to Meteorology's building. I took a point off for those.

**Answer:**

```
Department of Meteorology
University of Edinburgh
Kings Buildings
Edinburgh EH9 3JZ
U.K.
```

## Question 6

*What color is the carpet in the Main Transporter Lobby at Cyberion City?*

**Method:**

```
Micromuse found in Yanoff's list
telnet michael.ai.mit.edu
Login as "guest"
    connect guest
    You are immediately given a description of "Cyberion City Main
    TransporterReceiving Station" and the Attendant welcomes you.
    "You step down off of the MTRS platform and walk out into the lobby.
    Main Transporter Lobby(#37055RJ)
    This room has high, vaulted ceilings and white walls. The
    thick, plush, black carpeting makes no sound beneath your
    feet. You are just inside the lobby of the Main Transporter
    Facility. ..."
```

**Rick's Note:** Cyberion City is the name of a scenario mounted on Micro Muse software and maintained by the Massachusetts Institute of Technology. Unlike many other MUDs, which focus on dungeons, this one focuses on education and environmentalism, or in their own words:

```
!-================================================================- !
! Welcome! MicroMUSE is our vision of the 24th century, a blend of   !
! high technology and social consciousness with emphasis on education, !
! concern for the environment, and communication. Our charter is    !
! available by anonymous ftp to michael.ai.mit.edu (18.43.0.177).    !
!-.................................................................- !
```

The tough part about answering this question is assuming that clues like Main Transporter Lobby, and Cyberion City are not real places. This starts you looking for science fiction, games, or simulations. The entry from the Yanoff list:

```
-MicroMUSE telnet michael.ai.mit.edu or telnet 18.43.0.177
     offers: Educational Multi-User Simulated Environment.
     (Login: guest)
```

**Answer:** Black.

## The Internet Columbus Award

And finally, the answers to the bordering-on-genius-if-you-got-them questions.

### Question 1

*Of those countries receiving more than a gigabyte of data from the U.S. National Science Foundation Network's national backbone in January, 1993, which country had the highest net user ratio of data out to data in, in bytes?*

**Method:**

```
telnet consultant.micro.umn.edu
Login as "gopher"
Select item 3. Internet file server (ftp) sites/
Select item 4. Query a specific ftp host <?>
Words to search for:  nis.nsf.net
Select item 1. Link to ftp server nis.nsf.net/
Select item 19. statistics/
Select item 2. nsfnet/
Select item 6. 1993/
Select item 3. nsf-9301.country
```

Look for the information given by bytes to and from the backbone, not by packet!

Here's a spreadsheet I generated from the data I found. This is a list of countries receiving more than 1 gigabyte from NSF, in descending order of the ratio of bytes out (from NSF) to bytes in (to NSF):

| Country | Bytes In To BB | Bytes Out From BB | % In | % Out | Gigs Recv | Ratio Out:In |
|---------|---------|---------|------|-------|------|---------|
| Hong Kong | 1.9E+09 | 1.5E+10 | 0.04 | 0.29 | 14 | 7.986719 |
| Greece | 3.6E+08 | 2.1E+09 | 0.01 | 0.04 | 2 | 5.881365 |
| Korea | 2.1E+09 | 1.2E+10 | 0.04 | 0.24 | 12 | 5.827162 |
| Singapore | 3.1E+09 | 1.7E+10 | 0.06 | 0.33 | 16 | 5.423357 |
| Brazil | 1.0E+09 | 5.4E+09 | 0.02 | 0.1 | 5 | 5.268544 |

| Ireland | 5.8E+08 | 3.0E+09 | 0.01 | 0.06 | 2 | 5.105389 |
|---|---|---|---|---|---|---|
| Poland | 4.8E+08 | 2.3E+09 | 0.01 | 0.04 | 2 | 4.808341 |
| Israel | 3.4E+09 | 1.5E+10 | 0.07 | 0.3 | 15 | 4.506155 |
| Czechoslovakia | 9.7E+08 | 4.4E+09 | 0.02 | 0.09 | 4 | 4.502612 |
| Spain | 1.5E+09 | 6.6E+09 | 0.03 | 0.13 | 6 | 4.46984 |
| New Zealand | 1.2E+09 | 5.3E+09 | 0.02 | 0.1 | 5 | 4.294803 |
| Italy | 9.1E+09 | 3.4E+10 | 0.18 | 0.67 | 34 | 3.73034 |
| Belgium | 1.6E+09 | 5.7E+09 | 0.03 | 0.11 | 5 | 3.641767 |
| South Africa | 1.6E+09 | 5.6E+09 | 0.03 | 0.11 | 5 | 3.530957 |
| Austria | 6.5E+09 | 2.1E+10 | 0.13 | 0.41 | 20 | 3.238235 |
| Hungary | 3.4E+08 | 1.1E+09 | 0.01 | 0.02 | 1 | 3.172214 |
| United Kingdom | 3.3E+10 | 1.0E+11 | 0.64 | 2.01 | 102 | 3.120415 |
| Mexico | 3.8E+09 | 1.1E+10 | 0.07 | 0.21 | 10 | 2.765493 |
| Canada | 8.4E+10 | 2.3E+11 | 1.64 | 4.51 | 230 | 2.75814 |
| Germany | 3.6E+10 | 9.7E+10 | 0.71 | 1.89 | 96 | 2.682364 |
| Norway | 1.0E+10 | 2.7E+10 | 0.2 | 0.53 | 26 | 2.652069 |
| Chile | 1.2E+09 | 3.3E+09 | 0.02 | 0.06 | 3 | 2.62276 |
| Taiwan | 1.2E+10 | 3.0E+10 | 0.23 | 0.58 | 29 | 2.486676 |
| Portugal | 9.3E+08 | 2.3E+09 | 0.02 | 0.04 | 2 | 2.476198 |
| Puerto Rico | 7.9E+08 | 1.5E+09 | 0.02 | 0.03 | 1 | 1.938452 |
| Japan | 1.2E+10 | 2.4E+10 | 0.24 | 0.46 | 23 | 1.923033 |
| Sweden | 3.1E+10 | 5.2E+10 | 0.6 | 1.02 | 52 | 1.686067 |
| France | 3.8E+10 | 6.0E+10 | 0.73 | 1.17 | 59 | 1.594334 |
| Australia | 4.5E+10 | 6.1E+10 | 0.88 | 1.19 | 61 | 1.353244 |
| Netherlands | 2.7E+10 | 3.6E+10 | 0.54 | 0.7 | 35 | 1.311529 |
| Switzerland | 4.0E+10 | 3.8E+10 | 0.77 | 0.75 | 38 | 0.968221 |
| Denmark | 1.5E+10 | 1.4E+10 | 0.28 | 0.27 | 13 | 0.934667 |
| United States | 4.7E+12 | 4.1E+12 | 90.89 | 80.93 | 4143 | 0.890443 |
| Finland | 4.0E+10 | 2.5E+10 | 0.79 | 0.5 | 25 | 0.628287 |

**Answer:** The answer to this question was Hong Kong, with a ratio of 8:1. Interestingly, 3 countries—Denmark, Switzerland, and Finland—had more data going into the backbone than going out.

**Rick's Note:** Of the 5.1 TB (that's terabytes, trillions of bytes) of data that traveled over the backbone in January 1993, 90% entered from somewhere in the U.S., and 80% exited to somewhere in the U.S. The difference in both cases is made up by traffic between the backbone and nets in other countries. Keep in mind that this is roughly accurate *sampled* data, and that it only accounts for connections using the Internet Protocol (IP). This leaves out mail gateways such as UUNet or BITNET.

## Question 2

*There's a tavern in England rumored to be the site from which the* Canterbury Tales' *pilgrims departed. What brands of ale do they serve there today?*

**Method:**

```
get the FAQ for the homebrewing Usenet group, rec.crafts.brewing.
In it, there's a mention of pub list at sierra.stanford.edu
ftp sierra.stanford.edu
Login as "anonymous"
cd pub/homebrew/docs
binary
get publist.Z
uncompress publist.Z
      search for Canterbury in your favorite editor or read
      through the whole thing for those interested in finding a
      good place to drink. An excerpt:
      Oxford:
          Turf Tavern Pub.
          It's a little hard to find, but everyone knows where it is
          (I think it's on Bath). This place has been around since
          the 14th century, and was featured in Chaucer's Canterbury
          Tales as the point of departure for the pilgrims, and is
          still a fave of college students. Absolutely wonderful
          atmosphere. They serve two ales from Hook Norton, Hook's
          Best and Old Hook's - the smoothest bitters I've had.
```

**Answer:** The Turf Tavern located in Oxford serves two ales from Hook Norton: Hook's Best and Old Hook's.

**Rick's Note:** Chaucerian scholars know that the pilgrims departed from the Tabard Inn, (the original inn, long since gone), in Southwark, near London, not from Oxford. This is why the question referred to a rumor. As with any resource, authority is always an issue.

# COMMAND
# REFERENCE

This appendix is a summary of the programs discussed in this book. We would like to be able to say that these are definitive. Unfortunately, that's impossible. The reason is that new versions of some of these programs are appearing almost daily. Check the version of the programs you're using for differences from the descriptions given here.

We've also covered only the standard versions of these programs. The fancy versions—those that run under graphical user interfaces such as X Window, Windows, and the Macintosh—are all changing so fast that it's difficult to be accurate about them.

**Navigator's Note:** The command lists for these programs are not exhaustive. We've left out the specialized commands for three reasons. First, some of them are very complicated and you don't need them unless you're going to get very fancy. Second, they may be version dependent. Third, we wanted to avoid making the book twice as thick (and twice as expensive).

**Navigator's Note:** Be very careful with the case used in options and commands. For example, if you get a message from someone, and that person has cc'ed (that is, sent copies to) other people, and you reply with the message, "Why did you copy your message to those losers?" by pressing R, you'll be embarrassed when all the people on the cc list also get the message. What you should have pressed was r, but it's too late now. If we've told you once, we've told you a thousand times, and why don't you ever pick up your clothes, and…

# Regular Expressions

Because most of the programs you use when navigating the Internet are UNIX software, you should have an appreciation of regular expressions.

**Navigator's Note:** This is a dry topic and really requires several pages to cover properly; we'll just give the fundamentals here. If you want to find out more (you wild creature, you), check out a book on UNIX or, if you are made of sterner stuff, a UNIX system manual. To make this topic even more complex than it is, many UNIX programs add their own tricks and extensions. If you want to use any UNIX utility in a sophisticated way, check what it says in its help screens about regular expressions.

A *regular expression* is a text pattern that you want a UNIX program to find a match to. This applies in database or text file searches, or anywhere you want to look for a sequence of characters. For example, if you gave navigator as the text to search for, it would match navigator, and not navigate or navigation.

Regular expressions enable you to be inexact—that is, to find text that is similar to a specification of text. For example, if you wanted to find all the words beginning with `pi` in the text `Peter Piper picked a peck` and didn't care whether the characters were upper- or lowercase (so that you'd find both `Piper` and `picked`), you'd use a regular expression.

Rule 1. The characters in the text to be matched can be anything except `.` (period), `*` (asterisk), `[` (left square bracket), and `\` (backslash).

Rule 2. At the beginning of a sentence, you can't use `^` (caret) in its regular sense.

Rule 3. At the end of a sentence, you can't use `$` (dollar sign) in its regular sense.

Rule 4. If you need to use one of the special characters in Rules 1, 2, or 3, precede it with the `\` (backslash) character. For example, if the text to be searched for is `$100`, `2*2=4`, `[note]`, or `Press \`, you need to enter them as `\$100`, `2\*2=4`, `\[note]`, and `Press \\`.

Rule 5. To accept any single character in a particular position in the text, use `.` (a period). So, `b..t` would match `boot` or `bait` but not `bite` (however, if you use `b...`, you get `bite` too). This is equivalent to the `?` wildcard in PC DOS.

Rule 6. To accept zero or more occurrences of the same character, use `*` after the character. Thus, `mis*` matches `mis`, `miss`, `misss`, and even `misssssssssss`.

Rule 7. To find the end of a line, use `$`. Thus, `end.$` would match only lines ending with `end.`.

Rule 8. To find the beginning of a line, use `^`. Thus, `^Start` matches any line starting with `Start`.

Rule 9. To find only certain, single characters in a specific position in text, called a set, use `[<characters>]`. Thus, `t[a o i]n` would match with `tan`, `ton`, and `tin`. The only special characters in a set are `-` (minus), `]` (right square bracket), and `^`. All other characters stand for themselves, including `\`. At least one of the characters must be found to make a match. For example, looking for any variety of capitalization of London could be done by `[L l][O o][N n][D d][O o][N n]`, which would accept `London`, `london`, `LONDON`, or even `LoNdOn`.

Rule 10. In a set, the `-` means that all the characters between the letter on the left of the minus and the letter on the right of the minus are acceptable. So, `[a-f p-z]` would exclude any character in the range `g` to `o`.

Note that if you wanted to accept the match or non-match of a set, you'd use [<characters>]*.

Rule 11. In a set, the ] indicates the end of the set specification, unless it's the first character in the set. So to search for a left or right bracket, you have to write [][].

Rule 12. In a set, using ^ at the start of the set excludes those characters. Thus, [a-f p-z] in Rule 10 could also be written as [^g-o]. To accept only alphabetic characters in a particular position, use [^0-9]; to exclude alphabetic characters, use [^a-z A-Z].

If, as an example of a more complicated search, you wanted to find any word starting with navigat—whether the n is upper- or lowercase (such as Navigator, navigation, or Navigating)—you'd use [N n]avigat[.]* (the [.] means look for any character in this position, and the * means it can occur zero or any number of times).

**Navigator's Note:** There's a lot more to regular expressions. Just coming to grips with the preceding rules will make your searches using Archie and other Internet tools much more effective.

# Archie

Archie can be used in three ways—as a local client, interactively, or by e-mail.

## Archie Local Client Commands

The general form of the local Archie client command is

```
archie [{options}] [<text>]
```

### <text>

<text> can include any text (including UNIX regular expressions) that you want Archie to search for. Note that you must use the -r option for UNIX regular expressions.

## {options}

The options are codes that tell Archie to do something in addition to, or modify, the search for <text>. These are all prefaced by a - (minus), and multiple options are separated from each other and anything else by a space.

| | |
|---|---|
| -c | Search substrings paying attention to upper- and lower-case. |
| -e | Exact string match (the default). |
| -r | Search using a regular expression. |
| -s | Search substrings, ignoring the case of the letters. |
| -o<filename> | Put the results of the search in the file <filename>. |
| -t | Sort the results, listing the oldest matches first. |
| -m<n> | Stop searching after <n> matches (the default is 95). |
| -h<hostname> | Specifies which Archie server to use. |
| -L | Lists the Archie servers known to the copy you're using. |
| -V | If you are the kind of user who, if you run a program and nothing happens, immediately assumes it has died, this option (V, for verbose) will print messages as it works, to keep you happy. Good for long searches by pessimistic users. |

Thus,

```
archie -c -ofred.txt -r -V [N n]avigat[.]*
```

means pay attention to case (-c), put the results in the file named fred.txt (-ofred.txt), interpret the search text as a regular expression (-r), tell me what's happening as you search or I may have to hit the reset button (-V), and use [N n]avigat[.]* as the search text.

# Archie Interactive Commands

To conduct an interactive session with an Archie server, you first telnet to an Archie site and log in as archie (usually, although there may be some exceptions). Current Archie server site addresses are

```
archie.funet.fi
archie.doc.ic.ac.uk
archie.cs.huji.ac.il
archie.wide.ad.jp
archie.ncu.edu.tw
archie.sogang.ac.kr
archie.nz
archie.kuis.kyoto-u.ac.jp
archie.th-darmstadt.de
archie.luth.se
```

The available commands are

| | |
|---|---|
| `mail <address>` | Mail the results to the given address. |
| `prog <text>` | Search for the given text, which may be a UNIX regular expression if the search type is set to `regexp`. |
| `quit` | I've had enough, I'm leaving. |
| `set search <search type>` | Set the type of search to perform. The allowed types are `case`, `exact`, `regexp`, or `subcase`. |
| `show search` | Display the type of search being used. |
| `whatis <text>` | Search the description database for the text, which may be a UNIX regular expression if the search type is set to `regexp`. |

## Archie E-Mail Commands

E-mail can be used with Archie to get much the same results you would get through the other methods—just more slowly. Remember to leave the subject line blank or ensure that a valid command is used there.

| | |
|---|---|
| `compress` | Compresses the results of the Archie search before e-mailing them to you. |
| `list <regular expression>` | Searches for all servers in the Archie database matching the UNIX regular expression (note that e-mail searches are only UNIX regular expressions). |

| | |
|---|---|
| path *<address>* | Sets the address to reply to. E-mail headers are often wrong, so this ensures that you get the message. This can also be used to send the file to another user address. |
| prog *<regular expression>* | Searches for files matching the UNIX regular expression (note that e-mail searches are only UNIX regular expressions). |
| site *<address>* | Returns a list of every file that Archie knows about on the specified site. |
| whatis *<regular expression>* | Searches the description database for the UNIX regular expression. |
| quit | End of commands. |

# Standard UNIX E-Mail Commands

These commands are taken from mail, a standard e-mail program for UNIX. Note that a <message list> consists of message numbers (as in 20 21 25), a range of message numbers (as in 20-25), or user names separated by spaces (rjsmith mgibbs bclinton). If omitted, Mail uses the current message.

To start the mail program, just type mail. Once mail is running, the following commands are available:

| | |
|---|---|
| d *<message list>* | Delete message(s). |
| e *<message list>* | Edit message(s). |
| f *<message list>* | Show the From: lines of message(s). |
| h | Display message headers. |
| m *<user list>* | Mail to users. |
| n | Type next message. |
| p *<message list>* | Print message(s). |
| q | Quit. |
| r *<message list>* | Reply to sender (only) of message(s). |
| R *<message list>* | Reply to sender and all recipients of message(s). |

s *<message list>* file     Save the message(s) to file.

t *<message list>*     Type message(s) (same as print, for no particularly good reason).

top *<message list>*     Show the first line of message(s).

u *<message list>*     Undelete the message(s) you've deleted in this session (if you exit, deleted messages are lost forever).

v *<message list>*     Edit message(s).

w *<message list>* file     Append message(s) to file, without the From: line.

x     Quit, undelete deleted messages, and make any messages you read this session unread.

z *<->*     Display next *<previous>* page of message headers.

# FTP Commands

To start FTP, enter

ftp *<address>* *<port>*

The basic commands used when FTP is running are

get *<remote filename>* *<local filename>*

> Retrieve the remote file and store it on the local machine. If the local file name is not specified, it's given the same name that it has on the remote machine, subject to how the FTP client on the local system handles file names that may be illegal (for example, the UNIX file name UsersManual.Version.001 wouldn't be legal under PC DOS).

put *<local filename>* *<remote filename>*

> Store a local file on the remote machine. If remote file name is left unspecified, it's given the same name that it has on the local machine, subject to how the FTP server on the remote system handles file names that may be illegal.

| | |
|---|---|
| `dir` or `ls` | Print a listing of the contents of a directory on the remote computer. If no directory is specified, the current working directory on the remote machine is used. |
| `binary` | Use this setting to send and receive nontext files (such as program files and databases). |
| `ascii` | Use this setting to send and receive text files. |
| `pwd` | Print the name of the current working directory on the remote machine. |
| `quit` or `bye` | Terminate the FTP session with the remote server and exit FTP. |

# FTPmail Commands

This is the equivalent of having an FTP session with a remote system but through mail messages. Remember that you should always use the FTP server nearest to you on the Internet or, if you don't know where that is, geographically nearest to you.

| | |
|---|---|
| `reply <address>` | Sets the address to reply to. E-mail headers are often wrong, so this ensures that you get the message. This can also be used to send the file to another user address. |
| `connect <host> (<user> (<pass> (<acct>)))` | |
| | Connects you to a particular FTP server, optionally as a named user (the default is `anonymous`), with an optional password (you'll be asked for one if needed), and an account name on the FTP server. |
| `ascii` | Files are to be transferred as ASCII. |
| `binary` | Files are to be transferred as binary. |
| `chdir <directory>` | `get` and `ls` commands are relative to the named directory. (Note that you can use only one `chdir` per FTPmail session, and it is executed before any `ls`, `dir`, or `get` commands). |
| `compress` | Compress binaries using Lempel-Ziv encoding. |

| | |
|---|---|
| `compact` | Compress binaries using Huffman encoding. |
| `uuencode` | Binary files will be mailed in uuencode format. |
| `btoa` | Binary files will be mailed in btoa format. |
| `chunksize <bytes>` | Splits files into chunks of the specified size (the default is 64,000 bytes) and sends each as a separate e-mail message. |
| `ls <directory>` | Short directory listing. |
| `dir <directory>` | Long directory listing. |
| `index <text>` | Search for the given text in FTP server's index |
| `get <filename>` | Gets a file and has it mailed to you (each FTPmail session has a maximum of ten `get` commands). |
| `quit` | This marks the end of the FTPmail commands; the FTPmail server will ignore the rest of the mail message (useful if you have a `.signature` file or are a VMSMAIL user). |

# Gopher Commands

These are the standard Gopher commands. Gopher is evolving very quickly, and some Gophers may have local modifications that could make them very different. If you have a local Gopher, it is started by

`gopher`

If you don't have a local Gopher, you'll need to telnet to a site that does. All the following commands are used when Gopher is running.

## General Gopher Commands

| | |
|---|---|
| `[up]` | Move to previous line. |
| `[down]` | Move to next line. |
| `[right]` or `[enter]` | Select and act upon the current item. |
| `[left]` or `u` | Exit the current item. |
| `>`, `+`, `[pgdn]`, or `[space]` | View next page. |

| | |
|---|---|
| <, -, [pgup], or b | View previous page. |
| <n> | Go to a specific line (if line numbering is shown). |
| m | Go back to the main menu. |

## Gopher Bookmark Commands

Bookmarks are placeholders that you can set to take you straight to a specific Gopher menu. This is really useful if you've had to traverse a dozen menus to get to a resource that you want to get back to more easily next time. Some Gophers don't support this feature.

| | |
|---|---|
| a | Add current item to the bookmark list. |
| A | Add current directory/search to bookmark list. |
| v | View bookmark list. |
| d | Delete a bookmark. |

## Other Gopher Commands

| | |
|---|---|
| q | Quit and be asked to confirm. |
| Q | Quit unconditionally. |
| = | Display technical information about current item. |
| o | Change options. |

# LISTSERV Commands

LISTSERV is run by

`listserv command`

The commands that you can use with Eric Thomas' Revised Listserv are

| | |
|---|---|
| subscribe <listname> <first name> <last name> | |
| | Subscribe to a list or change your name if you've already subscribed. |
| signoff <listname> | Unsubscribe to the specified list. |

signoff *              Unsubscribe from all lists on that server.

signoff * netwide      Unsubscribe from all lists in the network.

confirm <listname1> (<listname2> (...))

                    Confirm your subscription (when LISTSERV requests it).

# News Commands

These commands are for the news reader program rn. Check the program and version your site is using; the commands may vary between releases. You start the program by simply typing rn.

The following commands are used when the program is running.

## Newsgroup Selection Commands

| | |
|---|---|
| y or [space] | Make this newsgroup current and read the first article. |
| = | Make this newsgroup current and list subjects before reading the articles. |
| u | Unsubscribe from this newsgroup. |
| c | Catch up (mark all articles in this newsgroup as read). |
| n | Go to the next newsgroup with unread news. |
| N | Go to the next newsgroup. |
| p | Go to the previous newsgroup with unread news. |
| P | Go to the previous newsgroup. |
| - | Go to the previously displayed newsgroup. |
| 1 | Go to the first newsgroup. |
| ^ | Go to the first newsgroup with unread news. |
| $ | Go to the last newsgroup. |
| g<name> | Go to the named newsgroup. Subscribe to new newsgroups this way too. |
| /<pattern> | Search forward for newsgroup matching pattern. (Use * and ? style patterns. Append r to include read newsgroups.) |

| | |
|---|---|
| ?*<pattern>* | Search backward for newsgroup matching pattern. (Use * and ? style patterns. Append r to include read news-groups.) |
| l*<pattern>* | List newsgroups that you haven't subscribed to that contain the text pattern. |
| o*<pattern>* | Display only newsgroups matching pattern. Omit pattern to display all newsgroups. |
| a*<pattern>* | Like o, but also scans for unsubscribed newsgroups matching text pattern. |
| L | List the newsgroups you currently subscribe to. |
| q | Quit. |
| x | Quit, restoring the news reader to the state it was in at the start of this session. |
| v | Print version. |

# Article Selection Commands

| | |
|---|---|
| n or [space] | Scan forward for next unread article. |
| N | Go to next article. |
| ^N | Scan forward for next unread article with same subject. |
| p, P, ^P | Same as n, N, and ^N, but going backwards. |
| - | Go to previously displayed article. |
| *<number>* | Go to specified article. |
| /*<pattern>*/*<modifiers>* | Scan forward for article containing pattern in the subject line. (Use ?*<pattern>*? to scan backwards; append h to scan headers, a to scan entire articles, r to scan read articles, and c to make case sensitive.) |
| f, F | Submit a follow-up article (F for include this article). |
| r, R | Reply through Internet mail (R for include this article). |
| s | Save to file. |

| C | Cancel this article, if it's your own. |
| ^R, v | Restart article (v for verbose). |
| ^X | Restart article, rot13 mode (encrypted, for potentially offensive material). |
| c | Catch up (mark all articles in the current newsgroup as read). |
| b | Back up one page. |
| ^ | Go to first unread article. Disables subject search mode. |
| $ | Go to end of newsgroup. Disables subject search mode. |
| # | Print last article number. |
| j | Junk this article (mark it read). Stays at end of article. |
| m | Mark article as still unread. |
| M | Mark article as still unread upon exiting newsgroup or after Y command. |
| k | Kill current subject (mark articles as read). |
| for | List subjects of unread articles. |
| u | Unsubscribe from this newsgroup. |
| q | Quit this newsgroup for now. |
| Q | Quit newsgroup, staying at current newsgroup. |

## Paging Commands

| [space] | Display the next page. |
| x | Display the next page decrypted (rot13). |
| d | Display half a page more. |
| [enter] | Display one more line. |
| ^R, v, ^X | Restart the current article (v for verbose header, ^X for rot13). |

| | |
|---|---|
| b | Back up one page. |
| g<*pattern*> | Search forward within article for pattern. |
| G | Search again for current pattern within article. |
| q | Quit the pager, go to end of article. Leave article read or unread. |
| j | Junk this article (mark it read). Go to end of article. |

The following commands skip the rest of the current article, then behave just as if typed to the What next? prompt at the end of the article:

| | |
|---|---|
| n | Scan forward for next unread article. |
| N | Go to next article. |
| ^N | Scan forward for next unread article with same title. |
| p, P, ^P | Same as n, N, ^N, but going backwards. |
| - | Go to previously displayed article. |

# Telnet Commands

You start telnet by specifying the address of the target computer and, optionally, the port number:

```
telnet <address> (<port>)
```

To issue commands to telnet, you need to use the escape character, which will be printed as the session starts. Take note of it because if you need it and don't know what it is, you'll have to either try several hundred key combinations or do something more drastic, like switch off your computer. The available commands when telnet is running are

| | |
|---|---|
| close | Close the current session and return to command mode. |
| open <address> (<port>) | Open a connection to the named host. If no port number is specified, telnet will attempt to contact a telnet server at the default port. |
| status | Report on the telnet session. |

quit                          Close any open telnet session and exit
                              telnet.

# WAIS (SWAIS) Commands

WAIS sessions are started by either running a local WAIS client with the command

wais

or using telnet to access a site such as quake.think.com that offers a WAIS client and logging in (usually) as WAIS. Once WAIS is running, you can use the following commands:

| | |
|---|---|
| j or [down] or ^N | Move down one source. |
| k or [up] or ^P | Move up one source. |
| J or ^V or ^D | Move down one screen. |
| K or [esc] v or ^U | Move up one screen. |
| ### | Position to source number. |
| /sss | Search for source sss. |
| [space] or [period] | Select current source. |
| = | Deselect all sources. |
| v or [comma] | View current source info. |
| [enter] | Perform search. |
| s | Select new sources (refresh the list of sources). |
| w | Select new keywords. |
| X or - | Remove current source for the rest of this session. |
| o | Set and show swais options. |
| h or ? | Show the help display. |
| H | Display program history. |
| q | Leave the program. |

# World Wide Web

To start WWW, you'll need to either telnet to info.cern.ch, which will connect you directly to its WWW server, or have your own WWW system locally. Once WWW is running, you can use the following commands:

| | |
|---|---|
| *<n>* | Follow the specified link in the current document. |
| [enter] | Go to the next page of the current document (noted on the command line as <RETURN>). |
| back | Go back to the previous document. |
| bottom | Go to the last screen of the current document. |
| help | Show help. |
| home | Go directly to the first page you saw when WWW started. |
| next | If you follow a link from a document and, when you're finished, you want to follow the next link on the document you came from, the next command will take you there. |
| previous | Just as the next command will take you to the next link on the last document you were on, the previous command will take you to the link prior to the one that you followed on the last document. |
| print | Print the current document (if you're not running a local version of WWW, don't do this). |
| quit | Exit WWW. |
| recall | Give a list of the documents you looked at. |
| recall *<n>* | Go to the nth document you looked at. The output from the recall command by itself gives the numbers of the documents. |
| top | Go to the first screen of the current document. |
| up | Go to the previous page of the current document. |

# INTERNET GLOSSARY

**alias**   A simple name substituted for a more complicated electronic mailing address. The alias might represent a single person or a group of people. For example, an alias such as "Sales" might be a list of the addresses of all the people in a company's sales department.

**anonymous FTP** (File Transfer Protocol)   The act of connecting to a remote computer as an anonymous user, in order to transfer files back to your own computer.

**ANSI** (American National Standards Institute)   The organization responsible for approving United States standards in several areas, including computers and communications.

**Archie**   A system for locating information on files and directories publicly available through anonymous FTP.

**archive**   A file that contains other files. Often used to store files that have related contents. Also used to refer to ftp sites that hold large collections of files for download.

**ARPANET** (Advanced Research Projects Agency Network)  An early research network that served as the "testing ground" for the theories and software upon which the Internet is based; forerunner of the Internet.

**ASCII** (American Standard Code for Information Interchange)  One of the standard formats for representing characters. This standard and others like it make sharing files between programs possible. A text file is usually in ASCII format.

**backbone**  A network that interconnects other networks.

**BBS**  Acronym for bulletin board system. See *bulletin board*.

**binary**  1. A system of counting that uses only the digits 0 and 1. 2. When used in connection with files (as in "binary file transfer"), it means that the file contains characters that are not printable.

**BITNET** (Because It's Time Network)  A network that connects academic and research institutions around the world. BITNET supports mail, mailing lists, and file transfer and connects to the Internet.

**bulletin board**  A service that enables users to enter information for others to read and that can store and retrieve files.

**client/server**  Describes a relationship between two pieces of software. One piece of software, the server, is responsible for servicing requests from the other piece, the client. These requests can be anything—from transferring files to searching databases to just about anything you can think of that one program can do for another.

**compress**  A technique for reducing the size of a data or program file. Compressed files are often stored in archives. See also *archive*.

**CompuServe**  A computer service available on the Internet and via modem connections. It offers an Internet e-mail gateway from its own e-mail system, discussion forums, access to hundreds of software vendors, and thousands of files for downloading.

**CWIS** (Campus Wide Information Systems)  Provides information and services available on campuses, including directory information, calendars, bulletin boards, databases, and interactive computing.

**DNS** (Domain Name System)  A system whose principal function is to locate host IP addresses based on host names. It consists of a hierarchical sequence of names (from the most specific to the most general) separated by dots (for example, ucs.usl.edu).

**downloading**  The electronic transfer of information from one computer to another, generally from a larger computer to a smaller one.

**e-mail** (electronic mail)   A system that enables the exchange of messages between network users or groups of users.

**e-mail address**   An identifier that is used to send electronic mail to a specific destination.

**emoticons**   See *smiley*.

**FAQ** (frequently asked question)   A listing of questions and answers provided for new subscribers to newsgroups and e-mail listings, usually published once a month. Also used by many service providers to answer questions that new Internet users might have concerning a service so that rather than having to repeat the same answers over and over, the FAQ can be sent to the user.

**finger**   A program that displays information about a particular user, or all users, logged on a system. It usually gives the full name, last login time, idle time, terminal time, and terminal location. May also display plan and project files left by the user.

**flame**   A strong opinion or criticism of some idea or statement expressed in an electronic mail message.

**freeware**   Software that is supplied by the author at no charge. Title and copyright is retained by the author.

**FTP** (File Transfer Protocol)   A protocol that enables a user to transfer files electronically from remote computers to the user's computer; part of the TCP/IP suite. Also the name of the program used to execute the protocol. See also *anonymous FTP*.

**gateway**   Software that translates data from the standards of one system to the standards of another.

**Gopher**   A distributed information service that uses a simple protocol to enable Gopher clients to access information from any other accessible Gopher server, creating a single "Gopherspace" of information.

**header**   Part of an electronic mail message that precedes the body of the message and provides the message originator, date, and time.

**host computer**   A term used with wild abandon to denote any computer attached directly to the Internet.

**hypertext**   Data in a document that is organized to provide links between key words or phrases, so that related concepts and issues can be linked together.

**internet**   Spelled with a small *i*, internet refers to a collection of interconnected networks.

**Internet**   The series of interconnected networks (a network of networks, in fact) that includes local area, regional, and national backbone networks; makes up the largest internet in the world. Networks in the Internet use the same telecommunications protocol (TCP/IP) and provide electronic mail, remote login, and file transfer services. Some networks attached to the Internet don't use TCP/IP, but they are not considered part of the Internet.

**Internet address**   The numeric address that uniquely identifies a computer on the Internet.

**Internetiquette**   Our term for netiquette on the Internet (just to be different). See *netiquette.*

**InterNIC** (Internet Network Information Center)   A Network Information Services Manager funded by the National Science Foundation, InterNIC provides registration, directory, database, and information services.

**IP** (Internet Protocol)   The Internet standard communications protocol; provides a common layer over dissimilar networks.

**IP Address**   The numeric address of a computer connected to the Internet.

**LISTSERV lists** (or listservers)   LISTSERVs are programs that act as message switches for e-mail on specific subjects. You subscribe to a list that is on a topic of interest to you on a LISTSERV and you will receive all messages that are sent to the list. You can reply to those messages, and all other list subscibers will see your message.

**lurking**   The act of "hanging around" a mailing list (a LISTSERV list) or USENET newsgroup without contributing to the discussion; sometimes used as a means of learning before becoming an active participant.

**mail gateway**   A machine that connects similar or dissimilar electronic mail systems and translates and transfers messages between them.

**mail server**   A software program that sends files or information in response to requests received via e-mail.

**mailing list**   A list of e-mail addresses used to forward messages (generally related to a specific topic) to groups of people. In some instances, moderators determine whether to send messages to the rest of the group or not.

**MIME** (Multipurpose Internet Mail Extensions)   An extension that provides the transfer of non-textual data, such as graphics and fax, by e-mail.

**MUD** (Multiuser Dungeon)   Role-playing games or simulations played on the Internet. Players interact in real-time and alter the game as they play it. MUDs are usually based on the telnet protocol for remote login.

**name server**   A computer on the Internet that manages a database of Internet names and their corresponding numeric addresses. Used by other computers to determine the correct address for e-mail, FTP, telnet, and other service connections.

**netiquette**   A pun on the word "etiquette" that refers to proper and tasteful behavior on a network communications system. See also *Internetiquette*.

**NIC** (Network Information Center)   A NIC provides administrative support, user assistance, and information services for a network.

**NIS** (Network Information Services)   The services provided by a NIC to assist users utilizing a network. See also *NIC*.

**NREN** (National Research and Education Network)   The proposed national computer network to be built upon the foundation of the NSF backbone network, NSFNET. NREN would provide high-speed interconnection between other national and regional networks.

**NSF** (National Science Foundation)   A United States government agency that promotes the advancement of science.

**NSFNET** (National Science Foundation Network)   Funded by the National Science Foundation, this network is a high speed "network of networks" that plays an essential part in academic and research communications. Part of the Internet, with connections to Canada, Mexico, and Europe, it is the backbone for the proposed NREN.

**OCLC** (Online Computer Library Catalog)   A nonprofit membership organization that offers computer-based services to libraries, educational organizations, and their users. OCLC connects over 10,000 libraries around the world.

**OPAC** (Online Public Access Catalog)   Any type of computerized library catalog.

**PING** (Packet InterNet Groper)   A program designed to test the accessibility of a particular destination.

**postmaster**   Person at a particular site responsible for handling electronic mail problems, answering queries about users, and other e-mail–related tasks.

**protocol**   A set of formats and procedures governing the exchange of information between systems.

**public domain**   Software with title and copyright explicitly relinquished by the author, so that anyone can use it as they please.

**relevance feedback**   A technique that involves the ordering of documents on the basis of the degree of relevance they have to the search request. The ordering is by a scoring system that tabulates the number of matches with the search criteria.

**remote access**   The ability to access a computer from outside the building in which it is housed. Remote access requires communications hardware, software, and actual physical links, such as telephone lines or a telnet login to another computer.

**remote login**   Connecting to a remote computer so that its screen display is sent to your computer, and your keyboard data is sent to it. This means that programs on the remote computer appear to be running locally. See also *telnet*.

**RFC** (Request for Comments)   The document series that describes the Internet suite of protocols and related experiments, begun in 1969. RFCs can be located through the Internet via anonymous FTP.

**rn**   The software program through which USENET news is accessed.

**RTFM**   An impolite acronym meaning "read the manual." Often posted by support staff to users who refuse to read a document that might actually help them.

**servers**   Computers that provide resources. There are many types of servers, including file servers, terminal servers, and name servers.

**shareware**   Software distributed through public channels for which the author hopes to receive monetary compensation.

**signature**   The message at the bottom of an e-mail message or USENET article that identifies the sender.

**smiley**   A group of characters that, when viewed sideways, constitute a face and are used to add "tone" to e-mail communications.

**tar**   A type of file archiving. See also *archive*.

**TCP/IP** (Transmission Control Protocol/Internet Protocol)   The combined set of protocols (or protocol suites) that performs the transfer of data between two computers. The standard protocol suite used on the Internet.

**telnet**   A portion of the TCP/IP suite of software protocols that enables a user to log in to a remote computer from the user's local computer.

**terminal emulator**   A program that enables a computer to communicate with a remote host as if it were a specific type of terminal directly connected to that computer or network.

**TN3270**   A version of telnet supplying IBM full-screen support.

**troughing**   See *lurking*.

**USENET**   A set of newsgroups considered to be of global interest and governed by a set of rules for passing and maintaining newsgroups.

**Veronica** (Very Easy Rodent-Oriented Net-wide Index to Computerized Archives)   A service that maintains an index of titles of Gopher items and provides keyword searches of those items.

**virus**   A program that replicates itself through incorporation into other programs.

**WAIS** (Wide Area Information Servers)   A distributed information system that offers natural language input, indexed searching, and "relevance feedback."

**whois**   A program that permits users to query a database of people or things, such as domains, networks, and hosts. The information provided includes a person's company name, address, phone number, and e-mail address.

**World-Wide Web**   A hypertext-based, distributed information system in which users may create, edit, or browse hypertext documents.

**WWW**   See *World-Wide Web*.

**Z39.50 Protocol**   A standard protocol for searching databases based on a client/server model.

**zoo**   A type of file compression and archiving. See also *archive* and *compress*.

# ADDRESSING E-MAIL TO OTHER SYSTEMS

Some of the networks that can receive e-mail from the Internet are based on different standards. This means that e-mail addresses must be translated so that they can be transferred from the Internet to the foreign system and vice versa. In some cases, the gateway software (the software that does the translation) needs a little extra help to figure out how to do the translation correctly. The following information should prove useful when you need to figure out how to do this.

## AT&T Mail to Bitnet

*internet!host.bitnet!user*

**Example:** To send from AT&T Mail to user Mickey at Bitnet host DISNEY:

```
internet!disney.bitnet!Mickey
```

## AT&T Mail to Internet

*internet!host.domain!user*

**Example:** Send from AT&T Mail to user Mickey at Internet host disney.world.com:

```
internet!disney.world.com!Mickey
```

## AT&T Mail to UUNET

*internet!uunet!system!user*

**Example:** Send from AT&T Mail to user Mickey on UUNET host DISNEY:

```
internet!uunet!disney!Mickey
```

## Bitnet and EARN to DECNET

Methods for routing mail from Bitnet to DECNET vary, depending on the specific mailer installed at the Bitnet node. Bitnet sites may route mail to DECNET hosts as shown in the following example:

*user%host.SPAN@DFTBIT*

*user%host.SPAN@STAR.STANFORD.EDU*

*user%host.SPAN@VLSI.JPL.NASA.GOV*

*user%host.SPAN@SDSC.BITNET*

## Bitnet and EARN to Internet

Methods for routing mail from Bitnet to Internet vary, depending on the specific mailer installed at the Bitnet node. Bitnet sites running the Croswell mailer are capable of directly addressing Internet hosts. For those sites that require the use of a Bitnet-to-Internet gateway, the logical Bitnet host INTERBIT should be used. This logical host name is translated into a real host name appropriate for the sender's location.

*user@host.domain* (with Croswell mailer)

*user%host.domain@INTERBIT* (without Croswell mailer)

**Example:** Send to user Mickey at Internet host disney.world.com:

```
Mickey@disney.world.com
```

or

```
Mickey%disney.world.com@INTERBIT
```

## CompuServe to Bitnet

>*INTERNET:user@HOST.BITNET*

**Example:** Send to user Mickey on Bitnet host Disney:

```
>INTERNET:Mickey@DISNEY.BITNET
```

**Note:** The >INTERNET: prefix is essential. A space after the >INTERNET: prefix is not required.

## CompuServe to Internet

>*INTERNET:user@host.domain*

**Example:** Send to user Mickey on Internet host disney.world.com:

```
>INTERNET:Mickey@disney.world.com
```

**Note:** The >INTERNET: prefix is essential. A space after the >INTERNET: prefix is not required.

## CompuServe to MCI Mail

>*MCIMAIL:firstname lastname*

or

>*MCIMAIL:user id*

**Example:** Send to MCI Mail user Mickey Mouse, ID 101-1001:

```
>MCIMAIL:Mickey Mouse
```

or

```
>MCIMAIL:101-1001
```

**Note:** The >MCIMAIL: prefix is essential. A space after the >MCIMAIL: prefix is not required. It is better to use the user ID, rather than the user's name, because more than one user might have the same name. A surcharge, based on message size, will be billed to the sending CompuServe account.

## DECNET to Bitnet and EARN

*DFTNIC::JNET%"user@host"*

*EAST::"user@host.BITNET"*

## DECNET to Internet

*NSFGW::"user@host.domain"* (NSF Gateway/NCAR)

*EAST::"user@host.domain"* (New GSFC Gateway)

*NSSDCA::SMTP%"user@host.domain"* (GSFC Gateway)

*DFTNIC::SMTP%"user@host.domain"* (GSFC Gateway)

*AMES::"user@host.domain"* (AMES Gateway)

*WITCH::"user@host.domain"* (JPL Gateway)

## Fidonet to Internet

*UUCP of FIDONET-UUCP-Gateway*

Then put Internet address as first line of message, followed by a blank line.

**Example:** Send to Mickey Mouse at disney.world.com:

```
UUCP of 1:382/39.9
```

Put Internet address on the first line of the message, followed by a blank line:

```
Mickey@disney.world.com
```

**Note:** This, of course, is done in Netmail (not in echo mail). To find the nearest gateway, look in your node list for the UUCP flag. For example, 1:382/39 is the gateway in Net 382.

## Internet to AT&T Mail

*user@attmail.com*

**Example:** Send to AT&T Mail subscriber Mickey:

```
Mickey@attmail.com
```

## Internet to AT&T Mail-Attached X.400 Gateway

Assume that there is an AT&T Mail X.400 gateway for XYZ Company. Given an X.400 address for someone at XYZ Company such as

```
/C=US/ADMD=ATTMAIL/PRMD=XYZ/O=TOPBRASS/PN=JOHN_DOE
```

this can be generalized to:

*/C=US/ADMD=ATTMAIL/PRMD=<PRMD-name>/<extra-X.400-stuff>*

You may then address a message as follows:

*@mhs.attmail.com:<PRMD-name>/<extra-X.400-stuff>*

**Example:** Send to /C=US/ADMD=attmail/PRMD=xyz/O=topbrass/ PN=mickey:

```
@mhs.attmail.com:xyz/o=topbrass/pn=mickey
```
 (for source-route)

or

```
xyz/o=topbrass/pn=mickey@mhs.attmail.com
```
 (non-source-route)

**Note:** Be careful of the return address when replying to mail. This gateway uses mixed UUCP, X.400, and Internet-style addressing in its return addresses. You may need to re-address your replies instead of letting your mailer do it for you.

## Internet to Bitnet and EARN

*user%host.BITNET@CUNYVM.CUNY.EDU* (CUNY gateway)

## Internet to CompuServe

*user@compuserve.com*

**Example:** Send to user 74055,412 (PC World) on CompuServe Mail:

```
74055.412@compuserve.com
```

**Note:** Note that the comma in the CompuServe user ID must be changed to a period when included in an Internet address.

## Internet to DECNET

*user%host.SPAN@LONGS.UCAR.EDU* (NSF Gateway/NCAR)

*user@host.dnet.nasa.gov* (New GSFC Gateway)

*user%host.dnet@east.gsfc.nasa.gov* (New GSFC Gateway)

*user@host.span.nasa.gov* (AMES Gateway)

*user%host.SPAN@AMES.ARCNASA.GOV*

*user%host.SPAN@WITCH.JPL.NASA.GOV* (JPL Gateway)

## Internet to Fidonet

*Firstname.Lastname@Fnodenumber.Nnet.Zzone.FIDONET.ORG*

*Firstname.Lastname@Ppoint.Fnodenumber.Nnet.Zzone.FIDONET.ORG*

**Example:** To send mail to Mickey Mouse at Fidonet address 1:10/101:

```
Mickey.Mouse@f101.n10.z1.fidonet.org
```

**Example:** To send mail to Minnie Mouse at Fidonet address 1:27/101.3:

```
Minnie.Mouse@p3.f101.n27.z1.fidonet.org
```

**Note:** Fido addresses are in the form: #:##/### (for example: 1:10/101).

To create an Internet address from a Fidonet address, start with the login name. If the login name includes both first and last name, separate them with a . character, then add an @. The three Fidonet numbers are reversed, then prefixed with f, n, and z.

**Example:** 1:10/101 becomes f101.n10.z1.

If the Fidonet address includes a point number other than zero, the point number is added with a p prefix.

**Example:** 1:27/101.3 becomes p3.f101.n27.z1.

After the encoded numbers, add .fidonet.org.

## Internet to MCI Mail

*userid@mcimail.com*

*firstname_lastname@mcimail.com*

**Example:** Send to MCI Mail subscriber Mickey Mouse with user ID 101-1001:

```
Mickey_Mouse@mcimail.com
```

or

```
101-1001@mcimail.com
```

**Note:** First name and last name are separated by a _. Because more than one user might share the same name, use the user ID as opposed to the user's name.

## Internet to UUNET

*alpha!user@uunet.uu.net*

*beta!alpha!user@uunet.uu.net*

**Example:** The uucp connection from UUNET to the destination host (alpha) must exist, or a uucp path from UUNET to the destination host (uunet!beta!alpha) must exist.

Send to user Mickey at UUCP host ALPHA:

```
alpha!Mickey@uunet.uu.net
```

```
beta!alpha!Mickey@uunet.uu.net
```

## MCI Mail to CompuServe

To: *username (EMS)*

EMS: *compuserve*

MBX: *P=CSMail*

MBX: *DDA=ID=CompuServe ID*

**Example:** Send to CompuServe user PC World, ID: 74055,412:

To: `PC World (EMS)`

EMS: `compuserve`

MBX: `P=CSMail`

MBX: `DDA=ID=74055,412`

## MCI Mail to Internet

To: *username (EMS)*

EMS: *Internet*

MBX: *Full Internet address*

**Example:** Send to Internet user Mickey Mouse:

To: `Mickey Mouse (EMS)`

EMS: `Internet`

MBX: `mickey@disney.world.com`

## UUNET to Internet

*uunet!user@host.domain*

*alpha!beta!uunet!user@host.domain*

**Example:** A uucp connection from the originating host to UUNET must exist, or a uucp path from the originating host to UUNET (alpha!beta!uunet) must exist.

Send to user Mickey at Internet host disney.world.com:

`uunet!Mickey@disney.world.com`

`alpha!beta!uunet!Mickey@disney.world.com`

# Credits

This information was adapted from a list compiled by the Louisiana State University Office of Telecommunications, with additions made by Scott Hoppe. Scott invites additions or changes to be addressed to him on CompuServe at 71641,2400 (for you Interneters, that's…hmmm, let's see…71641.2400@compuserve.com).

**Navigator's Note:** A special note about the @ (at) symbol. Many of the address structures listed in this chapter contain the @ symbol. The @ symbol is also defined as a delete character on some systems. This means that you must "escape" this character from the operating system so that it is not interpreted.

On some VM systems, for example, the address `user@host.domain` could be entered as `user"@host.domain`. When the mail entry screen appears, you should see the address written properly. On many UNIX systems, a backslash (\) can be used to escape a single character. Thus, the preceding example would be entered as `user\@host.domain`.

Unless you already know that you need to escape a particular character, it is usually best to attempt the normal (un-escaped) address first. If you have trouble with specific characters in the address, contact your local system administrator for information on how to escape the problem character.

# THE INTERNET NAVIGATOR'S GAZETTEER

This resource guide to the Internet is but a starting point for future exploration. The size and complexity of the Internet make it impossible to create a permanent, comprehensive list of everything available at a given time. Before you finish listing everything, something has already been added, deleted, or moved.

This list has been created to provide the widest variety of topics available to you, the fledgling Internet navigator, and to give you just a sample of what is out there. A quick browse through the guide will reveal that it focuses on list and e-mail resources (with a few other types thrown in for good measure). There are a few reasons for this:

⚓ The Internet is very e-mail and list oriented.

⚓ Many e-mail lists and discussion groups send letters of introduction when you subscribe, or they regularly post an FAQ (frequently asked question) that will often list related resources.

These resources may be in the form of other lists, archives of previous postings, or reference information available via FTP, USENET groups, or telnet sites.

⚓ Lists and e-mail provide a method of interacting with other people. This means that by joining lists focusing on your areas of interest, you'll receive (and eventually send!) messages that contain information about other related Internet resources. This will usually take the form of "...because of the interest in $x$, I've uploaded this file (or created this FTP site)..." or "...I've heard that $y$ is available by $z$...."

# When All Else Fails...

Use your Navigator's tools. This book has provided you with the means to find and use just about everything available on the Internet (at the time of this writing—remember, things change quickly on the Internet), including e-mail, FTP, telnet, WAIS, Gopher, WWW, Archie, Veronica, and USENET. Be patient. Remember, you are plugging yourself into the whole world. That's a lot to tackle right away.

As you use your tools and gain experience and confidence, you'll learn that it's possible to find just about anything, and if you can't find it, you may just have to create it yourself. After all, someone had to create everything else out there. You'll probably find that no subject is too bizarre, exotic, or specialized for someone else to be interested in and contribute to. It's just a matter of finding them—and sometimes they move around.

In the meantime, here are some other places to pursue your interests:

⚓ Keep an eye on USENET. USENET groups are constantly being created and voted upon. There are hundreds of lists with varying degrees of activity.

⚓ Periodically send the LIST GLOBAL command to a LISTSERV. New lists are being created daily. The size of the global list makes daily retrieval prohibitive, but you'll find many changes over time. Also, just as the LISTSERV software has a lot of user-oriented functions, it has a lot of behind-the-scenes (administrative) power as well. One of those features is relocation. Lists have a tendency to move around. This is one reason a subscription request doesn't have to be sent to the host machine, just to a LISTSERV machine (which then forwards your request to the appropriate machine).

⚓ Subscribe to the NEW-LIST LISTSERV. This list is a sounding board for anyone creating a new list (not just LISTSERV) as well as a place for people to ask things like "does anyone know of a list that discusses salt well drilling techniques in ancient China?"

⚓ Yanoff's List. Scott Yanoff regularly updates his "Internet Services List." This can be retrieved via anonymous FTP (or FTPmail) at csd4.csd.uwm.edu (in the directory /pub, the file is named inet.services.txt). This is a list of lists, FTP sites, telnet sites, and all-around interesting tidbits.

⚓ List of mailing lists. This can be retrieved via anonymous FTP (or FTPmail) at rtfm.mit.edu in the directory /pub/usenet/news.answers/mail. You should retrieve the file mailing-lists.

⚓ List of lists. This is available via anonymous FTP at ftp.nisc.sri.com in the directory /netinfo. The filename is interest-groups.

⚓ Smith's BigFun List. This is a general list of Internet resources. It can be retrieved via anonymous FTP from cerebus.cor.epa.gov in the directory /pub. The file is bigfun.

⚓ Send a request to LISTSERV@vm1.nodak.edu stating GET LISTSOF LISTS. This will return a list of lists as well as information for retrieving other files that will help you find interesting things.

⚓ Join the Internet Hunt. Have you ever noticed that while you are looking for something (usually something you've lost) you find lots of other interesting things? The Hunt is the same way. Not only do you learn how to use the Internet resources more efficiently, you find other things along the way to sidetrack you. Check out Appendix A, "Testing Your Navigation Skills," for more information on the Hunt.

⚓ Birds of a feather flock together. If you are interested in a specific topic, subject, or hobby that is part of a larger theme, see what the people who hang out there know. If you are interested in discussing a specific breed of dog, say a dachshund, check out lists where other pet or dog owners hang out and see if they know about such a list or if the interest level warrants creating one.

# Activism

## ACTUP

**Resource:**   List
**Address:**   `act-up@world.std.com`
Discussion and information exchange related to the ACTUP organization
(AIDS Coalition To Unleash Power). Send subscription requests to
`act-up-request@world.std.com`.

## Amnesty International

**Resource:**   LISTSERV
**Address:**   `amnesty@vms.cis.pitt.edu`
A list for distributing information about persons on the Amnesty International
list who are victims of human rights abuse. To subscribe, address a message in
the following manner:
**To:**        `LISTSERV@vms.cis.pitt.edu`
**From:**      `<your address>`
**Subject:**   *LISTSERV ignores this*
`SUBSCRIBE amnesty <firstname> <lastname>`

## Animal Rights

**Resource:**   List
**Address:**   `ar-alerts@ny.neavs.com`
Animal rights discussion and information exchange. Send your subscription
request to `majordomo@ny.neavs.com`. The message should contain the phrase
`subscribe ar-alerts`.

## College

**Resource:**   LISTSERV
**Address:**   `actnow-l@brownvm.brown.edu`
This is for anyone interested in college activism. To subscribe, address a
message in the following manner:
**To:**        `LISTSERV@brownvm.brown.edu`
**From:**      `<your address>`
**Subject:**   *LISTSERV ignores this*
`SUBSCRIBE actnow-l <firstname> <lastname>`

## Feminism

**Resource:**   LISTSERV
**Address:**   femisa@mach1.wlu.ca

A network for exchange of information by the members of the Feminism branch of the International Studies Association. To subscribe, address a message in the following manner:

**To:**   LISTSERV@mach1.wlu.ca
**From:**   <your address>
**Subject:**   *LISTSERV ignores this*

SUBSCRIBE femisa <firstname> <lastname>

## General

**Resource:**   LISTSERV
**Address:**   activ-l@mizzou1.bitnet

This is a general forum for activists to meet and exchange ideas and opinions. To subscribe, address a message in the following manner:

**To:**   LISTSERV@mizzou1.bitnet
**From:**   <your address>
**Subject:**   *LISTSERV ignores this*

SUBSCRIBE activ-l <firstname> <lastname>

## Human Rights

**Resource:**   LISTSERV
**Address:**   hrs-l@bingvmb.bitnet

This list discusses and exchanges information about the systematic studies of human rights. To subscribe, address a message in the following manner:

**To:**   LISTSERV@bingvmb.bitnet
**From:**   <your address>
**Subject:**   *LISTSERV ignores this*

SUBSCRIBE hrs-l <firstname> <lastname>

**Resource:**   LISTSERV
**Address:**   hr-l@vms.cis.pitt.edu

Devoted to the discussion of human rights. To subscribe, address a message in the following manner:

**To:**   LISTSERV@vms.cis.pitt.edu
**From:**   <your address>
**Subject:**   *LISTSERV ignores this*

SUBSCRIBE hr-l <firstname> <lastname>

## Media

**Resource:** List
**Address:** prog-pubs@fuggles.acc.virginia.edu
For persons interested in alternate, progressive media. Send your administrative information to prog-pubs-request@fuggles.acc.virginia.edu.

## Parental Rights

**Resource:** LISTSERV
**Address:** free-l@indycms.iupui.edu
A discussion list for supporters of Fathers' Rights and Equality Exchange. To subscribe, address a message in the following manner:

**To:**       LISTSERV@indycms.iupui.edu
**From:**     <your address>
**Subject:**  *LISTSERV ignores this*
SUBSCRIBE free-l <firstname> <lastname>

# Architecture

## Landscaping

**Resource:** LISTSERV
**Address:** larchnet@uoguelph.bitnet
This list is for anyone involved in landscape architecture. To subscribe, address a message in the following manner:

**To:**       LISTSERV@uoguelph.bitnet
**From:**     <your address>
**Subject:**  *LISTSERV ignores this*
SUBSCRIBE larchnet <firstname> <lastname>

# Art

## Ceramics

**Resource:** LISTSERV
**Address:** clayart@ukcc.uky.edu
For everyone who enjoys and appreciates ceramic arts of all shapes and sizes. To subscribe, address a message in the following manner:

```
To:        LISTSERV@ukcc.uky.edu
From:      <your address>
Subject:   LISTSERV ignores this
SUBSCRIBE clayart <firstname> <lastname>
```

## Support

**Resource:** List
**Address:** art-support@newcastle.ac.uk
A discussion list for all persons (creators, teachers, and fans) supporting the arts. Subscribe by sending a mail message containing the phrase subscribe art-support to mailbase@newcastle.ac.uk.

## Visual

**Resource:** LISTSERV
**Address:** artcrit@vm1.yorku.ca
Devoted to the exchange of information about and critical examination of the visual arts. To subscribe, address a message in the following manner:

```
To:        LISTSERV@vm1.yorku.ca
From:      <your address>
Subject:   LISTSERV ignores this
SUBSCRIBE artcrit <firstname> <lastname>
```

# Automotive

## BMW

**Resource:** List
**Address:** BMW@balltown.cma.com
A general discussion about BMW-manufactured automobiles. Subscriptions should be directed to bmw-request@balltown.cms.com.

## British

**Resource:** List
**Address:** British-Cars@autox.team.net
For anyone who wants to discuss any aspect of British-made cars. Send subscription requests to british-cars-request@autox.team.net or british-cars-request@hoosier.cs.utah.edu.

## Camaros and Firebirds

**Resource:**  List
**Address:**   `f-body@boogie.ebay.sun.com`
A discussion group for those who own or just appreciate Camaros or Firebirds.
Send subscriptions to `f-body-request@boogie.ebay.sun.com`.

## Classic

**Resource:**  LISTSERV
**Address:**   `autos-l@tritu.bitnet`
This list is for anyone who owns or just appreciates classic and sports cars. To
subscribe, address a message in the following manner:
**To:**        `LISTSERV@tritu.bitnet`
**From:**      `<your address>`
**Subject:**   *LISTSERV ignores this*
`SUBSCRIBE autos-l <firstname> <lastname>`

## Datsun

**Resource:**  List
**Address:**   `Datsun-Roadsters@autox.team.net`
For anyone interested in discussing Datsun roadsters. Send subscription
requests to `datsun-roadsters-request@autox.team.net`.

## Dodge Stealth

**Resource:**  List
**Address:**   `Stealth@jim.uucp@wupost.wustl.edu`
A discussion group for persons interested in the Dodge Stealth or Mitsubishi
automobiles. Send your subscriptions to
`stealth-request%jim.uucp@wupost.wustl.edu`.

## Electric Vehicles

**Resource:**  LISTSERV
**Address:**   `ev@sjsuvm1.sjsu.edu`
A discussion list for the current and future status of electric vehicles. To
subscribe, address a message in the following manner:
**To:**        `LISTSERV@sjsuvm1.sjsu.edu`
**From:**      `<your address>`
**Subject:**   *LISTSERV ignores this*
`SUBSCRIBE ev <firstname> <lastname>`

## Exotic

**Resource:**   List
**Address:**   `exotic-cars@sol.asl.hitachi.com`
For anyone involved with exotic cars. Send your subscription requests to
`exotic-cars-request@sol.asl.hitachi.com`.

## General

**Resource:**   LISTSERV
**Address:**   `cars-1@saupm00.bitnet`
This is a general discussion forum about cars. To subscribe, address a message
in the following manner:
**To:**   `LISTSERV@saupm00.bitnet`
**From:**   `<your address>`
**Subject:**   *LISTSERV ignores this*
`SUBSCRIBE cars-1 <firstname> <lastname>`

## Honda

**Resource:**   LISTSERV
**Address:**   `honda-1@brownvm.brown.edu`
This list is dedicated to the discussion of Honda automobiles. To subscribe,
address a message in the following manner:
**To:**   `LISTSERV@brownvm.brown.edu`
**From:**   `<your address>`
**Subject:**   *LISTSERV ignores this*
`SUBSCRIBE honda-1 <firstname> <lastname>`

## Racing

**Resource:**   LISTSERV
**Address:**   `autorace@indycms.iupui.edu`
A general discussion list about automobile racing—located in Indianapolis, the
home of auto racing. To subscribe, address a message in the following manner:
**To:**   `LISTSERV@indycms.iupui.edu`
**From:**   `<your address>`
**Subject:**   *LISTSERV ignores this*
`SUBSCRIBE autorace <firstname> <lastname>`

## VW

**Resource:**   List
**Address:**   `vintagevw@rocky.er.usgs.gov`
For anyone interested in vintage VW cars. Send your subscription request to `robert@whiplash.er.usgs.gov`.

# Aviation

## General

**Resource:**   LISTSERV
**Address:**   `aircraft@grearn.bitnet`
Focuses on airplanes and helicopters, both new and old. Includes updates about air shows. To subscribe, address a message in the following manner:

**To:**   `LISTSERV@grearn.bitnet`
**From:**   `<your address>`
**Subject:**   *LISTSERV ignores this*
`SUBSCRIBE aircraft <firstname> <lastname>`

# Biology

## Aquariums

**Resource:**   LISTSERV
**Address:**   `aquarium@emuvm1.bitnet`
For everyone who has or studies aquariums and fish. To subscribe, address a message in the following manner:

**To:**   `LISTSERV@emuvm1.bitnet`
**From:**   `<your address>`
**Subject:**   *LISTSERV ignores this*
`SUBSCRIBE aquarium <firstname> <lastname>`

## Brine Shrimp

**Resource:**   LISTSERV
**Address:**   `brine-l@uga.cc.uga.edu`
A discussion list devoted to the topic of brine shrimp. To subscribe, address a message in the following manner:

**To:**      `LISTSERV@uga.cc.uga.edu`
**From:**    `<your address>`
**Subject:** *LISTSERV ignores this*
`SUBSCRIBE brine-l <firstname> <lastname>`

## Camels

**Resource:** LISTSERV
**Address:** `camel-l@sakfu00.bitnet`
This is an open forum for all camel researchers. To subscribe, address a message in the following manner:
**To:**      `LISTSERV@sakfu00.bitnet`
**From:**    `<your address>`
**Subject:** *LISTSERV ignores this*
`SUBSCRIBE camel-l <firstname> <lastname>`

## Sea Turtles

**Resource:** LISTSERV
**Address:** `cturtle@nervm.bitnet`
This list is for everyone who has an interest in sea turtle biology and conservation. To subscribe, address a message in the following manner:
**To:**      `LISTSERV@nervm.bitnet`
**From:**    `<your address>`
**Subject:** *LISTSERV ignores this*
`SUBSCRIBE cturtle <firstname> <lastname>`

# Business

## Deming, W. Edwards

**Resource:** LISTSERV
**Address:** `deming-l@uhccvm.bitnet`
This forum is for the exchange of ideas and research about W. Edwards Deming, the man who almost single-handedly rebuilt Japan's business economy after World War II. To subscribe, address a message in the following manner:
**To:**      `LISTSERV@uhccvm.bitnet`
**From:**    `<your address>`
**Subject:** *LISTSERV ignores this*
`SUBSCRIBE deming-l <firstname> <lastname>`

## Ethics

**Resource:**  LISTSERV
**Address:**  `buseth-l@ubvm.cc.buffalo.edu`
This list exchanges viewpoints about business ethics. To subscribe, address a message in the following manner:
**To:**  `LISTSERV@ubvm.cc.buffalo.edu`
**From:**  `<your address>`
**Subject:**  *LISTSERV ignores this*
`SUBSCRIBE buseth-l <firstname> <lastname>`


## Tax Research

**Resource:**  LISTSERV
**Address:**  `taxres@waynest1.bitnet`
This list is dedicated to the discussion of tax research. To subscribe, address a message in the following manner:
**To:**  `LISTSERV@waynest1.bitnet`
**From:**  `<your address>`
**Subject:**  *LISTSERV ignores this*
`SUBSCRIBE taxres <firstname> <lastname>`


# Computers


## 3D

**Resource:**  LISTSERV
**Address:**  `catia-l@suvm.bitnet`
For everyone interested in supporting or developing computer-aided three-dimensional interactive applications. To subscribe, address a message in the following manner:
**To:**  `LISTSERV@suvm.bitnet`
**From:**  `<your address>`
**Subject:**  *LISTSERV ignores this*
`SUBSCRIBE catia-l <firstname> <lastname>`


## AI/Law

**Resource:**  LISTSERV
**Address:**  `ail-l@austin.onu.edu`
Devoted to discussions of how the law is affected by artificial intelligence (AI). To subscribe, address a message in the following manner:

**To:**        LISTSERV@austin.onu.edu
**From:**      <your address>
**Subject:**   *LISTSERV ignores this*
SUBSCRIBE ail-l <firstname> <lastname>

## Amiga

**Resource:**   LISTSERV
**Address:**    i-amiga@rutgers.edu
For all users and developers of the Amiga computer. To subscribe, address a message in the following manner:
**To:**        LISTSERV@rutgers.edu
**From:**      <your address>
**Subject:**   *LISTSERV ignores this*
SUBSCRIBE i-amiga <firstname> <lastname>

## Apple

**Resource:**   List
**Address:**    info-apple@brl.mil
For users and enthusiasts of the Apple Computer. Send your subscription requests to info-apple-request@brl.mil.

## Apple II

**Resource:**   LISTSERV
**Address:**    apple2-l@brownvm.brown.edu
For all users and developers of the Apple II computer. To subscribe, address a message in the following manner:
**To:**        LISTSERV@brownvm.brown.edu
**From:**      <your address>
**Subject:**   *LISTSERV ignores this*
SUBSCRIBE apple2-l <firstname> <lastname>

## Applications

**Resource:**   LISTSERV
**Address:**    wpcorp-l@ubvm.cc.buffalo.edu
All WordPerfect Corporation products are fair game in this discussion list. To subscribe, address a message in the following manner:

**To:**       `LISTSERV@ubvm.cc.buffalo.edu`
**From:**   `<your address>`
**Subject:**  *LISTSERV ignores this*
`SUBSCRIBE wpcorp-l <firstname> <lastname>`

**Resource:**  LISTSERV
**Address:**   `ovision@vtvm1.bitnet`
Application development and use of Borland's ObjectVision are the primary topics in this list. To subscribe, address a message in the following manner:
**To:**       `LISTSERV@vtvm1.bitnet`
**From:**   `<your address>`
**Subject:**  *LISTSERV ignores this*
`SUBSCRIBE ovision <firstname> <lastname>`

**Resource:**  LISTSERV
**Address:**   `simedu-l@nmsuvm1.bitnet`
A discussion list regarding modeling and simulation applications in business and education. To subscribe, address a message in the following manner:
**To:**       `LISTSERV@nmsuvm1.bitnet`
**From:**   `<your address>`
**Subject:**  *LISTSERV ignores this*
`SUBSCRIBE simedu-l <firstname> <lastname>`

**Resource:**  LISTSERV
**Address:**   `clipper@brufpb.bitnet`
This list is for exchange of information and support of the Clipper DBMS. To subscribe, address a message in the following manner:
**To:**       `LISTSERV@brufpb.bitnet`
**From:**   `<your address>`
**Subject:**  *LISTSERV ignores this*
`SUBSCRIBE clipper <firstname> <lastname>`

**Resource:**  LISTSERV
**Address:**   `quatro-l@yalevm.ycc.yale.edu`
This is a discussion group about Borland's Quattro Pro software product. To subscribe, address a message in the following manner:
**To:**       `LISTSERV@yalevm.ycc.yale.edu`
**From:**   `<your address>`
**Subject:**  *LISTSERV ignores this*
`SUBSCRIBE quatro-l <firstname> <lastname>`

**Resource:**  LISTSERV
**Address:**   `allin1-l@ccvm.sunysb.edu`
Discussion group focusing on the software product All-in-1. To subscribe, address a message in the following manner:

```
To:        LISTSERV@ccvm.sunysb.edu
From:      <your address>
Subject:   LISTSERV ignores this
SUBSCRIBE allin1-l <firstname> <lastname>
```

## Artificial Intelligence

**Resource:**   List
**Address:**    nl-kr@cs.rpi.edu
This list is devoted to the interpretation and creation of natural language processing in artificial intelligence (AI). Send administrative information to nl-kr-request@cs.rpi.edu.

**Resource:**   LISTSERV
**Address:**    ainnonce@trmetu.bitnet
This list is for announcements about artificial intelligence. To subscribe, address a message in the following manner:

```
To:        LISTSERV@trmetu.bitnet
From:      <your address>
Subject:   LISTSERV ignores this
SUBSCRIBE ainnonce <firstname> <lastname>
```

## Artificial Life

**Resource:**   List
**Address:**    ailife@cognet.ucla.edu
Devoted to the study and information exchange about artificial life. Send your subscription requests to ailife-request@cognet.ucla.edu.

## AS/400

**Resource:**   LISTSERV
**Address:**    as400-l@pccvm.bitnet
A discussion forum on the use and support of IBM AS/400 computer systems. To subscribe, address a message in the following manner:

```
To:        LISTSERV@pccvm.bitnet
From:      <your address>
Subject:   LISTSERV ignores this
SUBSCRIBE as400-l <firstname> <lastname>
```

## BBS

**Resource:** LISTSERV
**Address:** `bbs-l@saupm00.bitnet`
This discussion forum is about BBSs, including creation, usage, and support.
To subscribe, address a message in the following manner:
**To:** `LISTSERV@saupm00.bitnet`
**From:** `<your address>`
**Subject:** *LISTSERV ignores this*
`SUBSCRIBE bbs-l <firstname> <lastname>`

## CAD

**Resource:** LISTSERV
**Address:** `cadlist@suvm.bitnet`
A general list devoted to CAD (computer-aided design). To subscribe, address
a message in the following manner:
**To:** `LISTSERV@suvm.bitnet`
**From:** `<your address>`
**Subject:** *LISTSERV ignores this*
`SUBSCRIBE cadlist <firstname> <lastname>`

## CAD/CAM

**Resource:** LISTSERV
**Address:** `cadam-l@suvm.bitnet`
This list discusses and exchanges information about CAD/CAM (computer-
aided design and manufacturing). To subscribe, address a message in the
following manner:
**To:** `LISTSERV@suvm.bitnet`
**From:** `<your address>`
**Subject:** *LISTSERV ignores this*
`SUBSCRIBE cadam-l <firstname> <lastname>`

## CASE

**Resource:** LISTSERV
**Address:** `case-l@uccvma.bitnet`
CASE (computer-aided software engineering) is the primary focus of this
discussion group. To subscribe, address a message in the following manner:
**To:** `LISTSERV@uccvma.bitnet`
**From:** `<your address>`
**Subject:** *LISTSERV ignores this*
`SUBSCRIBE case-l <firstname> <lastname>`

## CD-ROM

**Resource:**   LISTSERV
**Address:**   cdpub@knex.via.mind.org
For persons interested in the CD-ROM industry. To subscribe, address a message in the following manner:
**To:**   LISTSERV@knex.via.mind.org
**From:**   <your address>
**Subject:**   *LISTSERV ignores this*
SUBSCRIBE cdpub <firstname> <lastname>

## CICS

**Resource:**   LISTSERV
**Address:**   cics-l@uga.cc.uga.edu
A discussion list created to exchange information and tips about the use and support of IBM's CICS software product. To subscribe, address a message in the following manner:
**To:**   LISTSERV@uga.cc.uga.edu
**From:**   <your address>
**Subject:**   *LISTSERV ignores this*
SUBSCRIBE cics-l <firstname> <lastname>

## Commodore

**Resource:**   LISTSERV
**Address:**   commodor@ubvm.cc.buffalo.edu
This discussion group is for all users, developers, and supporters of the Commodore computer system. To subscribe, address a message in the following manner:
**To:**   LISTSERV@ubvm.cc.buffalo.edu
**From:**   <your address>
**Subject:**   *LISTSERV ignores this*
SUBSCRIBE commodor <firstname> <lastname>

## Cryptography

**Resource:**   List
**Address:**   rsaref-users@rsa.com
For persons interested in all aspects of public key encryption, including how it relates to sending and receiving electronic mail. Send subscription requests to rsaref-users-request@rsa.com.

**Resource:** LISTSERV
**Address:** `crypto-l@jpntuvm0.bitnet`
This forum discusses cryptography, exchanges information about ongoing research, and distributes information on related mathematics. To subscribe, address a message in the following manner:
**To:** `LISTSERV@jpntuvm0.bitnet`
**From:** `<your address>`
**Subject:** *LISTSERV ignores this*
`SUBSCRIBE crypto-l <firstname> <lastname>`

**Resource:** List
**Address:** `info-pgp@lucpul.it.luc.edu`
Devoted to the discussion of the public-key encryption software package PGP. Send subscription requests to `info-pgp-request@lucpul.it.luc.edu`.

## Cybernetics

**Resource:** LISTSERV
**Address:** `cybsys-l@bingvmb.bitnet`
This list is for the discussion and exchange of ideas and research about cybernetics and systems. To subscribe, address a message in the following manner:
**To:** `LISTSERV@bingvmb.bitnet`
**From:** `<your address>`
**Subject:** *LISTSERV ignores this*
`SUBSCRIBE cybsys-l <firstname> <lastname>`

## Cyberspace

**Resource:** LISTSERV
**Address:** `ejvc-l@kentvm.bitnet`
This list is the Electronic Journal on Virtual Culture. To subscribe, address a message in the following manner:
**To:** `LISTSERV@kentvm.bitnet`
**From:** `<your address>`
**Subject:** *LISTSERV ignores this*
`SUBSCRIBE ejvc-l <firstname> <lastname>`

**Resource:** LISTSERV
**Address:** `cyber-l@marist.bitnet`
Devoted to the cyberspace phenomenon. To subscribe, address a message in the following manner:

**To:**       `LISTSERV@marist`
**From:**    `<your address>.bitnet`
**Subject:**  *LISTSERV ignores this*
`SUBSCRIBE cyber-l <firstname> <lastname>`

**Resource:**   LISTSERV
**Address:**    `virtu-l@vmd.cso.uiuc.edu`
This list is a gateway to the USENET group `sci.virtual-worlds` and is devoted to a discussion of virtual reality worlds. To subscribe, address a message in the following manner:
**To:**       `LISTSERV@vmd.cso.uiuc.edu`
**From:**    `<your address>`
**Subject:**  *LISTSERV ignores this*
`SUBSCRIBE virtu-l <firstname> <lastname>`

**Resource:**   LISTSERV
**Address:**    `vrapp-l@vmd.cso.uiuc.edu`
This list is gatewayed to the USENET group `sci.virtual-worlds.apps` and is for the exchange of information about virtual reality applications. To subscribe, address a message in the following manner:
**To:**       `LISTSERV@vmd.cso.uiuc.edu`
**From:**    `<your address>`
**Subject:**  *LISTSERV ignores this*
`SUBSCRIBE vrapp-l <firstname> <lastname>`

## Databases

**Resource:**   LISTSERV
**Address:**    `oracle-l@sbccvm.bitnet`
The Oracle DBMS software product is the primary focus of this discussion group. To subscribe, address a message in the following manner:
**To:**       `LISTSERV@sbccvm.bitnet`
**From:**    `<your address>`
**Subject:**  *LISTSERV ignores this*
`SUBSCRIBE oracle-l <firstname> <lastname>`

**Resource:**   LISTSERV
**Address:**    `access-l@indycms.iupui.edu`
A discussion list for all users, developers, and supporters of the Microsoft Access DBMS product. To subscribe, address a message in the following manner:
**To:**       `LISTSERV@indycms.iupui.edu`
**From:**    `<your address>`
**Subject:**  *LISTSERV ignores this*
`SUBSCRIBE access-l <firstname> <lastname>`

**Resource:** LISTSERV
**Address:** `foxpro-l@polarbear.rankin-inlet.nt.ca`
For the exchange of information, tips, design advice, and just about anything affiliated with the FoxPro DBMS. To subscribe, address a message in the following manner:
**To:** `LISTSERV@polarbear.rankin-inlet.nt.ca`
**From:** `<your address>`
**Subject:** *LISTSERV ignores this*
`SUBSCRIBE foxpro-l <firstname> <lastname>`

**Resource:** LISTSERV
**Address:** `sybase-l@ucsbvm.bitnet`
A discussion list for those using Sybase products on various platforms. To subscribe, address a message in the following manner:
**To:** `LISTSERV@ucsbvm.bitnet`
**From:** `<your address>`
**Subject:** *LISTSERV ignores this*
`SUBSCRIBE sybase-l <firstname> <lastname>`

**Resource:** LISTSERV
**Address:** `db2-l@auvm.bitnet`
A discussion list about IBM's DB2 database software product. To subscribe, address a message in the following manner:
**To:** `LISTSERV@auvm.bitnet`
**From:** `<your address>`
**Subject:** *LISTSERV ignores this*
`SUBSCRIBE db2-l <firstname> <lastname>`

**Resource:** LISTSERV
**Address:** `access-l@brufpb.bitnet`
Another list created for Microsoft Access DBMS users. To subscribe, address a message in the following manner:
**To:** `LISTSERV@brufpb.bitnet`
**From:** `<your address>`
**Subject:** *LISTSERV ignores this*
`SUBSCRIBE access-l <firstname> <lastname>`

**Resource:** List
**Address:** `ms-access@eunet.co.at`
This is an open list for the purpose of discussing and exchanging information about Microsoft's Access DBMS. Send your subscription request to `ms-access-request@eunet.co.at`.

**Resource:** LISTSERV
**Address:** `paradox@brufpb.bitnet`
This list is for all Borland Paradox users. To subscribe, address a message in the following manner:
**To:** `LISTSERV@brufpb.bitnet`
**From:** `<your address>`
**Subject:** *LISTSERV ignores this*
`SUBSCRIBE paradox <firstname> <lastname>`

**Resource:** LISTSERV
**Address:** `dbase-l@nmsuvm1.bitnet`
For everyone involved with the Borland dBASE software product. To subscribe, address a message in the following manner:
**To:** `LISTSERV@nmsuvm1.bitnet`
**From:** `<your address>`
**Subject:** *LISTSERV ignores this*
`SUBSCRIBE dbase-l <firstname> <lastname>`

## Desktop Publishing

**Resource:** LISTSERV
**Address:** `pagemakr@indycms.iupui.edu`
A discussion list devoted to PageMaker. To subscribe, address a message in the following manner:
**To:** `LISTSERV@indycms.iupui.edu`
**From:** `<your address>`
**Subject:** *LISTSERV ignores this*
`SUBSCRIBE pagemakr <firstname> <lastname>`

**Resource:** LISTSERV
**Address:** `dtp-l@yalevm.ycc.yale.edu`
Devoted to all aspects of desktop publishing. This includes (but is not limited to) product selection, tips, tricks, workarounds, known problems, and other ways of improving productivity using almost every known desktop publishing software package. To subscribe, address a message in the following manner:
**To:** `LISTSERV@yalevm.ycc.yale.edu`
**From:** `<your address>`
**Subject:** *LISTSERV ignores this*
`SUBSCRIBE dtp-l <firstname> <lastname>`

## Digital Video

**Resource:** List
**Address:** DVI-List@calvin.dgbt.doc.ca
For discussions, tips, and techniques for using Intel's DVI (Digital Video Interactive) product.

## Distributed Processing

**Resource:** LISTSERV
**Address:** pdppl@plwrtu11.bitnet
The emerging technologies of parallel and distributed processing are discussed and researched here. To subscribe, address a message in the following manner:

**To:** LISTSERV@plwrtu11.bitnet
**From:** <your address>
**Subject:** *LISTSERV ignores this*
SUBSCRIBE pdppl <firstname> <lastname>

## EDI

**Resource:** LISTSERV
**Address:** edi-l@uccvma.bitnet@vm1.nodak.edu
Devoted to the exchange of information about the burgeoning EDI industry. To subscribe, address a message in the following manner:

**To:** LISTSERV@uccvma.bitnet@vm1.nodak.edu
**From:** <your address>
**Subject:** *LISTSERV ignores this*
SUBSCRIBE edi-l <firstname> <lastname>

## Education

**Resource:** LISTSERV
**Address:** appl-l@pltumk11.bitnet
For users, developers, and supporters of computer applications in science and education. To subscribe, address a message in the following manner:

**To:** LISTSERV@pltumk11.bitnet
**From:** <your address>
**Subject:** *LISTSERV ignores this*
SUBSCRIBE appl-l <firstname> <lastname>

## E-Mail

**Resource:**    LISTSERV
**Address:**    `ccmail-l@vm1.ucc.okstate.edu`
A group to discuss ideas, tips, and support of the cc:mail software product. To subscribe, address a message in the following manner:

**To:**    `LISTSERV@vm1.ucc.okstate.edu`
**From:**    `<your address>`
**Subject:**    *LISTSERV ignores this*
`SUBSCRIBE ccmail-l <firstname> <lastname>`

## Engineering

**Resource:**    LISTSERV
**Address:**    `caeds-l@suvm.bitnet`
A discussion list about computer-aided engineering design. To subscribe, address a message in the following manner:

**To:**    `LISTSERV@suvm.bitnet`
**From:**    `<your address>`
**Subject:**    *LISTSERV ignores this*
`SUBSCRIBE caeds-l <firstname> <lastname>`

## Ethics

**Resource:**    LISTSERV
**Address:**    `ethcse-l@utkvm1.bitnet`
A forum for the exchange of ideas about ethical issues in software engineering. To subscribe, address a message in the following manner:

**To:**    `LISTSERV@utkvm1.bitnet`
**From:**    `<your address>`
**Subject:**    *LISTSERV ignores this*
`SUBSCRIBE ethcse-l <firstname> <lastname>`

**Resource:**    LISTSERV
**Address:**    `ethics-l@uga.cc.uga.edu`
A discussion list for the exchange of ideas and opinions about ethics in computing. To subscribe, address a message in the following manner:

**To:**    `LISTSERV@uga.cc.uga.edu`
**From:**    `<your address>`
**Subject:**    *LISTSERV ignores this*
`SUBSCRIBE ethics-l <firstname> <lastname>`

## Files—Compression

**Resource:** FTP
**Address:** `ftp.cso.uiuc.edu`
**Directory:** `doc/pcnet/compression`

**Resource:** FTP
**Address:** `ftp.cso.uiuc.edu`
**Directory:** `doc/pcnet`

## Flight Simulators

**Resource:** List
**Address:** `flight-sim@grove.iup.edu`
An open list for flight simulator enthusiasts and designers. Send your subscription requests to `flight-sim-request@grove.iup.edu`. An archive of previous material posted to the list can be found via anonymous FTP at `acorn.grove.iup.edu`.

## Fractals

**Resource:** LISTSERV
**Address:** `frac-l@gitvm1.bitnet`
A discussion list about fractals, image processing, and related graphics and mathematics. To subscribe, address a message in the following manner:
**To:** `LISTSERV@gitvm1.bitnet`
**From:** `<your address>`
**Subject:** *LISTSERV ignores this*
`SUBSCRIBE frac-l <firstname> <lastname>`

## Fuzzy Logic

**Resource:** LISTSERV
**Address:** `nafips-l@gsuvm1.bitnet`
North American Fuzzy Information Processing. A list devoted to the exchange of information and research about the emerging technology known as "fuzzy logic." To subscribe, address a message in the following manner:
**To:** `LISTSERV@gsuvm1.bitnet`
**From:** `<your address>`
**Subject:** *LISTSERV ignores this*
`SUBSCRIBE nafips-l <firstname> <lastname>`

# Games

**Resource:**  LISTSERV
**Address:**  `games-l@brownvm.brown.edu`
Computer games list. To subscribe, address a message in the following manner:
**To:**  `LISTSERV@brownvm.brown.edu`
**From:**  `<your address>`
**Subject:**  *LISTSERV ignores this*
`SUBSCRIBE games-l <firstname> <lastname>`

**Resource:**  List
**Address:**  `digital-games-submissions@digital-games.intuitive.com`
A list devoted to distributing reviews of video games for all electronic platforms. Subscription requests should be sent to `digital-games-request@digital-games.intuitive.com`.

# General

**Resource:**  FTP
**Address:**  `soda.berkeley.edu (128.32.149.19)`
**Directory:**  `pub/cypherpunks`
This directory contains instructions and helper scripts for the purpose of securing communications.

# Graphics

**Resource:**  LISTSERV
**Address:**  `graph-l@brufpb.bitnet`
Mathematical aspects of computer graphics. To subscribe, address a message in the following manner:
**To:**  `LISTSERV@brufpb.bitnet`
**From:**  `<your address>`
**Subject:**  *LISTSERV ignores this*
`SUBSCRIBE graph-l <firstname> <lastname>`

# Hand-held

**Resource:**  List
**Address:**  `handhelds@csl.sri.com`
For the discussion of calculators and hand-held computers (a.k.a. PDAs—Personal Digital Assistants).

## Hardware

**Resource:**     LISTSERV
**Address:**      pcbuild@list.dsu.edu
This is an open list for persons interested in many aspects of PC hardware, including building, upgrading, and fixing. To subscribe, address a message in the following manner:
**To:**           LISTSERV@list.dsu.edu
**From:**         <your address>
**Subject:**      *LISTSERV ignores this*
SUBSCRIBE pcbuild <firstname> <lastname>

## Health

**Resource:**     LISTSERV
**Address:**      c+health@iubvm.bitnet
This list discusses various health effects of computer use. To subscribe, address a message in the following manner:
**To:**           LISTSERV@iubvm.bitnet
**From:**         <your address>
**Subject:**      *LISTSERV ignores this*
SUBSCRIBE c+health <firstname> <lastname>

## History

**Resource:**     LISTSERV
**Address:**      ahc-l@dgogwdg1.bitnet
Association for History and Computing. To subscribe, address a message in the following manner:
**To:**           LISTSERV@dgogwdg1.bitnet
**From:**         <your address>
**Subject:**      *LISTSERV ignores this*
SUBSCRIBE ahc-l <firstname> <lastname>

**Resource:**     List
**Address:**      sigpast@list.kean.edu
A discussion list devoted to the history of computers and computing. Send your subscription requests to sigpast-subscribe@list.kean.edu.

## HyperCard

**Resource:**   LISTSERV
**Address:**    `hypercrd@purccvm.cc.vm.edu`
A discussion list for persons interested in the Macintosh software product HyperCard. To subscribe, address a message in the following manner:
**To:**       `LISTSERV@purccvm.cc.vm.edu`
**From:**    `<your address>`
**Subject:**  *LISTSERV ignores this*
`SUBSCRIBE hypercrd <firstname> <lastname>`

## IBM PCs

**Resource:**   LISTSERV
**Address:**    `i-ibmpc@vmd.cso.uiuc.edu`
A discussion list for all IBM PC users and owners. To subscribe, address a message in the following manner:
**To:**       `LISTSERV@vmd.cso.uiuc.edu`
**From:**    `<your address>`
**Subject:**  *LISTSERV ignores this*
`SUBSCRIBE i-ibmpc <firstname> <lastname>`

## Image Processing

**Resource:**   LISTSERV
**Address:**    `image-l@trearn.bitnet`
A discussion list for image processing and applications. To subscribe, address a message in the following manner:
**To:**       `LISTSERV@trearn.bitnet`
**From:**    `<your address>`
**Subject:**  *LISTSERV ignores this*
`SUBSCRIBE image-l <firstname> <lastname>`

## Kermit

**Resource:**   LISTSERV
**Address:**    `kermit-l@jpnsut30.bitnet`
A discussion list devoted to the Kermit software product. To subscribe, address a message in the following manner:
**To:**       `LISTSERV@jpnsut30.bitnet`
**From:**    `<your address>`
**Subject:**  *LISTSERV ignores this*
`SUBSCRIBE kermit-l <firstname> <lastname>`

## LANs

**Resource:**    LISTSERV
**Address:**    `nmg@nrcvm01.bitnet`
Novell NetWare Masters' Group. To subscribe, address a message in the
following manner:
**To:**    `LISTSERV@nrcvm01.bitnet`
**From:**    `<your address>`
**Subject:**    *LISTSERV ignores this*
`SUBSCRIBE nmg <firstname> <lastname>`

**Resource:**    LISTSERV
**Address:**    `novell@suvm.bitnet`
Novell LAN interest group for all users and supporters. To subscribe, address
a message in the following manner:
**To:**    `LISTSERV@suvm.bitnet`
**From:**    `<your address>`
**Subject:**    *LISTSERV ignores this*
`SUBSCRIBE novell <firstname> <lastname>`

## Latest Advances

**Resource:**    LISTSERV
**Address:**    `adv-info@utfsm.bitnet`
A discussion list for the announcement of the latest computing advances. To
subscribe, address a message in the following manner:
**To:**    `LISTSERV@utfsm.bitnet`
**From:**    `<your address>`
**Subject:**    *LISTSERV ignores this*
`SUBSCRIBE adv-info <firstname> <lastname>`

## Law

**Resource:**    LISTSERV
**Address:**    `cyberlaw@wmvm1.bitnet`
For the discussion and ongoing exchange of opinions about the laws and
policies of computer networks. To subscribe, address a message in the follow-
ing manner:
**To:**    `LISTSERV@wmvm1.bitnet`
**From:**    `<your address>`
**Subject:**    *LISTSERV ignores this*
`SUBSCRIBE cyberlaw <firstname> <lastname>`

## Legal Education

**Resource:**   LISTSERV
**Address:**    comlaw-l@ualtavm.bitnet
The use of computers and legal education. To subscribe, address a message in the following manner:
**To:**         LISTSERV@ualtavm.bitnet
**From:**       <your address>
**Subject:**    *LISTSERV ignores this*
SUBSCRIBE comlaw-l <firstname> <lastname>

## Macintosh

**Resource:**   LISTSERV
**Address:**    macprog@wuvmd.bitnet
For everyone interested in programming on the Macintosh computer. To subscribe, address a message in the following manner:
**To:**         LISTSERV@wuvmd.bitnet
**From:**       <your address>
**Subject:**    *LISTSERV ignores this*
SUBSCRIBE macprog <firstname> <lastname>

**Resource:**   LISTSERV
**Address:**    sys7-l@uafsysb.uark.edu
A list specifically for the discussion of Macintosh System 7.0. To subscribe, address a message in the following manner:
**To:**         LISTSERV@uafsysb.uark.edu
**From:**       <your address>
**Subject:**    *LISTSERV ignores this*
SUBSCRIBE sys7-l <firstname> <lastname>

**Resource:**   LISTSERV
**Address:**    macsystm@dartcms1.dartmouth.edu
Devoted to the discussion and support of Macintosh system software. To subscribe, address a message in the following manner:
**To:**         LISTSERV@dartcms1.dartmouth.edu
**From:**       <your address>
**Subject:**    *LISTSERV ignores this*
SUBSCRIBE macsystm <firstname> <lastname>

**Resource:**   List
**Address:**    mac-security@eclectic.com
For persons interested in sharing information about security related to the Macintosh computer. Send your subscription request to mac-security-request@eclectic.com.

**Resource:**   LISTSERV
**Address:**   macpb-l@yalevm.ycc.yale.edu
A discussion list for users of the Apple Powerbook. To subscribe, address a message in the following manner:
**To:**   LISTSERV@yalevm.ycc.yale.edu
**From:**   <your address>
**Subject:**   *LISTSERV ignores this*
SUBSCRIBE macpb-l <firstname> <lastname>

**Resource:**   LISTSERV
**Address:**   macnet-l@yalevm.ycc.yale.edu
For those interested in networking Macintosh computers. To subscribe, address a message in the following manner:
**To:**   LISTSERV@yalevm.ycc.yale.edu
**From:**   <your address>
**Subject:**   *LISTSERV ignores this*
SUBSCRIBE macnet-l <firstname> <lastname>

**Resource:**   LISTSERV
**Address:**   macmail@utoronto.bitnet
For users and supporters of Macintosh mail systems. To subscribe, address a message in the following manner:
**To:**   LISTSERV@utoronto.bitnet
**From:**   <your address>
**Subject:**   *LISTSERV ignores this*
SUBSCRIBE macmail <firstname> <lastname>

**Resource:**   LISTSERV
**Address:**   mac-l@yalevm.ycc.yale.edu
A forum to share and distribute Macintosh news and information. To subscribe, address a message in the following manner:
**To:**   LISTSERV@yalevm.ycc.yale.edu
**From:**   <your address>
**Subject:**   *LISTSERV ignores this*
SUBSCRIBE mac-l <firstname> <lastname>

**Resource:**   LISTSERV
**Address:**   macappli@dartcms1.dartmouth.edu
This list distributes usage tips about Macintosh applications. To subscribe, address a message in the following manner:
**To:**   LISTSERV@dartcms1.dartmouth.edu
**From:**   <your address>
**Subject:**   *LISTSERV ignores this*
SUBSCRIBE macappli <firstname> <lastname>

## Mainframe Operations

**Resource:** LISTSERV
**Address:** `opers-l@vm1.cc.uakron.edu`
For persons involved in the operation of mainframe computers. To subscribe, address a message in the following manner:
**To:** `LISTSERV@vm1.cc.uakron.edu`
**From:** `<your address>`
**Subject:** *LISTSERV ignores this*
`SUBSCRIBE opers-l <firstname> <lastname>`

## Mainframes

**Resource:** LISTSERV
**Address:** `ibm-main@ricevm1.rice.edu`
A discussion list for everyone involved in the use and support of IBM mainframe computers. To subscribe, address a message in the following manner:
**To:** `LISTSERV@ricevm1.rice.edu`
**From:** `<your address>`
**Subject:** *LISTSERV ignores this*
`SUBSCRIBE ibm-main <firstname> <lastname>`

## Materials Design

**Resource:** LISTSERV
**Address:** `mat-dsgn@jpntuvm0.bitnet`
A forum for discussing computer-aided materials design. To subscribe, address a message in the following manner:
**To:** `LISTSERV@jpntuvm0.bitnet`
**From:** `<your address>`
**Subject:** *LISTSERV ignores this*
`SUBSCRIBE mat-dsgn <firstname> <lastname>`

## Multimedia

**Resource:** LISTSERV
**Address:** `imamedia@umdd.bitnet`
This list is for the purpose of achieving compatibility of multimedia applications. To subscribe, address a message in the following manner:
**To:** `LISTSERV@umdd.bitnet`
**From:** `<your address>`
**Subject:** *LISTSERV ignores this*
`SUBSCRIBE imamedia <firstname> <lastname>`

**Resource:** LISTSERV
**Address:** `macmulti@fccj.bitnet`
A discussion list about Macintosh multimedia. To subscribe, address a message in the following manner:
**To:** `LISTSERV@fccj.bitnet`
**From:** `<your address>`
**Subject:** *LISTSERV ignores this*
`SUBSCRIBE macmulti <firstname> <lastname>`

**Resource:** List
**Address:** `mmm-people@isi.edu`
A discussion list for persons interested in developing and supporting multimedia mail, including the formation of standards. Send your subscription requests to `mmm-people-request@isi.edu`.

**Resource:** LISTSERV
**Address:** `toaster-list@karazm.math.uh.edu`
For persons interested in discussing aspects of the NewTek Video Toaster. To subscribe, address a message in the following manner:
**To:** `LISTSERV@karazm.math.uh.edu`
**From:** `<your address>`
**Subject:** *LISTSERV ignores this*
`SUBSCRIBE toaster-list <firstname> <lastname>`

**Resource:** LISTSERV
**Address:** `mmedia-l@vmtecmex.bitnet`
A discussion list for the purpose of using multimedia in education. To subscribe, address a message in the following manner:
**To:** `LISTSERV@vmtecmex.bitnet`
**From:** `<your address>`
**Subject:** *LISTSERV ignores this*
`SUBSCRIBE mmedia-l <firstname> <lastname>`

**Resource:** LISTSERV
**Address:** `mmedia-l@itesmvf1.bitnet`
This is a general multimedia discussion list. To subscribe, address a message in the following manner:
**To:** `LISTSERV@itesmvf1.bitnet`
**From:** `<your address>`
**Subject:** *LISTSERV ignores this*
`SUBSCRIBE mmedia-l <firstname> <lastname>`

## Networking

**Resource:** LISTSERV
**Address:** wfw-l@umdd.bitnet
Devoted to the support and use of Microsoft's Windows for Workgroups software product. To subscribe, address a message in the following manner:
**To:** LISTSERV@umdd.bitnet
**From:** <your address>
**Subject:** *LISTSERV ignores this*
SUBSCRIBE wfw-l <firstname> <lastname>

**Resource:** LISTSERV
**Address:** shoptalk@mcgill1.bitnet
An "info-line" for all Novell network supervisors. To subscribe, address a message in the following manner:
**To:** LISTSERV@mcgill1.bitnet
**From:** <your address>
**Subject:** *LISTSERV ignores this*
SUBSCRIBE shoptalk <firstname> <lastname>

**Resource:** LISTSERV
**Address:** banyan-l@akronvm.bitnet
A discussion list for supporters of the Banyan network software system. To subscribe, address a message in the following manner:
**To:** LISTSERV@akronvm.bitnet
**From:** <your address>
**Subject:** *LISTSERV ignores this*
SUBSCRIBE banyan-l <firstname> <lastname>

## Neural Nets

**Resource:** LISTSERV
**Address:** neural-n@andescol.bitnet
For the discussion and development of artificial neural networks. To subscribe, address a message in the following manner:
**To:** LISTSERV@andescol.bitnet
**From:** <your address>
**Subject:** *LISTSERV ignores this*
SUBSCRIBE neural-n <firstname> <lastname>

**Resource:** LISTSERV
**Address:** inns-l@umdd.bitnet
The International Neural Network Society discussion list. To subscribe, address a message in the following manner:

**To:**        LISTSERV@umdd.bitnet
**From:**      <your address>
**Subject:**   *LISTSERV ignores this*
SUBSCRIBE inns-l <firstname> <lastname>

## Next

**Resource:**   LISTSERV
**Address:**    next-l@antigone.com
For persons involved in the support of Next systems. To subscribe, address a message in the following manner:
**To:**        LISTSERV@antigone.com
**From:**      <your address>
**Subject:**   *LISTSERV ignores this*
SUBSCRIBE next-l <firstname> <lastname>

## NextStep

**Resource:**   LISTSERV
**Address:**    nextstep@indycms.iupui.edu
An open list dedicated to the exchange of information by persons using the NextStep operating system. To subscribe, address a message in the following manner:
**To:**        LISTSERV@indycms.iupui.edu
**From:**      <your address>
**Subject:**   *LISTSERV ignores this*
SUBSCRIBE nextstep <firstname> <lastname>

## Operating Systems

**Resource:**   LISTSERV
**Address:**    os2users@mcgill1.bitnet
For users of the IBM OS/2 operating system. To subscribe, address a message in the following manner:
**To:**        LISTSERV@mcgill1.bitnet
**From:**      <your address>
**Subject:**   *LISTSERV ignores this*
SUBSCRIBE os2users <firstname> <lastname>

**Resource:**   LISTSERV
**Address:**    os2@blekul11.bitnet
A moderated discussion forum about IBM's OS/2 PC operating system. To subscribe, address a message in the following manner:

**To:**        `LISTSERV@blekul11.bitnet`
**From:**     `<your address>`
**Subject:**   *LISTSERV ignores this*
`SUBSCRIBE os2 <firstname> <lastname>`

**Resource:**   LISTSERV
**Address:**    `unix-wiz@ndsuvm1.ndsu.edu`
A mailing list for all UNIX wizards. To subscribe, address a message in the following manner:
**To:**        `LISTSERV@ndsuvm1.ndsu.edu`
**From:**     `<your address>`
**Subject:**   *LISTSERV ignores this*
`SUBSCRIBE unix-wiz <firstname> <lastname>`

## Patents

**Resource:**   LISTSERV
**Address:**    `softpats@uvmvm.uvm.edu`
The discussion and exchange of information related to computer software patents. To subscribe, address a message in the following manner:
**To:**        `LISTSERV@uvmvm.uvm.edu`
**From:**     `<your address>`
**Subject:**   *LISTSERV ignores this*
`SUBSCRIBE softpats <firstname> <lastname>`

## PC Applications

**Resource:**   List
**Address:**    `clay=xldev@cs.cmu.edu`
Excel developers discussion list. To join, send an e-mail request to `clay=xldev-add@cs.cmu.edu`. Send other administrative information to `clay=xldev-request@cs.cmu.edu`.

## PC Programming Languages

**Resource:**   LISTSERV
**Address:**    `tasm-l@brufpb.bitnet`
A discussion list about Borland's Turbo Assembler and Debugger software products. To subscribe, address a message in the following manner:
**To:**        `LISTSERV@brufpb.bitnet`
**From:**     `<your address>`
**Subject:**   *LISTSERV ignores this*
`SUBSCRIBE tasm-l <firstname> <lastname>`

**Resource:** LISTSERV
**Address:** tcplus-l@ucf1vm.cc.ucf.edu
For all users and developers using Turbo C++. To subscribe, address a message in the following manner:
**To:** LISTSERV@ucf1vm.cc.ucf.edu
**From:** <your address>
**Subject:** *LISTSERV ignores this*
SUBSCRIBE tcplus-l <firstname> <lastname>

## PCs

**Resource:** LISTSERV
**Address:** msmail-l@yalevm.ycc.yale.edu
A discussion list for users and supporters of the Microsoft Mail software product. To subscribe, address a message in the following manner:
**To:** LISTSERV@yalevm.ycc.yale.edu
**From:** <your address>
**Subject:** *LISTSERV ignores this*
SUBSCRIBE msmail-l <firstname> <lastname>

**Resource:** LISTSERV
**Address:** pc-eval@irlearn.ucd.ie
A discussion list for the purpose of exchanging evaluations about personal computers. To subscribe, address a message in the following manner:
**To:** LISTSERV@irlearn.ucd.ie
**From:** <your address>
**Subject:** *LISTSERV ignores this*
SUBSCRIBE pc-eval <firstname> <lastname>

## PowerGlove

**Resource:** LISTSERV
**Address:** Glove-list@boxer.nas.nasa.gov
For anyone who wants to discuss and share information about the Nintendo PowerGlove. To subscribe, address a message in the following manner:
**To:** LISTSERV@boxer.nas.nasa.gov
**From:** <your address>
**Subject:** *LISTSERV ignores this*
SUBSCRIBE Glove-list <firstname> <lastname>

## Printers

**Resource:**   List
**Address:**    `INFO-PRINTERS@eddie.mil.edu`
This is a general printers discussion list. Send your request for subscriptions to `info-printers-request@eddie.mil.edu`.

## Privacy Issues

**Resource:**   List
**Address:**    `comp-privacy@pica.army.mil`
Dedicated to the discussion of how computers, and technology in general, affect privacy. Send subscriptions and other administrative traffic to `comp-privacy-request@pica.army.mil`.

## Programming Languages

**Resource:**   LISTSERV
**Address:**    `figi-l@scfvm.bitnet@cunyvm.cuny.edu`
FIGI is the FORTH Interest Groups International. Everything related to the FORTH programming language happens here! To subscribe, address a message in the following manner:
**To:**         `LISTSERV@scfvm.bitnet@cunyvm.cuny.edu`
**From:**       `<your address>`
**Subject:**    *LISTSERV ignores this*
`SUBSCRIBE figi-l <firstname> <lastname>`

**Resource:**   LISTSERV
**Address:**    `pascal-l@yalevm.ycc.yale.edu`
A discussion group about Borland's Pascal compiler. To subscribe, address a message in the following manner:
**To:**         `LISTSERV@yalevm.ycc.yale.edu`
**From:**       `<your address>`
**Subject:**    *LISTSERV ignores this*
`SUBSCRIBE pascal-l <firstname> <lastname>`

**Resource:**   LISTSERV
**Address:**    `actor-l@hearn.bitnet`
This list provides a platform for those developing applications with the Actor object-oriented programming language. To subscribe, address a message in the following manner:
**To:**         `LISTSERV@hearn.bitnet`
**From:**       `<your address>`
**Subject:**    *LISTSERV ignores this*
`SUBSCRIBE actor-l <firstname> <lastname>`

**Resource:**    LISTSERV
**Address:**    `smalk@finhutc.bitnet`
A discussion list for developers using the Smalltalk programming language. To subscribe, address a message in the following manner:
**To:**    `LISTSERV@finhutc.bitnet`
**From:**    `<your address>`
**Subject:**    *LISTSERV ignores this*
`SUBSCRIBE smalk <firstname> <lastname>`

**Resource:**    LISTSERV
**Address:**    `c-l@indycms.iupui.edu`
A general discussion list about the C programming language. To subscribe, address a message in the following manner:
**To:**    `LISTSERV@indycms.iupui.edu`
**From:**    `<your address>`
**Subject:**    *LISTSERV ignores this*
`SUBSCRIBE c-l <firstname> <lastname>`

**Resource:**    LISTSERV
**Address:**    `rexx-l@vmd.cso.uiuc.edu`
A discussion list to exchange ideas and information about the REXX programming language. To subscribe, address a message in the following manner:
**To:**    `LISTSERV@vmd.cso.uiuc.edu`
**From:**    `<your address>`
**Subject:**    *LISTSERV ignores this*
`SUBSCRIBE rexx-l <firstname> <lastname>`

**Resource:**    LISTSERV
**Address:**    `visbas-l@tamvm1.tamu.edu`
This discussion list is for those who develop and support applications with Microsoft's Visual Basic programming language. To subscribe, address a message in the following manner:
**To:**    `LISTSERV@tamvm1.tamu.edu`
**From:**    `<your address>`
**Subject:**    *LISTSERV ignores this*
`SUBSCRIBE visbas-l <firstname> <lastname>`

**Resource:**    LISTSERV
**Address:**    `pl1-l@vmd.cso.uiuc.edu`
A discussion list about the PL/I programming language. To subscribe, address a message in the following manner:
**To:**    `LISTSERV@vmd.cso.uiuc.edu`
**From:**    `<your address>`
**Subject:**    *LISTSERV ignores this*
`SUBSCRIBE pl1-l <firstname> <lastname>`

**Resource:**   LISTSERV
**Address:**   `info-m2@ucf1vm.cc.ucf.edu`
A discussion list for programmers using the Modula-2 programming language.
To subscribe, address a message in the following manner:
**To:**   `LISTSERV@ucf1vm.cc.ucf.edu`
**From:**   `<your address>`
**Subject:**   *LISTSERV ignores this*
`SUBSCRIBE info-m2 <firstname> <lastname>`

**Resource:**   LISTSERV
**Address:**   `apl-l@unb.ca`
Devoted to the discussion of the APL programming language. To subscribe,
address a message in the following manner:
**To:**   `LISTSERV@unb.ca`
**From:**   `<your address>`
**Subject:**   *LISTSERV ignores this*
`SUBSCRIBE apl-l <firstname> <lastname>`

**Resource:**   List
**Address:**   `franz-friends@berkeley.edu`
This list is for the discussion of Franz Lisp, a public domain version of
the computer programming language frequently used in the field of
artificial intelligence. Submit your subscription requests to
`franz-friends-request@berkeley.edu`.

## Programming Languages/Amiga

**Resource:**   List
**Address:**   `amiga-m2@virginia.edu`
A discussion group for persons interested in the use of Modula-2 on the
Amiga. Send subscription requests to `amiga-m2-request@virginia.edu`.

## Programming Languages/PC

**Resource:**   LISTSERV
**Address:**   `assmpc-l@usachvm1.bitnet@vm1.nodak.edu`
Assembler language for the PC. To subscribe, address a message in the follow-
ing manner:
**To:**   `LISTSERV@usachvm1.bitnet@vm1.nodak.edu`
**From:**   `<your address>`
**Subject:**   *LISTSERV ignores this*
`SUBSCRIBE assmpc-l <firstname> <lastname>`

## Publishing

**Resource:**   List
**Address:**    publish@chron.com
Devoted to the discussion of using computers to improve productivity in the publishing industry. Send subscription requests to publish-request@chron.com.

## Research

**Resource:**   LISTSERV
**Address:**    carr-l@ulkyvm.louisville.edu
Devoted to the exchange of information about computer-assisted reporting and research. To subscribe, address a message in the following manner:

**To:**         LISTSERV@ulkyvm.louisville.edu
**From:**       <your address>
**Subject:**    *LISTSERV ignores this*
SUBSCRIBE carr-l <firstname> <lastname>

## Software

**Resource:**   FTP
**Address:**    ftp.cica.indiana.edu
**Directory:**  pub/pc/win3
The best site in the world for Windows software. From games to utilities to new fonts, this is where everyone seems to upload their new material! For best results, retrieve the INDEX first and get the "lay of the land."

## Software—File Compression

**Resource:**   FTP
**Address:**    ftp.cso.uiuc.edu
Compression/decompression programs for many different operating systems.

## Software Licensing

**Resource:**   LISTSERV
**Address:**    license@uga.cc.uga.edu
A discussion list about software licensing. To subscribe, address a message in the following manner:

| | |
|---|---|
| **To:** | `LISTSERV@uga.cc.uga.edu` |
| **From:** | `<your address>` |
| **Subject:** | *LISTSERV ignores this* |

`SUBSCRIBE license <firstname> <lastname>`

## Software Patents

| | |
|---|---|
| **Resource:** | FTP |
| **Address:** | `mintaka.lcs.mit.edu:` |
| **Directory:** | `/mitlpf/ai/patent-list` |

This file contains a list of software patents and related information.

## Software Publishing

| | |
|---|---|
| **Resource:** | List |
| **Address:** | `softpub@toolz.uucp@mathcs.emory.edu` |

A list for the exchange of information related to computer software publishing activities, including the topic of shareware. Send your requests for subscription to `softpub-request%toolz.uucp@mathcs.emory.edu`.

## Software Reviews

| | |
|---|---|
| **Resource:** | LISTSERV |
| **Address:** | `softrevu@brownvm.brown.edu` |

A discussion list for the exchange of software evaluations. To subscribe, address a message in the following manner:

| | |
|---|---|
| **To:** | `LISTSERV@brownvm.brown.edu` |
| **From:** | `<your address>` |
| **Subject:** | *LISTSERV ignores this* |

`SUBSCRIBE softrevu <firstname> <lastname>`

## Sound Cards

| | |
|---|---|
| **Resource:** | LISTSERV |
| **Address:** | `ibmsnd-l@brownvm.brown.edu` |

This is a forum for the discussion and support of sound cards. To subscribe, address a message in the following manner:

| | |
|---|---|
| **To:** | `LISTSERV@brownvm.brown.edu` |
| **From:** | `<your address>` |
| **Subject:** | *LISTSERV ignores this* |

`SUBSCRIBE ibmsnd-l <firstname> <lastname>`

## Support/Help Desk

**Resource:** LISTSERV
**Address:** hdesk-l@wvnvm.wvnet.edu
For persons involved in supporting and staffing Help Desks, including problem-tracking, frustration, retraining users, and creating your own Help Desk. To subscribe, address a message in the following manner:
**To:** LISTSERV@wvnvm.wvnet.edu
**From:** <your address>
**Subject:** *LISTSERV ignores this*
SUBSCRIBE hdesk-l <firstname> <lastname>

## Tandy

**Resource:** LISTSERV
**Address:** coco@pucc.bitnet@cunyvm.cuny.edu
A discussion list for the Tandy Color Computer OS-9 operating system and related topics. To subscribe, address a message in the following manner:
**To:** LISTSERV@pucc.bitnet@cunyvm.cuny.edu
**From:** <your address>
**Subject:** *LISTSERV ignores this*
SUBSCRIBE coco <firstname> <lastname>

## TCP/IP

**Resource:** LISTSERV
**Address:** ibmtcp-l@pucc.bitnet
A list for users and supporters of IBM's TCP/IP software product. To subscribe, address a message in the following manner:
**To:** LISTSERV@pucc.bitnet
**From:** <your address>
**Subject:** *LISTSERV ignores this*
SUBSCRIBE ibmtcp-l <firstname> <lastname>

**Resource:** LISTSERV
**Address:** pcip@irlearn.ucd.ie
A discussion list about how to implement the TCP/IP protocol on PCs. To subscribe, address a message in the following manner:
**To:** LISTSERV@irlearn.ucd.ie
**From:** <your address>
**Subject:** *LISTSERV ignores this*
SUBSCRIBE pcip <firstname> <lastname>

## Utilities

**Resource:** List
**Address:** `info-zip@wsmr-simtel20.army.mil`
For the discussion of information related to the porting of ZIP software compression to the mainframe environment. Send your subscription requests to `inf-zip-request@wsmr-simtel20.army.mil`.

**Resource:** List
**Address:** `i-finger@spcvxa.bitnet@cunyvm.cuny.edu`
For the discussion and sharing of information related to user lookup facilities, particularly finger. Send your subscription requests to `i-fingreq%spcvxa@cunyvm.cuny.edu`.

## Viruses

**Resource:** LISTSERV
**Address:** `virus-l@lehiibm1.bitnet@cunyvm.cuny.edu`
This is the motherlode list for the exchange of information about computer viruses. The regular traffic and archives here provide ongoing advice and education about how to best protect yourself from and restrict the spread of a computer virus. To subscribe, address a message in the following manner:
**To:** `LISTSERV@lehiibm1.bitnet@cunyvm.cuny.edu`
**From:** `<your address>`
**Subject:** *LISTSERV ignores this*
`SUBSCRIBE virus-l <firstname> <lastname>`

**Resource:** LISTSERV
**Address:** `mibsrv-l@ua1vm.bitnet`
This list is about IBM PC (and compatible) antiviral software products and programs. To subscribe, address a message in the following manner:
**To:** `LISTSERV@ua1vm.bitnet`
**From:** `<your address>`
**Subject:** *LISTSERV ignores this*
`SUBSCRIBE mibsrv-l <firstname> <lastname>`

**Resource:** FTP
**Address:** `cert.org`
**Directory:** `pub/virus-l/docs/vtc`

**Resource:** FTP
**Address:** `cert.org`
**Directory:** `pub/virus-l/FAQ.virus-l`
This is the archive/respository of previous VIRUS-L postings.

**Resource:**   LISTSERV
**Address:**    `Virus-L@listserv@lehigh.edu`
A general list for alerts and information about software viruses. Forget the news hype. This is the best way to keep an eye on the current status of all known computer viruses. To subscribe, address a message in the following manner:

**To:**         `LISTSERV@listserv@lehigh.edu`
**From:**       `<your address>`
**Subject:**    *LISTSERV ignores this*
`SUBSCRIBE Virus-L <firstname> <lastname>`

**Resource:**   LISTSERV
**Address:**    `VALERT-L@listserv@VALERT-L@LEHIIBM1.BITNET`
Virus alerts (no discussion). All VALERT-L postings eventually reach VIRUS-L and comp.virus. To subscribe, address a message in the following manner:

**To:**         `LISTSERV@listserv@LISTSERV@LEHIIBM1.BITNET`
**From:**       `<your address>`
**Subject:**    *LISTSERV ignores this*
`SUBSCRIBE VALERT-L <firstname> <lastname>`

**Resource:**   FTP
**Address:**    `ftp.informatik.uni-hamburg.de`
**Directory:**  `pub/virus/texts/catalog`

**Resource:**   FTP
**Address:**    `cert.org`
**Directory:**  `pub/virus-l/docs/reviews`
Retrieve the file `slade.quickref.rvw`.

## Windows

**Resource:**   LISTSERV
**Address:**    `WIN3-L@UICVM.uic.cc.edu`
A forum for the discussion of all aspects of Microsoft's Windows product. Just about everything you could want to know about Windows is discussed here. To subscribe, address a message in the following manner:

**To:**         `LISTSERV@UICVM.uic.cc.edu`
**From:**       `<your address>`
**Subject:**    *LISTSERV ignores this*
`SUBSCRIBE WIN3-L <firstname> <lastname>`

## Word Processing

**Resource:**    LISTSERV
**Address:**     `word-pc@ufobi1.uni-forst.gwdg.de`
An open list for the support of and ongoing information exchange about
Microsoft Word for DOS and Windows. To subscribe, address a message in the
following manner:
**To:**          `LISTSERV@ufobi1.uni-forst.gwdg.de`
**From:**      `<your address>`
**Subject:**   *LISTSERV ignores this*
`SUBSCRIBE word-pc <firstname> <lastname>`

**Resource:**    LISTSERV
**Address:**     `word-mac@alsvid.une.edu.au`
A moderated list for the purposes of exchanging information about Microsoft
Word for the Macintosh. To subscribe, address a message in the following
manner:
**To:**          `LISTSERV@alsvid.une.edu.au`
**From:**      `<your address>`
**Subject:**   *LISTSERV ignores this*
`SUBSCRIBE word-mac <firstname> <lastname>`

**Resource:**    LISTSERV
**Address:**     `wpwin-l@ubvm.cc.buffalo.edu`
This discussion list is for users of WordPerfect for Windows. To subscribe,
address a message in the following manner:
**To:**          `LISTSERV@ubvm.cc.buffalo.edu`
**From:**      `<your address>`
**Subject:**   *LISTSERV ignores this*
`SUBSCRIBE wpwin-l <firstname> <lastname>`

**Resource:**    LISTSERV
**Address:**     `wp51-l@uottawa.bitnet`
For all users of the WordPerfect word processing software. To subscribe,
address a message in the following manner:
**To:**          `LISTSERV@uottawa.bitnet`
**From:**      `<your address>`
**Subject:**   *LISTSERV ignores this*
`SUBSCRIBE wp51-l <firstname> <lastname>`

## Zenith/Heath

**Resource:**    List
**Address:**     `heath-people@mc.lcs.mit.edu`

For persons interested in all aspects of Zenith and Heath computers and related components. Send your subscription request and related administrative information to `heath-people-request@mc.lcs.mit.edu`.

# Culture

## Celtic

**Resource:**   LISTSERV
**Address:**   `celtic-l@irlearn.ucd.ie`
This list is for everyone interested in the study of Celtic cultures. To subscribe, address a message in the following manner:

**To:**   `LISTSERV@irlearn.ucd.ie`
**From:**   `<your address>`
**Subject:**   *LISTSERV ignores this*
`SUBSCRIBE celtic-l <firstname> <lastname>`

## Islam

**Resource:**   LISTSERV
**Address:**   `islam-l@ulkyvm.louisville.edu`
This is a discussion list for the exchange of information about the history of Islam. To subscribe, address a message in the following manner:

**To:**   `LISTSERV@ulkyvm.louisville.edu`
**From:**   `<your address>`
**Subject:**   *LISTSERV ignores this*
`SUBSCRIBE islam-l <firstname> <lastname>`

## Japanese

**Resource:**   LISTSERV
**Address:**   `j-food-l@jpnknu01.bitnet`
This is a Japanese food and culture discussion list. To subscribe, address a message in the following manner:

**To:**   `LISTSERV@jpnknu01.bitnet`
**From:**   `<your address>`
**Subject:**   *LISTSERV ignores this*
`SUBSCRIBE j-food-l <firstname> <lastname>`

# Dancing

## Ballroom

**Resource:** List
**Address:** ballroom@athena.mit.edu
For the discussion of all aspects of ballroom (and related) dancing. Send your subscriptions to ballroom-request@athena.mit.edu.

## International

**Resource:** LISTSERV
**Address:** dance-l@hearn.bitnet
For everyone who appreciates or participates in international folk and traditional dancing. To subscribe, address a message in the following manner:

**To:** LISTSERV@hearn.bitnet
**From:** <your address>
**Subject:** *LISTSERV ignores this*
SUBSCRIBE dance-l <firstname> <lastname>

# Disabilities

## Attention Deficit Disorder

**Resource:** LISTSERV
**Address:** add-parents@n7kbt.rain.com
Support, research, and information about attention deficit disorder (ADD) for those whose lives are affected by it. To subscribe, address a message in the following manner:

**To:** LISTSERV@n7kbt.rain.com
**From:** <your address>
**Subject:** *LISTSERV ignores this*
SUBSCRIBE add-parents <firstname> <lastname>

## Autism

**Resource:** LISTSERV
**Address:** autism@sjuvm.bitnet
A discussion list for everyone affected by autism and developmental disabilities. To subscribe, address a message in the following manner:

**To:**      `LISTSERV@sjuvm.bitnet`
**From:**    `<your address>`
**Subject:**  *LISTSERV ignores this*
`SUBSCRIBE autism <firstname> <lastname>`

## Blindness

**Resource:**    LISTSERV
**Address:**    `blindnws@ndsuvm1.ndsu.edu`
This is the blind news digest. To subscribe, address a message in the following manner:
**To:**      `LISTSERV@ndsuvm1.ndsu.edu`
**From:**    `<your address>`
**Subject:**  *LISTSERV ignores this*
`SUBSCRIBE blindnws <firstname> <lastname>`

**Resource:**    LISTSERV
**Address:**    `blind-l@uafsysb.uark.edu`
A discussion list dedicated to computer use by and for the blind. To subscribe, address a message in the following manner:
**To:**      `LISTSERV@uafsysb.uark.edu`
**From:**    `<your address>`
**Subject:**  *LISTSERV ignores this*
`SUBSCRIBE blind-l <firstname> <lastname>`

## Carpal Tunnel

**Resource:**    LISTSERV
**Address:**    `sorehand@ucsfvm.bitnet`
An ongoing discussion and exchange of information about carpal tunnel syndrome and related problems. To subscribe, address a message in the following manner:
**To:**      `LISTSERV@ucsfvm.bitnet`
**From:**    `<your address>`
**Subject:**  *LISTSERV ignores this*
`SUBSCRIBE sorehand <firstname> <lastname>`

## Deaf and Blind

**Resource:**   LISTSERV
**Address:**    `deafblnd@ukcc.uky.edu`
This is the deaf-blind mailing list. To subscribe, address a message in the following manner:
**To:**       `LISTSERV@ukcc.uky.edu`
**From:**   `<your address>`
**Subject:**  *LISTSERV ignores this*
`SUBSCRIBE deafblnd <firstname> <lastname>`

## Deafness

**Resource:**   LISTSERV
**Address:**    `deaf-l@siucvmb.bitnet`
A list for those whose lives are affected by deafness. To subscribe, address a message in the following manner:
**To:**       `LISTSERV@siucvmb.bitnet`
**From:**   `<your address>`
**Subject:**  *LISTSERV ignores this*
`SUBSCRIBE deaf-l <firstname> <lastname>`

## Diabetes

**Resource:**   LISTSERV
**Address:**    `diabetic@pccvm.bitnet`
This is an open discussion forum for diabetics and persons affected by diabetes. To subscribe, address a message in the following manner:
**To:**       `LISTSERV@pccvm.bitnet`
**From:**   `<your address>`
**Subject:**  *LISTSERV ignores this*
`SUBSCRIBE diabetic <firstname> <lastname>`

## General

**Resource:**   LISTSERV
**Address:**    `ddfind-l@gitvm1`
This is a general forum for information networking on disabilities. To subscribe, address a message in the following manner:
**To:**       `LISTSERV@gitvm1`
**From:**   `<your address>`
**Subject:**  *LISTSERV ignores this*
`SUBSCRIBE ddfind-l <firstname> <lastname>`

## Speech

**Resource:** LISTSERV
**Address:** commdis@rpitsvm.bitnet
This is a forum providing ongoing exchange of support and ideas about speech disorders. To subscribe, address a message in the following manner:
**To:** LISTSERV@rpitsvm.bitnet
**From:** <your address>
**Subject:** *LISTSERV ignores this*
SUBSCRIBE commdis <firstname> <lastname>

## Stroke/CVA/TIA

**Resource:** LISTSERV
**Address:** stroke-l@ukcc.uky.edu
This is for persons whose lives are affected by strokes (CVAs), transient ischemic attacks (TIAs), and for ongoing research and rehabilitation. To subscribe, address a message in the following manner:
**To:** LISTSERV@ukcc.uky.edu
**From:** <your address>
**Subject:** *LISTSERV ignores this*
SUBSCRIBE stroke-l <firstname> <lastname>

## Stuttering

**Resource:** LISTSERV
**Address:** stutt-l@templevm.bitnet
This forum provides an exchange of information about stuttering, including research and clinical practice. To subscribe, address a message in the following manner:
**To:** LISTSERV@templevm.bitnet
**From:** <your address>
**Subject:** *LISTSERV ignores this*
SUBSCRIBE stutt-l <firstname> <lastname>

## Technology

**Resource:** LISTSERV
**Address:** l-hcap@ndsuvm1.ndsu.edu
A discussion list about how best to serve the needs of the disabled or handicapped with technology. To subscribe, address a message in the following manner:

**To:**        `LISTSERV@ndsuvm1.ndsu.edu`
**From:**      `<your address>`
**Subject:**   *LISTSERV ignores this*
`SUBSCRIBE l-hcap <firstname> <lastname>`

# Education

## French Business Schools

**Resource:**  LISTSERV
**Address:**   `fbs-l@freia11.bitnet`
A discussion list about French business schools. To subscribe, address a
message in the following manner:
**To:**        `LISTSERV@freia11.bitnet`
**From:**      `<your address>`
**Subject:**   *LISTSERV ignores this*
`SUBSCRIBE fbs-l <firstname> <lastname>`

## General

**Resource:**  LISTSERV
**Address:**   `ashe-l@mizzou1.bitnet`
Association for the Study of Higher Education. To subscribe, address a mes-
sage in the following manner:
**To:**        `LISTSERV@mizzou1.bitnet`
**From:**      `<your address>`
**Subject:**   *LISTSERV ignores this*
`SUBSCRIBE ashe-l <firstname> <lastname>`

**Resource:**  LISTSERV
**Address:**   `newedu-l@vm.usc.edu`
For the exchange of information related to new and improved methods of
education. To subscribe, address a message in the following manner:
**To:**        `LISTSERV@vm.usc.edu`
**From:**      `<your address>`
**Subject:**   *LISTSERV ignores this*
`SUBSCRIBE newedu-l <firstname> <lastname>`

## Gifted

**Resource:**    LISTSERV
**Address:**    `tag-l@ndsuvm1.ndsu.edu`
Devoted to the discussion of talented and gifted students. To subscribe, address a message in the following manner:
**To:**    `LISTSERV@ndsuvm1.ndsu.edu`
**From:**    `<your address>`
**Subject:**    *LISTSERV ignores this*
`SUBSCRIBE tag-l <firstname> <lastname>`

## History

**Resource:**    telnet
**Address:**    `ukanaix.cc.ukans.edu`
**User id:**    `history`

## Home Education

**Resource:**    List
**Address:**    `home-ed@think.com`
A place for advocates of home education to share and discuss ideas and techniques. Send subscription requests to `home-ed-request@think.com`.

## Law

**Resource:**    LISTSERV
**Address:**    `edlaw@ukcc.uky.edu`
Law and education discussion list. To subscribe, address a message in the following manner:
**To:**    `LISTSERV@ukcc.uky.edu`
**From:**    `<your address>`
**Subject:**    *LISTSERV ignores this*
`SUBSCRIBE edlaw <firstname> <lastname>`

## Law School

**Resource:**    LISTSERV
**Address:**    `lawsch-l@auvm.bitnet`
A law school discussion list. For everyone currently attending law school, teaching, or investigating the possibility of becoming a law student. To subscribe, address a message in the following manner:

| | |
|---|---|
| **To:** | `LISTSERV@auvm.bitnet` |
| **From:** | `<your address>` |
| **Subject:** | *LISTSERV ignores this* |

`SUBSCRIBE lawsch-l <firstname> <lastname>`

**Resource:** LISTSERV
**Address:** `lawaid@rutgers.edu`
Law school financial aid discussion. To subscribe, address a message in the following manner:

| | |
|---|---|
| **To:** | `LISTSERV@rutgers.edu` |
| **From:** | `<your address>` |
| **Subject:** | *LISTSERV ignores this* |

`SUBSCRIBE lawaid <firstname> <lastname>`

## Learning

**Resource:** LISTSERV
**Address:** `altlearn@sjuvm.bitnet`
This list provides a forum for the exchange of information about alternative approaches to learning. To subscribe, address a message in the following manner:

| | |
|---|---|
| **To:** | `LISTSERV@sjuvm.bitnet` |
| **From:** | `<your address>` |
| **Subject:** | *LISTSERV ignores this* |

`SUBSCRIBE altlearn <firstname> <lastname>`

## MBA Studies

**Resource:** LISTSERV
**Address:** `mba-l@marist.bitnet`
This discussion list is devoted to MBA student curricula. To subscribe, address a message in the following manner:

| | |
|---|---|
| **To:** | `LISTSERV@marist.bitnet` |
| **From:** | `<your address>` |
| **Subject:** | *LISTSERV ignores this* |

`SUBSCRIBE mba-l <firstname> <lastname>`

## Science

**Resource:** LISTSERV
**Address:** `ascd-sci@psuvm.psu.edu`
This is the Alliance for Science Teaching forum. To subscribe, address a message in the following manner:

**To:**      `LISTSERV@psuvm.psu.edu`
**From:**    `<your address>`
**Subject:**   *LISTSERV ignores this*
`SUBSCRIBE ascd-sci <firstname> <lastname>`

# Electronics

## Cellular

**Resource:**   List
**Address:**    `cellular@mail-server@yngbld.gwinnett.com`
Discussion list for the cellular industry and related technologies. Send a
message containing the following command lines:
`SUBSCRIBE CELLULAR`
`ECHOMAIL CELLULAR`

# Employment

## Federal Government

**Resource:**   LISTSERV
**Address:**    `fedjobs@dartcms1.dartmouth.edu`
Postings of the Federal Job Openings list are distributed through this list. To
subscribe, address a message in the following manner:
**To:**      `LISTSERV@dartcms1.dartmouth.edu`
**From:**    `<your address>`
**Subject:**   *LISTSERV ignores this*
`SUBSCRIBE fedjobs <firstname> <lastname>`

## Flexible Work

**Resource:**   LISTSERV
**Address:**    `flexwork@psuhmc.bitnet`
A discussion list for all aspects of a flexible working environment, including
telecommuting, flex-time, and other nontraditional work scenarios. To subscribe, address a message in the following manner:

| To: | LISTSERV@psuhmc.bitnet |
|---|---|
| **From:** | <your address> |
| **Subject:** | *LISTSERV ignores this* |

SUBSCRIBE flexwork <firstname> <lastname>

# Engineering

## Chemical

**Resource:**   LISTSERV
**Address:**   cheme-l@psuvm.psu.edu
A list for the purpose of discussing chemical engineering. To subscribe, address a message in the following manner:

| To: | LISTSERV@psuvm.psu.edu |
|---|---|
| **From:** | <your address> |
| **Subject:** | *LISTSERV ignores this* |

SUBSCRIBE cheme-l <firstname> <lastname>

## Mechanical

**Resource:**   LISTSERV
**Address:**   mech-l@utarlvm1.bitnet
This is the mechanical engineering discussion list. To subscribe, address a message in the following manner:

| To: | LISTSERV@utarlvm1.bitnet |
|---|---|
| **From:** | <your address> |
| **Subject:** | *LISTSERV ignores this* |

SUBSCRIBE mech-l <firstname> <lastname>

# Entertainment

## Anime

**Resource:**   FTP
**Address:**   wpi.wpi.edu
**Directory:**   /anime/Scripts

**Resource:**   LISTSERV
**Address:**    `anime-l@vtvm1.bitnet`
A discussion list for Japanese animedia and other animation news. To subscribe, address a message in the following manner:
**To:**         `LISTSERV@vtvm1.bitnet`
**From:**       `<your address>`
**Subject:**    *LISTSERV ignores this*
`SUBSCRIBE anime-l <firstname> <lastname>`

## Cinema

**Resource:**   LISTSERV
**Address:**    `cinema-l@auvm.bitnet`
This is a forum for discussion of all forms of cinema. To subscribe, address a message in the following manner:
**To:**         `LISTSERV@auvm.bitnet`
**From:**       `<your address>`
**Subject:**    *LISTSERV ignores this*
`SUBSCRIBE cinema-l <firstname> <lastname>`

## Dylan Dog

**Resource:**   LISTSERV
**Address:**    `dylandog@igecuniv.bitnet`
This is the fan club list for Dylan Dog. To subscribe, address a message in the following manner:
**To:**         `LISTSERV@igecuniv.bitnet`
**From:**       `<your address>`
**Subject:**    *LISTSERV ignores this*
`SUBSCRIBE dylandog <firstname> <lastname>`

## Film and Television

**Resource:**   LISTSERV
**Address:**    `screen-l@ua1vm.bitnet`
This is a list that discusses television and film. To subscribe, address a message in the following manner:
**To:**         `LISTSERV@ua1vm.bitnet`
**From:**       `<your address>`
**Subject:**    *LISTSERV ignores this*
`SUBSCRIBE screen-l <firstname> <lastname>`

## Film Music

**Resource:**    LISTSERV
**Address:**    `filmus-l@iubvm.bitnet`
This discussion list is devoted to film music. To subscribe, address a message in the following manner:
**To:**    `LISTSERV@iubvm.bitnet`
**From:**    `<your address>`
**Subject:**    *LISTSERV ignores this*
`SUBSCRIBE filmus-l <firstname> <lastname>`

## Medieval

**Resource:**    LISTSERV
**Address:**    `perform@iubvm.bitnet`
This list is for everyone interested in the medieval performing arts. To subscribe, address a message in the following manner:
**To:**    `LISTSERV@iubvm.bitnet`
**From:**    `<your address>`
**Subject:**    *LISTSERV ignores this*
`SUBSCRIBE perform <firstname> <lastname>`

## Movies

**Resource:**    LISTSERV
**Address:**    `amia-l@ukcc.uky.edu`
This list is frequented by the Association for Moving Image Archivists. To subscribe, address a message in the following manner:
**To:**    `LISTSERV@ukcc.uky.edu`
**From:**    `<your address>`
**Subject:**    *LISTSERV ignores this*
`SUBSCRIBE amia-l <firstname> <lastname>`

**Resource:**    LISTSERV
**Address:**    `horror@pacevm.bitnet`
This list is about horror films and fiction. To subscribe, address a message in the following manner:
**To:**    `LISTSERV@pacevm.bitnet`
**From:**    `<your address>`
**Subject:**    *LISTSERV ignores this*
`SUBSCRIBE horror <firstname> <lastname>`

**Resource:** LISTSERV
**Address:** `film-l@itesmvf1.bitnet`
This list is about filmmaking and reviews. To subscribe, address a message in the following manner:
**To:** `LISTSERV@itesmvf1.bitnet`
**From:** `<your address>`
**Subject:** *LISTSERV ignores this*
`SUBSCRIBE film-l <firstname> <lastname>`

## Public Radio

**Resource:** LISTSERV
**Address:** `pubradio@idbsu.bitnet`
This is the public radio discussion group. To subscribe, address a message in the following manner:
**To:** `LISTSERV@idbsu.bitnet`
**From:** `<your address>`
**Subject:** *LISTSERV ignores this*
`SUBSCRIBE pubradio <firstname> <lastname>`

## Stage Work

**Resource:** List
**Address:** `stagecraft@jaguar.cs.utah.edu`
A discussion list devoted to all aspects of stage work in the theater. Send your subscription requests to `stagecraft-request@jaguar.cs.utah.edu`.

## Theater

**Resource:** LISTSERV
**Address:** `comedia@arizvm1.bitnet`
This list discusses Hispanic classic theater. To subscribe, address a message in the following manner:
**To:** `LISTSERV@arizvm1.bitnet`
**From:** `<your address>`
**Subject:** *LISTSERV ignores this*
`SUBSCRIBE comedia <firstname> <lastname>`

# Farming

## Beef

**Resource:**  LISTSERV
**Address:**  `beef-l@wsuvm1.bitnet`
This list was created for those considered to be beef specialists and provides a common arena for information exchange. To subscribe, address a message in the following manner:
**To:**  `LISTSERV@wsuvm1.bitnet`
**From:**  `<your address>`
**Subject:**  *LISTSERV ignores this*
`SUBSCRIBE beef-l <firstname> <lastname>`

## Dairy

**Resource:**  LISTSERV
**Address:**  `automilk@umdd.bitnet`
This list specializes in the discussion of automatic milking systems. To subscribe, address a message in the following manner:
**To:**  `LISTSERV@umdd.bitnet`
**From:**  `<your address>`
**Subject:**  *LISTSERV ignores this*
`SUBSCRIBE automilk <firstname> <lastname>`

**Resource:**  LISTSERV
**Address:**  `dairy-l@umdd.bitnet`
This list is for those involved in the dairy industry. To subscribe, address a message in the following manner:
**To:**  `LISTSERV@umdd.bitnet`
**From:**  `<your address>`
**Subject:**  *LISTSERV ignores this*
`SUBSCRIBE dairy-l <firstname> <lastname>`

## Potatoes

**Resource:**  LISTSERV
**Address:**  `spud@wsuvm1.bitnet`
This list was created to discuss potato research. To subscribe, address a message in the following manner:

**To:**      `LISTSERV@wsuvm1.bitnet`
**From:**    `<your address>`
**Subject:**   *LISTSERV ignores this*
`SUBSCRIBE spud <firstname> <lastname>`

# Finance

## General

**Resource:**   LISTSERV
**Address:**    `finance@templevm.bitnet`
This is the electronic journal of finance. To subscribe, address a message in the following manner:
**To:**      `LISTSERV@templevm.bitnet`
**From:**    `<your address>`
**Subject:**   *LISTSERV ignores this*
`SUBSCRIBE finance <firstname> <lastname>`

# Food

## Food and Wine

**Resource:**   LISTSERV
**Address:**    `foodwine@cmuvm.csv.cmich.edu`
This is a discussion list for those who appreciate food and wine. To subscribe, address a message in the following manner:
**To:**      `LISTSERV@cmuvm.csv.cmich.edu`
**From:**    `<your address>`
**Subject:**   *LISTSERV ignores this*
`SUBSCRIBE foodwine <firstname> <lastname>`

## Recipes

**Resource:**   FTP
**Address:**    `mthvax.cs.miami.edu`
**Directory:**  `pub/recipes`

**Resource:**    LISTSERV
**Address:**    `eat-l@vtvm2.bitnet`
Devoted to foodlore and recipe exchange. To subscribe, address a message in the following manner:
**To:**          `LISTSERV@vtvm2.bitnet`
**From:**       `<your address>`
**Subject:**   *LISTSERV ignores this*
`SUBSCRIBE eat-l <firstname> <lastname>`

**Resource:**    FTP
**Address:**    `GATEKEEPER.DEC.COM (16.1.0.2)`
**Directory:**  `/pub/recipes`

# Fun

## Answers

**Resource:**    LISTSERV
**Address:**    `misc@trearn.bitnet`
This list provides a common area for miscellaneous questions and requests. To subscribe, address a message in the following manner:
**To:**          `LISTSERV@trearn.bitnet`
**From:**       `<your address>`
**Subject:**   *LISTSERV ignores this*
`SUBSCRIBE misc <firstname> <lastname>`

**Resource:**    List
**Address:**    `oracle@iuvax.cs.indiana.edu`
Where to turn when you need an answer. Send your administrative mail and subscription requests to `oracle-request@iuvax.cs.indiana.edu`.

## Fun

**Resource:**    telnet
**Address:**    `astro.temple.edu 12345`
Telnet to this site—it will return something different every time!

## Jokes

**Resource:**    FTP
**Address:**    `pc10868.pc.cc.cmu.edu`
An archive of the Rec.Humor and Rec.Humor.D USENET groups.

## Mardi Gras

**Resource:**   List
**Address:**   mardi-gras@mintir.new-orleans.la.us
For those interested in celebrating the annual festival known as Mardi Gras.
Send your subscription request to mail-server@mintir.new-orleans.la.us with
the following command in the message: subscribe mardi-gras.

## On This Day

Contact geiser@pictel.com and you'll receive a daily message containing
important events in history, astronomical events, religious holidays, and so on.

## Open Discussion

**Resource:**   LISTSERV
**Address:**   causerie@uquebec.bitnet
A free-talk, chat list. All correspondence is in French. What a way to practice!
To subscribe, address a message in the following manner:
**To:**   LISTSERV@uquebec.bitnet
**From:**   <your address>
**Subject:**   *LISTSERV ignores this*
SUBSCRIBE causerie <firstname> <lastname>

**Resource:**   LISTSERV
**Address:**   freetalk@brownvm.brown.edu
This is an open list for free talking. All subjects are fair game. To subscribe,
address a message in the following manner:
**To:**   LISTSERV@brownvm.brown.edu
**From:**   <your address>
**Subject:**   *LISTSERV ignores this*
SUBSCRIBE freetalk <firstname> <lastname>

## Puzzles

**Resource:**   List
**Address:**   cube-lovers@ai.ai.mit.edu
A discussion list for information about Rubik's Cube and related puzzles. Send
your subscription request to cube-lovers-request@ai.ai.mit.edu.

## Smiley

**Resource:**   FTP
**Address:**    `nic.funet.fi`
**Directory:**  `pub/doc/fun/smiley.txt`
This is the ultimate smiley dictionary.

## Thought for the Day

**Resource:**   LISTSERV
**Address:**    `tftd-l@tamvm1.tamu.edu`
This list provides a "Thought for the Day." To subscribe, address a message in the following manner:
**To:**         `LISTSERV@tamvm1.tamu.edu`
**From:**       `<your address>`
**Subject:**    *LISTSERV ignores this*
`SUBSCRIBE tftd-l <firstname> <lastname>`

## Weird Stuff

**Resource:**   LISTSERV
**Address:**    `weird-l@brownvm.brown.edu`
The stranger the better! Know of anything disturbing, weird, bizarre? Here's where you should hang out! To subscribe, address a message in the following manner:
**To:**         `LISTSERV@brownvm.brown.edu`
**From:**       `<your address>`
**Subject:**    *LISTSERV ignores this*
`SUBSCRIBE weird-l <firstname> <lastname>`

# Games

## Backgammon

**Resource:**   telnet
**Address:**    `ouzo.rog.rwth-aachen.de 8765`
Watch or participate in online backgammon games.

**Resource:**   LISTSERV
**Address:**    `bkgammon@indycms.iupui.edu`
This list is devoted to the discussion and exchange of backgammon strategy.
To subscribe, address a message in the following manner:

```
To:        LISTSERV@indycms.iupui.edu
From:      <your address>
Subject:   LISTSERV ignores this
SUBSCRIBE bkgammon <firstname> <lastname>
```

## Chess

**Resource:**   telnet
**Address:**   `valkyries.andrew.cmu.edu 5000`
Play or watch chess games with real people in real-time.

**Resource:**   telnet
**Address:**   `aragorn.andrew.cmu.edu 5000`
Watch or participate in chess games online.

**Resource:**   LISTSERV
**Address:**   `chess-l@grearn`
This list is devoted to international chess. Strategies, analysis, tournament information, and a position ladder are available. To subscribe, address a message in the following manner:

```
To:        LISTSERV@grearn
From:      <your address>
Subject:   LISTSERV ignores this
SUBSCRIBE chess-l <firstname> <lastname>
```

## Conflict Simulation

**Resource:**   LISTSERV
**Address:**   `consim-l@ualtavm.bitnet`
This list was created for those interested in conflict simulation games. To subscribe, address a message in the following manner:

```
To:        LISTSERV@ualtavm.bitnet
From:      <your address>
Subject:   LISTSERV ignores this
SUBSCRIBE consim-l <firstname> <lastname>
```

## Go

**Resource:**   List
**Address:**   `go-l@smcvax.bitnet@vm1.nodak.edu`
For the exchange of information and strategies as well as an opportunity to find electronic (e-mail) opponents. Send your subscription requests in the form of SUBSCRIBE GO-L to MailServ%SmcVax.Bitnet@VM1.NoDak.Edu.

**Resource:** telnet
**Address:** `icsib18.icsi.berkeley.edu 6969`
This provides a real-time connection for you to watch or play games of Go.


## Role-Playing Games

**Resource:** LISTSERV
**Address:** `ud-l@uriacc.bitnet`
This is the "ultimate dungeon list." To subscribe, address a message in the following manner:
**To:** `LISTSERV@uriacc.bitnet`
**From:** `<your address>`
**Subject:** *LISTSERV ignores this*
`SUBSCRIBE ud-l <firstname> <lastname>`

**Resource:** LISTSERV
**Address:** `stargame@pccvm.bitnet`
For persons involved in the FASA Star Trek role-playing game. To subscribe, address a message in the following manner:
**To:** `LISTSERV@pccvm.bitnet`
**From:** `<your address>`
**Subject:** *LISTSERV ignores this*
`SUBSCRIBE stargame <firstname> <lastname>`

**Resource:** LISTSERV
**Address:** `gmast-l@utcvm.bitnet`
This is for everyone who is or wants to be a role-playing gamemaster. To subscribe, address a message in the following manner:
**To:** `LISTSERV@utcvm.bitnet`
**From:** `<your address>`
**Subject:** *LISTSERV ignores this*
`SUBSCRIBE gmast-l <firstname> <lastname>`

**Resource:** LISTSERV
**Address:** `adnd-l@utarlvm1.bitnet`
This is the advanced Dungeons & Dragons discussion list. To subscribe, address a message in the following manner:
**To:** `LISTSERV@utarlvm1.bitnet`
**From:** `<your address>`
**Subject:** *LISTSERV ignores this*
`SUBSCRIBE adnd-l <firstname> <lastname>`

### Shogi/Japanese Chess

**Resource:**  LISTSERV
**Address:**  shogi-l@technion.technion.ac.il
This is a discussion list for the exchange of ideas, analysis, and tournament information for Shogi, also known as Japanese chess. To subscribe, address a message in the following manner:

**To:**  LISTSERV@technion.technion.ac.il
**From:**  <your address>
**Subject:**  *LISTSERV ignores this*
SUBSCRIBE shogi-l <firstname> <lastname>

# Gardening

### General

**Resource:**  LISTSERV
**Address:**  gardens@ukcc.uky.edu
This is a list devoted to the discussion of gardens and gardening. To subscribe, address a message in the following manner:

**To:**  LISTSERV@ukcc.uky.edu
**From:**  <your address>
**Subject:**  *LISTSERV ignores this*
SUBSCRIBE gardens <firstname> <lastname>

### Master

**Resource:**  LISTSERV
**Address:**  mgarden@wsuvm1.bitnet
This is a list for master gardeners. Show off your green thumb! To subscribe, address a message in the following manner:

**To:**  LISTSERV@wsuvm1.bitnet
**From:**  <your address>
**Subject:**  *LISTSERV ignores this*
SUBSCRIBE mgarden <firstname> <lastname>

# General

## Folklore

**Resource:**     LISTSERV
**Address:**     `FOLKLORE@vm1.nodak.edu`
A moderated list for the discussion of urban legends and folklore. To subscribe, address a message in the following manner:
**To:**     `LISTSERV@vm1.nodak.edu`
**From:**     `<your address>`
**Subject:**     *LISTSERV ignores this*
`SUBSCRIBE FOLKLORE <firstname> <lastname>`

**Resource:**     LISTSERV
**Address:**     `LORE-L@vm1.nodak.edu`
An unmoderated list devoted to the discussion of folklore and urban legends. To subscribe, address a message in the following manner:
**To:**     `LISTSERV@vm1.nodak.edu`
**From:**     `<your address>`
**Subject:**     *LISTSERV ignores this*
`SUBSCRIBE LORE-L <firstname> <lastname>`

## Problem Solving

**Resource:**     LISTSERV
**Address:**     `cre8tv-l@psuvm.psu.edu`
This list discusses how to teach creative problem solving to engineers. To subscribe, address a message in the following manner:
**To:**     `LISTSERV@psuvm.psu.edu`
**From:**     `<your address>`
**Subject:**     *LISTSERV ignores this*
`SUBSCRIBE cre8tv-l <firstname> <lastname>`

## Words

**Resource:**     LISTSERV
**Address:**     `words-l@uga.cc.uga.edu`
The formal description of this list is "A discussion of the English language." In reality, the sky is the limit! Many posters from a variety of disciplines, countries, and backgrounds post and read this list. Because nearly everything can be expressed in words, it is appropriate. To subscribe, address a message in the following manner:

```
To:          LISTSERV@uga.cc.uga.edu
From:        <your address>
Subject:     LISTSERV ignores this
SUBSCRIBE words-l <firstname> <lastname>
```

# Geography

## General

**Resource:**  LISTSERV
**Address:**   geograph@searn.sunet.se
This is a general-purpose geography discussion list. To subscribe, address a message in the following manner:

```
To:          LISTSERV@searn.sunet.se
From:        <your address>
Subject:     LISTSERV ignores this
SUBSCRIBE geograph <firstname> <lastname>
```

## Mapping

**Resource:**  LISTSERV
**Address:**   maps-l@uga.cc.uga.edu
This forum is for persons interested in maps and air photo systems. To subscribe, address a message in the following manner:

```
To:          LISTSERV@uga.cc.uga.edu
From:        <your address>
Subject:     LISTSERV ignores this
SUBSCRIBE maps-l <firstname> <lastname>
```

# Government

## State Department

**Resource:**  List
**Address:**   travel-advisories@stolaf.edu
Travel advisories from the United States State Department are posted here.

## Supreme Court Decisions

**Resource:** FTP
**Address:** po.CWRU.Edu
**Directory:** /hermes/ascii

## White House

**Resource:** e-mail
**Address:** President@WhiteHouse.Gov
Send a message to President Clinton!

**Resource:** e-mail
**Address:** Vice.President@WhiteHouse.Gov
Send a message to Vice President Gore!

# Health

## Addiction

**Resource:** LISTSERV
**Address:** addict-l@kentvm.bitnet
This list was formed for the academic and scholarly discussion of addictions.
To subscribe, address a message in the following manner:
**To:** LISTSERV@kentvm.bitnet
**From:** <your address>
**Subject:** *LISTSERV ignores this*
SUBSCRIBE addict-l <firstname> <lastname>

**Resource:** LISTSERV
**Address:** alcohol@lmuacad.bitnet
This list is for alcohol and drug studies. To subscribe, address a message in the
following manner:
**To:** LISTSERV@lmuacad.bitnet
**From:** <your address>
**Subject:** *LISTSERV ignores this*
SUBSCRIBE alcohol <firstname> <lastname>

## Cancer

**Resource:** LISTSERV
**Address:** clan@frmop11.bitnet
This is the cancer liaison and action network discussion list. To subscribe, address a message in the following manner:
**To:** LISTSERV@frmop11.bitnet
**From:** <your address>
**Subject:** *LISTSERV ignores this*
SUBSCRIBE clan <firstname> <lastname>

## Chronic Fatigue

**Resource:** LISTSERV
**Address:** cfs-news@nihlist.bitnet
This is the chronic fatigue syndrome newsletter discussion list. To subscribe, address a message in the following manner:
**To:** LISTSERV@nihlist.bitnet
**From:** <your address>
**Subject:** *LISTSERV ignores this*
SUBSCRIBE cfs-news <firstname> <lastname>

**Resource:** LISTSERV
**Address:** cfs-med@nihlist.bitnet
This list provides a general forum to discuss chronic fatigue syndrome. To subscribe, address a message in the following manner:
**To:** LISTSERV@nihlist.bitnet
**From:** <your address>
**Subject:** *LISTSERV ignores this*
SUBSCRIBE cfs-med <firstname> <lastname>

## Diabetes

**Resource:** LISTSERV
**Address:** diabetes@irlearn.ucd.ie
This is the international research project on diabetes discussion forum. To subscribe, address a message in the following manner:
**To:** LISTSERV@irlearn.ucd.ie
**From:** <your address>
**Subject:** *LISTSERV ignores this*
SUBSCRIBE diabetes <firstname> <lastname>

## Dieting

**Resource:**     LISTSERV
**Address:**     `diet@ubvm.cc.buffalo.edu`
This list is for the support and discussion of weight loss. To subscribe, address a message in the following manner:
**To:**     `LISTSERV@ubvm.cc.buffalo.edu`
**From:**     `<your address>`
**Subject:**     *LISTSERV ignores this*
`SUBSCRIBE diet <firstname> <lastname>`

## Multiple Sclerosis

**Resource:**     LISTSERV
**Address:**     `mslist-l@technion.technion.ac.il`
This list focuses on multiple sclerosis discussion and support. To subscribe, address a message in the following manner:
**To:**     `LISTSERV@technion.technion.ac.il`
**From:**     `<your address>`
**Subject:**     *LISTSERV ignores this*
`SUBSCRIBE mslist-l <firstname> <lastname>`

# History

## 18th Century

**Resource:**     LISTSERV
**Address:**     `c18-l@psuvm.psu.edu`
This is an interdisciplinary list devoted to the discussion of the 18th century. To subscribe, address a message in the following manner:
**To:**     `LISTSERV@psuvm.psu.edu`
**From:**     `<your address>`
**Subject:**     *LISTSERV ignores this*
`SUBSCRIBE c18-l <firstname> <lastname>`

## America

**Resource:**     LISTSERV
**Address:**     `earam-l@kentvm.bitnet`
This is the Society of Early Americanists distribution list. To subscribe, address a message in the following manner:

**To:**      LISTSERV@kentvm.bitnet
**From:**    <your address>
**Subject:** *LISTSERV ignores this*
SUBSCRIBE earam-l <firstname> <lastname>

## China

**Resource:**  LISTSERV
**Address:**   emedch-l@uscvm.bitnet
This list is for the discussion and exchange of information about early medieval China. To subscribe, address a message in the following manner:
**To:**      LISTSERV@uscvm.bitnet
**From:**    <your address>
**Subject:** *LISTSERV ignores this*
SUBSCRIBE emedch-l <firstname> <lastname>

## Columbus

**Resource:**  LISTSERV
**Address:**   nat-1492@tamvm1.tamu.edu
This is a moderated list for the discussion of how Christopher Columbus's voyage in 1492 has affected the world in the last 500 years. To subscribe, address a message in the following manner:
**To:**      LISTSERV@tamvm1.tamu.edu
**From:**    <your address>
**Subject:** *LISTSERV ignores this*
SUBSCRIBE nat-1492 <firstname> <lastname>

## England

**Resource:**  LISTSERV
**Address:**   victoria@iubvm.bitnet
This list discusses all aspects of 18th century Great Britain. To subscribe, address a message in the following manner:
**To:**      LISTSERV@iubvm.bitnet
**From:**    <your address>
**Subject:** *LISTSERV ignores this*
SUBSCRIBE victoria <firstname> <lastname>

## Genealogy

**Resource:** LISTSERV
**Address:** roots-l@vm1.nodak.edu
This list is for those interested in and involved with genealogy. To subscribe, address a message in the following manner:
**To:** LISTSERV@vm1.nodak.edu
**From:** <your address>
**Subject:** *LISTSERV ignores this*
SUBSCRIBE roots-l <firstname> <lastname>

## General

**Resource:** LISTSERV
**Address:** history@psuvm.psu.edu
A general history discussion forum. To subscribe, address a message in the following manner:
**To:** LISTSERV@psuvm.psu.edu
**From:** <your address>
**Subject:** *LISTSERV ignores this*
SUBSCRIBE history <firstname> <lastname>

## Holocaust

**Resource:** LISTSERV
**Address:** holocaus@UICVM.uic.cc.edu
This list is devoted to the discussion of the Holocaust. To subscribe, address a message in the following manner:
**To:** LISTSERV@UICVM.uic.cc.edu
**From:** <your address>
**Subject:** *LISTSERV ignores this*
SUBSCRIBE holocaus <firstname> <lastname>

## Law

**Resource:** LISTSERV
**Address:** hislaw-l@ulkyvm.louisville.edu
This list is about the history of law (feudal, common, canon). To subscribe, address a message in the following manner:
**To:** LISTSERV@ulkyvm.louisville.edu
**From:** <your address>
**Subject:** *LISTSERV ignores this*
SUBSCRIBE hislaw-l <firstname> <lastname>

## Medieval

**Resource:** LISTSERV
**Address:** mediev-1@ukanvm.cc.ukans.edu
This list is devoted to the topic of medieval history. To subscribe, address a message in the following manner:
**To:** LISTSERV@ukanvm.cc.ukans.edu
**From:** <your address>
**Subject:** *LISTSERV ignores this*
SUBSCRIBE mediev-1 <firstname> <lastname>

## Military

**Resource:** LISTSERV
**Address:** milhst-1@ukanvm.cc.ukans.edu
This list provides a forum for those interested in military history. To subscribe, address a message in the following manner:
**To:** LISTSERV@ukanvm.cc.ukans.edu
**From:** <your address>
**Subject:** *LISTSERV ignores this*
SUBSCRIBE milhst-1 <firstname> <lastname>

## Renaissance

**Resource:** LISTSERV
**Address:** renais-1@ulkyvm.louisville.edu
This list focuses on the Renaissance. To subscribe, address a message in the following manner:
**To:** LISTSERV@ulkyvm.louisville.edu
**From:** <your address>
**Subject:** *LISTSERV ignores this*
SUBSCRIBE renais-1 <firstname> <lastname>

## Theoretical

**Resource:** LISTSERV
**Address:** cliology@msu.bitnet
This list is devoted to the theories of history. To subscribe, address a message in the following manner:
**To:** LISTSERV@msu.bitnet
**From:** <your address>
**Subject:** *LISTSERV ignores this*
SUBSCRIBE cliology <firstname> <lastname>

## United Kingdom

**Resource:** LISTSERV
**Address:** `albion-l@ucsbvm.bitnet`
This list was created to provide a forum concerning British and Irish history.
To subscribe, address a message in the following manner:
**To:** `LISTSERV@ucsbvm.bitnet`
**From:** `<your address>`
**Subject:** *LISTSERV ignores this*
`SUBSCRIBE albion-l <firstname> <lastname>`

## Vietnam War

**Resource:** LISTSERV
**Address:** `vwar-l@ubvm.cc.buffalo.edu`
This is the Vietnam War discussion list. To subscribe, address a message in the
following manner:
**To:** `LISTSERV@ubvm.cc.buffalo.edu`
**From:** `<your address>`
**Subject:** *LISTSERV ignores this*
`SUBSCRIBE vwar-l <firstname> <lastname>`

## World War II

**Resource:** LISTSERV
**Address:** `wwii-l@ubvm.cc.buffalo.edu`
This is the World War II discussion list. To subscribe, address a message in the
following manner:
**To:** `LISTSERV@ubvm.cc.buffalo.edu`
**From:** `<your address>`
**Subject:** *LISTSERV ignores this*
`SUBSCRIBE wwii-l <firstname> <lastname>`

# Hobbies

## Beer/Zymurgy

**Resource:** LISTSERV
**Address:** `beer-l@ua1vm.bitnet`
This is the homebrew digest distribution list. To subscribe, address a message
in the following manner:

**To:**      `LISTSERV@ua1vm`
**From:**   `<your address>`
**Subject:**  *LISTSERV ignores this*
`SUBSCRIBE beer-l <firstname> <lastname>`

**Resource:**  List
**Address:**   `homebrew%hpfcmr@hplabs.hp.com`
For the discussion and sharing of information related to zymurgy (beer brewing). Send your subscription request to `homebrew-request%hpfcmr@hplabs.hp.com`.


## Birds

**Resource:**  LISTSERV
**Address:**   `birdband@arizvm1.bitnet`
This is the bird bander's forum. To subscribe, address a message in the following manner:
**To:**      `LISTSERV@arizvm1.bitnet`
**From:**   `<your address>`
**Subject:**  *LISTSERV ignores this*
`SUBSCRIBE birdband <firstname> <lastname>`

**Resource:**  LISTSERV
**Address:**   `bird_rba@arizvm1.bitnet`
This is the national birding hotline cooperative. To subscribe, address a message in the following manner:
**To:**      `LISTSERV@arizvm1.bitnet`
**From:**   `<your address>`
**Subject:**  *LISTSERV ignores this*
`SUBSCRIBE bird_rba <firstname> <lastname>`


## Birdwatching

**Resource:**  LISTSERV
**Address:**   `birdeast@arizvm1.bitnet@cornellc.cit.cornell.edu`
National Birding Hotline Cooperative. This list is for the Eastern United States. To subscribe, address a message in the following manner:
**To:**      `LISTSERV@arizvm1.bitnet@cornellc.cit.cornell.edu`
**From:**   `<your address>`
**Subject:**  *LISTSERV ignores this*
`SUBSCRIBE birdeast <firstname> <lastname>`

**Resource:** LISTSERV
**Address:** `birdwest@arizvm1.bitnet`
This is the west branch of the national birding hotline cooperative. To subscribe, address a message in the following manner:
**To:** `LISTSERV@arizvm1.bitnet`
**From:** `<your address>`
**Subject:** *LISTSERV ignores this*
`SUBSCRIBE birdwest <firstname> <lastname>`

**Resource:** LISTSERV
**Address:** `birdeast@arizvm1.bitnet`
This is the east branch of the national birding hotline cooperative. To subscribe, address a message in the following manner:
**To:** `LISTSERV@arizvm1.bitnet`
**From:** `<your address>`
**Subject:** *LISTSERV ignores this*
`SUBSCRIBE birdeast <firstname> <lastname>`

**Resource:** LISTSERV
**Address:** `birdcntr@arizvm1.bitnet`
This is the central branch of the national birding hotline cooperative. To subscribe, address a message in the following manner:
**To:** `LISTSERV@arizvm1.bitnet`
**From:** `<your address>`
**Subject:** *LISTSERV ignores this*
`SUBSCRIBE birdcntr <firstname> <lastname>`

## Bonsai

**Resource:** LISTSERV
**Address:** `bonsai@cms.cc.wayne.edu`
This is for anyone interested in bonsai. To subscribe, address a message in the following manner:
**To:** `LISTSERV@cms.cc.wayne.edu`
**From:** `<your address>`
**Subject:** *LISTSERV ignores this*
`SUBSCRIBE bonsai <firstname> <lastname>`

## Books

**Resource:** LISTSERV
**Address:** `exlibris@rutgers.edu`
This is the forum for rare books and special collections. To subscribe, address a message in the following manner:

**To:**        `LISTSERV@rutgers.edu`
**From:**      `<your address>`
**Subject:**   *LISTSERV ignores this*
`SUBSCRIBE exlibris <firstname> <lastname>`

## Coin Collecting/Numismatics

**Resource:**  List
**Address:**   `coins@rocky.er.usgs.gov`
Send subscription requests and other administrative information to
`ROBERT@WHIPLASH.ER.USGS.GOV`.

## Comix

**Resource:**  List
**Address:**   `Comix@world.std.com`
Devoted to the discussion of nontraditional comix. Send your subscription
requests to `comix-request@world.std.com`.

## Dollhouses

**Resource:**  LISTSERV
**Address:**   `dollh-l@ferris.bitnet`
This list will be of interest to those involved in designing, building, and just
enjoying dollhouses. To subscribe, address a message in the following manner:
**To:**        `LISTSERV@ferris.bitnet`
**From:**      `<your address>`
**Subject:**   *LISTSERV ignores this*
`SUBSCRIBE dollh-l <firstname> <lastname>`

## Flowers/Gardens

**Resource:**  List
**Address:**   `orchids@scu.bitnet@cunyvm.cuny.edu`
For persons interested in growing orchids. Send the text `subscribe orchids` to
`mailserv%scu@cunyvm.cuny.edu`.

## Juggling

**Resource:**    List
**Address:**    Juggling@Moocow.Cogsci.Indiana.Edu
This list is for everyone who wants to juggle as a hobbyist or professional. An elaborate FAQ explains various techniques, terminology, how to obtain festival listings, vendor contact information, and how to retrieve juggling software. Send a message containing the command ADD to Juggling-Request@Moocow.Cogsci.Indiana.Edu.

## Kites

**Resource:**    List
**Address:**    Kites@Harvard.Harvard.Edu
This list is for anyone who flies or makes kites. Send your subscription request to kites-request@harvard.harvard.edu.

## Magic

**Resource:**    List
**Address:**    magic@maillist.crd.ge.com
Devoted to the subjects of illusion and sleight of hand, this list is for serious practitioners only. Send your request for a questionnaire to magic-request@mailllist.crd.ge.com.

## Mensa

**Resource:**    List
**Address:**    mensatalk@psg.com
This list is open to all Mensa members. Send your subscription request to mensatalk-request@psg.com.

## Motorcycles

**Resource:**    List
**Address:**    moto.chassis@oce.orst.edu
For persons interested in building and designing a motorcycle chassis. Send your subscription requests and related administrative information to moto.chassis-request@oce.orst.edu.

## Origami

**Resource:** List
**Address:** origami-l@nstn.ns.ca
For those interested in the exchange of information related to the art of origami (paper folding). Send your subscription request to origami-l-request@nstn.ns.ca.

## Paintball

**Resource:** LISTSERV
**Address:** paintbol@tcsvm.bitnet
This is the paintball discussion list. To subscribe, address a message in the following manner:
**To:** LISTSERV@tcsvm.bitnet
**From:** <your address>
**Subject:** *LISTSERV ignores this*
SUBSCRIBE paintbol <firstname> <lastname>

## Pen Pals

**Resource:** LISTSERV
**Address:** penpal-l@unccvm.bitnet
This is for anyone interested in pen pals. To subscribe, address a message in the following manner:
**To:** LISTSERV@unccvm.bitnet
**From:** <your address>
**Subject:** *LISTSERV ignores this*
SUBSCRIBE penpal-l <firstname> <lastname>

## Photography

**Resource:** List
**Address:** pinhole@mintir.fidonet.org
A discussion list for persons interested in all aspects of pinhole photography. Send your subscription requests to pinhole-request@mintir.fidonet.org.

**Resource:** LISTSERV
**Address:** photo-l@buacca.bu.edu
This is a general photography forum. To subscribe, address a message in the following manner:

| To: | LISTSERV@buacca.bu.edu |
|-----|------------------------|
| From: | <your address> |
| Subject: | *LISTSERV ignores this* |

SUBSCRIBE photo-l <firstname> <lastname>

## Postcards/Deltiology

**Resource:** LISTSERV

**Address:** postcard@idbsu.bitnet

For those interested in the world's third-most popular hobby! Discussions include history, finding others with similar interest areas, and exchanging. To subscribe, address a message in the following manner:

| To: | LISTSERV@idbsu.bitnet |
|-----|------------------------|
| From: | <your address> |
| Subject: | *LISTSERV ignores this* |

SUBSCRIBE postcard <firstname> <lastname>

## Quilting

**Resource:** LISTSERV

**Address:** quilt@cornell.edu

For persons interested in quilts: patterns, tips, mail-order houses, and stores. To subscribe, address a message in the following manner:

| To: | LISTSERV@cornell.edu |
|-----|------------------------|
| From: | <your address> |
| Subject: | *LISTSERV ignores this* |

SUBSCRIBE quilt <firstname> <lastname>

## Radio

**Resource:** LISTSERV

**Address:** swl$l@cuvmb.bitnet

This is the shortwave listener's list. To subscribe, address a message in the following manner:

| To: | LISTSERV@cuvmb.bitnet |
|-----|------------------------|
| From: | <your address> |
| Subject: | *LISTSERV ignores this* |

SUBSCRIBE swl$l <firstname> <lastname>

## Railroading

**Resource:**    LISTSERV
**Address:**    `railroad@cunyvm.cuny.edu`
This is a general list for those interested in railroading. To subscribe, address a
message in the following manner:
**To:**           `LISTSERV@cunyvm.cuny.edu`
**From:**        `<your address>`
**Subject:**    *LISTSERV ignores this*
`SUBSCRIBE railroad <firstname> <lastname>`

## Remote Control

**Resource:**    LISTSERV
**Address:**    `remote-l@suvm.bitnet`
This is a discussion group for those interested in remote control hobbies. To
subscribe, address a message in the following manner:
**To:**           `LISTSERV@suvm.bitnet`
**From:**        `<your address>`
**Subject:**    *LISTSERV ignores this*
`SUBSCRIBE remote-l <firstname> <lastname>`

## Sailing

**Resource:**    LISTSERV
**Address:**    `yacht-l@grearn.bitnet`
This list focuses on yachting, sailing, and amateur boatbuilding. To subscribe,
address a message in the following manner:
**To:**           `LISTSERV@grearn.bitnet`
**From:**        `<your address>`
**Subject:**    *LISTSERV ignores this*
`SUBSCRIBE yacht-l <firstname> <lastname>`

## Scouting

**Resource:**    LISTSERV
**Address:**    `scouts-l@tcubvm.bitnet`
This is the scouting and youth volunteer discussion forum. To subscribe,
address a message in the following manner:
**To:**           `LISTSERV@tcubvm.bitnet`
**From:**        `<your address>`
**Subject:**    *LISTSERV ignores this*
`SUBSCRIBE scouts-l <firstname> <lastname>`

## Scuba Diving

**Resource:** LISTSERV
**Address:** scuba-l@brownvm.brown.edu
This list is for anyone interested in scuba diving. To subscribe, address a message in the following manner:
**To:** LISTSERV@brownvm.brown.edu
**From:** <your address>
**Subject:** *LISTSERV ignores this*
SUBSCRIBE scuba-l <firstname> <lastname>

**Resource:** LISTSERV
**Address:** scuba-d@brownvm.brown.edu
This is a redistribution (digest) of the scuba-l LISTSERV. To subscribe, address a message in the following manner:
**To:** LISTSERV@brownvm.brown.edu
**From:** <your address>
**Subject:** *LISTSERV ignores this*
SUBSCRIBE scuba-d <firstname> <lastname>

## Smoking

**Resource:** List
**Address:** Pipes@Paul.Rutgers.Edu
This list is for anyone who enjoys smoking and collecting pipes and tobacco.
Send your subscription requests to pipes-request@paul.rutgers.edu.

## Sports Cards

**Resource:** List
**Address:** cards@tanstaafl.uchicago.edu
For persons interested in the collecting, trading, and speculating of baseball, football, and hockey cards. Send your subscription requests to cards-request@tanstaafl.uchicago.edu.

## Stamps/Philately

**Resource:** LISTSERV
**Address:** stamps@cunyvm.cuny.edu
This list is for those who appreciate and collect postage stamps. To subscribe, address a message in the following manner:
**To:** LISTSERV@cunyvm.cuny.edu
**From:** <your address>
**Subject:** *LISTSERV ignores this*
SUBSCRIBE stamps <firstname> <lastname>

## Ultralight Aircraft

**Resource:**   List
**Address:**   ultralight-flight@ms.uky.edu
For anyone interested in flying ultralight aircraft. All aspects, including the sharing of experiences and how-to, are fair game. Send your subscription request to ultralight-flight-request@ms.uky.edu with the command subscribe as the first word after **Subject:**.

## VHF Radio

**Resource:**   List
**Address:**   vhf@w6yx.stanford.edu
A discussion list devoted to VHF and amateur radio. Send your subscription requests to vhf-request@w6yx.stanford.edu.

## Woodworking

**Resource:**   LISTSERV
**Address:**   woodwork@ipfwvm.bitnet
Anyone interested in woodworking can find a home here. All information related to tools, techniques, methods, and plans are open for discussion. To subscribe, address a message in the following manner:
**To:**   LISTSERV@ipfwvm.bitnet
**From:**   <your address>
**Subject:**   *LISTSERV ignores this*
SUBSCRIBE woodwork <firstname> <lastname>

# Human Sexuality

### Bisexual Women

**Resource:**   LISTSERV
**Address:**   bifem-d@brownvm.brown.edu
This is the bisexual women's digest. To subscribe, address a message in the following manner:
**To:**   LISTSERV@brownvm.brown.edu
**From:**   <your address>
**Subject:**   *LISTSERV ignores this*
SUBSCRIBE bifem-d <firstname> <lastname>

**Resource:** LISTSERV
**Address:** `bifem-l@Brownvm.Brown.Edu`
This is the bisexual women's discussion list. To subscribe, address a message in the following manner:
**To:** `LISTSERV@Brownvm.Brown.Edu`
**From:** `<your address>`
**Subject:** *LISTSERV ignores this*
`SUBSCRIBE bifem-l <firstname> <lastname>`

## Bisexuality

**Resource:** LISTSERV
**Address:** `bisexu-l@brownvm.brown.edu`
This is an open forum devoted to the subject of bisexuality. To subscribe, address a message in the following manner:
**To:** `LISTSERV@brownvm.brown.edu`
**From:** `<your address>`
**Subject:** *LISTSERV ignores this*
`SUBSCRIBE bisexu-l <firstname> <lastname>`

**Resource:** LISTSERV
**Address:** `biact-l@brownvm.brown.edu`
This is the bisexual activist list. To subscribe, address a message in the following manner:
**To:** `LISTSERV@brownvm.brown.edu`
**From:** `<your address>`
**Subject:** *LISTSERV ignores this*
`SUBSCRIBE biact-l <firstname> <lastname>`

## Feminism

**Resource:** LISTSERV
**Address:** `FIST@hamp.hampshire.edu`
Feminism in Science and Technology discussion forum. To subscribe, address a message in the following manner:
**To:** `LISTSERV@hamp.hampshire.edu`
**From:** `<your address>`
**Subject:** *LISTSERV ignores this*
`SUBSCRIBE FIST <firstname> <lastname>`

**Resource:** LISTSERV
**Address:** `FEMINIST@mitvma.mit.edu`
ALA Féminist Task Force discussion. To subscribe, address a message in the following manner:

**To:** `LISTSERV@mitvma.mit.edu`
**From:** `<your address>`
**Subject:** *LISTSERV ignores this*
`SUBSCRIBE FEMINIST <firstname> <lastname>`


## Gay and Lesbian Issues

**Resource:** List
**Address:** `qn@queernet.org`
For those involved in the activities of Queer Nation. Send your subscription request to `qn-request@queernet.org`.

**Resource:** List
**Address:** `gaynet@athena.mit.edu`
A digest form list for the purpose of discussing gay and lesbian issues and concerns on college campuses. Send subscription requests to `gaynet-request@athena.mit.edu`.

**Resource:** LISTSERV
**Address:** `glb-news@brownvm.brown.edu`
A moderated, "blind" (the author's name is removed from the original message) discussion list for the exchange of information related to LesBiGay issues and news. To subscribe, address a message in the following manner:
**To:** `LISTSERV@brownvm.brown.edu`
**From:** `<your address>`
**Subject:** *LISTSERV ignores this*
`SUBSCRIBE glb-news <firstname> <lastname>`


## Men's Studies

**Resource:** List
**Address:** `mail-men@usl.com`
This list is dedicated to the male movement. Send your subscription requests to `mail-men-request@attunix.att.com`.


## QueerNet

**Resource:** FTP
**Address:** `nifty.andrew.cmu.edu`
**Directory:** `Pub/QRD/README`

## Research

**Resource:**    LISTSERV
**Address:**    `sssstalk@tamvm1.tamu.edu`
A discussion list for all persons involved in the research of human sexuality.
To subscribe, address a message in the following manner:
**To:**    `LISTSERV@tamvm1.tamu.edu`
**From:**    `<your address>`
**Subject:**    *LISTSERV ignores this*
`SUBSCRIBE sssstalk <firstname> <lastname>`

## Transsexual/Transvestite

**Resource:**    LISTSERV
**Address:**    `transgen@brownvm.brown.edu`
TS/TV/TG list. To subscribe, address a message in the following manner:
**To:**    `LISTSERV@brownvm.brown.edu`
**From:**    `<your address>`
**Subject:**    *LISTSERV ignores this*
`SUBSCRIBE transgen <firstname> <lastname>`

# Humor

## General

**Resource:**    LISTSERV
**Address:**    `nutworks@tcsvm.bitnet`
This is the nutworks distribution list. More jokes than you'll ever know what to
do with! To subscribe, address a message in the following manner:
**To:**    `LISTSERV@tcsvm.bitnet`
**From:**    `<your address>`
**Subject:**    *LISTSERV ignores this*
`SUBSCRIBE nutworks <firstname> <lastname>`

# Internet

## Archie

**Resource:**  telnet
**User id:**  Archie
**Address:**  Use one of the following addresses:
        `archie.ans.net`
        `archie.au`
        `archie.doc.ic.ac.uk`
        `archie.funet.fi`
        `archie.kuis.kyoto-u.ac.jp`
        `archie.luth.se`
        `archie.ncu.edu.tw`
        `archie.nz`
        `archie.rutgers.edu`
        `archie.sogang.ac.kr`
        `archie.sura.net`
        `archie.th-darmstadt.de`
        `archie.univie.ac.at`
        `archie.unl.edu`

## BBS

**Resource:**  telnet
**Address:**  `bbs.oit.unc.edu`
**User id:**  `bbs`
University of North Carolina "laUNChpad" BBS.

**Resource:**  telnet
**Address:**  `lambada.oit.unc.edu`
**User id:**  `bbs`
This is a "freenet" site. A menu-oriented system will direct you to a public USENET feed, electronic libraries, and so on.

## CARL

**Resource:**  telnet
**Address:**  `pac.carl.org`
**User id:**  `wais`

**Resource:**    telnet
**Address:**    `quake.think.com (192.31.181.1)`
**User id:**    `wais`

**Resource:**    LISTSERV
**Address:**    `carl-l@uhccvm`
CARL user information list. To subscribe, address a message in the following manner:
**To:**    `LISTSERV@uhccvm`
**From:**    `<your address>`
**Subject:**    *LISTSERV ignores this*
`SUBSCRIBE carl-l <firstname> <lastname>`

## Commercialization

**Resource:**    List
**Address:**    `com-priv@uu.psi.com`
An electronic list dedicated to the commercialization of the Internet. Send subscription requests to `COM-PRIV-REQUEST@UU.PSI.COM`.

## CompuServe Gateway

**Resource:**    telnet
**Address:**    `HERMES.MERIT.EDU`
When prompted for the system, specify `CIS`. This is a telnet gateway to CompuServe.

## CWIS

**Resource:**    telnet
**Address:**    `info.rutgers.edu`
**User id:**    `wais`

**Resource:**    FTP
**Address:**    `ftp.oit.unc.edu`
**Directory:**    `pub/docs/cwis-1`

## Electronic Journals

**Resource:**    FTP
**Address:**    `ftp.eff.org`
**Directory:**    `/pub/journals`

## Freenet

**Resource:** telnet
**Address:** yfn.ysu.edu
**User id:** visitor
This is the Youngstown Freenet/Electronic Village.

**Resource:** telnet
**Address:** freenet.scri.fsu.edu
**User id:** visitor
This is the Tallahassee Freenet/Electronic Village.

**Resource:** telnet
**Address:** FREENET.HSC.COLORADO.EDU
Telnet to the electronic version of the city of Denver.

## FTP

**Resource:** FTP
**Address:** pilot.njin.net
Retrieve the file /ftp.list.

## FTPmail

**Resource:** e-mail
**Address:** FTPMAIL@decwrl.dec.com
Send a message containing the word HELP for full instructions.

## Fun

**Resource:** FTP
**Address:** cerberus.cor.epa.gov
**Directory:** /pub/bigfun

## Gopher—Telnet

Note: Telnet to these locations when you don't have your own Gopher software:

> ux1.cso.uiuc.edu (userid: gopher)
> consultant.micro.umn.edu
> panda.uiowa.edu
> gdunix.gd.chalmers.se
> gopher.uiuc.edu
> gopher.unt.edu

```
tolten.puc.cl
wsuaix.csc.wsu.edu (Login: wsuinfo)
una.hh.lib.um1mich.edu
harpoon.cso.uiuc.edu (Login: gopher)
```

## Gopher—List of Gopher Sites

**Resource:**  FTP
**Address:**  `liberty.uc.wlu.edu`
**Directory:**  `/pub/lawlib`
Retrieve the file `veronica.gopher.sites`.

## Hytelnet

**Resource:**  telnet
**Address:**  `info.anu.edu.au`
**User id:**  `hytelnet`

**Resource:**  telnet
**Address:**  `access.usask.ca`
**User id:**  `hytelnet`

**Resource:**  FTP
**Address:**  `access.usask.ca`
**Directory:**  `pub/hytelnet`

**Resource:**  LISTSERV
**Address:**  `hytel-l@kentvm.bitnet`
Hytelnet updates distribution. To subscribe, address a message in the following manner:
**To:**  `LISTSERV@kentvm.bitnet`
**From:**  `<your address>`
**Subject:**  *LISTSERV ignores this*
`SUBSCRIBE hytel-l <firstname> <lastname>`

**Resource:**  telnet
**Address:**  `laguna.epcc.edu`
**User id:**  `library`

## Indexes/How-To

**Resource:**  LISTSERV
**Address:**  `ann-lots@vm1.nodak.edu`
Indexing forum for annotated lists of things. To subscribe, address a message in the following manner:

| **To:** | LISTSERV@vm1.nodak.edu |
|---|---|
| **From:** | \<your address\> |
| **Subject:** | *LISTSERV ignores this* |

SUBSCRIBE ann-lots \<firstname\> \<lastname\>

## Internet

| **Resource:** | FTP |
|---|---|
| **Address:** | nic.merit.edu |
| **Directory:** | documents/rfc |

Retrieve the file `rfc1394.txt`.

## Internet Info/Doc

| **Resource:** | FTP |
|---|---|
| **Address:** | pit-manager.mit.edu |

Text files of frequently asked questions, from *artifical intelligence* to *z-faq*. Over 275 subjects.

## Link Failures

| **Resource:** | LISTSERV |
|---|---|
| **Address:** | linkfail@uga.cc.uga.edu |

This list posts "downed" network sites. To subscribe, address a message in the following manner:

| **To:** | LISTSERV@uga.cc.uga.edu |
|---|---|
| **From:** | \<your address\> |
| **Subject:** | *LISTSERV ignores this* |

SUBSCRIBE linkfail \<firstname\> \<lastname\>

## List Management

| **Resource:** | List |
|---|---|
| **Address:** | list-managers@greatcircle.com |

A discussion group devoted to the management of mailing lists. Send the text `subscribe list-managers` in an e-mail message to `majordomo@greatcircle.com`.

## List Ownership

**Resource:**   LISTSERV
**Address:**   `listownl@indycms.iupui.edu`
This list is for anyone involved in creating, supporting, or moderating a
LISTSERV list. To subscribe, address a message in the following manner:
**To:**   `LISTSERV@indycms.iupui.edu`
**From:**   `<your address>`
**Subject:**   *LISTSERV ignores this*
`SUBSCRIBE listownl <firstname> <lastname>`

## List of Lists

**Resource:**   FTP
**Address:**   `ftp.nisc.sri.com`
**Directory:**   `netinfo`
Retrieve `interest-groups`.

## Lists

**Resource:**   LISTSERV
**Address:**   `new-list@vm1.nodak.edu`
New list announcements are generally made here. This is also a good place to
inquire about the existence of lists.
**To:**   `LISTSERV@vm1.nodak.edu`
**From:**   `<your address>`
**Subject:**   *LISTSERV ignores this*
`SUBSCRIBE new-list <firstname> <lastname>`

## MUDs

**Resource:**   FTP
**Address:**   `caisr2.caisr.cwru.edu`
**Directory:**   `/pub/mud`

## Navigating

**Resource:**   LISTSERV
**Address:**   `navigate@ubvm.cc.buffalo.edu`
Navigating the Internet workshop list. To subscribe, address a message in the
following manner:

**To:**        LISTSERV@ubvm.cc.buffalo.edu
**From:**      <your address>
**Subject:**   *LISTSERV ignores this*
SUBSCRIBE navigate <firstname> <lastname>

**Resource:**   LISTSERV
**Address:**    k12nav-l@kentvm.bitnet
This discussion list is for K-12 educators investigating Internet navigation. To subscribe, address a message in the following manner:
**To:**        LISTSERV@kentvm.bitnet
**From:**      <your address>
**Subject:**   *LISTSERV ignores this*
SUBSCRIBE k12nav-l <firstname> <lastname>

**Resource:**   LISTSERV
**Address:**    k12nav-n@kentvm.bitnet
This is the Internet navigation course for K-12 educators. To subscribe, address a message in the following manner:
**To:**        LISTSERV@kentvm.bitnet
**From:**      <your address>
**Subject:**   *LISTSERV ignores this*
SUBSCRIBE k12nav-n <firstname> <lastname>

## Project Gutenberg

**Resource:**   LISTSERV
**Address:**    gutnberg@vmd.cso.uiuc.edu
Project Gutenberg e-mail list. To subscribe, address a message in the following manner:
**To:**        LISTSERV@vmd.cso.uiuc.edu
**From:**      <your address>
**Subject:**   *LISTSERV ignores this*
SUBSCRIBE gutnberg <firstname> <lastname>

**Resource:**   FTP
**Address:**    MRCNEXT.CSO.UIUC.EDU

**Resource:**   FTP
**Address:**    mrcnext.cso.uiuc.edu
**Directory:**   /pub/etext

## Public Access

**Resource:** FTP
**Address:** nnsc.nsf.net
**Directory:** nsfnet
Retrieve the file nixpub.

## Public USENET

**Resource:** telnet
**Address:** tolten.puc.cl

## Resources

**Resource:** telnet
**Address:** stis.nsf.gov
**User id:** public

## USENET

**Resource:** telnet
**Address:** suntan.ec.usf.edu 119
Retrieve the file maps.

**Resource:** FTP
**Address:** pit-manager.mit.edu
**Directory:** pub/usenet

**Resource:** FTP
**Address:** ftp.uu.net
**Directory:** uunet-info

**Resource:** FTP
**Address:** gator.netcom.com
**Directory:** /pub/profile

**Resource:** FTP
**Address:** pit-manager.mit.edu [18.172.1.27]
**Directory:** /pub/usenet/news.answers/news-answers
Retrieve the file introduction.

**Resource:** telnet
**Address:** vaxc.cc.monash.edu.au 119

**Resource:** FTP
**Address:** ftp.netcom.com
**Directory:** /pub/profile
Retrieve the file ftp-list.

**Resource:** telnet
**Address:** m-net.ann-arbor.mi.us
When prompted for **Which host:**, enter um-m-net. Enter g for guest.
**Login:** newuser

**Resource:** telnet
**Address:** hermes.merit.edu

**Resource:** telnet
**Address:** quip.eecs.umich.edu 119

**Resource:** telnet
**Address:** nyx.cs.du.edu
**User id:** new

## USENET—Maps

**Resource:** FTP
**Address:** gatekeeper.dec.com
**Directory:** /pub

## USENET Search

**Resource:** telnet
**Address:** mudhoney.micro.umn.edu

## Utilities

**Resource:** telnet
**Address:** wugate.wustl.edu
**Userid:** services

## Veronica

**Resource:** FTP
**Address:** cs.dal.ca
**Directory:** pub/comp.archives/bionet.software
Retrieve the file veronica.

## WAIS

**Resource:** telnet
**Address:** nnsc.nsf.net
**User id:** wais

**Resource:** FTP
**Address:** julian.uwo.ca
**Directory:** doc/wais

**Resource:** FTP
**Address:** think.com
**Directory:** wais

**Resource:** telnet
**Address:** info.funet.fi
**User id:** info

**Resource:** telnet
**Address:** swais.cwis.uci.edu
**User id:** swais

**Resource:** telnet
**Address:** sunsite.unc.edu
**User id:** swais

## Whois

**Resource:** FTP
**Address:** sipb.mit.edu
**Directory:** /pub/whois
Retrieve the file whois-servers.list.

## World-Wide Web (WWW)

**Resource:** telnet
**Address:** nxoc01.cern.ch

**Resource:** telnet
**Address:** ukanaix.cc.ukans.edu
**User id:** www

**Resource:** telnet
**Address:** fatty.law.cornell.edu
**User id:** www

**Resource:** FTP
**Address:** `info.cem.ch`
**Directory:** `pub/www/doc`
Retrieve the file `the_www_book`.

# Journalism

## Editing

**Resource:** LISTSERV
**Address:** `copyediting-l@cornell.edu`
This list is for anyone involved in the copyediting process. To subscribe, address a message in the following manner:
**To:** `LISTSERV@cornell.edu`
**From:** `<your address>`
**Subject:** *LISTSERV ignores this*
`SUBSCRIBE copyediting-l <firstname> <lastname>`

# Languages

## Esperanto

**Resource:** LISTSERV
**Address:** `esper-l@trearn.bitnet@cunyvm.cuny.edu`
A discussion group about the language Esperanto. To subscribe, address a message in the following manner:
**To:** `LISTSERV@trearn.bitnet@cunyvm.cuny.edu`
**From:** `<your address>`
**Subject:** *LISTSERV ignores this*
`SUBSCRIBE esper-l <firstname> <lastname>`

**Resource:** List
**Address:** `esperanto@lll-crg.llnl.gov`
A discussion list devoted to the language Esperanto, gatewayed to the USENET group `mail.esperanto`.

## Gaelic

**Resource:** LISTSERV
**Address:** GAELIC-L@irlearn.ucd.ie
A discussion of the Gaelic (Irish) language. To subscribe, address a message in the following manner:
**To:** LISTSERV@irlearn.ucd.ie
**From:** <your address>
**Subject:** *LISTSERV ignores this*
SUBSCRIBE GAELIC-L <firstname> <lastname>

## General

**Resource:** LISTSERV
**Address:** linguist@tamvm1.tamu.edu
This list is for everyone involved in the research of linguistics. To subscribe, address a message in the following manner:
**To:** LISTSERV@tamvm1.tamu.edu
**From:** <your address>
**Subject:** *LISTSERV ignores this*
SUBSCRIBE linguist <firstname> <lastname>

## Iroquois

**Resource:** LISTSERV
**Address:** iroquois@utoronto.bitnet
This list is for the discussion and exchange of ideas about the Iroquois language. To subscribe, address a message in the following manner:
**To:** LISTSERV@utoronto.bitnet
**From:** <your address>
**Subject:** *LISTSERV ignores this*
SUBSCRIBE iroquois <firstname> <lastname>

## Japanese

**Resource:** LISTSERV
**Address:** nihongo@mitvma.mit.edu
This is the Japanese language discussion list. To subscribe, address a message in the following manner:
**To:** LISTSERV@mitvma.mit.edu
**From:** <your address>
**Subject:** *LISTSERV ignores this*
SUBSCRIBE nihongo <firstname> <lastname>

## Latin

**Resource:**   LISTSERV
**Address:**    `latin-l@psuvm.psu.edu`
This list is devoted to Latin and Neo-Latin. To subscribe, address a message in the following manner:

**To:**    `LISTSERV@psuvm.psu.edu`
**From:**   `<your address>`
**Subject:**  *LISTSERV ignores this*
`SUBSCRIBE latin-l <firstname> <lastname>`

## Loglan

**Resource:**   List
**Address:**    `lojban-list@snark.thyrsus.com`
For supporters of the language Loglan. Send your subscription request to `lojban-list-request@snark.thyrsus.com`.

## Older Germanic

**Resource:**   LISTSERV
**Address:**    `GERLINGL@cso.uiuc.edu`
This list discusses and researches older (to 1500) Germanic languages. To subscribe, address a message in the following manner:

**To:**    `LISTSERV@cso.uiuc.edu`
**From:**   `<your address>`
**Subject:**  *LISTSERV ignores this*
`SUBSCRIBE GERLINGL <firstname> <lastname>`

## Russian

**Resource:**   LISTSERV
**Address:**    `russian@asuacad.bitnet`
This is the Russian language discussion forum. To subscribe, address a message in the following manner:

**To:**    `LISTSERV@asuacad.bitnet`
**From:**   `<your address>`
**Subject:**  *LISTSERV ignores this*
`SUBSCRIBE russian <firstname> <lastname>`

## Sign Language

**Resource:**    LISTSERV
**Address:**    `slling-l@yalevm.ycc.yale.edu`
This is the sign language list. To subscribe, address a message in the following manner:
**To:**    `LISTSERV@yalevm.ycc.yale.edu`
**From:**    `<your address>`
**Subject:**    *LISTSERV ignores this*
`SUBSCRIBE slling-l <firstname> <lastname>`

## Swahili

**Resource:**    LISTSERV
**Address:**    `SWAHILI-L@macc.wisc.edu`
Readers and writers of Kiswahili. To subscribe, address a message in the following manner:
**To:**    `LISTSERV@macc.wisc.edu`
**From:**    `<your address>`
**Subject:**    *LISTSERV ignores this*
`SUBSCRIBE SWAHILI-L <firstname> <lastname>`

## Telugu

**Resource:**    LISTSERV
**Address:**    `TELUGU@vm1.nodak.edu`
Telegu (Andhra Pradesh) language and culture. To subscribe, address a message in the following manner:
**To:**    `LISTSERV@vm1.nodak.edu`
**From:**    `<your address>`
**Subject:**    *LISTSERV ignores this*
`SUBSCRIBE TELUGU <firstname> <lastname>`

## Welsh

**Resource:**    LISTSERV
**Address:**    `WELSH-L@irlearn.ucd.ie`
Welsh language bulletin board (bilingual). To subscribe, address a message in the following manner:
**To:**    `LISTSERV@irlearn.ucd.ie`
**From:**    `<your address>`
**Subject:**    *LISTSERV ignores this*
`SUBSCRIBE WELSH-L <firstname> <lastname>`

## Yiddish

**Resource:**   List
**Address:**   mail.yiddish@dave@lsuc.on.ca
For those interested in the Yiddish language. Send your subscription request to
dave@lsuc.on.ca.

**Resource:**   LISTSERV
**Address:**   Mendele@yalevm.ycc.yale.edu
For the discussion of the Yiddish language. To subscribe, address a message in
the following manner:
**To:**   LISTSERV@yalevm.ycc.yale.edu
**From:**   <your address>
**Subject:**   *LISTSERV ignores this*
SUBSCRIBE Mendele <firstname> <lastname>

# Legal

## Criminal Justice

**Resource:**   LISTSERV
**Address:**   cjust-l@cunyvm.cuny.edu
Criminal justice discussion list. To subscribe, address a message in the follow-
ing manner:
**To:**   LISTSERV@cunyvm.cuny.edu
**From:**   <your address>
**Subject:**   *LISTSERV ignores this*
SUBSCRIBE cjust-l <firstname> <lastname>

# Literature

## American Literature

**Resource:**   LISTSERV
**Address:**   amlit-l@umcvmb.missouri.edu
This list was created for the exchange of ideas, opinions, and information
related to American Literature. To subscribe, address a message in the follow-
ing manner:
**To:**   LISTSERV@umcvmb.missouri.edu
**From:**   <your address>
**Subject:**   *LISTSERV ignores this*
SUBSCRIBE amlit-l <firstname> <lastname>

## Asimov, Isaac

**Resource:**   LISTSERV
**Address:**    `asimov-l@utdallas.bitnet`
Discussion of Isaac Asimov's works. To subscribe, address a message in the following manner:
**To:**         `LISTSERV@utdallas.bitnet`
**From:**       `<your address>`
**Subject:**    *LISTSERV ignores this*
`SUBSCRIBE asimov-l <firstname> <lastname>`

## Austen, Jane

**Resource:**   LISTSERV
**Address:**    `austen-l@vm1.mcgill.ca`
Jane Austen discussion list. To subscribe, address a message in the following manner:
**To:**         `LISTSERV@vm1.mcgill.ca`
**From:**       `<your address>`
**Subject:**    *LISTSERV ignores this*
`SUBSCRIBE austen-l <firstname> <lastname>`

## Chicano

**Resource:**   LISTSERV
**Address:**    `chicle@unmvma.bitnet`
Chicano literature discussion list. To subscribe, address a message in the following manner:
**To:**         `LISTSERV@unmvma.bitnet`
**From:**       `<your address>`
**Subject:**    *LISTSERV ignores this*
`SUBSCRIBE chicle <firstname> <lastname>`

## Children

**Resource:**   LISTSERV
**Address:**    `kidlit-l@bingvmb.bitnet`
Children and youth literature list. To subscribe, address a message in the following manner:
**To:**         `LISTSERV@bingvmb.bitnet`
**From:**       `<your address>`
**Subject:**    *LISTSERV ignores this*
`SUBSCRIBE kidlit-l <firstname> <lastname>`

## Chinese Poetry

**Resource:**   LISTSERV
**Address:**   `chpoem-l@ubvm.cc.buffalo.edu`
Chinese poem exchange and discussion list. To subscribe, address a message in the following manner:
**To:**   `LISTSERV@ubvm.cc.buffalo.edu`
**From:**   `<your address>`
**Subject:**   *LISTSERV ignores this*
`SUBSCRIBE chpoem-l <firstname> <lastname>`

## Classics

**Resource:**   LISTSERV
**Address:**   `classics@uwavm.bitnet`
Classical Greek and Latin discussion group. To subscribe, address a message in the following manner:
**To:**   `LISTSERV@uwavm.bitnet`
**From:**   `<your address>`
**Subject:**   *LISTSERV ignores this*
`SUBSCRIBE classics <firstname> <lastname>`

## Comic Writing

**Resource:**   LISTSERV
**Address:**   `comicw-l@unlvm.bitnet`
Workshop for comic writers. To subscribe, address a message in the following manner:
**To:**   `LISTSERV@unlvm.bitnet`
**From:**   `<your address>`
**Subject:**   *LISTSERV ignores this*
`SUBSCRIBE comicw-l <firstname> <lastname>`

## Comics

**Resource:**   LISTSERV
**Address:**   `comics-l@unlvm.bitnet`
Comics discussion list. To subscribe, address a message in the following manner:
**To:**   `LISTSERV@unlvm.bitnet`
**From:**   `<your address>`
**Subject:**   *LISTSERV ignores this*
`SUBSCRIBE comics-l <firstname> <lastname>`

## Dickens, Charles

**Resource:** LISTSERV
**Address:** dickns-l@ucsbvm.bitnet
Charles Dickens forum. To subscribe, address a message in the following manner:
**To:** LISTSERV@ucsbvm.bitnet
**From:** <your address>
**Subject:** *LISTSERV ignores this*
SUBSCRIBE dickns-l <firstname> <lastname>

## Disney Comics

**Resource:** List
**Address:** Disney-Comics@Student.Docs.Uu.Se
A discussion group devoted to Disney comics. Send your subscription requests to disney-comics-request@student.docs.uu.se.

## Electronic

**Resource:** telnet
**Address:** bbs.oit.unc.edu
**User id:** bbs

## Fiction

**Resource:** LISTSERV
**Address:** vampyres@guvm.bitnet
Vampiric lore, fact and fiction. To subscribe, address a message in the following manner:
**To:** LISTSERV@guvm.bitnet
**From:** <your address>
**Subject:** *LISTSERV ignores this*
SUBSCRIBE vampyres <firstname> <lastname>

## Finnegans Wake

**Resource:** LISTSERV
**Address:** fwaken-l@irlearn.ucd.ie
*Finnegans Wake* - textual notes. To subscribe, address a message in the following manner:

| **To:** | LISTSERV@irlearn.ucd.ie |
|---|---|
| **From:** | <your address> |
| **Subject:** | *LISTSERV ignores this* |

SUBSCRIBE fwaken-l <firstname> <lastname>

## King Arthur/Camelot

**Resource:** List
**Address:** camelot@castle.ed.ac.uk
For the discussion of King Arthur and the Holy Grail. Send your subscription requests to camelot-request@castle.ed.ac.uk.

## Magazines

**Resource:** LISTSERV
**Address:** magazine@rpitsvm.bitnet
Magazines. To subscribe, address a message in the following manner:

| **To:** | LISTSERV@rpitsvm.bitnet |
|---|---|
| **From:** | <your address> |
| **Subject:** | *LISTSERV ignores this* |

SUBSCRIBE magazine <firstname> <lastname>

## Medieval English

**Resource:** LISTSERV
**Address:** chaucer@unlinfo.unl.edu
Medieval English literature and culture (1100-1500). To subscribe, address a message in the following manner:

| **To:** | LISTSERV@unlinfo.unl.edu |
|---|---|
| **From:** | <your address> |
| **Subject:** | *LISTSERV ignores this* |

SUBSCRIBE chaucer <firstname> <lastname>

## Mystery

**Resource:** LISTSERV
**Address:** dorothyl@kentvm.Kent.Edu
This is a mystery literature electronic conference. To subscribe, address a message in the following manner:

| **To:** | LISTSERV@kentvm.Kent.Edu |
|---|---|
| **From:** | <your address> |
| **Subject:** | *LISTSERV ignores this* |

SUBSCRIBE dorothyl <firstname> <lastname>

## Nabokov, Vladimir

**Resource:** LISTSERV
**Address:** `nabokv-l@ucsbvm.bitnet`
This list discusses the life and works of Vladimir Nabokov. To subscribe, address a message in the following manner:
**To:** `LISTSERV@ucsbvm.bitnet`
**From:** `<your address>`
**Subject:** *LISTSERV ignores this*
`SUBSCRIBE nabokv-l <firstname> <lastname>`

## Online Books

**Resource:** FTP
**Address:** `wiretap.spies.com`

## Poetry

**Resource:** LISTSERV
**Address:** `poet@scruz.ucsc.edu`
This is a works-in-progress list. This means that you can submit your poems and receive feedback, as well as critique the work of others. Send your subscription request to `poet-request@scruz.ucsc.edu`. To subscribe, address a message in the following manner:
**To:** `LISTSERV@scruz.ucsc.edu`
**From:** `<your address>`
**Subject:** *LISTSERV ignores this*
`SUBSCRIBE poet <firstname> <lastname>`

**Resource:** LISTSERV
**Address:** `e-poetry@ubvm.cc.buffalo.edu`
Electronic poetry distribution list. To subscribe, address a message in the following manner:
**To:** `LISTSERV@ubvm.cc.buffalo.edu`
**From:** `<your address>`
**Subject:** *LISTSERV ignores this*
`SUBSCRIBE e-poetry <firstname> <lastname>`

## Robin Hood

**Resource:** FTP
**Address:** `rtfm.mit.edu`
**Directory:** `/pub/usenet/news.answers/books`
Retrieve the file `robin-hood`.

## Romance

**Resource:**    LISTSERV
**Address:**    `rra-l@kentvm.kent.edu`
For everyone (open and closeted) interested in romance novels. To subscribe, address a message in the following manner:

**To:**    `LISTSERV@kentvm.kent.edu`
**From:**    `<your address>`
**Subject:**    *LISTSERV ignores this*
`SUBSCRIBE rra-l <firstname> <lastname>`

## Science Fiction

**Resource:**    LISTSERV
**Address:**    `sf-lovers@rutgers.edu`
This is a list gatewayed to the USENET. Science fiction fans flock here to exchange information about forthcoming books, magazines, conventions, television shows, movies, and "spoilers." The FTP archives have nearly every message posted since 1980 and a collection of author lists, which contain a list of known works by that author. To subscribe, address a message in the following manner:

**To:**    `LISTSERV@rutgers.edu`
**From:**    `<your address>`
**Subject:**    *LISTSERV ignores this*
`SUBSCRIBE sf-lovers <firstname> <lastname>`

**Resource:**    List
**Address:**    `quanta@andrew.cmu.edu`
An e-magazine devoted to the science fiction genre. Send your subscription request to `quanta+request-ascii@andrew.cmu.edu`.

## Screenwriting

**Resource:**    LISTSERV
**Address:**    `scrnwrit@tamvm1.tamu.edu`
For people interested in screenwriting for television or movies. Anything related to this challenging industry is fair game! To subscribe, address a message in the following manner:

**To:**    `LISTSERV@tamvm1.tamu.edu`
**From:**    `<your address>`
**Subject:**    *LISTSERV ignores this*
`SUBSCRIBE scrnwrit <firstname> <lastname>`

## Shakespeare

**Resource:**     LISTSERV
**Address:**     shaksper@utoronto.bitnet
Shakespeare electronic conference. To subscribe, address a message in the following manner:
**To:**          LISTSERV@utoronto.bitnet
**From:**        <your address>
**Subject:**     *LISTSERV ignores this*
SUBSCRIBE shaksper <firstname> <lastname>

## Technical Writing

**Resource:**     LISTSERV
**Address:**     techwr-l@vm1.ucc.okstate.edu
For anyone involved in technical writing and technical communications, including documentation and specifications. To subscribe, address a message in the following manner:
**To:**          LISTSERV@vm1.ucc.okstate.edu
**From:**        <your address>
**Subject:**     *LISTSERV ignores this*
SUBSCRIBE techwr-l <firstname> <lastname>

## Tolkien, J.R.R.

**Resource:**     LISTSERV
**Address:**     tolkien@jhuvm.bitnet
This is for all fans who wish to discuss the literary works of J.R.R. Tolkien. To subscribe, address a message in the following manner:
**To:**          LISTSERV@jhuvm.bitnet
**From:**        <your address>
**Subject:**     *LISTSERV ignores this*
SUBSCRIBE tolkien <firstname> <lastname>

## Twain, Mark

**Resource:**     LISTSERV
**Address:**     twain-l@vm1.yorku.ca
This is the Mark Twain/Samuel Clemens forum. To subscribe, address a message in the following manner:
**To:**          LISTSERV@vm1.yorku.ca
**From:**        <your address>
**Subject:**     *LISTSERV ignores this*
SUBSCRIBE twain-l <firstname> <lastname>

## Writing/Fiction

**Resource:** List
**Address:** fiction-writers@studguppy@lanl.gov
For the exchange and support of issues related to persons interested in writing fiction. Also an arena where works in progress can be distributed for feedback. Submit subscription requests to fiction-writers-request%studguppy@lanl.gov.

**Resource:** LISTSERV
**Address:** fiction@psuvm.psu.edu
Fiction writers' workshop. To subscribe, address a message in the following manner:
**To:** LISTSERV@psuvm.psu.edu
**From:** <your address>
**Subject:** *LISTSERV ignores this*
SUBSCRIBE fiction <firstname> <lastname>

# Medicine

## AIDS

**Resource:** LISTSERV
**Address:** aids@wuvmd.bitnet
Sci.med.aids newsgroup. To subscribe, address a message in the following manner:
**To:** LISTSERV@wuvmd.bitnet
**From:** <your address>
**Subject:** *LISTSERV ignores this*
SUBSCRIBE aids <firstname> <lastname>

**Resource:** LISTSERV
**Address:** aids@rutgers.edu
This list is gatewayed to the USENET group sci.med.aids. To subscribe, address a message in the following manner:
**To:** LISTSERV@rutgers.edu
**From:** <your address>
**Subject:** *LISTSERV ignores this*
SUBSCRIBE aids <firstname> <lastname>

**Resource:**    LISTSERV
**Address:**    aidsbkrv@UICVM.uic.cc.edu
This is an AIDS book review forum. To subscribe, address a message in the following manner:
**To:**    LISTSERV@UICVM.uic.cc.edu
**From:**    <your address>
**Subject:**    *LISTSERV ignores this*
SUBSCRIBE aidsbkrv <firstname> <lastname>

## Anesthesiology

**Resource:**    LISTSERV
**Address:**    anest-1@ubvm.cc.buffalo.edu
Anesthesiology discussion list. To subscribe, address a message in the following manner:
**To:**    LISTSERV@ubvm.cc.buffalo.edu
**From:**    <your address>
**Subject:**    *LISTSERV ignores this*
SUBSCRIBE anest-1 <firstname> <lastname>

## Back Pain

**Resource:**    LISTSERV
**Address:**    backs-1@uvmvm.uvm.edu
This list is for the exchange of information on lower back pain and related disabilities. To subscribe, address a message in the following manner:
**To:**    LISTSERV@uvmvm.uvm.edu
**From:**    <your address>
**Subject:**    *LISTSERV ignores this*
SUBSCRIBE backs-1 <firstname> <lastname>

## Brain Tumors

**Resource:**    LISTSERV
**Address:**    braintmr@mitvma.mit.edu
This list was created to exchange brain tumor research and support information. To subscribe, address a message in the following manner:
**To:**    LISTSERV@mitvma.mit.edu
**From:**    <your address>
**Subject:**    *LISTSERV ignores this*
SUBSCRIBE braintmr <firstname> <lastname>

## Fitness

**Resource:**   LISTSERV
**Address:**   `fit-l@etsuadmn.etsu.edu`
This is an exercise, diet, and wellness discussion list. To subscribe, address a message in the following manner:
**To:**   `LISTSERV@etsuadmn.etsu.edu`
**From:**   `<your address>`
**Subject:**   *LISTSERV ignores this*
`SUBSCRIBE fit-l <firstname> <lastname>`


## Free Radicals

**Resource:**   LISTSERV
**Address:**   `oxygen-l@mizzou1.bitnet`
This list discusses oxygen-free radical biology and medicine. To subscribe, address a message in the following manner:
**To:**   `LISTSERV@mizzou1.bitnet`
**From:**   `<your address>`
**Subject:**   *LISTSERV ignores this*
`SUBSCRIBE oxygen-l <firstname> <lastname>`


## Holistic

**Resource:**   LISTSERV
**Address:**   `herb@trearn.bitnet`
Medicinal and aromatic plants discussion list. To subscribe, address a message in the following manner:
**To:**   `LISTSERV@trearn.bitnet`
**From:**   `<your address>`
**Subject:**   *LISTSERV ignores this*
`SUBSCRIBE herb <firstname> <lastname>`

**Resource:**   LISTSERV
**Address:**   `holistic@siucvmb.bitnet`
This discussion list exchanges information about holistic medicine and practices. To subscribe, address a message in the following manner:
**To:**   `LISTSERV@siucvmb.bitnet`
**From:**   `<your address>`
**Subject:**   *LISTSERV ignores this*
`SUBSCRIBE holistic <firstname> <lastname>`

## Hyperbaric

**Resource:**  LISTSERV
**Address:**  hypbar-l@technion.technion.ac.il
This list is for hyperbaric and diving medicine research and information exchange. To subscribe, address a message in the following manner:
**To:**  LISTSERV@technion.technion.ac.il
**From:**  <your address>
**Subject:**  *LISTSERV ignores this*
SUBSCRIBE hypbar-l <firstname> <lastname>

## Immune Disorders

**Resource:**  List
**Address:**  immune@weber.ucsd.edu
A discussion list for persons whose lives are affected by immune disorders. Send your subscription requests to immune-request@weber.ucsd.edu.

## Ingestive Disorders

**Resource:**  LISTSERV
**Address:**  ingest@cuvmb.bitnet
This list is for persons with ingestive disorders. To subscribe, address a message in the following manner:
**To:**  LISTSERV@cuvmb.bitnet
**From:**  <your address>
**Subject:**  *LISTSERV ignores this*
SUBSCRIBE ingest <firstname> <lastname>

## Laser

**Resource:**  LISTSERV
**Address:**  lasmed-l@taunivm.tau.ac.il
Laser medicine. To subscribe, address a message in the following manner:
**To:**  LISTSERV@taunivm.tau.ac.il
**From:**  <your address>
**Subject:**  *LISTSERV ignores this*
SUBSCRIBE lasmed-l <firstname> <lastname>

## Lyme Disease

**Resource:**    LISTSERV
**Address:**    `lymenet-1@lehigh.edu`
For the discussion of Lyme Disease, including current treatment, research, and information related to its spread. To subscribe, address a message in the following manner:
**To:**    `LISTSERV@lehigh.edu`
**From:**    `<your address>`
**Subject:**    *LISTSERV ignores this*
`SUBSCRIBE lymenet-1 <firstname> <lastname>`

## Medical Imaging

**Resource:**    LISTSERV
**Address:**    `medimage@polyvm.bitnet`
Medical imaging discussion list. To subscribe, address a message in the following manner:
**To:**    `LISTSERV@polyvm.bitnet`
**From:**    `<your address>`
**Subject:**    *LISTSERV ignores this*
`SUBSCRIBE medimage <firstname> <lastname>`

## Medical Students

**Resource:**    LISTSERV
**Address:**    `medstu-1@unmvma.bitnet`
This list is where medical students can exchange ideas, experiences, and general information. To subscribe, address a message in the following manner:
**To:**    `LISTSERV@unmvma.bitnet`
**From:**    `<your address>`
**Subject:**    *LISTSERV ignores this*
`SUBSCRIBE medstu-1 <firstname> <lastname>`

## Mind-Brain

**Resource:**    LISTSERV
**Address:**    `brain-1@mcgill1.bitnet`
Mind-brain discussion group. To subscribe, address a message in the following manner:
**To:**    `LISTSERV@mcgill1.bitnet`
**From:**    `<your address>`
**Subject:**    *LISTSERV ignores this*
`SUBSCRIBE brain-1 <firstname> <lastname>`

## Motor Skills

**Resource:**   LISTSERV
**Address:**   `motordev@umdd.bitnet`
Human motor skill development list. To subscribe, address a message in the following manner:

**To:**   `LISTSERV@umdd.bitnet`
**From:**   `<your address>`
**Subject:**   *LISTSERV ignores this*
`SUBSCRIBE motordev <firstname> <lastname>`

## Neuroscience

**Resource:**   LISTSERV
**Address:**   `neuro1-l@UICVM.uic.cc.edu`
Neuroscience information forum. To subscribe, address a message in the following manner:

**To:**   `LISTSERV@UICVM.uic.cc.edu`
**From:**   `<your address>`
**Subject:**   *LISTSERV ignores this*
`SUBSCRIBE neuro1-l <firstname> <lastname>`

## Nutrition

**Resource:**   LISTSERV
**Address:**   `nutepi@db0tui11.bitnet`
Nutritional epidemiology. To subscribe, address a message in the following manner:

**To:**   `LISTSERV@db0tui11.bitnet`
**From:**   `<your address>`
**Subject:**   *LISTSERV ignores this*
`SUBSCRIBE nutepi <firstname> <lastname>`

## Transplantation

**Resource:**   LISTSERV
**Address:**   `brit-l@ksuvm.bitnet`
Behavioral research in transplantation. To subscribe, address a message in the following manner:

**To:**   `LISTSERV@ksuvm.bitnet`
**From:**   `<your address>`
**Subject:**   *LISTSERV ignores this*
`SUBSCRIBE brit-l <firstname> <lastname>`

# Music

## Accordion

**Resource:** List
**Address:** Accordion@marie.stat.uga.edu
For everyone interested in playing, appreciating, acquiring, or repairing all types of accordions. Send your subscription in the form of e-mail to accordion@marie.stat.uga.edu.

## Allman Brothers

**Resource:** List
**Address:** Allman@world.std.com
Devoted to discussion of the Allman Brothers Band and subsequent groups. Send your subscription requests to allman-request@world.std.com.

## Bagpipe

**Resource:** List
**Address:** Pipes@sunapee.dartmouth.edu
Any topic related to bagpipes or related instruments. Send your subscriptions to pipes-request@sunapee.dartmouth.edu.

## Barbershop

**Resource:** List
**Address:** barbershop@bigd.cray.com
For anyone interested in barbershop harmony and singing. Send your e-mail subscription requests to barbershop-request@bigd.cray.com.

## Bluegrass

**Resource:** LISTSERV
**Address:** bgrass-l@ukcc.uky.edu
Bluegrass music discussion. To subscribe, address a message in the following manner:
**To:**       LISTSERV@ukcc.uky.edu
**From:**     <your address>
**Subject:**  *LISTSERV ignores this*
SUBSCRIBE bgrass-l <firstname> <lastname>

## Blues

**Resource:**     LISTSERV
**Address:**     `blues-l@brownvm.brown.edu`
Blues music list. To subscribe, address a message in the following manner:
**To:**     `LISTSERV@brownvm.brown.edu`
**From:**     `<your address>`
**Subject:**     *LISTSERV ignores this*
`SUBSCRIBE blues-l <firstname> <lastname>`

## Brass Lovers

**Resource:**     List
**Address:**     `brass@geomag.gly.fsu.edu`
For persons interested in performing with brass musical instruments. Send your subscription requests to `brass-request@geomag.gly.fsu.edu`.

## Chinese Music

**Resource:**     LISTSERV
**Address:**     `acmr-l@uhccvm.bitnet`
Association for Chinese Music Research network. To subscribe, address a message in the following manner:
**To:**     `LISTSERV@uhccvm.bitnet`
**From:**     `<your address>`
**Subject:**     *LISTSERV ignores this*
`SUBSCRIBE acmr-l <firstname> <lastname>`

## Clarinet

**Resource:**     LISTSERV
**Address:**     `klarinet@vccscent.bitnet`
For fans and performers of the clarinet. To subscribe, address a message in the following manner:
**To:**     `LISTSERV@vccscent.bitnet`
**From:**     `<your address>`
**Subject:**     *LISTSERV ignores this*
`SUBSCRIBE klarinet <firstname> <lastname>`

## Concrete Blonde

**Resource:**   List
**Address:**    `concrete-blonde@ferkel.ucsb.edu`
A list devoted to Concrete Blonde. Send subscriptions and related administrative information to `concrete-blonde-request@ferkel.ucsb.edu`.


## Cooper, Alice

**Resource:**   LISTSERV
**Address:**    `alicefan@wkuvx1.bitnet`
This list is for all fans who wish to discuss and exchange information about Alice Cooper. To subscribe, address a message in the following manner:
**To:**         `LISTSERV@wkuvx1.bitnet`
**From:**       `<your address>`
**Subject:**    *LISTSERV ignores this*
`SUBSCRIBE alicefan <firstname> <lastname>`


## Costello, Elvis

**Resource:**   List
**Address:**    `costello@gnu.ai.mit.edu`
For fans of Elvis Costello. Send your subscriptions and administrative information to `costello-request@gnu.ai.mit.edu`.


## Davis, Miles

**Resource:**   LISTSERV
**Address:**    `miles@hearn.bitnet`
A discussion list for all fans of jazz trumpeter Miles Davis. To subscribe, address a message in the following manner:
**To:**         `LISTSERV@hearn.bitnet`
**From:**       `<your address>`
**Subject:**    *LISTSERV ignores this*
`SUBSCRIBE miles <firstname> <lastname>`


## Dire Straits

**Resource:**   List
**Address:**    `Dire-Straits@Merrimack.Edu`
A discussion list for the fans of Dire Straits. Send a message containing `subscribe` to `dire-straits-request@merrimack.edu`.

## Electronic

**Resource:** LISTSERV
**Address:** `emusic-d@auvm.bitnet`
This is a digest for electronic music discussion. To subscribe, address a message in the following manner:
**To:** `LISTSERV@auvm.bitnet`
**From:** `<your address>`
**Subject:** *LISTSERV ignores this*
`SUBSCRIBE emusic-d <firstname> <lastname>`

**Resource:** LISTSERV
**Address:** `emusic-l@auvm.bitnet`
This is the electronic music discussion list. To subscribe, address a message in the following manner:
**To:** `LISTSERV@auvm.bitnet`
**From:** `<your address>`
**Subject:** *LISTSERV ignores this*
`SUBSCRIBE emusic-l <firstname> <lastname>`

## ELP

**Resource:** List
Contact `J.Arnold@bull.com` for information about subscribing to a list devoted to the music group Emerson, Lake, and Palmer.

## Folk Music

**Resource:** LISTSERV
**Address:** `folk_music@nysernet.org`
Fans of the resurgence in folk music hang out here. To subscribe, address a message in the following manner:
**To:** `LISTSERV@nysernet.org`
**From:** `<your address>`
**Subject:** *LISTSERV ignores this*
`SUBSCRIBE folk_music <firstname> <lastname>`

**Resource:** LISTSERV
**Address:** `folktalk@wmvm1.bitnet`
This is a general discussion list devoted to folk music. To subscribe, address a message in the following manner:
**To:** `LISTSERV@wmvm1.bitnet`
**From:** `<your address>`
**Subject:** *LISTSERV ignores this*
`SUBSCRIBE folktalk <firstname> <lastname>`

## General

**Resource:**     List
**Address:**     `allmusic@auvm.bitnet@vm1.nodak.edu`
Devoted to the discussion and exchange of information and viewpoints about all forms of music. Direct subscriptions and administrative information to `U6183%wvnvm.bitnet@vm1.nodak.edu`.

**Resource:**     LISTSERV
**Address:**     `rmusic-l@gitvm1.bitnet`
A general discussion about the music industry, including concert, albums, song lyrics, performers, and anything else related to general music. To subscribe, address a message in the following manner:

**To:**     `LISTSERV@gitvm1.bitnet`
**From:**     `<your address>`
**Subject:**     *LISTSERV ignores this*
`SUBSCRIBE rmusic-l <firstname> <lastname>`

## Gibson, Debbie

**Resource:**     List
**Address:**     `btl @mkwong@scf.nmsu.edu`
For fans of Debbie Gibson. Send subscription requests to `mkwong@scf.nmsu.edu`.

## Grateful Dead

**Resource:**     List
**Address:**     `dead-heads@virginia.edu`
"Deadicated" to the discussion of nonmusic aspects of Deadhead culture. Your subscription requests should be sent to `dead-heads-request@virginia.edu`.

**Resource:**     List
**Address:**     `dead-flames@virginia.edu`
Gatewayed to the USENET group `rec.music.gdead`. For all Deadheads! Send your subscription requests to `dead-flames-request@virginia.edu`.

## Grunge

**Resource:**     LISTSERV
**Address:**     `Grunge-L@ubvm.cc.buffalo.edu`
For anyone who is a fan of the grunge music scene. To subscribe, address a message in the following manner:

```
To:          LISTSERV@ubvm.cc.buffalo.edu
From:        <your address>
Subject:     LISTSERV ignores this
SUBSCRIBE Grunge-L <firstname> <lastname>
```

## Indigo Girls

**Resource:**  List
**Address:**  indigo@athena.mit.edu
For fans and enthusiasts of the Indigo Girls. Send your subscription requests to indigo-request@athena.mit.edu.

## Irish

**Resource:**  LISTSERV
**Address:**  irtrad-l@irlearn.ucd.ie
Irish traditional music list. To subscribe, address a message in the following manner:

```
To:          LISTSERV@irlearn.ucd.ie
From:        <your address>
Subject:     LISTSERV ignores this
SUBSCRIBE irtrad-l <firstname> <lastname>
```

## Jane's Addiction

**Resource:**  List
**Address:**  janes-addiction@ms.uky.edu
For fans of Jane's Addiction. Send your subscription requests to janes-addiction-request@ms.uky.edu.

## Japanese

**Resource:**  List
**Address:**  jpop@ferkel.ucsb.edu
For fans and devotees of Japanese popular music and the related culture. Send your subscription requests to jpop-request@ferkel.ucsb.edu.

## Jazz

**Resource:**  LISTSERV
**Address:**  jazz-l@templevm.bitnet
For jazz lovers. To subscribe, address a message in the following manner:

```
To:        LISTSERV@templevm.bitnet
From:      <your address>
Subject:   LISTSERV ignores this
SUBSCRIBE jazz-l <firstname> <lastname>
```

## KISS

**Resource:** LISTSERV
**Address:** kissarmy@wkuvx1.bitnet
This list is for all fans of the KISS rock band. To subscribe, address a message in the following manner:

```
To:        LISTSERV@wkuvx1.bitnet
From:      <your address>
Subject:   LISTSERV ignores this
SUBSCRIBE kissarmy <firstname> <lastname>
```

## Library

**Resource:** LISTSERV
**Address:** mla-l@iubvm.bitnet
Music Library Association mailing list. To subscribe, address a message in the following manner:

```
To:        LISTSERV@iubvm.bitnet
From:      <your address>
Subject:   LISTSERV ignores this
SUBSCRIBE mla-l <firstname> <lastname>
```

## Lutes

**Resource:** List
**Address:** Lute@sunapee.dartmouth.edu
This discussion list focuses on playing lutes and researching lute music. Send your subscription request to lute-request@sunapee.dartmouth.edu.

## Lyrics

**Resource:** FTP
**Address:** ftp.uwp.edu
**Directory:** /pub/lyrics

| Resource: | FTP |
|---|---|
| Address: | `ftp.iastate.edu` |
| Directory: | `/pub/lyrics` |

## Opera

| Resource: | LISTSERV |
|---|---|
| Address: | `opera-(@brfapq.bitnet` |

For everyone who loves opera. To subscribe, address a message in the following manner:

| To: | `LISTSERV@brfapq.bitnet` |
|---|---|
| From: | `<your address>` |
| Subject: | *LISTSERV ignores this* |

`SUBSCRIBE opera-l <firstname> <lastname>`

## Pink Floyd

| Resource: | List |
|---|---|
| Address: | `Echoes@Fawnya.tcs.com` |

A discussion group devoted to the rock band Pink Floyd. Send your subscriptions to `echoes-request@fawnya.tcs.com`.

## Pipe Organs

| Resource: | LISTSERV |
|---|---|
| Address: | `piporg-l@albnyvm1` |

This list is for the discussion of pipe organs and related topics. To subscribe, address a message in the following manner:

| To: | `LISTSERV@albnyvm1` |
|---|---|
| From: | `<your address>` |
| Subject: | *LISTSERV ignores this* |

`SUBSCRIBE piporg-l <firstname> <lastname>`

## Rave

| Resource: | LISTSERV |
|---|---|
| Address: | `dcraves@auvm` |

This list is for the discussion of the Washington D.C. rave culture. To subscribe, address a message in the following manner:

| To: | `LISTSERV@auvm` |
|---|---|
| From: | `<your address>` |
| Subject: | *LISTSERV ignores this* |

`SUBSCRIBE dcraves <firstname> <lastname>`

**Resource:**    LISTSERV
**Address:**    uk-rave@orbital.demon.co.uk
This list is devoted to the rave subculture in the U.K. To subscribe, address a
message in the following manner:
**To:**    LISTSERV@orbital.demon.co.uk
**From:**    <your address>
**Subject:**    *LISTSERV ignores this*
SUBSCRIBE uk-rave <firstname> <lastname>

## Renaissance

**Resource:**    LISTSERV
**Address:**    VW5EARN@awiwuw11.bitnet
Renaissance and Reformation music. To subscribe, address a message in the
following manner:
**To:**    LISTSERV@awiwuw11.bitnet
**From:**    <your address>
**Subject:**    *LISTSERV ignores this*
SUBSCRIBE VW5EARN <firstname> <lastname>

## Rock 'n' Roll

**Resource:**    LISTSERV
**Address:**    rock@tritu.bitnet
Rock 'n' roll music discussion list. To subscribe, address a message in the
following manner:
**To:**    LISTSERV@tritu.bitnet
**From:**    <your address>
**Subject:**    *LISTSERV ignores this*
SUBSCRIBE rock <firstname> <lastname>

## Rolling Stones

**Resource:**    List
**Address:**    undercover@snowhite.cis.uoguelph.ca
This is an open list for fans of the Rolling Stones. Send your subscription
requests and related administrative information to undercover-
request@snowhite.cis.uoguelph.ca.

## Siouxsie and the Banshees

**Resource:**  List
**Address:**  `siouxsie+@andrew.cmu.edu`
A list for all fans of Siouxsie and the Banshees. Send your subscription request
to `siouxsie-request+@andrew.cmu.edu`.

## Springsteen, Bruce

**Resource:**  List
**Address:**  `backstreets@virginia.edu`
Bruce Springsteen fans, this is your list. Send your subscription requests to
`backstreets-request@virginia.edu`.

## Sun Ra

**Resource:**  LISTSERV
**Address:**  `saturn@hearn.bitnet`
For fans of the late Sun Ra and his Arkestra. To subscribe, address a message in
the following manner:
**To:**  `LISTSERV@hearn.bitnet`
**From:**  `<your address>`
**Subject:**  *LISTSERV ignores this*
`SUBSCRIBE saturn <firstname> <lastname>`

## Tangerine Dream

**Resource:**  List
**Address:**  `tadream@vacs.uwp.wisc.edu`
This list provides a common forum for fans of the band Tangerine Dream.
Send your subscription request to `tadream-request@vacs.uwp.wisc.edu`.

## Tuba

**Resource:**  LISTSERV
**Address:**  `tuba-l@vtvm2.bitnet`
This is the tuba players' mailing list. To subscribe, address a message in the
following manner:
**To:**  `LISTSERV@vtvm2.bitnet`
**From:**  `<your address>`
**Subject:**  *LISTSERV ignores this*
`SUBSCRIBE tuba-l <firstname> <lastname>`

## U2

**Resource:**   LISTSERV
**Address:**   U2@jhuvms.hcf.jhu.edu
An electronic magazine for U2 fans. Send your subscription requests to
metz@jhuvms.hcf.jhu.edu. To subscribe, address a message in the following
manner:
**To:**   LISTSERV@jhuvms.hcf.jhu.edu
**From:**   <your address>
**Subject:**   *LISTSERV ignores this*
SUBSCRIBE U2 <firstname> <lastname>

# Parapsychology

### Astrology

**Resource:**   LISTSERV
**Address:**   astrol-l@brufpb.bitnet
This is a forum for astrological discussion. To subscribe, address a message in
the following manner:
**To:**   LISTSERV@brufpb.bitnet
**From:**   <your address>
**Subject:**   *LISTSERV ignores this*
SUBSCRIBE astrol-l <firstname> <lastname>

### General

**Resource:**   LISTSERV
**Address:**   psi-l@rpitsvm.bitnet
This is the parapsychology discussion forum. To subscribe, address a message
in the following manner:
**To:**   LISTSERV@rpitsvm.bitnet
**From:**   <your address>
**Subject:**   *LISTSERV ignores this*
SUBSCRIBE psi-l <firstname> <lastname>

### Skeptics

**Resource:**   LISTSERV
**Address:**   skeptic@vm1.yorku.ca
This is the skeptic discussion group. To subscribe, address a message in the
following manner:

**To:**       LISTSERV@vm1.yorku.ca
**From:**     <your address>
**Subject:**  *LISTSERV ignores this*
SUBSCRIBE skeptic <firstname> <lastname>

## UFOs

**Resource:**  LISTSERV
**Address:**   ufo-l@psuvm.psu.edu
This is for everyone interested in UFO-related phenomena. To subscribe, address a message in the following manner:
**To:**       LISTSERV@psuvm.psu.edu
**From:**     <your address>
**Subject:**  *LISTSERV ignores this*
SUBSCRIBE ufo-l <firstname> <lastname>

# Pets

## Cats

**Resource:**  LISTSERV
**Address:**   feline-l@psuvm.psu.edu
This is a discussion list created just for cat fanciers. To subscribe, address a message in the following manner:
**To:**       LISTSERV@psuvm.psu.edu
**From:**     <your address>
**Subject:**  *LISTSERV ignores this*
SUBSCRIBE feline-l <firstname> <lastname>

## Dogs

**Resource:**  LISTSERV
**Address:**   canine-l@psuvm.psu.edu
This is a discussion list for all dog lovers and fanciers. To subscribe, address a message in the following manner:
**To:**       LISTSERV@psuvm.psu.edu
**From:**     <your address>
**Subject:**  *LISTSERV ignores this*
SUBSCRIBE canine-l <firstname> <lastname>

**Resource:** LISTSERV
**Address:** golden@hobbes.ucsd.edu
All aspects of golden retriever ownership (pets, shows, etc.). To subscribe, address a message in the following manner:
**To:** LISTSERV@hobbes.ucsd.edu
**From:** <your address>
**Subject:** *LISTSERV ignores this*
SUBSCRIBE golden <firstname> <lastname>

## Dogs—Obedience Training

**Resource:** List
**Address:** obed@reepicheep.gcn.uoknor.edu
For the discussion of all aspects of training and showing dogs. Send administrative information to obedreq@reepicheep.gcn.uoknor.edu.

## Ferrets

**Resource:** List
**Address:** Ferret@Ferret.ocunix.on.ca
For anyone interested in the ferret. Send subscriptions to ferret-request@ferret.ocunix.on.ca.

## General

**Resource:** LISTSERV
**Address:** pets-l@itesmvf1.bitnet
This list is for the discussion of domestic animal care and education. To subscribe, address a message in the following manner:
**To:** LISTSERV@itesmvf1.bitnet
**From:** <your address>
**Subject:** *LISTSERV ignores this*
SUBSCRIBE pets-l <firstname> <lastname>

## Horses

**Resource:** LISTSERV
**Address:** equine-d@pccvm.bitnet
This is a gateway digest to the USENET group rec.equestrian. To subscribe, address a message in the following manner:

```
To:         LISTSERV@pccvm.bitnet
From:       <your address>
Subject:    LISTSERV ignores this
SUBSCRIBE equine-d <firstname> <lastname>
```

# Philosophy

## General

**Resource:** LISTSERV
**Address:** philosop@vm1.yorku.ca
Philosophy discussion forum. To subscribe, address a message in the following manner:

```
To:         LISTSERV@vm1.yorku.ca
From:       <your address>
Subject:    LISTSERV ignores this
SUBSCRIBE philosop <firstname> <lastname>
```

## Holistic

**Resource:** LISTSERV
**Address:** urantial@listserv%uafsysb.bitnet@cunyvm.cuny.edu
An open forum for the discussion of ideas presented in the Urantia book. To subscribe, address a message in the following manner:

```
To:         LISTSERV@listserv%uafsysb.bitnet@cunyvm.cuny.edu
From:       <your address>
Subject:    LISTSERV ignores this
SUBSCRIBE urantial <firstname> <lastname>
```

## Rand, Ayn

**Resource:** LISTSERV
**Address:** ayn-rand@iubvm.bitnet
This is a moderated list for the discussion of objectivist philosophy. To subscribe, address a message in the following manner:

```
To:         LISTSERV@iubvm.bitnet
From:       <your address>
Subject:    LISTSERV ignores this
SUBSCRIBE ayn-rand <firstname> <lastname>
```

# Politics

## Democratic

**Resource:** LISTSERV
**Address:** `clinton@marist.bitnet`
This list was created for the discussion of campaigning for Bill Clinton's Presidency. To subscribe, address a message in the following manner:
**To:** `LISTSERV@marist.bitnet`
**From:** `<your address>`
**Subject:** *LISTSERV ignores this*
`SUBSCRIBE clinton <firstname> <lastname>`

## Disarmament

**Resource:** LISTSERV
**Address:** `disarm-d@albnyvm1.bitnet`
Disarmament discussion monthly digest. To subscribe, address a message in the following manner:
**To:** `LISTSERV@albnyvm1.bitnet`
**From:** `<your address>`
**Subject:** *LISTSERV ignores this*
`SUBSCRIBE disarm-d <firstname> <lastname>`

## Environment

**Resource:** LISTSERV
**Address:** `ecology@emuvm1.bitnet`
This list is devoted to the discussion of politics and the environment. To subscribe, address a message in the following manner:
**To:** `LISTSERV@emuvm1.bitnet`
**From:** `<your address>`
**Subject:** *LISTSERV ignores this*
`SUBSCRIBE ecology <firstname> <lastname>`

## Firearms/Gun Control

**Resource:** List
**Address:** `firearms-politics@cs.cmu.edu`
Discussion group for the exchange of information related to the 2nd Amendment. Send your subscription requests to `firearms-politics-request@cs.cmu.edu`.

## General

**Resource:**   LISTSERV
**Address:**    POLITICS@ucf1vm.cc.ucf.edu
Politics. To subscribe, address a message in the following manner:
**To:**         LISTSERV@ucf1vm.cc.ucf.edu
**From:**       <your address>
**Subject:**    *LISTSERV ignores this*
SUBSCRIBE POLITICS <firstname> <lastname>

## Republican

**Resource:**   LISTSERV
**Address:**    gop-l@pccvm.bitnet
A discussion of the Grand Old Party. To subscribe, address a message in the following manner:
**To:**         LISTSERV@pccvm.bitnet
**From:**       <your address>
**Subject:**    *LISTSERV ignores this*
SUBSCRIBE gop-l <firstname> <lastname>

## Senate Bills

**Resource:**   FTP
**Address:**    gaia.ucs.orst.edu
**Directory:**  /OLIS/Working Directory/Senate

# Professional

## Clocks

**Resource:**   LISTSERV
**Address:**    clocks@suvm.bitnet
Devoted to all aspects of clock/watch repair, collecting, and construction. To subscribe, address a message in the following manner:
**To:**         LISTSERV@suvm.bitnet
**From:**       <your address>
**Subject:**    *LISTSERV ignores this*
SUBSCRIBE clocks <firstname> <lastname>

## Consultant

**Resource:**  LISTSERV
**Address:**  `cons-l@mcgill1.bitnet`
This is the consultant's discussion list. To subscribe, address a message in the following manner:
**To:**  `LISTSERV@mcgill1.bitnet`
**From:**  `<your address>`
**Subject:**  *LISTSERV ignores this*
`SUBSCRIBE cons-l <firstname> <lastname>`


## Dentistry

**Resource:**  LISTSERV
**Address:**  `dblist@umab.umd.edu`
This list discusses databases for dentistry. To subscribe, address a message in the following manner:
**To:**  `LISTSERV@umab.umd.edu`
**From:**  `<your address>`
**Subject:**  *LISTSERV ignores this*
`SUBSCRIBE dblist <firstname> <lastname>`


## Emergency Services

**Resource:**  LISTSERV
**Address:**  `emerg-l@marist.bitnet`
This list is for the discussion and exchange of information for those involved in emergency services. To subscribe, address a message in the following manner:
**To:**  `LISTSERV@marist.bitnet`
**From:**  `<your address>`
**Subject:**  *LISTSERV ignores this*
`SUBSCRIBE emerg-l <firstname> <lastname>`


## Exhibitionists/Projectionists

**Resource:**  List
**Address:**  `exhibitionists@jvnc.net`
For anyone in the cinema who shows movies. Send your subscription requests to `exhibitionists-request@jvnc.net`.

## Filmmakers

**Resource:**    List
**Address:**     Filmmakers@Grissom.Larc.nasa.gov
For anyone interested in the film industry. Send subscriptions to
filmmakers-request@grissom.larc.nasa.gov.

## Human Resources

**Resource:**    LISTSERV
**Address:**     perdir-l@ubvm.cc.buffalo.edu
This is for everyone involved in human resources: personnel directors, associates, managers. To subscribe, address a message in the following manner:
**To:**          LISTSERV@ubvm.cc.buffalo.edu
**From:**        <your address>
**Subject:**     *LISTSERV ignores this*
SUBSCRIBE perdir-l <firstname> <lastname>

**Resource:**    LISTSERV
**Address:**     hrd-l@mizzou1.bitnet
This is the human resource development group list. To subscribe, address a message in the following manner:
**To:**          LISTSERV@mizzou1.bitnet
**From:**        <your address>
**Subject:**     *LISTSERV ignores this*
SUBSCRIBE hrd-l <firstname> <lastname>

## Insurance

**Resource:**    LISTSERV
**Address:**     risk@utxvm.bitnet
This list discusses risk and insurance issues. To subscribe, address a message in the following manner:
**To:**          LISTSERV@utxvm.bitnet
**From:**        <your address>
**Subject:**     *LISTSERV ignores this*
SUBSCRIBE risk <firstname> <lastname>

## Janitorial

**Resource:**    LISTSERV
**Address:**     janitors@ukanvm.cc.ukans.edu
This list was created for all college and university housekeeping personnel. To subscribe, address a message in the following manner:

```
To:          LISTSERV@ukanvm.cc.ukans.edu
From:        <your address>
Subject:     LISTSERV ignores this
SUBSCRIBE janitors <firstname> <lastname>
```

## Physical Plants

**Resource:**   LISTSERV
**Address:**    erappa-l@psuvm.psu.edu
This is a list for the association of physical plant administrators. To subscribe, address a message in the following manner:

```
To:          LISTSERV@psuvm.psu.edu
From:        <your address>
Subject:     LISTSERV ignores this
SUBSCRIBE erappa-l <firstname> <lastname>
```

## Play-by-Play

**Resource:**   LISTSERV
**Address:**    pbp-l@etsuadmn.etsu.edu
For all persons involved in being or desiring to be a play-by-play sportscaster. To subscribe, address a message in the following manner:

```
To:          LISTSERV@etsuadmn.etsu.edu
From:        <your address>
Subject:     LISTSERV ignores this
SUBSCRIBE pbp-l <firstname> <lastname>
```

## Real Estate

**Resource:**   LISTSERV
**Address:**    re-forum@utarlvm1.bitnet
This is the real estate forum. To subscribe, address a message in the following manner:

```
To:          LISTSERV@utarlvm1.bitnet
From:        <your address>
Subject:     LISTSERV ignores this
SUBSCRIBE re-forum <firstname> <lastname>
```

## Veterinary

**Resource:** LISTSERV
**Address:** `vetmed-1@uga.cc.uga.edu`
This is a list for the discussion and exchange of information and research for persons involved in veterinary medicine. To subscribe, address a message in the following manner:

**To:** `LISTSERV@uga.cc.uga.edu`
**From:** `<your address>`
**Subject:** *LISTSERV ignores this*
`SUBSCRIBE vetmed-1 <firstname> <lastname>`

**Resource:** LISTSERV
**Address:** `vetinfo@ucdcvdls.bitnet`
This list enables those in the veterinary profession to exchange information, ideas, and research information. To subscribe, address a message in the following manner:

**To:** `LISTSERV@ucdcvdls.bitnet`
**From:** `<your address>`
**Subject:** *LISTSERV ignores this*
`SUBSCRIBE vetinfo <firstname> <lastname>`

## Writing

**Resource:** LISTSERV
**Address:** `writers@ndsuvm1.ndsu.edu`
This is a list for the purpose of exchanging information by current and would-be professional writers. To subscribe, address a message in the following manner:

**To:** `LISTSERV@ndsuvm1.ndsu.edu`
**From:** `<your address>`
**Subject:** *LISTSERV ignores this*
`SUBSCRIBE writers <firstname> <lastname>`

# Psychology

## Aging/Geriatrics

**Resource:** LISTSERV
**Address:** `humage-1@asuacad.bitnet`
This list discusses the humanistic effects of aging. To subscribe, address a message in the following manner:

**To:**  LISTSERV@asuacad.bitnet
**From:** &lt;your address&gt;
**Subject:** *LISTSERV ignores this*
SUBSCRIBE humage-l &lt;firstname&gt; &lt;lastname&gt;

## Children

**Resource:** LISTSERV
**Address:** behavior@asuacad.bitnet
This forum discusses behavioral and emotional disorders in children. To subscribe, address a message in the following manner:
**To:**  LISTSERV@asuacad.bitnet
**From:** &lt;your address&gt;
**Subject:** *LISTSERV ignores this*
SUBSCRIBE behavior &lt;firstname&gt; &lt;lastname&gt;

## Consciousness

**Resource:** LISTSERV
**Address:** bridge-l@ucsbvm.bitnet
This forum is devoted to the bridge across consciousness. To subscribe, address a message in the following manner:
**To:**  LISTSERV@ucsbvm.bitnet
**From:** &lt;your address&gt;
**Subject:** *LISTSERV ignores this*
SUBSCRIBE bridge-l &lt;firstname&gt; &lt;lastname&gt;

## Creativity

**Resource:** LISTSERV
**Address:** crea-cps@hearn.bitnet
This list is for the discussion of creativity and creative problem solving. To subscribe, address a message in the following manner:
**To:**  LISTSERV@hearn.bitnet
**From:** &lt;your address&gt;
**Subject:** *LISTSERV ignores this*
SUBSCRIBE crea-cps &lt;firstname&gt; &lt;lastname&gt;

## Drug Abuse

**Resource:**   LISTSERV
**Address:**   `drugabus@umab.umd.edu`
Community drug abuse education and related issues. To subscribe, address a
message in the following manner:
**To:**   `LISTSERV@umab.umd.edu`
**From:**   `<your address>`
**Subject:**   *LISTSERV ignores this*
`SUBSCRIBE drugabus <firstname> <lastname>`

## Family Relations

**Resource:**   LISTSERV
**Address:**   `famcomm@rpitsvm.bitnet`
For the discussion of marital/family and relational communication. To sub-
scribe, address a message in the following manner:
**To:**   `LISTSERV@rpitsvm.bitnet`
**From:**   `<your address>`
**Subject:**   *LISTSERV ignores this*
`SUBSCRIBE famcomm <firstname> <lastname>`

## Industrial

**Resource:**   LISTSERV
**Address:**   `ioobf-l@uga.cc.uga.edu`
This is the industrial psychology forum. To subscribe, address a message in the
following manner:
**To:**   `LISTSERV@uga.cc.uga.edu`
**From:**   `<your address>`
**Subject:**   *LISTSERV ignores this*
`SUBSCRIBE ioobf-l <firstname> <lastname>`

## Smoking/Support

**Resource:**   LISTSERV
**Address:**   `smoke-free@ra.msstate.edu`
A discussion list used as a support group for persons who want to quit smok-
ing or for persons supporting others who want to quit. To subscribe, address a
message in the following manner:
**To:**   `LISTSERV@ra.msstate.edu`
**From:**   `<your address>`
**Subject:**   *LISTSERV ignores this*
`SUBSCRIBE smoke-free <firstname> <lastname>`

## Support Groups

**Resource:**  List
**Address:**   12Step@trwrb.dsd.trw.com
This group discusses and shares information and experiences related to 12-step programs such as Alcoholics Anonymous, Alanon, etc. Contact suhre@trwrb.dsd.trw.com for subscription requests.

## Technology

**Resource:**  LISTSERV
**Address:**   mind-l@asylum.sf.ca.us
A discussion list exchanging information about the use of mind-altering technology. To subscribe, address a message in the following manner:

**To:**        LISTSERV@asylum.sf.ca.us
**From:**      <your address>
**Subject:**   *LISTSERV ignores this*
SUBSCRIBE mind-l <firstname> <lastname>

## Thinking

**Resource:**  LISTSERV
**Address:**   fnord-l@ubvm.cc.buffalo.edu
This is the list for new ways of thinking. To subscribe, address a message in the following manner:

**To:**        LISTSERV@ubvm.cc.buffalo.edu
**From:**      <your address>
**Subject:**   *LISTSERV ignores this*
SUBSCRIBE fnord-l <firstname> <lastname>

## Violence

**Resource:**  LISTSERV
**Address:**   violen-l@bruspvm.bitnet
This list discusses all forms of violence. To subscribe, address a message in the following manner:

**To:**        LISTSERV@bruspvm.bitnet
**From:**      <your address>
**Subject:**   *LISTSERV ignores this*
SUBSCRIBE violen-l <firstname> <lastname>

# Reference

## Acronyms

**Resource:**   telnet
**Address:**    info.mcc.ac.uk

## Dictionary

**Resource:**   telnet
**Address:**    cs.indiana.edu 2627

**Resource:**   telnet
**Address:**    chem.ucsd.edu
**User id:**    webster

## Law Libraries

**Resource:**   telnet
**Address:**    pegasus.law.columbia.edu
**User id:**    pegasus

**Resource:**   telnet
**Address:**    liberty.uc.wlu.edu
**User id:**    lawlib

## Library

**Resource:**   telnet
**Address:**    library.dartmouth.edu
**User id:**    dante

## Reference

**Resource:**   telnet
**Address:**    CHEM.UCSD.EDU
**User id:**    webster

### Thesaurus

**Resource:**   LISTSERV
**Address:**    `libthea@kentvm.bitnet`
This list is devoted to thesaurus science. To subscribe, address a message in the following manner:
**To:**         `LISTSERV@kentvm.bitnet`
**From:**       `<your address>`
**Subject:**    *LISTSERV ignores this*
`SUBSCRIBE libthea <firstname> <lastname>`

# Religion

### Anglican

**Resource:**   LISTSERV
**Address:**    `anglican@auvm.bitnet`
This is the Episcopal mailing list. To subscribe, address a message in the following manner:
**To:**         `LISTSERV@auvm.bitnet`
**From:**       `<your address>`
**Subject:**    *LISTSERV ignores this*
`SUBSCRIBE anglican <firstname> <lastname>`

### Baha'i

**Resource:**   List
**Address:**    `Bahai-faith@oneworld.wa.com`
A peaceful, open forum for discussing the Baha'i faith. Send your subscription requests to `bahai-faith-request@oneworld.wa.com`.

### Baptist

**Resource:**   LISTSERV
**Address:**    `baptist@ukcc.uky.edu`
This is an open discussion list for all things Baptist. To subscribe, address a message in the following manner:
**To:**         `LISTSERV@ukcc.uky.edu`
**From:**       `<your address>`
**Subject:**    *LISTSERV ignores this*
`SUBSCRIBE baptist <firstname> <lastname>`

## Buddhism

**Resource:** LISTSERV
**Address:** `hindu-d@arizvm1.bitnet`
This is the Hindu digest. To subscribe, address a message in the following manner:

**To:** `LISTSERV@arizvm1.bitnet`
**From:** `<your address>`
**Subject:** *LISTSERV ignores this*
`SUBSCRIBE hindu-d <firstname> <lastname>`

**Resource:** LISTSERV
**Address:** `buddha-l@ulkyvm.louisville.edu`
This is the Buddhist academic discussion forum. To subscribe, address a message in the following manner:

**To:** `LISTSERV@ulkyvm.louisville.edu`
**From:** `<your address>`
**Subject:** *LISTSERV ignores this*
`SUBSCRIBE buddha-l <firstname> <lastname>`

## Catholicism

**Resource:** LISTSERV
**Address:** `amercath@ukcc.uky.edu`
Devoted to the exchange of information about American Catholicism. To subscribe, address a message in the following manner:

**To:** `LISTSERV@ukcc.uky.edu`
**From:** `<your address>`
**Subject:** *LISTSERV ignores this*
`SUBSCRIBE amercath <firstname> <lastname>`

**Resource:** List
**Address:** `catholic-action @rfreeman@vpnet.chi.il.us`
A moderated list for the discussion of the Catholic religion. Send your subscription requests to `rfreeman.vpnet.chi.il.us`.

**Resource:** LISTSERV
**Address:** `catholic@auvm`
This is an open list for all Catholics. To subscribe, address a message in the following manner:

**To:** `LISTSERV@auvm`
**From:** `<your address>`
**Subject:** *LISTSERV ignores this*
`SUBSCRIBE catholic <firstname> <lastname>`

## Christianity

**Resource:**   LISTSERV
**Address:**   `conchr-l@templevm.bitnet`
This is a conservative Christian discussion list. To subscribe, address a message
in the following manner:
**To:**   `LISTSERV@templevm.bitnet`
**From:**   `<your address>`
**Subject:**   *LISTSERV ignores this*
`SUBSCRIBE conchr-l <firstname> <lastname>`

**Resource:**   LISTSERV
**Address:**   `globlx-l@qucdn.bitnet`
This is a list for the discussion of global Christianity. To subscribe, address a
message in the following manner:
**To:**   `LISTSERV@qucdn.bitnet`
**From:**   `<your address>`
**Subject:**   *LISTSERV ignores this*
`SUBSCRIBE globlx-l <firstname> <lastname>`

**Resource:**   LISTSERV
**Address:**   `christia@asuacad.bitnet`
This is a list for discussing practical Christian life. To subscribe, address a
message in the following manner:
**To:**   `LISTSERV@asuacad.bitnet`
**From:**   `<your address>`
**Subject:**   *LISTSERV ignores this*
`SUBSCRIBE christia <firstname> <lastname>`

**Resource:**   LISTSERV
**Address:**   `elenchus@acadvm1.uottawa.ca`
Dedicated to the events and literature of early Christianity. To subscribe,
address a message in the following manner:
**To:**   `LISTSERV@acadvm1.uottawa.ca`
**From:**   `<your address>`
**Subject:**   *LISTSERV ignores this*
`SUBSCRIBE elenchus <firstname> <lastname>`

**Resource:**   List
**Address:**   `mailjc@grian.cps.altadena.ca.us`
For the open discussion of Christianity. Send your subscription requests to
`mailjc-request@grian.cps.altadena.ca.us`.

**Resource:**    LISTSERV
**Address:**    `histec-l@ukanvm.cc.ukans.edu`
This list discusses the history of evangelical Christianity. To subscribe, address a message in the following manner:
**To:**    `LISTSERV@ukanvm.cc.ukans.edu`
**From:**    `<your address>`
**Subject:**    *LISTSERV ignores this*
`SUBSCRIBE histec-l <firstname> <lastname>`

## Feminism

**Resource:**    LISTSERV
**Address:**    `femrel-l@mizzou1.bitnet`
This is an open discussion of women, religion, and feminism. To subscribe, address a message in the following manner:
**To:**    `LISTSERV@mizzou1.bitnet`
**From:**    `<your address>`
**Subject:**    *LISTSERV ignores this*
`SUBSCRIBE femrel-l <firstname> <lastname>`

## General

**Resource:**    LISTSERV
**Address:**    `contents@uottawa.bitnet`
This is the religious studies publications journal. To subscribe, address a message in the following manner:
**To:**    `LISTSERV@uottawa.bitnet`
**From:**    `<your address>`
**Subject:**    *LISTSERV ignores this*
`SUBSCRIBE contents <firstname> <lastname>`

## General Beliefs

**Resource:**    LISTSERV
**Address:**    `belief-l@Brownvm.Brown.Edu`
This is the personal ideologies discussion list. To subscribe, address a message in the following manner:
**To:**    `LISTSERV@Brownvm.Brown.Edu`
**From:**    `<your address>`
**Subject:**    *LISTSERV ignores this*
`SUBSCRIBE belief-l <firstname> <lastname>`

## Hare Krishna

**Resource:**    LISTSERV
**Address:**    `krsnanet@arizvm1.bitnet`
This list discusses the Krishna consciousness club. To subscribe, address a message in the following manner:
**To:**    `LISTSERV@arizvm1.bitnet`
**From:**    `<your address>`
**Subject:**    *LISTSERV ignores this*
`SUBSCRIBE krsnanet <firstname> <lastname>`

## Jewish Studies

**Resource:**    LISTSERV
**Address:**    `jstudy@UICVM.uic.cc.edu`
The forum for Jewish studies. To subscribe, address a message in the following manner:
**To:**    `LISTSERV@UICVM.uic.cc.edu`
**From:**    `<your address>`
**Subject:**    *LISTSERV ignores this*
`SUBSCRIBE jstudy <firstname> <lastname>`

## Ministry

**Resource:**    LISTSERV
**Address:**    `ministry-l@gacvax1.bitnet@vm1.nodak.edu`
This list is for everyone involved in or desiring to be involved in the ministry. To subscribe, address a message in the following manner:
**To:**    `LISTSERV@gacvax1.bitnet@vm1.nodak.edu`
**From:**    `<your address>`
**Subject:**    *LISTSERV ignores this*
`SUBSCRIBE ministry-l <firstname> <lastname>`

## New Testament

**Resource:**    LISTSERV
**Address:**    `nt-greek@virginia.edu`
This list is for anyone wishing to exchange information about the Greek language and its use in the New Testament. To subscribe, address a message in the following manner:
**To:**    `LISTSERV@virginia.edu`
**From:**    `<your address>`
**Subject:**    *LISTSERV ignores this*
`SUBSCRIBE nt-greek <firstname> <lastname>`

## Old Testament

**Resource:**  List
**Address:**  `ot-hebrew@virginia.edu`
For those interested in studying Old Testament Hebrew. Send your subscription requests to `ot-hebrew-request@virginia.edu`.

## Orthodox

**Resource:**  LISTSERV
**Address:**  `orthodox@indycms.iupui.edu`
A moderated list for the purpose of discussing the Orthodox Christian Church. To subscribe, address a message in the following manner:

**To:**       `LISTSERV@indycms.iupui.edu`
**From:**     `<your address>`
**Subject:**  *LISTSERV ignores this*
`SUBSCRIBE orthodox <firstname> <lastname>`

## Paganism

**Resource:**  List
**Address:**  `pagan@drycas.club.cc.cmu.edu`
For those interested in pursuing Paganism. Send administrative information to `pagan-request@drycas.clu.cc.cmu.edu`.

## Quaker

**Resource:**  LISTSERV
**Address:**  `quaker-l@vmd.cso.uiuc.edu`
This list is devoted to Quaker concerns. To subscribe, address a message in the following manner:

**To:**       `LISTSERV@vmd.cso.uiuc.edu`
**From:**     `<your address>`
**Subject:**  *LISTSERV ignores this*
`SUBSCRIBE quaker-l <firstname> <lastname>`

## Scientific Study

**Resource:**  LISTSERV
**Address:**  `ssrel-l@utkvm1.bitnet`
This forum is for the scientific study of religion. To subscribe, address a message in the following manner:

```
To:        LISTSERV@utkvm1.bitnet
From:      <your address>
Subject:   LISTSERV ignores this
SUBSCRIBE ssrel-l <firstname> <lastname>
```

## Seventh-Day Adventists

**Resource:**  LISTSERV
**Address:**   sda-l@lluvm.bitnet
This list was created for Seventh-Day Adventists. To subscribe, address a message in the following manner:

```
To:        LISTSERV@lluvm.bitnet
From:      <your address>
Subject:   LISTSERV ignores this
SUBSCRIBE sda-l <firstname> <lastname>
```

## Shaker

**Resource:**  LISTSERV
**Address:**   shaker@ukcc.uky.edu
This is the Shaker forum. To subscribe, address a message in the following manner:

```
To:        LISTSERV@ukcc.uky.edu
From:      <your address>
Subject:   LISTSERV ignores this
SUBSCRIBE shaker <firstname> <lastname>
```

## Unitarians

**Resource:**  LISTSERV
**Address:**   uus-l@ubvm.cc.buffalo.edu
This is a list for Unitarian Universalists. To subscribe, address a message in the following manner:

```
To:        LISTSERV@ubvm.cc.buffalo.edu
From:      <your address>
Subject:   LISTSERV ignores this
SUBSCRIBE uus-l <firstname> <lastname>
```

# Science

## Agriculture

**Resource:**   LISTSERV
**Address:**    newcrops@purccvm.cc.vm.edu

A discussion list for new crops. To subscribe, address a message in the following manner:

**To:**        LISTSERV@purccvm.cc.vm.edu
**From:**      <your address>
**Subject:**  *LISTSERV ignores this*
SUBSCRIBE newcrops <firstname> <lastname>

## Anthropology

**Resource:**   LISTSERV
**Address:**    anthro-l@ubvm.cc.buffalo.edu

Devoted to all aspects of anthropology research and information exchange. To subscribe, address a message in the following manner:

**To:**        LISTSERV@ubvm.cc.buffalo.edu
**From:**      <your address>
**Subject:**  *LISTSERV ignores this*
SUBSCRIBE anthro-l <firstname> <lastname>

## Aquaculture

**Resource:**   LISTSERV
**Address:**    aqua-l@vm.uoguelph.ca

This is the aquaculture discussion list. To subscribe, address a message in the following manner:

**To:**        LISTSERV@vm.uoguelph.ca
**From:**      <your address>
**Subject:**  *LISTSERV ignores this*
SUBSCRIBE aqua-l <firstname> <lastname>

## Archaeology

**Resource:**   LISTSERV
**Address:**    arch-l@tamvm1.tamu.edu

This is the all-purpose archaeology list. To subscribe, address a message in the following manner:

**To:**        `LISTSERV@tamvm1.tamu.edu`
**From:**    `<your address>`
**Subject:**  *LISTSERV ignores this*
`SUBSCRIBE arch-l <firstname> <lastname>`

## Aviation

**Resource:**    List
**Address:**     `aviation-theory@mc.lcs.mit.edu`
Devoted to the discussion of all matters related to aerospace engineering. Send subscription requests to `aviation-theory-request@mc.lcs.mit.edu`.

**Resource:**    List
**Address:**     `aviation@mc.lcs.mit.edu`
A discussion list devoted to subject matter of interest to pilots. Send subscription requests to `aviation-request@mc.lcs.mit.edu`.

## Bees (Apiary)

**Resource:**    LISTSERV
**Address:**     `bee-l@albnyvm1.bitnet`
A general discussion of bee biology and beekeeping. To subscribe, address a message in the following manner:
**To:**        `LISTSERV@albnyvm1.bitnet`
**From:**    `<your address>`
**Subject:**  *LISTSERV ignores this*
`SUBSCRIBE bee-l <firstname> <lastname>`

## Biology

**Resource:**    LISTSERV
**Address:**     `deepsea@uvvm.uvic.ca`
Devoted to a discussion of all aspects of deep-sea diving and underwater science. To subscribe, address a message in the following manner:
**To:**        `LISTSERV@uvvm.uvic.ca`
**From:**    `<your address>`
**Subject:**  *LISTSERV ignores this*
`SUBSCRIBE deepsea <firstname> <lastname>`

## Botany

**Resource:**   LISTSERV
**Address:**    `CP@hp1-opus.hpl.hp.com`

Devoted to the topic of carnivorous plants. To subscribe, address a message in the following manner:

**To:**         `LISTSERV@hp1-opus.hpl.hp.com`
**From:**       `<your address>`
**Subject:**    *LISTSERV ignores this*

`SUBSCRIBE CP <firstname> <lastname>`

## Cryonics

**Resource:**   List
**Address:**    `cryonics @kqb@whscad1.att.com`

Dedicated to the discussion and dissemination of information about cryonics. Send your subscription information to `kqb@whscad1.att.com`.

## Dentistry

**Resource:**   LISTSERV
**Address:**    `amalgam@ibmvm.rus.uni-stuttgart.de`

A list devoted to the exchange of information about amalgam fillings and the potential health hazards of mercury poisoning for those with silver fillings. To subscribe, address a message in the following manner:

**To:**         `LISTSERV@ibmvm.rus.uni-stuttgart.de`
**From:**       `<your address>`
**Subject:**    *LISTSERV ignores this*

`SUBSCRIBE amalgam <firstname> <lastname>`

## Dinosaurs

**Resource:**   List
**Address:**    `dinosaur@wichitaks.ncr.com`

An open list for the discussion of dinosaurs. Send your subscription requests to `dinosaur-request@wichitaks.ncr.com`.

## Earthquakes

**Resource:**   telnet
**Address:**    `geophys.washington.edu`
**User id:**    `quake`

## Ecology

**Resource:** LISTSERV
**Address:** `biosph-l@ubvm.cc.buffalo.edu`
This is the biosphere and ecology discussion list. To subscribe, address a message in the following manner:
**To:** `LISTSERV@ubvm.cc.buffalo.edu`
**From:** `<your address>`
**Subject:** *LISTSERV ignores this*
`SUBSCRIBE biosph-l <firstname> <lastname>`

## Electromagnetics

**Resource:** LISTSERV
**Address:** `emflds-l@ubvm.cc.buffalo.edu`
This is a list devoted to electromagnetics in medicine, science, and communications. To subscribe, address a message in the following manner:
**To:** `LISTSERV@ubvm.cc.buffalo.edu`
**From:** `<your address>`
**Subject:** *LISTSERV ignores this*
`SUBSCRIBE emflds-l <firstname> <lastname>`

## Environment

**Resource:** LISTSERV
**Address:** `envbeh-l@polyvm.bitnet`
This is a forum on environment and human behavior. To subscribe, address a message in the following manner:
**To:** `LISTSERV@polyvm.bitnet`
**From:** `<your address>`
**Subject:** *LISTSERV ignores this*
`SUBSCRIBE envbeh-l <firstname> <lastname>`

**Resource:** LISTSERV
**Address:** `envst-l@brownvm.brown.edu`
This is the environmental studies discussion list. To subscribe, address a message in the following manner:
**To:** `LISTSERV@brownvm.brown.edu`
**From:** `<your address>`
**Subject:** *LISTSERV ignores this*
`SUBSCRIBE envst-l <firstname> <lastname>`

## Fraud

**Resource:**   LISTSERV
**Address:**    `scifraud@albnyvm1.bitnet`
This list provides an open forum for the discussion of fraud in science. To subscribe, address a message in the following manner:
**To:**         `LISTSERV@albnyvm1.bitnet`
**From:**       `<your address>`
**Subject:**    *LISTSERV ignores this*
`SUBSCRIBE scifraud <firstname> <lastname>`

## Fuller, Buckminster

**Resource:**   LISTSERV
**Address:**    `geodesic@ubvm.cc.buffalo.edu`
A list for the discussion of the life and science of Buckminster Fuller. To subscribe, address a message in the following manner:
**To:**         `LISTSERV@ubvm.cc.buffalo.edu`
**From:**       `<your address>`
**Subject:**    *LISTSERV ignores this*
`SUBSCRIBE geodesic <firstname> <lastname>`

## Fusion

**Resource:**   LISTSERV
**Address:**    `fusion@vm1.nodak.edu`
Created for the purpose of discussing the current status of and information related to the energy of the future: fusion. To subscribe, address a message in the following manner:
**To:**         `LISTSERV@vm1.nodak.edu`
**From:**       `<your address>`
**Subject:**    *LISTSERV ignores this*
`SUBSCRIBE fusion <firstname> <lastname>`

## Future

**Resource:**   List
**Address:**    `info-futures@world.std.com`
A list for persons who like to speculate about the future and what it might be like. Send your subscription requests to `info-futures-request@world.std.com`.

## Geology

**Resource:**   LISTSERV
**Address:**   `geology@ptearn.bitnet`
Geology discussion list. To subscribe, address a message in the following manner:
**To:**   `LISTSERV@ptearn.bitnet`
**From:**   `<your address>`
**Subject:**   *LISTSERV ignores this*
`SUBSCRIBE geology <firstname> <lastname>`


## Marine Studies

**Resource:**   LISTSERV
**Address:**   `marine-l@uoguelph.bitnet`
Marine studies/shipboard education discussion. To subscribe, address a message in the following manner:
**To:**   `LISTSERV@uoguelph.bitnet`
**From:**   `<your address>`
**Subject:**   *LISTSERV ignores this*
`SUBSCRIBE marine-l <firstname> <lastname>`


## Mathematics

**Resource:**   LISTSERV
**Address:**   `nmbrthry@ndsuvm1.ndsu.edu`
This list is devoted to number theory and related mathematics. To subscribe, address a message in the following manner:
**To:**   `LISTSERV@ndsuvm1.ndsu.edu`
**From:**   `<your address>`
**Subject:**   *LISTSERV ignores this*
`SUBSCRIBE nmbrthry <firstname> <lastname>`


## Medieval

**Resource:**   LISTSERV
**Address:**   `medsci-l@brownvm.brown.edu`
This is the medieval science discussion list. To subscribe, address a message in the following manner:
**To:**   `LISTSERV@brownvm.brown.edu`
**From:**   `<your address>`
**Subject:**   *LISTSERV ignores this*
`SUBSCRIBE medsci-l <firstname> <lastname>`

## Military Technology

**Resource:**    List
**Address:**    `military@att.att.com`
This list is a gateway to the USENET group `sci.military` for those who do not have USENET access. Send your subscription request to `military-request@att.att.com`.

## Museums

**Resource:**    LISTSERV
**Address:**    `museum-l@unmvma.bitnet`
The museum discussion list. To subscribe, address a message in the following manner:
**To:**    `LISTSERV@unmvma.bitnet`
**From:**    `<your address>`
**Subject:**    *LISTSERV ignores this*
`SUBSCRIBE museum-l <firstname> <lastname>`

## Optics

**Resource:**    LISTSERV
**Address:**    `optics-l@taunivm.tau.ac.il`
This is the optics newsletter. To subscribe, address a message in the following manner:
**To:**    `LISTSERV@taunivm.tau.ac.il`
**From:**    `<your address>`
**Subject:**    *LISTSERV ignores this*
`SUBSCRIBE optics-l <firstname> <lastname>`

## Parapsychology

**Resource:**    LISTSERV
**Address:**    `parapsych @psi-l%rpicicge@vm1.nodak.edu`
For those interested in pursuing ESP and related phenomena. To subscribe, address a message in the following manner:
**To:**    `LISTSERV@psi-l%rpicicge@vm1.nodak.edu`
**From:**    `<your address>`
**Subject:**    *LISTSERV ignores this*
`SUBSCRIBE parapsych <firstname> <lastname>`

## Photosynthesis

**Resource:**   LISTSERV
**Address:**   photosyn@taunivm.tau.ac.il
Photosynthesis research list. To subscribe, address a message in the following manner:
**To:**   LISTSERV@taunivm.tau.ac.il
**From:**   <your address>
**Subject:**   *LISTSERV ignores this*
SUBSCRIBE photosyn <firstname> <lastname>


## Research Methodologies

**Resource:**   LISTSERV
**Address:**   methods@rpitsvm.bitnet
This list discusses research methodology. To subscribe, address a message in the following manner:
**To:**   LISTSERV@rpitsvm.bitnet
**From:**   <your address>
**Subject:**   *LISTSERV ignores this*
SUBSCRIBE methods <firstname> <lastname>


## Seismology

**Resource:**   LISTSERV
**Address:**   quake-l@vm1.nodak.edu
Earthquake discussion list. To subscribe, address a message in the following manner:
**To:**   LISTSERV@vm1.nodak.edu
**From:**   <your address>
**Subject:**   *LISTSERV ignores this*
SUBSCRIBE quake-l <firstname> <lastname>

**Resource:**   LISTSERV
**Address:**   seismd-l@bingvmb.bitnet
This is for seismological discussion. To subscribe, address a message in the following manner:
**To:**   LISTSERV@bingvmb.bitnet
**From:**   <your address>
**Subject:**   *LISTSERV ignores this*
SUBSCRIBE seismd-l <firstname> <lastname>

## Superconductivity

**Resource:** LISTSERV
**Address:** `sup-cond@taunivm.tau.ac.il`
This is the superconductivity list. To subscribe, address a message in the following manner:

**To:** `LISTSERV@taunivm.tau.ac.il`
**From:** `<your address>`
**Subject:** *LISTSERV ignores this*
`SUBSCRIBE sup-cond <firstname> <lastname>`

## Volcanoes

**Resource:** LISTSERV
**Address:** `volcano@asuacad.bitnet`
For everyone interested in volcanoes. To subscribe, address a message in the following manner:

**To:** `LISTSERV@asuacad.bitnet`
**From:** `<your address>`
**Subject:** *LISTSERV ignores this*
`SUBSCRIBE volcano <firstname> <lastname>`

## Water

**Resource:** LISTSERV
**Address:** `aquifer@ibacsata.bitnet`
This list discusses pollution and groundwater recharge. To subscribe, address a message in the following manner:

**To:** `LISTSERV@ibacsata.bitnet`
**From:** `<your address>`
**Subject:** *LISTSERV ignores this*
`SUBSCRIBE aquifer <firstname> <lastname>`

## Weather

**Resource:** LISTSERV
**Address:** `wx-misc@vmd.cso.uiuc.edu`
This is a miscellaneous weather discussion list. To subscribe, address a message in the following manner:

**To:** `LISTSERV@vmd.cso.uiuc.edu`
**From:** `<your address>`
**Subject:** *LISTSERV ignores this*
`SUBSCRIBE wx-misc <firstname> <lastname>`

**Resource:** LISTSERV
**Address:** wx-swo@vmd.cso.uiuc.edu
This list distributes severe weather outlook information. To subscribe, address
a message in the following manner:
**To:** LISTSERV@vmd.cso.uiuc.edu
**From:** <your address>
**Subject:** *LISTSERV ignores this*
SUBSCRIBE wx-swo <firstname> <lastname>

**Resource:** LISTSERV
**Address:** wx-talk@vmd.cso.uiuc.edu
This is a general weather discussion and talk list. To subscribe, address a
message in the following manner:
**To:** LISTSERV@vmd.cso.uiuc.edu
**From:** <your address>
**Subject:** *LISTSERV ignores this*
SUBSCRIBE wx-talk <firstname> <lastname>

**Resource:** LISTSERV
**Address:** wx-watch@vmd.cso.uiuc.edu
For the distribution of weather watches and cancellations. To subscribe,
address a message in the following manner:
**To:** LISTSERV@vmd.cso.uiuc.edu
**From:** <your address>
**Subject:** *LISTSERV ignores this*
SUBSCRIBE wx-watch <firstname> <lastname>

**Resource:** LISTSERV
**Address:** wx-wstat@vmd.cso.uiuc.edu
Weather watch status and storm reports. To subscribe, address a message in
the following manner:
**To:** LISTSERV@vmd.cso.uiuc.edu
**From:** <your address>
**Subject:** *LISTSERV ignores this*
SUBSCRIBE wx-wstat <firstname> <lastname>

**Resource:** List
**Address:** met-stud@metw3.met.fu-berlin.de
An open list for meteorology students to meet and exchange information. Send
your subscription request to dennis@metw3.met.fu-berlin.de.

**Resource:** LISTSERV
**Address:** wx-tropl@vmd.cso.uiuc.edu
This list distributes tropical storm and hurricane information. To subscribe,
address a message in the following manner:

| To: | LISTSERV@vmd.cso.uiuc.edu |
|---|---|
| From: | <your address> |
| Subject: | *LISTSERV ignores this* |

SUBSCRIBE wx-tropl <firstname> <lastname>

**Resource:**    LISTSERV
**Address:**    wx-natnl@vmd.cso.uiuc.edu

A list for distribution of weather summaries for the nation and selected cities. To subscribe, address a message in the following manner:

| To: | LISTSERV@vmd.cso.uiuc.edu |
|---|---|
| From: | <your address> |
| Subject: | *LISTSERV ignores this* |

SUBSCRIBE wx-natnl <firstname> <lastname>

**Resource:**    LISTSERV
**Address:**    wxspot@vmd.cso.uiuc.edu

This list is devoted to severe weather spotters and trackers, including the exchange of training information and tips. To subscribe, address a message in the following manner:

| To: | LISTSERV@vmd.cso.uiuc.edu |
|---|---|
| From: | <your address> |
| Subject: | *LISTSERV ignores this* |

SUBSCRIBE wxspot <firstname> <lastname>

**Resource:**    telnet
**Address:**    downwind.sprl.umich.edu

University of Michigan WEATHER UNDERGROUND

**Resource:**    LISTSERV
**Address:**    wx-lsr@vmd.cso.uiuc.edu

Local storm reports and related weather information. To subscribe, address a message in the following manner:

| To: | LISTSERV@vmd.cso.uiuc.edu |
|---|---|
| From: | <your address> |
| Subject: | *LISTSERV ignores this* |

SUBSCRIBE wx-lsr <firstname> <lastname>

# Social Groups

## Masons

**Resource:**    List
**Address:**    masonic@ptrei@asgard.bbn.com

A discussion list for those involved in Freemasonry and related groups. All subscription requests should be directed to ptrei@asgard.bbn.com.

# Sports

## Balloon

**Resource:** List
**Address:** Balloon@lut.ac.uk
For all balloonists. Send your subscription requests and related administrative information to balloon-request@lut.ac.uk.

## Baseball

**Resource:** telnet
**Address:** culine.colorado.edu 862
Schedules online.

**Resource:** LISTSERV
**Address:** statlg-l@brownvm.brown.edu
Baseball (and lesser sports) discussion list. To subscribe, address a message in the following manner:
**To:** LISTSERV@brownvm.brown.edu
**From:** <your address>
**Subject:** *LISTSERV ignores this*
SUBSCRIBE statlg-l <firstname> <lastname>

## Baseball—Toronto Blue Jays

**Resource:** List
**Address:** jays@hivnet.ubc.ca
For fanatics of the Toronto Blue Jays baseball team. Submit your subscription request to jays-request@hivnet.ubc.ca.

## Basketball

**Resource:** telnet
**Address:** culine.colorado.edu 859
Schedules online.

## Bicycling

**Resource:**  List
**Address:**  `bicycles@bbn.com`
A discussion list for all topics related to bicycling, both recreational and racing. Send your subscription request to `bicycles-request@bbn.com`.

## Caving/Spelunking

**Resource:**  List
**Address:**  `Cavers@M2c.Org`
For anyone interested in caving. Send subscription requests to `cavers-request@m2c.org`.

## Cleveland

**Resource:**  List
**Address:**  `@cleveland.freenet.edu`
A general support list for all Cleveland sports activities. Contact `aj755@cleveland.freenet.edu` for more information about subscribing.

## Cricket

**Resource:**  LISTSERV
**Address:**  `cricket@ndsuvm1.ndsu.edu`
This is a redistribution of cricket information. To subscribe, address a message in the following manner:
**To:**  `LISTSERV@ndsuvm1.ndsu.edu`
**From:**  `<your address>`
**Subject:**  *LISTSERV ignores this*
`SUBSCRIBE cricket <firstname> <lastname>`

## Figure Skating

**Resource:**  LISTSERV
**Address:**  `skating@umab.umd.edu`
For all fans of figure skating. To subscribe, address a message in the following manner:
**To:**  `LISTSERV@umab.umd.edu`
**From:**  `<your address>`
**Subject:**  *LISTSERV ignores this*
`SUBSCRIBE skating <firstname> <lastname>`

## Fly Fishing

**Resource:**    LISTSERV
**Address:**    `flyfish@umab.umd.edu`
This is the fly-fishing digest. To subscribe, address a message in the following manner:
**To:**    `LISTSERV@umab.umd.edu`
**From:**    `<your address>`
**Subject:**    *LISTSERV ignores this*
`SUBSCRIBE flyfish <firstname> <lastname>`

## Football

**Resource:**    LISTSERV
**Address:**    `coordcom@msu.bitnet`
This is a football information list. To subscribe, address a message in the following manner:
**To:**    `LISTSERV@msu.bitnet`
**From:**    `<your address>`
**Subject:**    *LISTSERV ignores this*
`SUBSCRIBE coordcom <firstname> <lastname>`

**Resource:**    telnet
**Address:**    `culine.colorado.edu 863`
Schedules online.

## Golf

**Resource:**    LISTSERV
**Address:**    `golf-l@ubvm.cc.buffalo.edu`
This is the golf discussion list. To subscribe, address a message in the following manner:
**To:**    `LISTSERV@ubvm.cc.buffalo.edu`
**From:**    `<your address>`
**Subject:**    *LISTSERV ignores this*
`SUBSCRIBE golf-l <firstname> <lastname>`

## Guns/Firearms

**Resource:**    List
**Address:**    `firearms@cs.cmu.edu`
Devoted to the nonpolitical aspects of guns and firearms. Send your subscription requests to `firearms-request@cs.cmu.edu`.

## Gymnastics

**Resource:**   List
This list discusses all aspects of gymnastics. Contact `raek@athena.mit.edu`.

## Hang Gliding

**Resource:**   List
**Address:**   `hang-gliding@virginia.edu`
This discussion list covers all aspects of hang gliding and ballooning. Send your subscription requests to `hang-gliding-request@virginia.edu`.

## Hockey

**Resource:**   List
**Address:**   `ahl-news@andrew.cmu.edu`
For people interested in discussing and following the American Hockey League. Send your subscription requests to `ahl-news-request@andrew.cmu.edu`.

**Resource:**   LISTSERV
**Address:**   `hockey-l@maine.maine.edu`
A college hockey discussion list. To subscribe, address a message in the following manner:
**To:**   `LISTSERV@maine.maine.edu`
**From:**   `<your address>`
**Subject:**   *LISTSERV ignores this*
`SUBSCRIBE hockey-l <firstname> <lastname>`

**Resource:**   LISTSERV
**Address:**   `olympuck@maine.maine.edu`
The Olympic ice hockey discussion list. To subscribe, address a message in the following manner:
**To:**   `LISTSERV@maine.maine.edu`
**From:**   `<your address>`
**Subject:**   *LISTSERV ignores this*
`SUBSCRIBE olympuck <firstname> <lastname>`

**Resource:**   telnet
**Address:**   `culine.colorado.edu 860`
Schedules online.

## Horse Racing

**Resource:**   List
**Address:**   Derby@Ekrl.Com
For anything related to horse racing, including gambling and handicapping.
Send subscriptions to Derby-Request@Ekrl.Com.

## Hunting

**Resource:**   LISTSERV
**Address:**   hunting@tamvm1.tamu.edu
This is a gateway to the USENET group Rec.Hunting. To subscribe, address a
message in the following manner:
**To:**   LISTSERV@tamvm1.tamu.edu
**From:**   <your address>
**Subject:**   *LISTSERV ignores this*
SUBSCRIBE hunting <firstname> <lastname>

## Lacrosse

**Resource:**   LISTSERV
**Address:**   lacros-l@villvm.bitnet@vm1.nodak.edu
For everyone interested in lacrosse. To subscribe, address a message in the
following manner:
**To:**   LISTSERV@villvm.bitnet@vm1.nodak.edu
**From:**   <your address>
**Subject:**   *LISTSERV ignores this*
SUBSCRIBE lacros-l <firstname> <lastname>

## Management

**Resource:**   LISTSERV
**Address:**   sportmgt@unbvm1.bitnet
For everyone who participates in or is interested in sport management. To
subscribe, address a message in the following manner:
**To:**   LISTSERV@unbvm1.bitnet
**From:**   <your address>
**Subject:**   *LISTSERV ignores this*
SUBSCRIBE sportmgt <firstname> <lastname>

## Martial Arts

**Resource:**  LISTSERV
**Address:**  `aikido-l@psuvm.psu.edu`
This is the aikido list. To subscribe, address a message in the following manner:
**To:**  `LISTSERV@psuvm.psu.edu`
**From:**  `<your address>`
**Subject:**  *LISTSERV ignores this*
`SUBSCRIBE aikido-l <firstname> <lastname>`

**Resource:**  LISTSERV
**Address:**  `kokikai@psuvm.psu.edu`
This list is devoted to kokikai aikido. To subscribe, address a message in the following manner:
**To:**  `LISTSERV@psuvm.psu.edu`
**From:**  `<your address>`
**Subject:**  *LISTSERV ignores this*
`SUBSCRIBE kokikai <firstname> <lastname>`

**Resource:**  List
**Address:**  `martial-arts@dragon.cso.uiuc.edu`
A general discussion list for martial artists. Send your subscription requests to `martial-arts-request@dragon.cso.uiuc.edu`.

## Mountaineering

**Resource:**  LISTSERV
**Address:**  `mount-l@trmetu.bitnet`
This is the mountaineering discussion list. To subscribe, address a message in the following manner:
**To:**  `LISTSERV@trmetu.bitnet`
**From:**  `<your address>`
**Subject:**  *LISTSERV ignores this*
`SUBSCRIBE mount-l <firstname> <lastname>`

## Orienteering

**Resource:**  List
**Address:**  `Orienteering@Graphics.Cornell.Edu`
This list is for the purpose of exchanging information on and discussing the sport of orienteering. Send your subscription requests to `orienteering-request@graphics.cornell.edu`.

## Psychology

**Resource:**   LISTSERV
**Address:**   `sportpsy@templevm.bitnet`
This list discusses exercise and sports psychology. To subscribe, address a message in the following manner:
**To:**   `LISTSERV@templevm.bitnet`
**From:**   `<your address>`
**Subject:**   *LISTSERV ignores this*
`SUBSCRIBE sportpsy <firstname> <lastname>`

## Running

**Resource:**   LISTSERV
**Address:**   `drs@dartcms1.dartmouth.edu`
This is the Dead Runners Society. To subscribe, address a message in the following manner:
**To:**   `LISTSERV@dartcms1.dartmouth.edu`
**From:**   `<your address>`
**Subject:**   *LISTSERV ignores this*
`SUBSCRIBE drs <firstname> <lastname>`

## Nordic Skiing

**Resource:**   List
**Address:**   `nordic-ski@graphics.cornell.edu`
This list discusses all aspects of Nordic skiing. Send your subscription requests to `nordic-ski-request@graphics.cornell.edu`.

## Soccer

**Resource:**   LISTSERV
**Address:**   `soccer-l@ukcc.uky.edu`
This is the soccer boosters list. To subscribe, address a message in the following manner:
**To:**   `LISTSERV@ukcc.uky.edu`
**From:**   `<your address>`
**Subject:**   *LISTSERV ignores this*
`SUBSCRIBE soccer-l <firstname> <lastname>`

## Swimming

**Resource:** LISTSERV
**Address:** `swim-l@uafsysb.uark.edu`
For persons interested in any aspect of swimming. To subscribe, address a message in the following manner:
**To:** `LISTSERV@uafsysb.uark.edu`
**From:** `<your address>`
**Subject:** *LISTSERV ignores this*
`SUBSCRIBE swim-l <firstname> <lastname>`

## Technology

**Resource:** LISTSERV
**Address:** `sportpc@unbvm1.bitnet`
This list discusses the use of computers in sporting events. To subscribe, address a message in the following manner:
**To:** `LISTSERV@unbvm1.bitnet`
**From:** `<your address>`
**Subject:** *LISTSERV ignores this*
`SUBSCRIBE sportpc <firstname> <lastname>`

## Training

**Resource:** LISTSERV
**Address:** `athtrn-l@iubvm.bitnet`
This is a discussion list for athletic trainers. To subscribe, address a message in the following manner:
**To:** `LISTSERV@iubvm.bitnet`
**From:** `<your address>`
**Subject:** *LISTSERV ignores this*
`SUBSCRIBE athtrn-l <firstname> <lastname>`

## Weight Lifting

**Resource:** List
**Address:** `weights@mickey.disney.com`
For the exchange of information related to all aspects of weight lifting. Send your subscription requests to `weights-request@mickey.disney.com`.

### Windsurfing

**Resource:**    List
**Address:**    `Windsurfing@gcm.com`
This list is for everyone interested in windsurfing and boardsailing. Send your subscription requests to `windsurfing-request@gcm.com`.

# Technology

### Biotechnology

**Resource:**    LISTSERV
**Address:**    `biotech@umdd.bitnet`
This is a biotechnology discussion list. To subscribe, address a message in the following manner:
**To:**    `LISTSERV@umdd.bitnet`
**From:**    `<your address>`
**Subject:**    *LISTSERV ignores this*
`SUBSCRIBE biotech <firstname> <lastname>`

### Current

**Resource:**    LISTSERV
**Address:**    `adv-eli@utfsm.bitnet`
A discussion list devoted to the latest advances in electrical engineering. To subscribe, address a message in the following manner:
**To:**    `LISTSERV@utfsm.bitnet`
**From:**    `<your address>`
**Subject:**    *LISTSERV ignores this*
`SUBSCRIBE adv-eli <firstname> <lastname>`

### Home Satellites

**Resource:**    LISTSERV
**Address:**    `homesat@ndsuvm1.ndsu.edu`
This list discusses home satellite technology. To subscribe, address a message in the following manner:
**To:**    `LISTSERV@ndsuvm1.ndsu.edu`
**From:**    `<your address>`
**Subject:**    *LISTSERV ignores this*
`SUBSCRIBE homesat <firstname> <lastname>`

## Laser Printers

**Resource:**   LISTSERV
**Address:**   laser-l@irlearn.ucd.ie
This is the laser printer information distribution list. To subscribe, address a message in the following manner:
**To:**       LISTSERV@irlearn.ucd.ie
**From:**      \<your address\>
**Subject:**   *LISTSERV ignores this*
SUBSCRIBE laser-l \<firstname\> \<lastname\>

## Latest Advances

**Resource:**   LISTSERV
**Address:**   adv-elo@utfsm.bitnet
This list discusses the latest electronic advances. To subscribe, address a message in the following manner:
**To:**       LISTSERV@utfsm.bitnet
**From:**      \<your address\>
**Subject:**   *LISTSERV ignores this*
SUBSCRIBE adv-elo \<firstname\> \<lastname\>

## Mass Communications

**Resource:**   LISTSERV
**Address:**   masscomm@rpitsvm.bitnet
This list discusses and exchanges information about mass communications and new or emerging technologies. To subscribe, address a message in the following manner:
**To:**       LISTSERV@rpitsvm.bitnet
**From:**      \<your address\>
**Subject:**   *LISTSERV ignores this*
SUBSCRIBE masscomm \<firstname\> \<lastname\>

## Touchtone

**Resource:**   LISTSERV
**Address:**   touchton@sjsuvm1.sjsu.edu
For the discussion of touchtone/voice response systems. To subscribe, address a message in the following manner:
**To:**       LISTSERV@sjsuvm1.sjsu.edu
**From:**      \<your address\>
**Subject:**   *LISTSERV ignores this*
SUBSCRIBE touchton \<firstname\> \<lastname\>

## Video

**Resource:** List
**Address:** videotech@wsmr-simtel20.army.mil
For the discussion and information exchange of all video technologies. Send
your subscription and related administrative information to
videotech-request@wsmr-simtel20.army.mil.

# Television

## 90210

**Resource:** List
**Address:** 90210@ferkel.ucsb.edu
The 90210 lover's discussion list. Send your subscription request and other
administrative information to 90210-request@ferkel.ucsb.edu.

## Cable Television

**Resource:** List
**Address:** catv@quack.sac.ca.us
A discussion list devoted to the cable television industry. Send your subscrip-
tion request to catv-request@quack.sac.ca.us.

## Clarissa

**Resource:** List
**Address:** clarissa@ferkel.ucsb.edu
Discussion of the Nickelodeon television show "Clarissa Explains It All." Send
your subscription requests to clarissa-request@ferkel.ucsb.edu.

## Class of '96

**Resource:** List
**Address:** Class96@dream.saigon.com
A discussion of the Fox TV show "Class of '96". Send an e-mail subscription
request to class96-request@dream.saigon.com.

## Dark Shadows

**Resource:**    List
**Address:**     shadows@sunee.waterloo.edu
Devoted to the daily soap opera "Dark Shadows." Send your subscriptions to shadows-request@sunee.waterloo.edu.

## General

**Resource:**    LISTSERV
**Address:**     tv-l@trearn.bitnet
General television discussions. To subscribe, address a message in the following manner:
**To:**          LISTSERV@trearn.bitnet
**From:**        <your address>
**Subject:**     *LISTSERV ignores this*
SUBSCRIBE tv-l <firstname> <lastname>

## Melrose Place

**Resource:**    List
**Address:**     melrose-place@ferkel.ucsb.edu
For fans and devotees of the television show "Melrose Place." Send subscription requests to melrose-place-request@ferkel.ucsb.edu.

## Mystery Science Theater 3000

**Resource:**    List
**Address:**     mst3k rsk@gynko.circ.upenn.edu
For fans and mavens of the television show "Mystery Science Theater 3000" (Comedy Channel). Send administrative information to rsk@gynko.circ.upenn.edu.

## Star Trek

**Resource:**    LISTSERV
**Address:**     strfleet@pccvm.bitnet
This is the Starfleet forum. To subscribe, address a message in the following manner:
**To:**          LISTSERV@pccvm.bitnet
**From:**        <your address>
**Subject:**     *LISTSERV ignores this*
SUBSCRIBE strfleet <firstname> <lastname>

**Resource:**   LISTSERV
**Address:**   `strek-l@pccvm.bitnet`
This is the Star Trek fan club list. To subscribe, address a message in the following manner:
**To:**   `LISTSERV@pccvm.bitnet`
**From:**   `<your address>`
**Subject:**   *LISTSERV ignores this*
`SUBSCRIBE strek-l <firstname> <lastname>`

**Resource:**   LISTSERV
**Address:**   `strek-d@pccvm.bitnet`
This is the Star Trek fan club digest. To subscribe, address a message in the following manner:
**To:**   `LISTSERV@pccvm.bitnet`
**From:**   `<your address>`
**Subject:**   *LISTSERV ignores this*
`SUBSCRIBE strek-d <firstname> <lastname>`

**Resource:**   LISTSERV
**Address:**   `trek-review-l@cornell.edu`
This is a forum dedicated to reviewing, rating, and giving commentary on all aspects of the Star Trek phenomenon. To subscribe, address a message in the following manner:
**To:**   `LISTSERV@cornell.edu`
**From:**   `<your address>`
**Subject:**   *LISTSERV ignores this*
`SUBSCRIBE trek-review-l <firstname> <lastname>`

# Travel

## Tourism

**Resource:**   LISTSERV
**Address:**   `travel-l@trearn.bitnet@vm1.nodak.edu`
For persons interested in discussing the tourist trade. To subscribe, address a message in the following manner:
**To:**   `LISTSERV@trearn.bitnet@vm1.nodak.edu`
**From:**   `<your address>`
**Subject:**   *LISTSERV ignores this*
`SUBSCRIBE travel-l <firstname> <lastname>`

# World Events

## Arms

**Resource:**   LISTSERV
**Address:**   arms-l@buacca.bu.edu
Focuses on the exchange of information and discussion related to national armaments. To subscribe, address a message in the following manner:
**To:**   LISTSERV@buacca.bu.edu
**From:**   <your address>
**Subject:**   *LISTSERV ignores this*
SUBSCRIBE arms-l <firstname> <lastname>

## Asia

**Resource:**   LISTSERV
**Address:**   cenasia@mcgill1.bitnet
This list discusses the former Soviet Republic and Central Asian politics. To subscribe, address a message in the following manner:
**To:**   LISTSERV@mcgill1.bitnet
**From:**   <your address>
**Subject:**   *LISTSERV ignores this*
SUBSCRIBE cenasia <firstname> <lastname>

## Canada

**Resource:**   LISTSERV
**Address:**   canada-l@vm1.mcgill.ca
This forum is for the exchange of ideas about Canadian issues. To subscribe, address a message in the following manner:
**To:**   LISTSERV@vm1.mcgill.ca
**From:**   <your address>
**Subject:**   *LISTSERV ignores this*
SUBSCRIBE canada-l <firstname> <lastname>

## Caribbean

**Resource:**   LISTSERV
**Address:**   carecon@vm1.yorku.ca
This list discusses the Caribbean economy. To subscribe, address a message in the following manner:

**To:**         `LISTSERV@vm1.yorku.ca`
**From:**    `<your address>`
**Subject:**  *LISTSERV ignores this*
`SUBSCRIBE carecon <firstname> <lastname>`

## Central America

**Resource:**   LISTSERV
**Address:**    `centam-l@ubvm.cc.buffalo.edu`
The Central America discussion list. To subscribe, address a message in the following manner:
**To:**         `LISTSERV@ubvm.cc.buffalo.edu`
**From:**    `<your address>`
**Subject:**  *LISTSERV ignores this*
`SUBSCRIBE centam-l <firstname> <lastname>`

## China

**Resource:**   LISTSERV
**Address:**    `china@pucc.bitnet`
This forum is for Chinese studies. To subscribe, address a message in the following manner:
**To:**         `LISTSERV@pucc.bitnet`
**From:**    `<your address>`
**Subject:**  *LISTSERV ignores this*
`SUBSCRIBE china <firstname> <lastname>`

## Cuba

**Resource:**   LISTSERV
**Address:**    `cuba-l@unmvma.bitnet`
Cuba today. This is a bilingual list in Spanish/English for the discussion of Cuba's current state of affairs. To subscribe, address a message in the following manner:
**To:**         `LISTSERV@unmvma.bitnet`
**From:**    `<your address>`
**Subject:**  *LISTSERV ignores this*
`SUBSCRIBE cuba-l <firstname> <lastname>`

## Diversity

**Resource:**  LISTSERV
**Address:**  `divers-l@psuvm.psu.edu`
For anyone interested in the diversity of the world's peoples. To subscribe, address a message in the following manner:
**To:**  `LISTSERV@psuvm.psu.edu`
**From:**  `<your address>`
**Subject:**  *LISTSERV ignores this*
`SUBSCRIBE divers-l <firstname> <lastname>`

## General

**Resource:**  LISTSERV
**Address:**  `val-l@ucf1vm.cc.ucf.edu`
Valentine Michael Smith's commentary. To subscribe, address a message in the following manner:
**To:**  `LISTSERV@ucf1vm.cc.ucf.edu`
**From:**  `<your address>`
**Subject:**  *LISTSERV ignores this*
`SUBSCRIBE val-l <firstname> <lastname>`

## India

**Resource:**  LISTSERV
**Address:**  `india-d@utarlvm1.bitnet`
India News Network. To subscribe, address a message in the following manner:
**To:**  `LISTSERV@utarlvm1.bitnet`
**From:**  `<your address>`
**Subject:**  *LISTSERV ignores this*
`SUBSCRIBE india-d <firstname> <lastname>`

## Middle Europe

**Resource:**  LISTSERV
**Address:**  `mideur-l@ubvm.cc.buffalo.edu`
An open list for the purpose of discussing all aspects of Middle European politics. To subscribe, address a message in the following manner:
**To:**  `LISTSERV@ubvm.cc.buffalo.edu`
**From:**  `<your address>`
**Subject:**  *LISTSERV ignores this*
`SUBSCRIBE mideur-l <firstname> <lastname>`

## South Asia

**Resource:**    LISTSERV
**Address:**    `currents@pccvm.bitnet`
South Asian news and culture electronic magazine. To subscribe, address a message in the following manner:
**To:**    `LISTSERV@pccvm.bitnet`
**From:**    `<your address>`
**Subject:**    *LISTSERV ignores this*
`SUBSCRIBE currents <firstname> <lastname>`

## Spain

**Resource:**    LISTSERV
**Address:**    `espana-l@albnyvm1.bitnet`
A discussion list dedicated to Spain and its people. To subscribe, address a message in the following manner:
**To:**    `LISTSERV@albnyvm1.bitnet`
**From:**    `<your address>`
**Subject:**    *LISTSERV ignores this*
`SUBSCRIBE espana-l <firstname> <lastname>`

# INDEX

# Add to Your Sams Library Today with the Best Books for Programming, Operating Systems, and New Technologies

## The easiest way to order is to pick up the phone and call

# 1-800-428-5331

## between 9:00 a.m. and 5:00 p.m. EST.

## For faster service please have your credit card available.

| ISBN | Quantity | Description of Item | Unit Cost | Total Cost |
|------|----------|---------------------|-----------|------------|
| 0-672-30318-3 | | Windows Sound FunPack (Book/Disk) | $19.95 | |
| 0-672-30310-8 | | Windows Graphics FunPack (Book/Disk) | $19.95 | |
| 0-672-30249-7 | | Multimedia Madness! (Book/Disk CD-ROM) | $44.95 | |
| 0-672-30248-9 | | FractalVision (Book/Disk) | $39.95 | |
| 0-672-30305-1 | | Computer Graphics Environments (Book/Disk) | $34.95 | |
| 0-672-30322-1 | | PC Video Madness! (Book/Disk CD-ROM) | $39.95 | |
| 0-672-30315-9 | | The Magic of Image Processing (Book/Disk) | $39.95 | |
| 0-672-30361-2 | | Virtual Reality and the Exploration of Cyberspace (Book/Disk) | $26.95 | |
| 0-672-30345-0 | | Wasting Time with Windows (Book/Disk) | $19.95 | |
| 0-672-30301-9 | | Artificial Life Explorer's Kit (Book/Disk) | $24.95 | |
| 0-672-30352-3 | | Blaster Mastery (Book/Disk CD-ROM) | $34.95 | |
| 0-672-30320-5 | | Morphing Magic (Book/Disk) | $29.95 | |
| 0-672-30308-6 | | Tricks of the Graphics Gurus (Book/Disk) | $49.95 | |
| ❏ 3 ½" Disk | | Shipping and Handling: See information below. | | |
| ❏ 5 ¼" Disk | | TOTAL | | |

Shipping and Handling: $4.00 for the first book, and $1.75 for each additional book. Floppy disk: add $1.75 for shipping and handling. If you need to have it NOW, we can ship product to you in 24 hours for an additional charge of approximately $18.00, and you will receive your item overnight or in two days. Overseas shipping and handling adds $2.00 per book and $8.00 for up to three disks. Prices subject to change. Call for availability and pricing information on latest editions.

### 11711 N. College Avenue, Suite 140, Carmel, Indiana 46032

**1-800-428-5331 — Orders     1-800-835-3202 — FAX     1-800-858-7674 — Customer Service**

Book ISBN 0-672-30362-0